W9-BKM-620

DESTINY'S CONSUL

DESTINY'S CONSUL

America's Ten Greatest Presidents

MICHAEL P. RICCARDS

ROWMAN & LITTLEFIELD PUBLISHERS, INC.
Lanham • Boulder • New York • Toronto • Plymouth, UK

Published by Rowman & Littlefield Publishers, Inc.
A wholly owned subsidiary of The Rowman & Littlefield Publishing Group, Inc.
4501 Forbes Boulevard, Suite 200, Lanham, Maryland 20706
www.rowman.com

10 Thornbury Road, Plymouth PL6 7PP, United Kingdom

British Library Cataloguing in Publication Information Available

Library of Congress Cataloging-in-Publication Data
Riccards, Michael P.
  Destiny's consul : America's ten greatest presidents / Michael P. Riccards.
    p. cm.
  Includes bibliographical references.
  ISBN 978-1-4422-1624-2 (cloth : alk. paper) — ISBN 978-1-4422-1626-6 (electronic)
  1. Presidents—United States—History. 2. Presidents—United States—Biography. I.
Title.
  JK511.R52 2012
  973.09'9—dc23   2012004246

∞™ The paper used in this publication meets the minimum requirements of American National Standard for Information Sciences—Permanence of Paper for Printed Library Materials, ANSI/NISO Z39.48-1992.

Printed in the United States of America

I have dedicated this book to my grandchildren in a paraphrase of John Adams:

To Michael, Anna, and Madison,

I have studied politics and government so that their parents could study education and the law, and that they may study art, music, philosophy, and poetry.

CONTENTS

Preface

FOR WELL OVER TWO EVENTFUL CENTURIES, the United States of America has struggled to adapt its eighteenth-century institutions to contemporary times. Now in the twenty-first century, those institutions, with their checks and balances, separation of powers, and federal-state divisions, place an emphasis on caution and also on inertia. Coupled with the Bill of Rights and complex legal systems, that environment has often protected Americans from the loss of liberties and personal freedoms. That very environment is so rare in the world that we must stop and look in awe sometimes at what we have sustained.

But that environment has also created a rigid status quo that makes it difficult to plan for the future or to meet the serious challenges of the present. Two historical developments have helped the United States be a great nation. First, the Supreme Court and the legal structure have established a national network of laws that unite us. And although we may hear silly talk of states' rights and state nullification (even in our times), it is still unity that brings strength. A weak union of states does not solidify great-power status in the world. The procedures of basic rights and united laws further a national citizenship.

The second major development is the presidency, known for its energy, dispatch, and prompt action—a set of defining characteristics that Alexander Hamilton used in extolling the new executive office.[1] Several times in American history, the presidency saved the Union—in a literal sense. Historically, the United States has faced some really terrible enemies, both abroad and even at home. The powerful presidents featured in this book have not been flawless leaders with a sure touch of history and purpose. They have made mistakes, drifted, and miscalculated, but in the long run they have made decisions that helped reshape the office, the nation, and often the world.

Some of our presidents were truly great historical figures, others were competent, and a few were dismal. This volume lists ten presidents as "great." The immediate questions are how this list was chosen—based on what hard criteria and sometimes on what historical judgments, which may at first appear elusive. But together, these criteria comprise a record that can be laid before students of this great and awesome office.

With all the complexities of defining greatness, it is obvious that most historians agree on the highest-ranking presidents. Generally the consensus is George Washington, Abraham Lincoln, and Franklin D. Roosevelt. The next tier is Thomas Jefferson, Theodore Roosevelt, Harry S Truman, Woodrow Wilson, Dwight D. Eisenhower, and Andrew Jackson. James K. Polk, a dark horse in his times and in ours, is also listed, as are Lyndon B. Johnson and John F. Kennedy.[2]

One major near-great president whose status has been rising over the last twenty or so years is Dwight D. Eisenhower, a five-star general who led the Allied armies in Western Europe during the Second World War. He was part of that extraordinary collection of diplomat-generals who ran much of the strategy and diplomacy of the war in both theaters. Ike was probably the most competent president of the modern era in creating and running a presidential bureaucracy, working on the army model with an assertive chief of staff, strong interdepartmental committees, and clear delegation of authority. Behind the scenes, he was also adept at providing leadership that the general public did not see and he did not acknowledge. He was probably more responsible for the demise of Senator Joe McCarthy than realized, but he also seemed to be oblivious to some of the moral issues that plagued the nation, most especially the rising tide of the civil rights movement. Ike upheld the law, but he did not seem to appreciate the crippling state of race relations. It very well may be that he simply did not sympathize with the aspirations of African Americans. In foreign policy, he was a president who used the U.S. intelligence forces rather than his beloved army for dangerous military operations. And most consequentially, he gave very bad advice to a neophyte president, John F. Kennedy, about the need eventually to go to war in Asia. Kennedy would have been better off listening to General Douglas MacArthur, who told him early in his term to stay away from that sinkhole.

John F. Kennedy's position in history is more due to the romantic and dashing profile he conveyed than to his brief and at times confusing presidency. He bungled the Bay of Pigs invasion of Cuba; pushed forward in Latin America in a moderately successful Alliance for Progress; led the nation through the Cuban Missile Crisis, which he and his brother were somewhat responsible for; and reluctantly embraced the civil rights movement. But his three years in office were too brief to offer a judgment on a man who experienced considerable growth in office.

His successor, Lyndon Baines Johnson, compiled one of the most extraordinary domestic legislative records since his mentor FDR. Johnson's extensive commitments to poverty legislation, civil rights, education access, and medical coverage were truly remarkable. He would be one of our greatest presidents if he had not embraced a massive military buildup in Vietnam, one that he knew from the start of his term was doomed. That huge miscalculation has clouded his leadership record.

So what makes a great president, and what makes an executive whom the nation can count on in its most dire times? Polls of presidential greatness, usually done by historians, have listed five general categories: leadership qualities, accomplishments and crisis management, political skill, appointments, and character and integrity. I could also add that the greatest presidents tend to be linked up with powerful themes that outlast their terms in office.[3] Such is the case with Washington and Federalism; Jefferson and republican self-government; Jackson and popular democracy; Polk and Manifest Destiny; Lincoln and the Union and emancipation; Theodore Roosevelt and national reform, and also environmentalism; Wilson and Progressivism and international democracy; Franklin D. Roosevelt and the welfare state and the Four Freedoms; Truman and the imperial presidency; and Reagan and the conservative crusade for limited government and personal freedom.[4]

Generally, these men left genuine legacies, and they struggled to educate the people and win their allegiance by rebuilding their parties and coalitions. Karl Rove, former presidential adviser under George W. Bush, has identified some major characteristics: clarity of vision, clarity about goals, an ability to benefit from the legacy left to them by other great presidents, and an "emotional intelligence" that sets them free from "any disturbing emotional perturbations." They must also have real self-confidence, a healthy respect for public opinion, and the ability to put together a good team. The president should organize his administration so he gets solid, straightforward advice. Finally, he must have a readiness to act and be comfortable in deciding among options.[5] And lastly, I would add, a president's decisions must ultimately be wise ones, for it is not all process, but rather making good, solid, historically valid decisions, that lives up to the test of time.

This study of great presidents tells us much about the office—it is a difficult job for even the most accomplished to hold. But this volume is also about the American people and the American nation—a lesson in how a free people may govern or misgovern themselves.

George Washington: Creating a Nation in War and Then in Peace
1

O F ALL THE LEADERS WHO EMERGED from the crucible of the Revolution, no one combined better the attributes of experience, sagacity, and "gravitas" that so captivated the imaginations of his fellow countrymen than George Washington. Many educated Americans regarded Washington as their Cincinnatus, the noble Roman who left his plow, saved his country, and then returned to his farm, personally uncorrupted by the lure of power. With a hint of jealousy and some admiration, John Adams once said that Washington's main assets were that he was tall and a Virginian. Indeed, he was both, but he was also a man of considerable means who had risked his life and his future in a seemingly hopeless gamble. While not one of the signers of the Declaration of Independence served in the Continental Army, Washington shared in the soldiers' misery and despair, and he went on to reap quite rightfully the powerful glory that only military victory can bring. Like so many of the Founding Fathers, he sought fame and desired to have posterity remember him for his patriotic services. To many Americans of his time, however, Washington was already the living embodiment of republican virtue, a testament that men raised by proper breeding might very well be able to handle honestly the lure and trappings of power.

Washington was born on February 22, 1732 (February 11, Old-Style Calendar), in Pope's Creek, Virginia, the first child of his father's second marriage. Although the family could trace its roots deep in English history and was closely aligned with the Stuarts, Washington's forebears in America were unable to move into the innermost circle of colonial society. George was raised in a family where his father was often absent, his mother overprotective, and his brothers off on their own. George grew up withdrawn, restrained, and often self-reliant. Frequently in his early career, he had difficulties relating to his elders, often appearing impetuous and headstrong. He spent a considerable amount of his time teaching himself personal control and creating in the process a public persona of aloofness and reserve under which flowed the strong torrents of pride, ambition, and temper.

He was on occasion a surveyor and a lieutenant colonel in the British army. Treated unfairly by some British senior officers, Washington finally resigned from the army, married a wealthy widow, and, at the age of twenty-seven, retired to his estate. Later he was elected to the Virginia House of Burgesses and became associated with George Mason in creating a network of opposition to British colonial policies. He was chosen in 1775 to lead the American Continental Army; in part, his selection was due to the fact that he was a Virginian in a conflict that was identified mainly with New England. Washington became a standard around which the new unformed America was to rally, and he persevered in what was to become a legendary struggle of a ragtag army under an inexperienced commander against the greatest empire on earth.

After a series of lucky engagements against the British and exploiting invaluable French assistance, the Americans prevailed. Washington, like Cincinnatus, returned to Mount Vernon wearing well his newfound glory and dedicated to the republican ideals of tolerance and civilian control of the military.

Although a few other names were occasionally mentioned for the presidency, there was near universal agreement that the office was Washington's if he wanted it. Washington, however, having established his reputation, was reluctant to risk it anew. He wondered if he was too old, at fifty-six, to take on another arduous public position, and he was sure his views were not acceptable to the Anti-Federalist elements. On the other hand, he was uncertain if his fellow citizens would criticize him for refusing to discharge his duty and answer the call to service. While he was debating with himself, his associates were already deciding whom to support for the vice presidency. Most of the Federalist leadership wanted John Adams, but Adams during the war had sought to curtail the general's power, citing the ever-present danger of standing armies. Recognizing the problem, an old friend of the general, Benjamin Lincoln, wrote to Washington and warned that those who opposed Adams really wanted to elect an opponent of the Constitution as vice president. Washington responded tactfully that he would support any true friend of the Constitution and later added that it might be wise for the independent electors to choose a vice president from Massachusetts. Privately, the general let it be known to his closest associates that he favored Adams over Governor George Clinton of New York, who had expressed reservations about the new Constitution. By the end of February, Washington was unanimously elected president and Adams garnered enough votes for the second slot.[1]

By April 14, 1789, Washington was officially notified of his election by Charles Thomson, the secretary of the Congress, who had traveled to Mount Vernon to make the formal announcement. Prepared already, Washington left two days later and began the week-long journey from his country estate to New York City. His trip prompted the most remarkable outpouring of public goodwill and affection ever shown in the new nation. As he passed through Virginia, he was honored at a farewell dinner at Alexandria, was greeted by large crowds in Maryland, and was presented in Delaware with an address thanking him for his willingness to give up retirement and once again come to the aid of his country. In Pennsylvania, he was greeted again by large crowds and a huge flower-covered arch bearing banners and slogans draped across laurel roses and green boughs. A chorus of young maidens sang his praises, as a flowered crown descended on his head from the overhanging structure.

Moving across New Jersey, Washington was greeted by more crowds and saw the faces of some of the old veterans of the last great war. By the time he reached Elizabethtown, he was surrounded by a vast throng of people who led him to a special barge, which was to take him across the river to the shores of New York City, the first capital of the new nation. Washington was saluted by bands, gunfire from ships, church bells, singers, and a school of porpoises that followed his barge part of the way. At the base of Manhattan, near what is now Wall Street, Washington was greeted by more celebrities and a military guard. He declined to ride in the elegant carriage held for him, and instead walked toward his new Cherry Street residence past a cheering and shouting crowd. The first administration was about to begin amid pageantry and pomp, in a republic dedicated nominally to the simple virtues of thrift and moderation.

The New York City that Washington entered in 1789 was the second-largest city in the new nation and, despite the migrations of German, French, English, and African inhabitants, it was still heavily influenced by the Dutch. Few of the streets were paved, and Benjamin Franklin once sarcastically observed that one could always spot a New Yorker by the way he shuffled. Livestock roamed the avenues and lanes, and thousands of pigs feasted on the garbage that people threw into the streets.

Many of the government leaders lived near Wall and Queen streets, and Abigail Adams described her house on Richmond Hill as "the most delicious spot I ever saw." Near the fields, today's City Hall Park, were an almshouse, bridewell, debtors' jail, and gallows. In 1789, ten persons were executed on the Chinese pagoda–style gallows, none for a crime more serious than burglary. Close to the gallows were the whipping posts and the stockades. In New York City, prices then as now seemed to travelers generally high. Washington paid $80 a month to livery his horses; a skilled worker earned 50¢ a day and an unskilled one about half that amount. A loaf of bread sold for 3¢, and it cost a working person a week's wages to buy a ticket to Philadelphia and two days' wages to see a theater production. There were numerous brothels and 330 licensed drinking places—more than one for every hundred inhabitants, including women and children.

The new republic that witnessed the inaugural of General George Washington was in many ways still a confederation. Although the Articles of Confederation had been discarded, the underlying assumptions of American life were really more decentralized and generally looser than the ardent Federalists could abide. Washington knew the sentiments of his people, and he was by temperament a conservative in many ways.

Nearly all Americans worked the land, and land was indeed plentiful in the United States. Many distrusted paper money, and at the time of the first inaugural there were only three commercial banks in business. In the Deep South states of South Carolina and Georgia, rice-producing plantations in the lowlands were worked by African American slaves. World markets were generally open, and 40 percent of those two states' rice crop was sold to England. In the tobacco areas, especially in Virginia and Maryland, the problem of overproduction was apparent. By 1788, prices for that commodity had dropped sharply, and some planters sought to renege on debts owed to the British, while others began to diversify their crops.

In the Northwest Territory, the British still had not honored the provisions of the Treaty of Paris, and they retained a dozen trading posts near the Native American tribes. South of the Ohio area, the flood of Americans met the constraints of the Spanish empire, which restricted travel down the Mississippi and its tributaries leading toward the great port of New Orleans. In the East, among the yeoman farmers there grew up three moderate-sized cities: Philadelphia (population 42,444), New York (33,131), and Baltimore (13,503), with the beginnings of a cosmopolitan culture in each. In New England, the seafaring business was the central source of wealth, with Boston, Providence, and (to a lesser extent) Newport all conducting a lively trade with Europe and the West Indies.

This complex and diverse society fascinated European visitors, as they noted the Americans' love of freedom, the lack of extremes of wealth and poverty, the emphasis on industry and hard work, and the absence of religious and hereditary distinctions. Americans were generally materialistic, at times crude, and usually enterprising. There were notable character differences between the practical and stingy Yankees, the uncouth frontiersmen, and the cultured tidewater aristocracy of the South, which were to produce tensions in the new nation.[2]

The First Months

After Washington's inaugural, the new president waited patiently while Congress debated what would be the outline of the new bureaucracy and executive agencies. The Confederation, both during the war and after, had a series of such offices, which oversaw the functions of the state, war, treasury, and the post office departments, and those agents continued their work during the first administration. As Washington watched the weeks pass by, Congress began its deliberations with an extremely difficult decision to make: who had the power to remove subordinates. The new Constitution said little about removing administrative officers, and it mentioned dismissal only by means of the cumbersome impeachment process.

The House of Representatives, including some nineteen members of the original Philadelphia Convention of 1787, should have known all too well what the Constitution said and what the delegates originally meant. Yet they were in disagreement as to whether the president had the power to remove such officials and if he needed the consent of Congress, or at least the Senate, which initially would approve many of those individuals. In fact, as the debate progressed, no fewer than four separate views emerged. Some congressmen, such as James Madison, argued that the power to remove the heads of the departments must rest with the executive alone. Others argued that the only method of removal was through the impeachment process. A third group argued that the Constitution delegated to Congress the authority to create new offices and to make laws, and that therefore it was the legislative branch that could determine tenure, duties, and compensation of officers. However, some of the congressmen who held this view still believed that Congress should delegate its removal power to the president. And last, some members felt that the president and the Senate shared the removal power. In the end, the president was "given" the power to remove subordinates, but whether the power was inherently his in the Constitution or whether it was delegated to him by the Congress never became clear. By the time of Reconstruction, the Radical Republicans would resurrect the controversy by charging that President Andrew Johnson had acted improperly in dismissing major cabinet officials against the express will of the legislative branch.[3]

While that issue was being decided, Washington was spending a considerable amount of time worrying about questions of etiquette. Although he was a republican by nature and by inclination, Washington was no democrat. He had worked long and hard to separate himself from the mass of his fellow citizens, and he was sure that a solid base for the presidency had to include a decent respect for ceremony and decorum. Privately, he admitted that without his wife Martha beside him in that first month, he found much of the socializing burdensome. He spent nearly every day receiving visitors, and many nights returning calls and going to civic events. Overwhelmed, he brooded that there was no time left for public business. As he was aware, the presiding officers of the Confederation Congress had entertained lavishly and their tables were often open to the public. Washington reviewed the situation and bluntly observed that the presiding officer was a "maître d'hôtel," and he was determined to avoid that fate.

In addition to being very time consuming, such entertainment was costly. In his first nine months in office, Washington spent nearly $2,000 on liquor alone—as astronomical figure in 1789. As some of the more vocal republican representatives watched the new president, they found him to be a bit pompous and rather pretentious. But Washington was anxious to present a good impression in office, and he personally exhibited an old soldier's awkwardness rather than entertaining any illusions about his own position. To one confidant, he wrote that he would rather be at Mount Vernon with a friend or two than to be "attended at the seat of government by the officers and representatives of every power in Europe." When Martha finally arrived, Washington began to relax somewhat, and at informal tea parties he was seen to pass by the men and spend more time with the ladies, whose gracious company he always enjoyed.[4]

The First Administration

The most pressing issue facing the new republic, though, was not etiquette or appointments, but the state of the economy. Much of the pressure to pass the new Constitution and create a new form of government was based on the widely held view, especially in the commercial classes, that the Confederation was too weak to promote economic development and guarantee financial stability. For those groups, it was fortuitous that the most brilliant and energetic cabinet member in the administration was Alexander Hamilton.

Hamilton took office as secretary of the treasury on September 11, 1789, and ten days later he received a request from the House of Representatives that he send to it a plan for the "adequate support of the public credit." That simple inquiry was the immediate cause of Hamilton's far-reaching design to expand the federal government's power and tie it to the merchants and bankers. Blessed with a remarkable mastery of detail and a gift for tactical leadership, Hamilton unfolded a monumental economic policy. In his own mind, he was the prime minister of this new administration and the mainstay of what was to become the Federalist faction.

The Revolutionary War had been financed by a crazy-quilt array of measures, and the states and national government had been unable to settle the problem of who owed what to whom. The largest part of the debt was intergovernmental credits and obligations. The total amount the state governments had spent for the war was somewhat over $100 million, and under the Articles of Confederation and various ordinances passed by Congress, those expenditures were to be credited and the costs reapportioned. Those states that had given more than their share would be reimbursed from the general treasury, and those that had paid less than their share would have to pay into it. Since the New Englanders kept more meticulous records than the Southerners, the reimbursement proposals were bound to create problems. Also, the United States owed $8 million to the government of France and $2 million to banks in Holland, and Congress had issued unsecured paper money that had depreciated enormously. Speculators had bought up a good number of governmental securities at a discount rate. Should they end up with a currency that was worth full value? Many of the speculators had purchased vast tracts of land from the federal government or the states, paying for them with securities at face value. In addition, some states had already repaid their debts, while others had not.

Facing those vexatious questions, Hamilton put forth a brilliant mosaic. He would have the federal government assume the war debt, refinance the old securities under a variety of options, make no distinctions between the original and current holders of governmental securities, allow purchasers of western lands to pay for them with the full value of inflated currencies, continue the tariff, and create a national bank.

Major opposition immediately came over the method of calculating the debts of the states. Facing intense opposition in Congress, Hamilton appealed in desperation to the new secretary of state, Thomas Jefferson, to secure important support. Hamilton, Jefferson, and Madison ended up approving a deal whereby the national capital would be moved to the Potomac River area, and the Commonwealth of Virginia received confirmation that the allowable debt assumption total in Hamilton's plan would jump to nearly $19 million. Thus, to Jefferson's later consternation, the first piece of the Hamiltonian system—the debt assumption scheme—passed with his help.[5]

Jefferson and his republican colleagues were less amenable to the next keystone, the establishment of a national bank. Jefferson and Madison openly challenged the constitutionality of the measure, insisting that the Constitution provided no specific grant of power to create such a bank. But Hamilton brilliantly demolished those criticisms and ended up making a case in the process for a broad interpretation of federal powers. In those major economic battles, the president retained his position of being above the fray, although he publicly supported the debt plan and had personal reservations, which he overcame, about a federal banking system.

While most accounts of the first term of the Washington administration concentrate on the economic program, another major issue that occupied the president's attention was the situation on the frontier. Some of the tribes constituted a clear danger, while others were still aligned with the British and Spanish. Western politicians demanded increased federal protection, and when they did not get it, some talked of setting up a new nation divorced from the weak American republic.

Congress was at that time engaged in a protracted debate over reorganizing the modest military establishment. Strong opposition to a standing army and its costs was expressed by New England representatives, while petitions of concern over the threat from the tribes came in from the Ohio Valley, Kentucky, and elsewhere. The administration resorted to the same strategies used by the Confederation government—peace treaties, bribes, and an occasional show of force. But not all the tribes were willing to be pushed or cheated into the deep hinterlands. In the Northwest Territory, the army suffered serious setbacks at the hands of the tribes, and Congress ordered an investigation.

After the demise of General Arthur St. Clair's forces, the House of Representatives insisted on getting relevant War Department documents, and the president and his cabinet secretaries discussed the question of invoking what later was called executive privilege, or the right to withhold information. Washington finally forwarded the papers to the House and sent the secretary of war and secretary of the treasury to testify in person before Congress. As a consequence of these developments, the president, through Secretary of War Henry Knox, exercised increasing responsibilities both in terms of frontier diplomacy and in the activities of the army in those regions. Dealing with General "Mad" Anthony Wayne, the president ordered reevaluations of court martial proceedings, instructed Wayne where to lay camp and how to discipline and train troops, identified where the destinations of the troops should be, approved all promotions to higher ranks, stopped a proposed expedition to the rapids of the Miami River, and laid out the terms of a peace treaty to be presented to the tribes. Wayne desperately wrote to Knox, "Would to God that my hands were untied."

The president also continued to meet with less bellicose tribal leaders, and in summit conferences with the Seneca chief Cornplanter in December 1790 and with the leaders of the Six Nations in late 1791 and early 1792, he urged moderation and friendship. At times, the administration's Indian policy seemed a confusing mixture of diplomacy and brute force. Faced with both tribal suspicion of the white man's push for more and more land and the restlessness of Western politicians, the president and Knox tried to curtail the excesses of land speculators and lawless elements. They resisted the brutality that so characterized later administrations' policies toward the tribes, thwarted as best they could the mischief making of the British and the Spanish, and tried to contain the strong pressures to enact measures for the wholesale removal of the Native Americans. Faced with a loose republic, a weak army, and limited options, the president walked a fine line between restraint and bellicose action.[6]

In another development, the impetus for political parties had been muted for a while by Washington's election. He was a symbol of unity and continuity with the Revolution. But in his own cabinet and in Congress, two factions were emerging that threatened to polarize the administration. The sources of that division lay embedded in many controversies: the Hamilton economic plan, the powerful sectional differences that were evident before the Constitution was ratified, the relative importance of a strong frontier defense and a standing army, and, most especially, the intense wars in Europe. By making the executive branch a center of initiative and the federal government a visible establishment, Washington inadvertently facilitated that division. At first, the partisan hostility swirled around him like currents around the calm. But by the middle of his second term, with Hamilton and Jefferson gone and Europe aflame, Washington provided the strong leadership that caused both opposition leaders and the opposition press to attack him openly. Steadfastly, Washington reached beyond the narrow confines of the capital and the elites in those controversies and prevailed again and again.

By December 1793, the two factions (which later became known as the Federalists and the Democratic-Republicans) were locked in a bitter controversy over the establishment of a national bank, then being discussed in the Senate. In the House during the next session, the two factions became increasingly cohesive in voting on issues involving the Whiskey Rebellion, Democratic-Republican societies, frontier security, and tribal affairs.

The growth of these factions and later full-fledged parties was facilitated by the increase in communications and the general rise in what one might call political consciousness. In the decade from 1790 to 1800, the number of newspapers doubled to two hundred, and by 1810 there were more journals of public opinion per capita in the United States than anywhere else in the world. There was also a dramatic upsurge in the number of post offices, from 28 in 1776 to 75 by 1790 and 453 in 1795. America was becoming a literate and participatory political culture, the likes of which were unknown in the world at that time.

Politics became more popularly covered, as news, even delayed news, was widely disseminated. Partisan clubs also began to grow up, the most visible being the "Democratic-Republican societies," first appearing in 1793 among the Germans in Philadelphia. Jefferson exuberantly called these clubs a rekindling of "the spirit of 1776." But the real focus of the partisan strife revolved around Hamilton and Jefferson, with the latter being supported by the energetic efforts of his fellow Virginian James Madison. Hamilton had laid out the Federalist agenda, an alliance of wealth and privilege harnessed to the new experiment. Jefferson, at first diffident but later surreptitiously involved in partisan intrigue, became the lightning rod for Federalist animosity and Republican acclaim. Actually, the real engine of the opposition was Madison, who had once been both a close Hamilton ally and a confidant to the president. But by the 1790s, Southern and Western ranks began to coalesce around regional leaders, who in turn opposed the Hamiltonian agenda. Joined with the unscrupulous and ambitious Aaron Burr in New York, the Democratic-Republicans of Virginia were creating the first real political party.

Through the early 1790s, Washington tried to ignore the controversies and attempted to mediate the differences, especially in his own cabinet. He pleaded with his secretaries for an end to "tearing our vitals out." Hamilton insisted he was the main victim in these partisan controversies, as attacks on his character and policies continued in the opposition newspapers. Jefferson's response was even more bitter: Hamilton was "a man whose history . . . is a tissue of machinations against the liberty of the country which had not only received and given him bread, but heaped honors on his head." The president tried reason, flattery—even a cabinet picnic! But nothing worked. Washington privately expressed a desire to retire from all this acrimony, but the leaders of both factions insisted on his continuing.

He was unanimously reelected in 1792, but partisanship flared up in the choice for the second office. Adams won reelection over Governor Clinton of New York, although the governor not only carried New York but also did very well in the South. Even with the national vote of confidence he received, Washington was not immune to the increasing controversies taking place. The major whirlwind he endured was the American division of opinion about the French Revolution and the wars in Europe.[7]

France had been the one true ally whose support made the American Revolution a success against incredible odds and turned Washington from a beleaguered guerrilla fighter into a national hero. The two nations—the new republic and the Ancien Régime—were bound together by treaty, self-interest, and affection. As a reminder of British presence after the peace, His Majesty's government still refused to abandon some of its forts in the West and helped stir up the tribes against the fragile American union, leaving the United States with strong positive sentiments toward its old ally France.

Washington at first joined with nearly all Americans in welcoming the French Revolution—seeing it as a child of his own nation's upheaval. He was deeply moved when the legendary Marquis de Lafayette sent him the main key of the Bastille prison, that "fortress of despotism." Linking up the two great revolutions he had been part of, Lafayette gave the key "as a tribute which I owe as a son to my adoptive father, as an aide-de-camp to my general, as a missionary of liberty to its patriarch."

But as the French Revolution became more extreme and violent, as the cycle of events began to eat its own fathers, Washington wondered if the French were not being overwhelmed by their "too great eagerness in swallowing something so delightful as liberty." Even Jefferson, who spoke of the need for a revolution every twenty years or so to water the tree of liberty, began to have misgivings about what was happening.

In politics, imitation is often more important than rational public discourse. The radical spirit of the French Revolution began to develop in the United States, and the Federalists regrouped to battle the influx of an ideology of atheism, anarchy, and excess. The new regime in France turned its energies to Europe, proclaiming the liberation of those enslaved by old monarchies and despots and using patriotism as a unifying cry for the French people. And so the wars of ideology began.

Faced with a meager military establishment and a clear sense of the folly of European wars, Washington insisted on announcing American neutrality. Hamilton pushed for a total repudiation of the treaties of friendship and armistice between France and the United States. Jefferson vigorously rejected any such step and opposed even using the word *neutrality*. But Washington was clearly unwilling to be drawn into conflicts not of his own making. The United States would stay out of those wars of ideology in Europe. Some Republicans denounced him in the capital and in the newspapers, but public sentiment was with the president. While Madison and Hamilton—each using pen names—debated in partisan newspapers whether the president had the authority in foreign affairs to issue a neutrality proclamation, Washington moved to implement his policy. He was soon attacked by the French minister to the United States, Edmond Genêt, for abandoning treaty commitments to his country, and Genêt eventually appealed to Republican leaders and to the nation as a whole.

At one cabinet meeting, the president lost his temper and denounced the criticisms of the pro-French Republican editor, that "rascal [Philip] Freneau." Years later, Adams remembered the opposition to Washington (probably in exaggerated terms): "Ten thousand people in the streets of Philadelphia, day after day, threatened to drag Washington out of his house, and effect a revolution in the government, or compel it to declare war in favor of the French Revolution and against England. The coolest and firmest minds, even among the Quakers in Philadelphia, have given their opinions to me, that nothing but the yellow fever . . . could have saved the United States from a fatal revolution of government."

But when Genêt threatened publicly to appeal over the president's head to the people, the patriotic response was swift and predictable. Genêt was bitterly denounced in all quarters for his foreign presumption, and public opinion quickly swung to the Washington of old. The Republicans quietly walked away from their French friend.

In the beginning of 1794, the Republicans in the Senate tried again and demanded from the president copies of correspondence from Gouverneur Morris, the American minister to France. Once again the cabinet discussed the question of invoking executive privilege, but Washington sent the correspondence, except for one sensitive dispatch. Meanwhile in France, the radical Jacobins had seized control of the faltering French republic, and they wanted Genêt sent home for arrest and probably the guillotine. Genêt pleaded for asylum, relief that the president graciously granted.[8]

Besides opposition to his foreign policy, the president was also faced with some nasty rumblings from western Pennsylvania. In several counties, excise taxes on whiskey enacted by Congress at Hamilton's request were the focal point for an insurrection. Hamilton saw the uprising as a fine opportunity to assert the power of the new federal government; Washington was more cautious and started with several warnings admonishing all to obey the law and respect the authority of revenue agents.

For the frontiersmen of western Pennsylvania, whiskey was more than a beverage at mealtimes or an elixir in extending hospitality. The farmers had little cash and were unable to transport lumber, grain, and meat at reasonable costs across the mountains to market. Instead, they often turned rye to whiskey, which could be easily transported in bulk and sold at a profit. The excise tax on whiskey, then, was a direct burden on their livelihoods and a restriction on one of the few sources of cash they could generate. From their point of view, the federal government provided little protection on the frontier against the tribes, and yet it demanded taxes to run its administration way back east.

While Hamilton continued to push for strict prosecution, Washington temporized; in 1792, the violence seemed to have been curtailed. But gradually through 1793 and into the next year, the controversy mounted, and an excise agent in western Pennsylvania was attacked. Finally, the president called up several state militias and rode with them to the areas supposedly in rebellion.

But as the president and the armed forces moved into the western counties, no real resistance was encountered. Several of the ringleaders of the rebellion were tried, and two were convicted and sentenced to death. Washington issued a proclamation pardoning all those who were not then under indictment or sentenced, and he pardoned the two found guilty, remarking that one was a simpleton and the other insane.

Hamilton regarded the whole episode as a sterling demonstration of the new assertiveness and power of the nascent national administration. Yet the rebels in their crude way were also correct in their assessment that this was an administration more sensitive to the problems of the bondholders, speculators, merchants, and bankers than those of laborers, farmers, and frontier democrats in the hinterlands. Meanwhile, the Federalists in the 1794 elections adroitly used the rebellion against the Republicans. Even Washington went out of his way to criticize the so-called Democratic-Republican clubs that he felt had instigated the rebellion. He called them "self-created societies," and the Federalist-controlled Senate approved a resolution censuring the groups, while the more Republican-oriented House refused to concur. The controversy was mild, however, compared to the intense controversies that swirled around the president's support for the Jay Treaty.[9]

The upheavals in Europe profoundly changed the Old World and the New. The wars of interest and ideology begun by revolutionary France and the wars of empire heralded by Napoleon resulted in the demise of parts of the Spanish colonial system and eventually in the curbing of the power of the French nation. The United States during Jefferson's presidency was to double its size as Napoleon gladly gave up the Louisiana Territory, and American leaders were soon after to proclaim confidently that European influence would no longer be expanded in the Western Hemisphere.

But in 1794, there was no way that Washington could have known what would be the benevolent outcomes of the brutal European war that was destroying the old regime and inflaming the hearts of many Americans. At first, the president also had to contend with an increasing number of British violations of American rights. Jefferson, leaving the position of secretary of state, and Madison in the House pushed Republicans to demand retaliatory steps against the British. But then the French increased their seizing of American ships bound for England. Federalist leaders fearful of hostilities with both countries pressed Washington to reach some accommodation with the British; finally, the president sent Chief Justice John Jay to England. Jay was an experienced diplomat and a former secretary of foreign affairs during the Confederation period. He negotiated a treaty that moderated many of the major points of contention between the two nations, fostered British–American amity, and led the Spanish to reevaluate their policies in the American Southwest, which finally culminated in the Pinckney Treaty approved by the Senate on March 3, 1796.

The Jay Treaty, however, was barely presented to the Senate when the Republican politicians and their newspapers began criticizing its provisions. In the midst of all this controversy, Washington received some evidence that his trusted secretary of state, Edmund Randolph, had been compromised in dealing with the French and had supposedly asked for bribes from the French ambassador. The charges were unsubstantiated, but Randolph resigned, and the last major Republican figure in the administration was gone.

Washington ended up signing the controversial Jay Treaty and then faced an intensified campaign in the House of Representatives against providing funds to implement the agreement. By 1796, the president was under varied attacks from Republican newspapers and leaders. One editor, Benjamin Bache of the Philadelphia *Aurora*, said Washington's behavior was more characteristic of an "omnipotent director of a seraglio instead of the first magistrate of a free people." Even Madison informed Jefferson, who had retired to Monticello, that Washington's popularity was ebbing and that he was marked "in indelible character as the head of a British faction."

When the Republicans in the House pushed for information on Jay's instructions and all relevant correspondence, the president dug in his heels and refused to bow to the request. He argued that the House had no role in the treaty-making process and pointedly remarked that the only relevant purpose for such a request would be to provide information for impeachment proceedings.

Federalist leaders appealed to the Constitution, the integrity of the president, and the economic interests most likely to be affected by continued stresses in U.S.-British relationships. Banks and insurance companies began to sound alarms about what the consequences would be if the treaty were rejected. The Federalist establishment demonstrated all too well how Hamilton's alliance of political power and economic influence could be quickly and effectively mobilized, just as the Republicans had feared. But the major factor in settling this controversy was once again the immense popularity of the president. Observing the unexpected setback to the Republican cause in the House, Jefferson simply concluded, "One man outweighs them all in influence over the people."

With the major figures of his administration gone—especially Hamilton and Jefferson—Washington took over more of the day-to-day responsibilities of his administration, especially in foreign affairs. He insisted on staying with his neutrality proclamation, and when the French ambassadors, Edmond Genêt and later Pierre Adet, tried to rally popular sentiment against the president, public support for Washington mounted instead. The administration squarely faced not just French discontent but also concerns over British attacks on U.S. ships and the impressment of American seamen.

Criticisms of the president came even from Thomas Paine, Randolph, Jefferson, and other notable Republican figures, and Washington at times wondered if he had in any way hurt his reputation by continuing on in public service. Weary with the burdens of office, Washington refused to consider a third term and issued on September 17, 1796, his farewell address to the American people. The Federalist mantle passed to John Adams, who was able to squeak out a victory over Thomas Jefferson, who in turn became vice president. Washington returned home to Mount Vernon, soon to be deified by the contentious people he had headed in war and peace.[10]

Thomas Jefferson: Establishing Popular Rule **2**

As the republic enlarged and the franchise expanded, the forces of democratic sentiment and popular reform became more apparent. In the South and in the West, Republican strength increased, and in the spring of 1800, the party even captured control of the New York legislature. The stage then was set for a changing of the guard.

As they approached the election, the Republicans nominated Thomas Jefferson for president and Aaron Burr for vice president, but in the process the party leaders forgot to make sure that Burr would receive one vote less in the Electoral College than Jefferson so there would be no tie. The result was that the lame-duck House of Representatives was forced to decide the contest, and the Federalists threw their support to Burr, resulting in a deadlock of thirty-five ballots each. Burr, a veteran intriguer, instead of disavowing that tactic, said nothing publicly and infuriated his own party's leaders. Finally, it was Hamilton who persuaded his fellow Federalists to support his old enemy, Thomas Jefferson, arguing quite rightly that while Jefferson was a dreamy ideologue, Burr was a dangerous man. Thus, the Founding Fathers, for all their differences, knew each other well enough to appreciate the conflicts between rhetoric and reality.

The election of 1800 and the long controversies after the Electoral College deadlock produced some understandable bitterness among Jefferson and his followers. But when the dust settled and the House of Representatives did its constitutional duty, the new nation witnessed a peaceful transition of power into the hands of the loyal opposition. Jefferson's response was typical of him: a generous sentiment captured in a felicitous phrase covering over real malice. In his first inaugural address, probably the finest ever given by a president, he pronounced, "We have called by different names brethren of the same principle. We are all republicans; we are all federalists."

Then in a vein of public confidence and political tolerance, he fell back on the familiar sentiments of the Enlightenment: "If there be any among us who would wish to dissolve this Union or to change its republican form, let them stand undisturbed as monuments of safety with which error of opinion may be tolerated where reason is left free to combat it."[1]

As Jefferson took office in 1801, the population had grown by 25 percent since 1790 and would grow at the same rate between 1800 and 1810. A sixth of Americans were slaves, and only one out of twenty-five people lived in a city. The capital was a swampy village with clusters of houses and the beginnings of a row of government buildings. There were about two hundred newspapers in the United States in 1801, and every political faction seemed to have its own organ of opinion. The country was an agricultural nation with substantial trading and commerce; the Land Act of 1800 provided for the sale of tracts of 320 acres for a minimum price of $2 per acre. From 1790 to 1810, the amount of cotton produced in the South jumped from 3,000 bales to 178,000 bales. There were very few free laborers, in a nation where free land was so abundant and the indentured servant system was dying. Workers in towns and cities made up 2 to 3 percent of the population, and by 1815, personal income was ranging from 80¢ a day in the rural areas to $1.50 in the cities. Roads were poor, although some privately run toll roads and canals were in place. The United States, in the language of the late twentieth century, had a third world economy with a fairly literate and politically aware population for that period.

The Jeffersonians, or Democratic-Republicans (as they were sometimes termed), were the party of the yeoman farmers, the small businessmen, the South, and the West. However, by the end of the Jeffersonian era, the Federalist Party would be thoroughly routed even in its stronghold of New England.

At the center of this first political party was Thomas Jefferson—his thought and his enigmatic personality. At six feet two inches tall, Jefferson dressed casually and had an easy way about him; he conveyed the impression of a dreamy, loose-limbed planter. His detractors saw him as a dangerous partisan and a subtle manipulator of people and events. But he was, in the words of one woman, "so meek and mild, yet dignified in his manners, with a voice so soft and low, with a countenance so benignant and intelligent." He avoided public controversies, but privately he could be a political operator not above recrimination and petty retaliation. Like many Southerners, he was imbued with a sense of formal manners and was unwilling to confront people directly. And like so many individuals from that region, because of his studied politeness, he gave people at times a sense of reassurance when he was simply avoiding disagreement, and this reticence often led to charges of hypocrisy. To Jefferson, the election of 1800 was a reaffirmation of the principles of the American Revolution, the "Spirit of '76," as he liked to characterize it. But at fifty-seven, he had spent nearly all his adult life thinking about politics and becoming aware that people are shaped by prejudices, moved by self-interest, and often swayed by the basest of sentiments.[2]

His stated intention was to split off the Federalist voters from their leaders, and to do that he insisted that his own followers and friends see the need for some public moderation, especially during his first term. Jefferson refused to begin his term with a radical agenda, arguing in part that slender majorities such as his do not lend themselves to political upheavals. He seemed to be satisfied with some patronage changes, a cut in military spending, and a balanced budget. To those moderate prescriptions, he attached the label "Revolution of 1800."

But under pressure from more radical Republican leaders and followers, Jefferson decided to make major changes in government offices, especially in the lucrative customs agent positions and in the law enforcement areas. During the period of the Alien and Sedition Acts, the Jeffersonians had learned all too well that the administration of justice was discretionary, and that politicians were not above using the law as a weapon to indict, try, and sentence opponents. Jefferson had not forgotten the "reign of the witches" and which individuals were the instruments of oppressive Federalist policies. In actuality, though, in the Adams administration there were only fifteen indictments and ten convictions under the Sedition Act of 1798. Still, Jefferson swept the enforcement stables clean and replaced them with Republicans. And retaining the bitterness of memory, he publicly approved the end of the Alien and Sedition Acts, citing them as inimical to a free people, while privately urging some of his closest and most discreet followers to undertake similar indictments on the state level against Federalists.

The Jeffersonians had to come to grips with the most difficult vestige of Federalist dominance—the federal judiciary. Critics charged that Adams had nominated judges and a chief justice up to the last days of his lame-duck term, and Congress had expanded the number of positions and court layers even while litigation declined. The people could cast the Federalists out of the presidency and trim down the number of elected Federalist congressmen and senators, but one branch of government was still beyond their reach. The Jeffersonians attacked the federal judiciary in two ways: impeachment and contraction. The new Congress in 1801 began with the repeal of the Judiciary Act in order to slice away at the new judgeships and the Federalists embedded in them. Congress then demanded that the Supreme Court go into recess so as to avoid reviewing its actions. The Republican-controlled House of Representatives and Senate also began to look at the impeachment option, focusing on Federalist judges who were obviously unfit or obnoxiously partisan. But the failed attempt to impeach Supreme Court Justice Samuel Chase ended the enthusiasm for that laborious process.[3]

The Jeffersonians accepted the basic economic structure put in place by Hamilton, and Jefferson and Madison—both critics of Washington's neutrality policy—proved to be less belligerent toward Britain than the Federalists expected. The president's chief economic adviser, the Swiss-born Albert Gallatin, accepted Hamilton's nationalism, although he advocated a more frugal and a less ambitious government. But the basic pillars of the Hamiltonian system remained: refinancing of the debt, the bank, and a strong treasury department. In setting its foreign policy, the Jefferson administration was filled with individuals who had served in past positions of responsibility. Jefferson and Madison, Monroe, and Robert Livingston may have engaged in pro-French rhetoric, but in the quiet parlors of diplomacy, when they were among friends, they detested the airs of Europe and struggled to promote American interests as firmly as Washington, Adams, and Jay. As Jefferson commented, it would have been better if the Atlantic were an ocean of fire to prevent the contamination of court politics and the decadence of European life from permeating pristine American shores.

To the Republicans, the presidency was the chief instrument of the very policies they were elected to end. Jefferson, as a symbolic concession and also because of his own predilections, refused to make the State of the Union address personally. It smacked of the speech from the throne. Instead, he had his speech hand-delivered to be read by the clerk of the House, a custom continued until Woodrow Wilson. To further differentiate himself from the Federalist presidents, he deliberately avoided balls, disregarded traditional court etiquette, wore slippers in his meetings with some foreign diplomats, and conducted bright cheery dinners where fine light wines and Renaissance-style conversation dominated the tone. He was the planter squire, the Enlightenment intellectual, the reserved but friendly man of letters. Gone were the Washington preoccupation with etiquette and the Adams obsession with mannered dignity. Jefferson walked to his own inaugural, rode to Congress on his own horse, and wrote his own speeches.

Although he did not publicly ask Congress to follow his prescriptions, Jefferson had spent too much time in legislative politics not to know that things do not happen by chance. While he avoided outward displays of leadership, in fact he and his cabinet ministers and friends in Congress served as conduits for his words, sentiments, and proposals. With respectable majorities in both houses of Congress, Jefferson's first term and the beginning of his second showed remarkable results. Because of the president's stature in the nation, his long record as a leader in Republican causes, and the lack of a structured leadership in Congress, Jefferson was able to provide strong guidance in a subtle but effective way. But as in all presidencies, the last several years are usually the undoing, and his undoing came over his foreign policy.[4]

The First Republican Agenda

Jefferson's attitude toward federal appointments drew some criticism from the ardent supporters of the Republican cause for being too lenient and from the Federalists for being too extreme. He did try to stop some last-minute Adams appointees from taking office, and later the new president enlarged that group to those appointed in the last three months of Adams's term. Many of the Republicans regarded the whole host of them as "midnight" appointments. One of them was William Marbury, who never received his formal notice as justice of the peace for the District of Columbia from the Jefferson administration after his appointment by Adams. Consequently he sued. The Supreme Court under Chief Justice John Marshall granted Marbury no relief, but proclaimed in a landmark decision the doctrine of judicial review instead.

Jefferson insisted that his appointments had to tilt toward the Republicans until they received a just proportion of the offices to make up for Federalist neglect over the years and to reflect better the true popular majority they commanded. The president also took a dim view of Federalist officeholders using their positions "to overthrow the cause," as he put it. However, he drew from the gentleman class in making his appointments, picking men who were more often similar in background to the Federalist civil servants than those chosen later by the more democratic Andrew Jackson.

Faced with his narrow election margin, Jefferson was pragmatic and limited in placing his public agenda before Congress. As he wrote to his friend Pierre Samuel DuPont de Nemours, "What is practicable must often control what is pure theory: and the habits of the governed determine in a great degree what is practicable."[5]

In the area of foreign policy, the president at first saw only peace on the horizons except along the Barbary coast of North Africa where Tripoli had committed acts of war against the United States. Jefferson's reaction to the pirate state was at first rather indecisive. He argued that he needed congressional sanction to act, a position attacked as another sign of weakness by Hamilton, writing under one of his many pen names. "What will the world think of the fold which has such a shepherd?" the New Yorker speculated. Jefferson did send the U.S. Navy to do battle, and after four years of conflict, the United States finally defeated the Tripoli pirate regime.[6]

Overall, Jefferson minimized America's presence in other ways. He retained missions only to Great Britain, France, and Spain, and he began an active campaign to cut the U.S. Navy, except the frigate fleet. Aided by Secretary of the Treasury Gallatin, the president pushed for retiring the national debt, then about $83 million. Jefferson as a matter of philosophy opposed a public debt that was passed on to future generations. As he once observed, "The earth belongs always to the living generation."[7]

Jefferson exercised considerable control over Congress even though the ideology of his party tended to depreciate presidential leadership. He accomplished his objectives through close informal relationships with his party's legislative leaders and because of the high regard in which he was held among the rank and file as a symbol of the very march of democracy. Not until Woodrow Wilson, with his very different, prime ministerial style of leadership, was Congress to be so dominated by the executive. As Jefferson once observed, if he just limited himself to formal recommendations, his administration would be "a government of chance and not of design."[8]

At the top on the president's and the party's agenda was the repeal of the Judiciary Act of 1801. That act had become effective three weeks before the end of the last Federalist Congress, and it was clearly meant to enlarge the judiciary branch in order to stack it with Federalist Party faithful. Not one Republican was seated on the federal bench at any level when Jefferson took office. The judiciary in general was a friend to creditors over debtors, and Republicans were worried about its attitude toward disputed land titles in the South and the West. The arrogance of the Federalist judiciary in the Alien and Sedition cases was legendary among the Jeffersonians, and the president shared in expressing those standard Republican criticisms. As noted, Congress repealed the Judiciary Act and then in a highly controversial step mandated that the Supreme Court would not meet for another fourteen months—a demand seen as a move to stop judi-cial review of its action.[9] During the dispute, Vice President Burr, already distrusted for his ambiguous role in the deadlocked election of 1800, let it be known that he opposed his party's policy on the repeal.

Although Jefferson's popularity grew enormously in his first years in office, he was subject to a continuing barrage of criticism. Some of it was harmless, such as Thomas Pinckney's characterization of the president as "the moonshine philosopher of Monticello."[10] But others were more vitriolic, such as James Thomson Callender, a former ally of Jefferson who turned on him and carried on a personal attack for months. Among other stories, Callender spread the rumor that Jefferson had a slave mistress named Sally (which was probably true), had tried to seduce his friend's wife years before (which was only partly true), and had tried to pay off a debt to a friend in depreciated currency. The "Dusty Sally" story remains in currency down to the present, being revived in biographies and in fiction. And the opposition press resurrected charges of corruption and incompetence during his lackluster term as wartime governor of Virginia.

One can see why Jefferson, who had so often praised a free press and once commented that if he had to he would prefer it to the government itself, began to change his mind. Midway through his first term, he con-cluded that "our newspapers, for the most part, present only the caricatures of disaffected minds. Indeed the abuses of the freedom of the press here have been carried to a length never before known or borne by any civilized nation."[11] As noted, he had early in his term recommended to Republicans on a state level a few selected prosecutions of opposition journalists—a po-sition similar to the Federalist objectives in passing the Sedition Act. Still, he returned almost as a reflex action to his faith in the people, concluding, "The firmness with which the people have withstood the late abuses of the press, the discernment they have manifested between truth and falsehood, show that they may safely be trusted to hear everything true and false, and form a correct judgment between them."[12]

The Louisiana Purchase

One persistent issue that concerned Americans of all parties and many areas of the nation was the fate of the Mississippi Valley region then held by Spain. The matter was complicated by the European wars begun as a consequence of revolutionary and later Napoleonic France's dreams of republican ideology and imperial conquest. Jefferson had hoped that a weakened Spain would continue to hold onto the Mississippi lands until the United States was able to assert itself and take them over. As Arthur Whitaker has written, "[N]either unionism nor disunionism was deeply rooted in the West at the end of the century."[13] Still, as with his Federalist predecessors, Jefferson understood that he had to show that the national government cared about the West, and his party's strength in that region was based heavily on his successes.

As for Spain, the royal court's ministers saw Louisiana and the Floridas as a buffer between the United States and its more valued empire around the Gulf of Mexico. To facilitate growth in population in those colonies, Spain had adopted a generous immigration policy, including religious toleration and commercial advantages. Administratively, Louisiana and West Florida were placed under a single governor with New Orleans as the capital; East Florida had a separate governor at Saint Augustine. Both governors were under the authority of the captain-general, who resided in Havana. About 80 percent of the colonists were concentrated in the lower areas of Louisiana and in the lands west of Mobile Bay in West Florida.

However, in 1795, Spanish Minister Manuel de Godoy signed the Treaty of San Lorenzo, which granted the Americans free navigation of the Mississippi River and the right of deposit at New Orleans port. He recognized the thirty-first parallel as the southern boundary of the United States and promised to withdraw Spanish garrisons from the areas his country was giving up. Godoy also had changed his views toward Louisiana, which he came to believe was unmanageable and a drain on the Spanish treasury. Consequently, he decided to offer France the Louisiana Territory in return for the Italian kingdom of Parma. Overall, the costs of being in Louisiana exceeded the modest revenues that came in from custom duties and other levies. Louisiana had to be supported by a Mexican subsidy for its administrative costs, and Godoy wearily examined the defense problems and concluded, "You can't lock up an open field."[14] The Spanish minister feared that conflict over Louisiana would involve his nation in controversies with both Great Britain and the United States, which he and the royal court did not want, and which they feared would jeopardize the more important southwestern empire of Mexico and New Spain. When Spain finally gave Louisiana to Napoleon, he typically insisted on possessing the Floridas as well, a demand they rejected. Napoleon then promised that he would not part with Louisiana without giving Spain the opportunity to reclaim it. In the end, he never turned over the Italian territory to the Spanish king, and he sold Louisiana to the Americans without Spanish approval.

Between the American Revolution and the Louisiana Purchase, commerce in the Mississippi Valley changed the very nature of that area. The major items exported from Louisiana were tobacco, indigo, furs and skins, and lumber; the Treaty of San Lorenzo increased the export trade for the Americans west to New Orleans and down to the West Indies. By the end of 1798, American goods were allowed to enter and leave New Orleans, but they could not be sold there.

Meanwhile on the frontier, there were increasing problems linked with the troubles in Natchez in 1797, with the Blount conspiracy, and with the Yazoo land scandal. William Blount had been a territorial governor and was later a United States senator who was nearly impeached before he left that body. He was charged by his enemies with seeking to split off the West and push the Spanish out of the hinterlands. Blount's path also crossed that of the roving Aaron Burr, who had his own visions of empire. In addition, there were also some ties between Blount and other Yazoo land companies, one of which was involved in rampant land speculation and illicit contacts with the Georgia legislature.

The West was a bubbling cauldron of intrigue and reckless adventurism. At that time, Alexander Hamilton was planning a campaign to attack Louisiana and the Floridas with troops from the South and West and to connect up with the British fleet. But Hamilton's plans were threatening to Adams, and the president pressed for peace rather than war with France. A war with France would have probably led to war with its surrogate, Spain, and Hamilton may have even envisioned a path of conquest down through New Spain with himself cast as the new Cortez. His primary concern was to dominate Louisiana and the Floridas; as he put it, "All on this side of the Mississippi must be ours including both Floridas." Characteristically, Hamilton was to conclude in 1802, "I have always held that the *unity of our Empire*, and the best interests of our nation, require that we should annex to the United States all the territory east of the Mississippi, New Orleans included." Thus, the Louisiana Territory, the Southwest, and the hinterlands fired the lustful ambitions of many individuals, some of them old-fashioned adventurers and some frustrated and out-of-power establishment figures.

Ironically, what provided the Louisiana Territory to the United States was not force but commerce, not the weakness of Spain but the shifting priorities of Napoleon. With the treaty in place, the port of New Orleans saw a steady and impressive flow of sugar, flour, and cotton from the Illinois region, the Ohio Valley, and the Natchez district, which moved down the Mississippi and into the West Indies and even to Europe. Then on October 18, 1802, the acting intendant of Louisiana, Juan Ventura Morales, closed American access to New Orleans, and the United States reacted with a sense of outrage and deep vulnerability. Americans responded that the declaration was a violation of the treaty, and national pressure was generated to consider even war in order to reassert U.S. rights. Jefferson carefully balanced his Western strength and European realpolitik, buying time while he himself talked and wrote tough statements linking honor and war.

Federalists led by Hamilton now attacked Jefferson for being too weak in his defense of the rights of the West. Using these public pronouncements, Jefferson shrewdly convinced the French and Spanish ministers to the United States that war was near and that he was holding it back as best he could. To pacify the West, he sent James Monroe—an avowed friend of that region—to Europe as a special envoy. The Republican-controlled Congress opposed extreme resolutions and instead gave the president the right to call up eighty thousand militia if he saw the need. Drawing on goodwill in the West, Jefferson kept that region in the fold while he practiced the uncertain arts of diplomacy.[15]

Added to the intrigue and problems in the West were the Yazoo land scandals. The word *yazoo* quietly entered the early American vocabulary as a shorthand for land fraud and greedy speculation. The state of Georgia laid claim to a huge tract west from the Chattahoochee River to the Mississippi and south from present-day Tennessee to western Spanish Florida. In the 1780s and 1790s, Georgia had pushed for a liberal policy granting land tracts to new prospective settlers, and officials decided to grant a "perpetual" title for twenty-nine million acres in an area that contained less than nine million acres.

The Georgia legislature agreed to sell three land companies nearly sixteen million acres for $200,000 in cash to be paid over two years. That deal fell through, but in the mid-1790s four new land companies with more capital—aided by powerful political friends and armed with extensive bribery money—pushed for a better proposal. They were successful in getting a bill passed in late 1794, and for a mere $500,000 the four companies received a grant of thirty-five million acres of land.

A wave of public indignation and charges of widespread corruption led to a political upheaval, and a new governor and legislature demanded that the state reverse the deal, which it did. But on the national level, the Federalists insisted on upholding the arrangement, citing the sanctity of contracts and knowing that important supporters of their causes in New England were involved with the land companies. Jefferson appointed three of his cabinet secretaries as a committee to negotiate and settle the issue with Georgia. Their recommendations were that Georgia should transfer its western lands to the federal government for $1,250,000 and hold back one-tenth of the Yazoo lands to satisfy land claims. But some Republicans in the House, led by John Randolph, refused to accept the administration's agreement, and for years it languished in the legislative branch. Finally, in *Fletcher v. Peck*, Chief Justice Marshall wrote an opinion for the Supreme Court that upheld the original Georgia legislature's corrupt bargain as an appropriate exercise of the contract power.[16]

By 1802, it was apparent that Louisiana had been given by Spain to France. In addition, Napoleon's brother-in-law, General Charles V. E. Leclerc, was sent to overthrow the black leader of Santo Domingo, General Pierre Toussaint L'Ouverture. In the end, Leclerc's disastrous defeats convinced Napoleon to forget for a while about reviving any dreams of a New World empire. Thus, ironically, it was a black liberator who helped the United States acquire the Louisiana Purchase and consequently open up that region to slavery.

Shrewdly, Jefferson warned the French that their occupation of the Louisiana province would change the relationship between France and the United States and that the only way of avoiding problems was to cede the island of New Orleans to the United States. Through other diplomatic channels, he and Madison began to talk about an alliance with Great Britain and, eventually, war with France. Jefferson's goal was to control New Orleans and the Floridas, but he insisted he had no designs on Mexico.

As has been noted, when the Spanish government demanded the end of the right of deposit in New Orleans, Congress and the American public were outraged, and Jefferson tried to embark on diplomatic overtures to calm what he called the fever and ferment that had seized the public mind. In an executive session, Congress approved his request for an appropriation of $2 million for the purpose of negotiating with the French and Spanish governments to purchase the island of New Orleans and the provinces of East and West Florida.

Jefferson's critics charged that he had so cut the defense budget that there was no military option left if diplomacy failed. Actually, the president and his aides had augmented troop strength in the Mississippi Territory near Natchez, and the administration had decided to push the Indians back even farther. Jefferson sought to acquire Indian lands along the Mississippi River so that the river would become a natural barrier. The Indians would then be forced into agriculture and made more dependent on trading posts. The president cynically hoped that in this way the tribes would accumulate debts and be made to give up even more of their lands. He concluded, "In this way our settlements will gradually circumscribe & approach the

Indians, & they will in time either incorporate with us as citizens of the United States or remove beyond the Mississippi." The president had also already decided to send Meriwether Lewis and William Clark out on what was really a reconnaissance mission as well as an exploratory nature walk across the Louisiana area, which the United States had acquired by the time they departed.

The Federalists watching the New Orleans problem continued to criticize the allegedly feeble response of the administration. When Jefferson sent Monroe to join Livingston in the negotiations, the *New York Evening Post* characterized it as "the weakest measure that ever disgraced the administration of any country." Hamilton, writing under the pen name of Pericles, called for more strength and advocated naval and military preparations. Only such determined measures "might yet retrieve his [Jefferson's] disaster." Federalists in the Senate, led by James Ross of Pennsylvania, took up the attack and asked that the president be authorized to take "immediate possession" of places necessary to secure the rights of Americans on the Mississippi and in New Orleans.

The Republicans, though, saw the resolution as a transparent attempt to embarrass Jefferson and substituted a motion to allow the president to organize and call up eighty thousand militia. Ironically, the warlike talk in Congress strengthened Jefferson's position in dealing with the Spanish minister to the United States, Don Carlos Martinez de Yrujo, who, watching the public outrage, pushed his government for a repeal of the intendant's restrictive orders in New Orleans.

On July 3, 1803, two months after Livingston's successful negotiations in France, Jefferson received formal notice of the outcome. Bonaparte had become disgusted with the New World and focused his attentions instead on the monumental war he was waging for hegemony over Europe. When he learned of the death of his brother-in-law in Santo Domingo, he is supposed to have cursed, "Damn sugar, damn coffee, damn colonies." He also probably was aware of Jefferson's deliberate tilting toward Great Britain and realized that he did not need to add to the strength of his major enemy.[17]

At home, a few Federalists grumbled about the purchase—the United States had given money, which was scarce, for land, which was already so plentiful in the new nation. Others saw the new territory as destroying the old Union as they knew it and adding land that would be divided into a large number of new states. Jefferson himself wondered whether the nation needed a constitutional amendment to acquire these lands, but more sensible Republicans prevailed and urged him simply to accept the windfall and abandon his usual constitutional scruples. The total price was $11,250,000 to go to France in stock and the assumption by the United

States of its own citizens' claims against France, which totaled about $3,750,000. Thus, for $15 million or so, the United States had more than doubled the size of its domain. Jefferson's empire of liberty was to become a reality not just for his generation and its children, but also for generations far beyond his dreams.

The administration was unsure where the boundaries were, and Jefferson and his ministers insisted that the grant included parts of West Florida—a claim about which Napoleon was ambiguous. Jefferson was also troubled about the proper administration of a vast area that contained unexplored regions in the north and west and a large concentration of people in the south. The president was concerned about emigration into the first area, seeking probably to postpone the establishment of territorial governments and the massive expansion of the Union. In addition, he and others were preoccupied with administering the New Orleans region with its very different legal code. In the past, Jefferson had foreseen not annexation, but a series of sister republics, and he was generally indifferent to the Federalist fear of an independent regime growing up in the Mississippi Valley.

Jefferson wisely abandoned his constitutional reservations, especially with the news that Napoleon was having second thoughts concerning the sale. Jefferson was later to remark,

> A strict observance of the written laws is doubtless *one* of the high duties of a good citizen, but it is not the highest. The laws of necessity, of self-preservation, of saving our country when in danger, are of higher obligation. To lose our country by a scrupulous adherence to written law, would be to lose the law itself, with life, liberty, property and all those who are enjoying them with us; thus absurdly sacrificing the end to the means.[18]

Even the most determined literalist can depart from prophecy if the price is right. Finally, Jefferson delivered the treaty to the Senate, where it was passed 24–7, and all ignored the question of whether France had true title to the Louisiana area after all.

When control of Louisiana passed from Spain to France to the United States on December 20, 1803, the provisional governor, William C. C. Claiborne, was faced with having no judicial system for the region. He promptly declared all past laws in effect, and on March 26, 1804, Congress divided Louisiana into two districts. The governor in the more populous New Orleans region was appointed by the president and was to be aided by a council of thirteen. A court system was set up and common law practices such as the writ of habeas corpus, the right to reasonable bail, and other guarantees were instituted. Still, the mixture of Spanish and French law and custom and the Anglo-American system of jurisprudence was confusing, as those various codes were based on very different views of landownership, family relationships, and personal liberties.

Jefferson was committed to guaranteeing the predominance of Anglo-American law, and he encouraged immigration into that region by American citizens. Claiborne urged a slower pace, opposing, for example, jury trials in civil suits, arguing that people wanted review not by their peers but by "great Personages."[19] Also, in the past, military commanders of Spanish garrisons had exercised considerable civil and quasi-judicial powers—a practice at variance with Anglo-American separation of powers. In 1804, objections to the new system were presented in the Louisiana Remonstrance. The petitioners complained about the use of English in the courts, the novel reliance on oral argument in cases, the uncertain mix of legal principles between civil and common law, and the general thrust of changes that had already taken place.

By March 2, 1805, Congress sought to apply the major provisions of the Northwest Ordinance to the territory and established in principle a government that was to be similar in all respects to those in the Mississippi Territory. That guarantee would have meant that the common law would have prevailed. But Congress then circumscribed that guarantee in certain ways in the Louisiana area in order to deal with the increasing controversy. The territorial legislature and Governor Claiborne were at loggerheads for a while over the issue, with the executive's position not being the popular one. Jefferson pushed for settling thirty thousand volunteers on the west side of the Mississippi River in order to change the political and ethnic balance in the region. His attitude toward the Louisiana natives was that they were "as yet as incapable of self-government as children."[20]

There is no question that Jefferson, aided by Madison, Monroe, and Livingston, had turned a difficult and politically explosive situation in the port of New Orleans into a brilliant diplomatic and political coup. In one fell swoop, the president silenced the Federalists, solidified the allegiance of the West to the Republican Party (and the seaboard Union), doubled the size of the United States, cleared the frontier of many of America's European opponents, and changed the very nature of the vague republican empire of land and liberty.

Domestic Controversies

In the capital, the Republican caucus refused to renominate Burr as vice president on its ticket and celebrated Jefferson's willingness to run for a second term. In the election of 1804, the president lost only the states of Connecticut and Delaware and two electors in Maryland as he and George Clinton, his new running mate from New York, swept the nation with 162 electoral votes to 14 for Charles Cotesworth Pinckney of South Carolina and Rufus King of New York. Jefferson had become the very symbol of democracy and the greatest practitioner of its politics of liberty and expansion. John Quincy Adams said Jefferson had an "itch of popularity"—and it was indeed contagious across the country, as the Republicans were to prove. Observing the Federalists, the president calculatingly wrote, "To me will have fallen the drudgery of putting them out of condition to do mischief."[21]

Yet, oddly, following this incredible triumph, Jefferson, by temperament a reserved person, became in the next congressional session rather passive and aloof in office. The major issues being discussed in Congress were the settlement of the Yazoo land claims and the impeachment and trial of Associate Justice Samuel Chase, a Federalist partisan of long standing. Jefferson had been used to dealing with a supportive leadership in Congress, but in the 1801 to 1802 term, the party's major leader in the House, William Branch Giles from Virginia, was succeeded by John Randolph, who provided Jefferson with less support and considerably less skill. Twenty-eight years old, Randolph represented the area of Bizarre, Virginia, which his critics insisted was a good description of his behavior—bizarre. He was tall and slight, with a rather high-pitched voice that led to rumors about his lack of virility. Randolph at first supported the administration, but he was especially vocal in attacking the administration's settlement of the Yazoo question, insisting that for Jefferson it would be "a libel on his whole political life."[22]

As noted, the Republicans had good reasons to despise Federalist judges and their hold on the bench over the years. After his election in 1800, Jefferson concluded that his political enemies had "retired into the judiciary as a stronghold. There the remains of federalism are to be preserved and fed from the treasury, and from that battery all the works of republicanism are to be beaten and erased." The Republicans in Pennsylvania had led the way and gone after the state Federalist judiciary, as the president gave those efforts his quiet support. On a national level, Republicans moved to impeach and convict Judge John Pickering, who was both insane and an ardent Federalist.

The president also called to the attention of his congressional supporters the conduct of Justice Chase, and the Republicans in the House formally brought charges against him. The major accusation was that he had acted improperly and in an outrageously partisan manner in instructing a grand jury in Baltimore in May 1803. Publicly staying quiet, the president privately encouraged his supporters to push on, for as he noted, "Ought the seditious and official attack on the principles of our Constitution, and on the proceedings of a State, to go unpunished?" Chase was impeached but not convicted, in part because some Northern Republican senators did not agree that he had committed "high crimes and misdemeanors." In the midst of all these activities, the president was working on a life of Jesus Christ, stripping the Gospels of the miracle stories and concentrating on what he took to be Christ's true philosophy.[23]

The Response to the European Wars

In June 1805, a treaty was finally signed ending the war with Tripoli, and in September, the president received news that Tobias Lear had successfully negotiated a treaty in Algiers, which included returning U.S. prisoners for a ransom of $60,000. Difficulties continued with the Barbary states, however, especially Tunis and Algiers, until the War of 1812. But in the more important European theater, the Monroe mission to Spain in 1805 was unsuccessful. The administration wanted the royal government to accept the Perdido River as the eastern boundary of the Louisiana Purchase and to give up the Floridas to the United States. Once again, Jefferson and Madison expressed in a guarded way how Spain's recalcitrance would hazard peace in the area. A frustrated Jefferson wrote to his secretary of state, "I do not view peace as within our choice." And once again as with Louisiana, the leaders of the administration rattled sabers among themselves as their imperialist visions were dimmed.[24]

The president at that time even indicated he would support a provisional alliance with England if and when the United States should go to war against France, Spain, or both. But the policies of the British government under William Pitt the Younger accentuated U.S. concerns about increasing interference with neutral shipping and the imprisonment of seamen. Then, in 1805, the British in the *Essex* case insisted that trade forbidden in times of peace could not be carried out in wartime. The policy was an important change from the so-called British Rule of 1756, which had allowed that if a ship had stopped and paid a nominal duty in a neutral port, that trip would be seen as a broken voyage, which would not fall under the tighter restrictions.

The greatest failure of the Jefferson administration's foreign policy, however, came out of the turmoil of the Napoleonic wars that the president and his advisers had so skillfully exploited initially in acquiring the

Louisiana Territory. While Great Britain stood alone against the French emperor, the United States, committed to decentralization, demobilization, and economy, insisted on both its neutrality and on profiting from the carrying trade. But America's historic demand for freedom of the seas ran directly counter to the British war strategy. Central to Britain's defense was control of the oceans and coastlines, and that nation vigorously and often arbitrarily impressed seamen from American merchant ships to man the Royal Navy, charging them with being, in the first place, deserters or British subjects.

By October 1805, Horatio Nelson had clearly established British supremacy on the seas, while Napoleon swept from one great land victory to another across the European continent. He easily defeated the Austrians and the Russians at Austerlitz and signed a peace treaty with the decimated Habsburg Empire. He then moved on to crush the Prussians at Jena and Auerstadt, and later in the spring, he humiliated the Russians at Friedland. July 1807 saw Napoleon and Czar Alexander reaching a personal peace at Tilsit, and consequently the Third Coalition against Bonaparte was ended. As in 1940–1941, Britain and her leaders felt that she alone stood between liberty and the triumph of barbarism.

Because British power was due predominantly to the Royal Navy, its policy toward neutrals, most especially the United States, was often harsh and arbitrary on the seas. Also, much of the English leadership class retained a deep disdain toward the former colonists in America and their peculiar form of government, an attitude galling to Republican politicians such as Jefferson and Madison. When the president rejected the Monroe-Pinkney Treaty with England because it did not deal with the impressment of seamen, the British government insisted that the Jeffersonians were pro-French after all. Later, though, the Crown went on to appoint the so-called Ministry of All the Talents, and Americans hoped that it would mean a salutary change in policy, especially with Charles James Fox's presence in the cabinet. Fox had been sympathetic to the United States in the past, but he died too soon to have any impact, and by 1807 the controlling faction in the government of George III was determined to pursue the European war vigorously and American concerns were secondary.

To some Englishmen, the Americans were also commercial rivals that used the war as a chance to supersede British mercantile interests. Indeed, America hurt British colonies in the Caribbean area by growing competing crops on their Southern plantations and also by carrying to Europe the non-British produce in that region. As Bradford Perkins has summarized, from 1801 to 1805, the British West Indies imported each year about

$6.5 million in U.S. goods. But soon the American cotton trade increased dramatically, and U.S. shipping was intensely involved in the reshipping trade. By 1806 and 1807, U.S. reexports totaled $60 million. Still, both nations remained linked by trade. Americans purchased about one-third of all British exports, and in 1806, more than $20 million worth of goods produced in the United States were shipped to Britain—over 40 percent of all domestic produce, much more than to France or Spain. As the British empire continued its war, U.S. trade with other nations increased; one result in that increase in trade was that the British blockade against Napoleon's empire was being weakened.

Napoleon, in turn, sought to crush Great Britain and called for a "remorseless war against English merchandise." In November 1806, he issued in Berlin a decree blockading the British Isles and prohibiting all trade with the British or in British merchandise, although Napoleon lacked the navy to enforce the decree. A year later, while in Milan, he expanded the scope of his decree by declaring that all ships that submitted to British regulations or allowed themselves to be searched at sea by the British navy would no longer be considered neutral and would therefore be subject to confiscation. By the end of 1807, both Britain and France were violating U.S. rights at sea.

One of the most explosive issues for Americans in that conflict was the impressment of seamen. Added to that insult was the controversy over the vessel *Essex* and the decision of the British courts to curtail the reexport trade. Many former Englishmen served on U.S. ships, and of the eleven hundred naturalized seamen who were registered with American papers in 1805, most had been British. Gallatin concluded that a total of nine thousand men fell into that category. Estimates of impressment reached sixty-five hundred, although about thirty-eight hundred is probably a closer count. To exploit U.S.-British tensions, Talleyrand informed the Americans that the emperor had decided to use his good offices to get the Spanish to give up the Floridas and to acknowledge the Colorado River in mid-Texas as the western boundary of the Louisiana Purchase. Spain would in turn get $7 million as payment.[25]

As noted, Jefferson confidentially informed Congress of the failure of Monroe's mission and also asked for authority to use $2 million of public money for negotiations with Spain. Several times in these frontier intrigues, the administration came close to the edge of indiscretion. One such incident that attracted attention was Jefferson's and Madison's contacts with General Francisco de Miranda, who wanted to liberate his native Venezuela from Spain. Miranda set sail with 180 to 200 men on an American-owned ship to accomplish his mission. Jefferson, hearing of those plans, decided to order an investigation to see if any federal laws had been violated, hoping in the process to head off French and Spanish authorities, who took a dim view of alleged U.S. involvement in Miranda's cause. Two individuals were arrested in New York after Jefferson's order, and at the trial it was asserted by the accused that the U.S. government had told Miranda that it would not thwart his plans. The acknowledgment that Miranda had spoken with Madison and had dined with Jefferson added to the credibility of the claim. In an extraordinary move, the defendants appealed to Congress against the executive branch for assistance and had the court subpoena cabinet officers. The Federalists lovingly exploited the controversy and the defendants were acquitted. As for the president, he was never able to reach a settlement with Spain, and his major biographer, Dumas Malone, has concluded that West Florida became an "obsession" for him.[26]

Meanwhile, Congress began to react to British intrusions on U.S. shipping and the impressment of seamen. Congressman Andrew Grigg of Pennsylvania introduced a resolution calling for the exclusion of all British imports until those issues were settled. The Senate, in turn, passed several strongly anti-British resolutions and asked the president to demand restoration of confiscated property and the indemnification of American citizens for loss. John Randolph deserted Jefferson and the party in the House on the issue and attacked the administration in general for its lack of leadership, but Republican congressmen as a group supported more moderate expressions drawn up by Joseph H. Nicholson of Maryland. Reports flew in the cabinet that only Madison supported the president's policies of economic retaliation. Finally, Congress passed the Non-Importation Act, based on Nicholson's resolutions, which banned a list of specific articles and commodities but would not go into effect until November 15, 1806. Randolph was somewhat correct when he observed, "What is it? A milk and water bill, a dose of chicken broth to be taken nine months hence. . . . It is too contemptible to be the object of consideration or to excite the feelings of the pettiest state in Europe." To add to Jefferson's problems, the British ship *Leander* off the New Jersey coast shot at a merchant vessel in American waters and killed one person. Jefferson issued a proclamation charging the captain of the vessel with murder, stipulating that he was to be tried if he landed on American territory, and ordering the three British vessels in that area out of American waters.

Jefferson was able to contain much of the American discontent on this and other issues because of his towering presence as both a symbol of the democratic faith and as a successful party leader, playing an important and decisive role behind the scenes. He was, Randolph bitterly concluded, a "political idol" whose "colossal popularity . . . seemed to mock at all opposition."[27] He skillfully used his natural hospitality and good manners to reassure people who frequented his table. The president was a master at both conversation and at conviviality, and he rarely dined alone when in the capital. Although he was the great Apostle of Freedom in the eyes of many, he in fact rarely appeared in public and made no presidential trips as did his successors. Nonetheless, in the period of 1806–1807, he received a barrage of messages from individuals and public resolutions that supported his policies and urged him to consider a third term.

Burr and the Conspiracies of the West

Jefferson's delight was increased in 1806 when he received the news that Lewis and Clark had successfully reached their destination at St. Louis. Surely the president's own vision now moved toward seeing the United States expand into the Oregon Territory and even to the Pacific coast. In 1803, he had written, "The object of your mission is single, the direct water communication from sea to sea formed by the bed of the Missouri and perhaps the Oregon." Later, he wrote to a friend, "The work we are now doing is, I trust, done for posterity, in such a way that they need not repeat it. . . . We shall delineate with the correctness the great arteries of this great country. Those who come after us will extend the ramifications as they become acquainted with them, and fill up the canvas we begin." He also approved a second expedition by Captain Zebulon Pike, who sent the president two grizzly bear cubs captured on his trip, which Jefferson in turn gave to Charles Willson Peale's museum.[28]

But there was more than exploration going on in the hinterlands, and the president at times was remarkably naive in his dealings with some of the unsavory characters there, most notably General James Wilkinson, an associate of Burr and a man on and off in the pay of the Spanish, who had been involved in so many intrigues that his biography is a string of plots and counterplots. Burr, apparently in 1805 after having left the vice presidency and after having the year before killed Hamilton in a duel in New Jersey, was hatching a vague plan to separate the Western states from the United States with British assistance and was contemplating leading armed forces to seize Spain's possessions and create perhaps a new empire of his own. In the scheme, Burr and Wilkinson quietly joined forces, while Jefferson, too often more loyal than wise, continued to heap honors on Wilkinson, including naming him governor of the Louisiana Territory.[29]

On December 1, 1805, the president received an anonymous letter concerning the intrigues of Burr, which alleged that Wilkinson was a Spanish agent, an accusation that Jefferson seems to have discounted. Whether Jefferson knew it or not, the files of the Adams administration contained charges that Wilkinson was indeed a pensioner of the Spanish government. The president surely must have heard of Burr's Western tour in the late spring and summer of 1805, which led to speculation about the latter's plans for the West. For some reason, as these rumors swirled around, Jefferson had Burr to dinner and explored possibilities of a future role in politics for the discredited vice president. Burr apparently also talked with the British minister to the United States, Anthony Merry, and his Spanish counterpart, the Marqués de Casa Yrujo, about splitting the West off from the United States. Burr also added to his web Senator Jonathan Dayton of New Jersey, with whom he explored the possibilities of a coup d'état in Washington.

Jefferson had faith in the loyalty of the West, so important to the Republican Party, but finally he confidentially ordered governors and district attorneys in those regions to have Burr watched, and the president concluded that Wilkinson was under "very general suspicion of infidelity." On November 6, 1806, Jefferson wrote his son-in-law that Burr was "unquestionably very actively engaged" in taking steps to sever the West from the United States. Wilkinson had caught the drift, began to abandon Burr, and suddenly emerged as a pillar of support for the administration, sending the president dispatches about conspiracies extending from New York to the West. The purpose of these conspiracies was allegedly to transport eight to ten thousand men to New Orleans and then join with naval forces going to Vera Cruz around February 1. There was also supposed to be support for a revolt against the Mexican government with some assistance from the British navy. Wilkinson claimed he was overwhelmed by "the magnitude of the enterprise, the desperation of the plan, and the stupendous consequences."

Jefferson decided to issue a presidential proclamation warning against any military adventures directed at Spain, a nation with which the United States was at peace. In addition, the president also asked an ally in Congress to introduce a bill to give him the authority to use land and naval forces to suppress domestic insurrections—shades of the federal government's response to the Whiskey Rebellion.

Burr's intentions and movements were confusing. He apparently indicated that the administration had given its approval to his ventures. He waxed eloquent: "The gods invite to glory and fortune; it remains to be seen whether we deserve the boon." In Congress, sentiment began to increase that the president should lay before the legislative branch information that he might have about such conspiracies. When the president responded and prejudged some of the developments, Burr had already surrendered to authorities in the Mississippi Territory. The Senate in secret session quickly passed a bill to suspend the writ of habeas corpus for three months, but the House, more imbued with Republican ideology, overwhelmingly rejected it.[30]

Burr was called before the grand jury, which found that he was not involved in any illegal action and he had not given any cause for alarm, but the court refused to allow him to be discharged. The prisoner vanished but surrendered after learning of Wilkinson's treachery and was incarcerated at Fort Stoddert on February 19, 1807. Finally, Burr was tried in the Fifth Circuit Court in Richmond, before Chief Justice Marshall with Judge Cyrus Griffin at Marshall's side. Burr was received as a celebrity there rather than as an accused traitor. His attorneys were astute in their strategy: they insisted on getting a subpoena to be issued to the president for correspondence essential to Burr's case. Jefferson, through the district attorney trying the case, informed the court that the government would turn over any evidence that was proper.

Marshall concluded that the president, like any citizen, could be subpoenaed but recognized that Jefferson obviously had other demands on his time as chief executive. Jefferson wrote to the district attorney that he was ready to cooperate but reminded him of "the necessary right of the President of the U.S. to decide, independently of all other authority, what papers, coming to him as president, the public interests permit to be communicated, & to whom." The president, in Edward Corwin's words, "neither obeyed the writ nor swore anything on its return, though he forwarded the papers required."[31] Richard Nixon was later to cite the Burr case as a precedent supporting the withholding of information under the claim of executive privilege. Nixon was criticized for having misquoted the case, but it appears from the confused record that Jefferson did recognize a claim of executive privilege as a principle, but probably did not press it in this instance. However, neither Jefferson nor Marshall wanted to convert the Burr trial into a major confrontation between the executive and judiciary branches of government.

The grand jury reported two indictments against Burr, one for treason and the other a misdemeanor. The Constitution defines treason specifically as levying war against the United States or adhering to their enemies, giving them aid and comfort. A person can only be convicted on the testimony of two witnesses "to the same overt act, or on confession in open court." Burr's attorneys argued that since he was two hundred miles from where the alleged conspiratorial activity took place, he could have advised war but could not have been involved in the overt act of levying war. Despite Marshall's previous opinion in a similar case in which he took a broader view of conspiracy, the chief justice accepted this limited interpretation, and the jury subsequently found Burr not guilty by the evidence submitted. An annoyed Jefferson pushed the district attorney to seek an indictment for the misdemeanor (attempting a military expedition against Spain), in order to get evidence for a possible impeachment of Marshall.

In addition, there was an attempt by Republicans to investigate the conduct of General Wilkinson and his ties to Spain, and the secretary of war set up a military tribunal to review the general's behavior. There was also some talk about removing federal judges on address of two-thirds of both houses of Congress, a Republican proposal that gathered some initial support. Others talked of redefining treason to overturn Marshall's precedent, but these changes all died on the vine.

The Burr trial does not represent one of the high points of Marshall's great legal career and illustrates some of the most partisan and shadowy aspects of Jefferson's leadership. The president influenced the district attorney beyond fair limits, encouraged the assault of the judiciary he never trusted, and was genuinely foolish in his dealings and loyalty to Wilkinson.

The gap between Jefferson's libertarian rhetoric and his encouragement of his followers to prosecute editors on a state level for their activities has already been noted. Despite their hatred of the Federalist Sedition Law, the Jeffersonians gave as good as they got. In intensely Federalist Connecticut, a Republican judge appointed by Jefferson charged a grand jury to look at the problem of a vitriolic press there. Six persons were indicted for libel in one such case. Jefferson had been subject to an incredible barrage of attacks on his philosophy, alleged atheism, sexual life, personal courage, and a variety of other areas. His policy was to refuse to answer them. Such attacks were delivered not just at political rallies and in the press, but in the church pulpit as well. While Jefferson did not encourage Connecticut officials, he probably took some quiet comfort that his enemies were getting some just retribution. As he put it, a spirit of indignation and retaliation should have been expected. Much later in his life, Jefferson observed that a newspaper should be divided into truths, probabilities, possibilities, and lies—a remark unusual for a man so canonized today as a proponent of a totally free press.[32]

Jefferson's main problems in his second term were not due to the New England remnants of Federalist orthodoxy or to Burr's ambiguous intrigues in the West. His second term was seriously damaged by the increasing difficulties of trying to balance American interests and national esteem with the imperatives of the British to use their naval power to strangle Napoleon and the French emperor's lack of sympathy for American sensitivities and commerce.

The president had instructed Monroe and William Pinkney to negotiate a treaty with the British and to pay particular attention to the issue of impressment. As noted, the Americans had counted on making some progress after Charles James Fox, a figure friendly toward the United States, was named foreign secretary, but Fox died on September 13, 1806. The American commissioners finally signed a treaty that ignored Jefferson's and Madison's admonitions on the impressment of seamen, and the president refused to submit the document to the Senate, fearing a domestic outcry and also a weakening of the American position toward Napoleon.

The impressment issue came to the forefront again in the *Chesapeake* affair. Some seamen had run away from British vessels and enlisted on U.S. vessels, one of them being the frigate *Chesapeake*, which was docked at Norfolk, Virginia. The British authorities demanded that these men be returned to British service, and Secretary of State Madison refused. After a war of nerves, the British vessel *Leopard* fired on the U.S. frigate, and British officers took several deserters off that vessel. The people of Norfolk were furious and refused to sell provisions and supplies to the British warships and their agents off their coast. The administration acknowledged that outrage and encouraged "honorable reparation" to get past the crisis. Jefferson ordered all British armed vessels out of U.S. waters, but instead of recognizing the president's steps as a moderate response, one British commodore responded by blockading Norfolk.

The British foreign secretary, George Canning, responded cautiously at first and insisted on knowing the nationality of the alleged deserters. Jefferson, meanwhile, presented the whole matter to Congress, although Gallatin insisted that the president tone down the message. Jefferson had already added to military and naval supplies beyond what had been previously authorized by Congress, and the president and the nation were clearly running out of options to the extremes of humiliation or war. In late 1807, the president concluded that Congress would have to choose "war, embargo or nothing," but one of the president's most astute critics (and a frequent ally), John Quincy Adams, saw him as engaged in simple procrastination toward Britain. Indeed, Jefferson was hoping to avoid war, believing that diplomacy might still work as it had in the New Orleans crisis.[33]

In late 1807 and early 1808, Jefferson watched as Napoleon tightened his grip on Europe and through his Berlin decree sought to close the Continent to all British products, including those carried by neutral nations. King George reasserted in even stronger terms the British right of impressment. As the president sought some encouragement from somewhere, he received Gallatin's warning: "In every point of view, privations, sufferings, revenue, effect on the enemy, politics at home, & c, I prefer war to a permanent embargo." But Jefferson was probably more realistic, and Congress, with its strong Republican majorities, approved an embargo, which severely limited American imports and exports with belligerents. The vote was more of a motion of confidence in the executive, than a clear understanding of the consequences of cutting off trade to and from European countries.

Jefferson's embargo has been, in his time and down to the present, much criticized as a naive pacifist response to a complex problem. There is still some dispute about whether the embargo affected Britain as seriously as the administration had hoped, and historians disagree as to whether the embargo crippled U.S. commerce as much as New England merchants and Federalist politicians claimed at the time. But there is no question that politically the anti-embargo pressure became too powerful to resist, and it was repealed just before Jefferson left office. The criticisms of the policy, however, have to be weighed against the judgment of what the alternatives were for a weak nation with no real navy, a small army, and only the loosest ties of nationalism. And if the United States went to war, on whose side would it enter? Both Britain and France were hurtful to American interests; should the Americans go to war against both great empires?[34]

Jefferson and his Republicans had been partially responsible for cutting the military and for the ideology of economy and loose union. Even while war loomed on the horizon, Gallatin presented an ambitious internal improvement plan of $20 million for roads, canals, and assorted projects. But in fairness, in 1805–1806 the president was personally more assertive in his defense buildup as he recognized what was happening in Europe where minor navies, such as the Danish fleet, had been destroyed rather easily. The administration favored gunboats, and the president asked Congress later for 188 more such vessels. His secretary of navy, Henry Dearborn, requested that Congress also increase the army by six thousand regulars and twenty-four thousand volunteers, but even then Congress had no real enthusiasm for the full plan, deciding instead to raise the strength of the regular army to a total of ten thousand men.

In late 1807, Jefferson noted that opposition to the embargo had quieted down when Americans learned of the British Order in Council of November 11, which declared that any vessels trading to or from the ports of France or her allies or colonies were liable to confiscation. Napoleon's response on December 17 was a decree that all vessels submitting to British regulations or sailing to or from any port under British control were subject to confiscation as British property.

Congress followed up those moves with supplemental acts to the original embargo, which gave the executive branch more enforcement powers. Added to the president's problems was the fact that talks on reparations over the *Chesapeake* incident were not going well. After criticism for his secrecy, the president sent Congress a mass of papers and reasserted the wisdom of the embargo. Defensively, Jefferson observed that the embargo was not imposed by him or his ministers but was a true expression of the will of the legislative branch.

Americans have historically talked tough and advocated strict enforcement of the laws except when those actions affect them personally. With regard to the embargo, this same backsliding occurred, and Jefferson faced a morass of legalisms and public petitions on his hands. In May of 1808, the president indicated to Gallatin, "I am clear we ought to use it freely that we may, by a fair experiment, know the power of this great weapon, the embargo." While the administration was concerned about the coastal trade, troubles multiplied in the northern borders. Soon the Republican administration, so associated with laissez-faire government and protestations of individual liberty during the Federalist era, was involved in a vigorous enforcement of what was becoming a rapidly unpopular act. Enforcement was more difficult where politicians were in the opposition party or not particularly enamored with Jefferson's rule. Candidly the president in August 1808 concluded, "This embargo law is certainly the most embarrassing one we have ever had to execute. I did not expect a crop of so sudden & rank growth of fraud & open opposition by force could have grown up in the U.S."

One authority on the embargo, Walter Wilson Jennings, has found:

> If, in conclusion, the effects of the embargo on industry can be epitomized in one final sentence, that sentence will read: "The embargo stimulated manufactures, injured agriculture, and prostrated commerce." In the years 1805, 1806, and 1807, the value of the exports of domestic produce and manufacture was $134,590,552 or an average of $44,863,517 per year;

during the same years the exports of foreign produce and manufacture amounted to \$173,105,813 or an average of \$57,701,937 per year. Re-exports thus exceeded domestic exports by \$38,515,261 for the three years or \$12,838,420 per year.[35]

The Federalists saw the embargo as giving them a new lease on life, a short-term calculation that proved correct but that did not hold for the long haul. Resolutions for an end to the embargo poured in, especially from New England town meetings. Jefferson's attitude was that the embargo was a national policy and that critics should be pointing to the cause of the problem—the British and the French. Later Jefferson was to admit, "I felt the foundations of the government shaken under my feet by the New England townships." Having in 1808 refused to consider a third term, Jefferson watched as Madison carried the nation by 122–49 electoral votes, running well except in New England and Delaware.

With months to go, Jefferson became a spectator overlooking the debacle of his own policies. He left deliberations on the embargo to Congress and called himself "an unmeddling listener." Gallatin and Madison asked for some leadership with the legislature, and Secretary of Navy Robert Smith called for preparations for war. Meanwhile, New England Federalists introduced resolutions to repeal the embargo. Congress wavered, first passing in January 1809 a rather tough enforcement act and then leaning toward eviscerating the embargo act altogether. The president received resolutions of support now from the legislatures of New York, Virginia, South Carolina, and Georgia, and from Philadelphia, and various groups and committees in Massachusetts, Connecticut, Maryland, and Delaware.

But it was apparent that the Republicans in Congress were ready for repeal, and an old Jefferson friend, Wilson Cary Nichols, introduced such a resolution and urged that the effective date be June 1. But other Republicans wanted the controversy over and done with in March, as sentiment in the New England and New York delegations proved too strong to stop quick repeal. Jefferson called it "a panic," and it certainly was a quick lurch. The bill's provisions embodied a limited control over commerce with nonintercourse toward Great Britain's and France's imports. President Jefferson signed the bill and prepared to return to Monticello. He was to write on March 2, 1809, "Nature intended me for the tranquil pursuits of science, by rendering them my supreme delight. But the enormities of the times in which I have lived have forced me to take a part in resisting them, and to commit myself on the boisterous ocean of political passions."[36]

Andrew Jackson: The President as a Tribune of the People

S OMETIMES IT SEEMS THAT THE FEDERALISTS and the Republicans would have had their partisans believe that the very directions of the earth depended on how completely their opinions prevailed. There surely were differences in policies, philosophies, and views of the ideal republic and the dangers of the outside world. But in many ways, there was a continuity that reflected the general homogeneity of the Founding Fathers. Jackson, however, was a very different sort of man, one who terrified Federalist descendants and elicited leery reviews from older Jeffersonian Democrats.

Jefferson had heard Jackson's name in connection with Aaron Burr's schemes to create a new republic in the West. The sage of Monticello concluded that Jackson was, at the very least, not dependable, and while his colleagues Madison and Monroe acknowledged the exploits of the man who became the hero of New Orleans—one of the few American generals who won a definitive victory in the War of 1812—they also had reservations. President James Monroe actually had presided over cabinet discussions as to whether to discipline Jackson for his actions in Florida, and it was his secretary of state, John Quincy Adams, who defended the headstrong military leader. As for Jackson, he had strong views about some of his predecessors. He had criticized Washington and Adams for what he felt was their abuse of office. He thought that Washington had grasped after power and often exercised authority that he was not constitutionally invested with; in fact, Jackson had proposed that Washington be impeached for his attempts to influence the passage of the Jay Treaty. As for Adams, Jackson suggested that he was guilty of violating constitutional liberties, and he said of Jefferson that he was "the best Republican in theory and the worst in practice."[1]

But even beyond all that, Andrew Jackson by the sheer drama of his personality came to be considered a national figure, and from 1824 to 1828 a systematic campaign was waged to gain him the White House and to discredit President John Quincy Adams and Secretary of State Henry Clay in the process. But Jackson was a strange choice, considering the state of the presidency at the time. The chief executive position had gone into a period of nonpartisanship and general decline. Jefferson had been somewhat successful in creating a presidency that was deeply enmeshed for over six years in the daily operations of Congress and in promoting the Republican Party on both the national and state levels. As has been seen, Jefferson was a superb behind-the-scenes operator, but his talents were sorely tried by the embargo, and his successor, Madison, was never able to exercise the level of leadership that one would have expected considering his previous successes in legislative bodies. Monroe substituted a patina of good feelings publicly while his own cabinet members attacked each other, and the second Adams tried to make his absence of a party base into a public virtue.

The Jacksonian model of the presidency was very different. Jackson was a product and a promoter of a plebiscite democracy. No president before and probably no president until Franklin D. Roosevelt so directly appealed to the people over and over again. The general did not use surrogates as the Jeffersonians did to deal with controversies or to prod Congress into action. He confronted the great disputes of his time, personalized them, and drew the restive farmers, frontiersmen, and artisans into his orbit. He regarded his elections and congressional elections in off years as personal votes of confidence, and he drew his inspiration and power from the approval of the people—in a way that would seem alien if not undignified to his predecessors and to most of his successors in the nineteenth century.

Obviously, then, the Jacksonian presidency was different from what had gone before. In its strongest expression under General Jackson, it was characterized by a plebiscite view of democracy, a strong affirmation of limited national government, an activist presidency, and an aggressive, expansionist foreign policy. Unlike the Federalist presidents, who maintained a judicious separation from Congress, and the Jeffersonian presidents, who provided leadership of the legislature in an informal, guileful way through associates, the Jacksonians were not very apologetic about direct intrusions into the legislative branch when they regarded them as warranted.

Jackson imagined he had a special and personal relationship with the common people, and all exaggeration aside, he did indeed. He was the first president to urge abolition of the Electoral College because it was undemocratic, the first to use the veto not just because of constitutional scruples but also on matters of public policy, the first to unashamedly exploit patronage to reward the faithful, and the first to engage in public campaigns to directly rally the people. Not until Teddy Roosevelt would a president so robustly use the office, and not until Franklin D. Roosevelt would the chief executive become so identified with popular hopes and democratic resentments.

The explosive style of Andrew Jackson was like gasoline poured on the fires of that period of democratic expansion. The 1830s were an epoch of major economic changes, social upheavals and reform movements, a passionate reaffirmation of tariff protectionism, and a strident form of American nationalism. Jackson was a product and also a promoter of those sentiments. He embodied them, he advocated them, he furthered their impetus. And his closest associate, Martin Van Buren, the new type of political man, saw that the old parties based on deference and Republican tradition were no longer viable vehicles for the movement that Jackson and he followed and eventually led.

The Jacksonian Personality

To Jackson's foes, he was an illiterate, ignorant, harsh, and vindictive man. One senator, Elijah Hunt Mills, judged that the general was only "a little advanced in civilization over the Indians with whom he made war."[2]

At times, he seemed to be a man possessed of only one genuine emotion—undifferentiated anger. But to his allies and friends, Andrew Jackson was a mythic man who exemplified the true strengths of democratic America. He was born in Waxhaw, South Carolina, in 1767, and at the age of fourteen he fought alongside adults against the British during the Revolutionary War. He and his brother were captured, and when they refused to clean the boots of a redcoat officer, they were both slashed by his sword. They were later imprisoned and caught smallpox, from which Jackson's brother died. In 1781, his mother, who had been nursing prisoners at Charleston, caught a fever and died as well. For forty years he unsuccessfully searched for her grave. All he had left was the memory of her last words: "Andy, . . . never tell a lie, nor take what is not your own, nor sue . . . for slander. *Settle them cases yourself.*"[3]

Like many individuals plagued by insecurity, Jackson came to exude in public a sense of incredible self-confidence and firmness. He grew in wealth and influence, becoming a military hero and slave owner on the

American frontier. As late as 1821, he dismissed the idea of being president by observing, "Do they think that I am such a demented fool as to think myself fit for the president of the United States? No, sir; I know what I am fit for. I can command a body of men in a rough way; but I am not fit to be president." But because of the controversy of 1824–1825, Jackson felt he was cheated out of the highest office, and so did a good number of Americans. His behavior began to change; by his mid-fifties, he had curtailed his famous temper. Either Jackson was mellowing or he had realized that his political ambitions required a more moderate public posture. When he arrived in Washington in 1824, he observed to a friend, "Many do indeed believe me unfit for civil life; and many here, strangers to me, had expected, I believe, to see a most uncivilized, unchristian man when they beheld me." Instead, observers saw a lean, tall, almost ascetic-looking gentleman, slightly stooped over, and personally courteous to a fault. He even patched up old rivalries, most importantly with Thomas Hart Benton of Missouri, whose bullet from an early duel was embedded for years in Jackson's body.

Throughout his career, he personalized differences and saw conspiracies all around him. Once, when informed that he had violated international law in Florida, he cursed the scholarly authorities: "Damn Grotius! Damn Pufendorf! Damn Vattel! This is a mere matter between Jim Monroe and myself." One obvious reason for his irritability was probably bad health, which would fray anyone's nerves. He suffered from chronic diarrhea and indigestion and had tuberculosis, rheumatism, and bouts of migraines. Until 1832, he carried Benton's bullet in his left arm and a ball in his chest, which rested close to his heart. This harsh warrior, though, was a true and kind companion and a devoted family man.

He had an incredible hold over the masses, being seen as a glorious military hero and a romantic spirit of the age. He fought duels of honor, killed Native Americans, beat the British and Spanish, and stood strong and straight. His nickname, "Old Hickory," summed it up best. As no other president, he was identified as a man of courage and audacity. At the age of sixty-eight, he was attacked by a would-be assassin carrying two pistols. The president charged forward with only a cane to fight off the miscreant. No one ever accused Jackson of being a superb and subtle democratic thinker, but he was not the ignorant savage he was portrayed to be by his enemies. His state paper against South Carolina's nullification is equal to Lincoln's logic and Webster's eloquence on the same topic.

Jackson's political philosophy might be summarized as entailing a simple faith in the people, majority rule, limited government, a Jeffersonian respect for states' rights, opposition to "class legislation," a distrust of banks and middlemen, and a profound commitment to the preservation of the Union. One scholar, Albert Somit, has noted that Jackson was different from most Jeffersonians in three ways: he emphasized the direct relationships between economic interests and political action, and he brought that issue into the campaigns; he emphasized a social conception of government's obligations to the people; and he expanded the Democratic Party's appeal to the masses, especially the nascent urban dwellers. This in the 1830s was remarkable.[4]

Jackson's major biographer, Robert V. Remini, has concluded that the candidate rode to victory on a wave of public indignation about alleged political corruption. There were numerous instances of fraud involving banks, especially the branches of the Bank of the United States, and many congressmen took money from corporations that wanted favorable legislation passed. In the Senate, Thomas Hart Benton started an investigation of the Office of Indian Trade within the War Department amid charges of improprieties; the conclusions exposed a swindle against both the tribes and the federal government. Other departments in the Monroe administration, it was charged, were also riddled with graft, bribery, and kickbacks. To add to those problems was James Monroe's decision to personally borrow $5,000 from businessman John Jacob Astor and his rescinding of a previous order prohibiting foreigners from engaging in the fur trade—seen by some as a quid pro quo.

The allies of presidential candidate Secretary of the Treasury William Crawford of Georgia especially went after the enlarged War Department, headed by rival John C. Calhoun of South Carolina, and sought to cut the army from twelve thousand to six thousand men.[5] Calhoun was also hurt by the so-called Yellowstone Expedition, when the secretary and Monroe threw good money after bad to support an expedition going up the Missouri River. The contracts had gone to the brother of Calhoun's ally in Kentucky, Colonel Richard M. Johnson. Still another contract of $300,000 was given by Calhoun's chief clerk to his brother-in-law for supply stores in the construction of Fortress Monroe. In addition, there was criticism of Calhoun's chief enemy in the cabinet, Secretary of Treasury William Crawford, for the handling of money received from the sale of public lands. Even Secretary of State John Quincy Adams was accused of being influenced by New England insurance interests in his negotiations of the Florida treaty. Thus, the whole cabinet seemed to be under scrutiny for misconduct.

Part of the talk about corruption was directly due to the intense cabinet jockeying for the right to succeed Monroe. His era of good feelings provided the veil behind which men of inordinate ambition promoted vicious attacks on each other and conveyed the overall impression of widespread corruption, malfeasance, and general disarray. From Jackson's point of view, they had already robbed him of the presidency once in 1824, when he lost to John Quincy Adams, and he was not surprised at any charges levied at them.

The Force of Democracy

Swept up in the tidal wave of "Jackson and Reform" and aided by the machinations of a new generation of professional politicians such as Martin Van Buren, the aging general came into the White House as the people's choice. Deprived of the love of his wife, who died after the bitter election, Jackson emerged in the public eye as even more of a solitary and courageous man, dressed in the very color of mourning. For that period, he was to form an extraordinary and at times personal attachment to the people and they to him.

Early on, Jackson let it be known that he wanted strict economy in government, a liquidation of the national debt, a "judicious" tariff, and a distribution of the budget surplus on the basis of representation to promote education and internal improvements. The key word in the Jackson lexicon was "reform." The administration saw itself as a period of cleansing after an era of corruption. Senator Daniel Webster caustically remarked, "Persons have come five hundred miles to see General Jackson, *and they really seem to think that the country is rescued from some dreadful danger!*"[6]

The inaugural itself reflected those initial feelings, as Jackson opened up the "president's palace" and people of all classes pressed into the house. Justice Joseph Story concluded, "The reign of KING MOB seemed triumphant." Barrels of orange punch were laid out, but as the mob rushed forward, pails of liquor fell to the floor, fixtures were broken, and china and glassware were smashed. Men with muddy boots stood on the fine furniture in order to see the famed general better. For his safety, Jackson was ushered out of the house, and he spent the night at Gadsby's Tavern. In a different tone, the *Argus of Western America* wrote on March 18, 1829, "General Jackson is *their own* president. Plain in his dress, venerable in his appearance, unaffected and familiar in his manners, he was greeted by them with an enthusiasm which bespoke him the Hero of a popular triumph."[7]

Jackson started his administration with a call for some changes in the distribution of patronage. He was confident that "rotation in office will perpetuate our liberty." In that way he would weed out corruption and prevent the growth of an "official aristocracy." Or, as one of Van Buren's allies in New York, William L. Marcy, in the Senate summarized it, shorn of any philosophical pretense, "To the victor belong the spoils of the enemy." An anti-Jacksonian critic, however, portrayed a different picture: "The government formerly served by the *elite* of the nation, is now served, to a considerable extent, by its refuse."[8]

The president's focus was a little different. He told one associate early in his first term, "Assure my friends we are getting on here *well*, we labour night and day, and will continue to do so, until we destroy all the rats, who have been plundering the Treasury." Within a year of taking office, the administration discovered that some $280,000 had been stolen from the Treasury Department alone—a further proof of the corruption of the previous administration. This was another indictment of the educated, trained elite that Jackson so hated, people "who are on the scent of Treasury pap. And if I had a *tit* for every one of these pigs to suck at they would still be my friends." While the president did insist that in a democracy "no one man has any more intrinsic right to official station than another," there were very few dismissals of incumbent officials—about 10 percent of the total over eight years.

Jackson's biographer Remini has concluded that with the combined episodes of misconduct involving Native American affairs, army and navy contracts, and the operations of the Bank of the United States, the previous period is more aptly called the "Era of Corruption" rather than the "Era of Good Feelings." Surely, if one compares the Monroe-Adams era to the corruptions of the Grant, Harding, Truman, or Reagan years, there is little fault. But coming as it did after the comparatively pristine Federalist and early Jeffersonian presidencies, there was surely some moral slippage during the Monroe-Adams period. However, what made Jackson also susceptible later to criticism was his overall poor record for judging candidates for major offices and his selection for his cabinet of men of very limited ability. His crusade against corruption, for example, was hurt by a very bad appointment of his own, the collector of the Port of New York, Samuel Swartwout, who vanished to Europe with over $1.2 million.[9]

His bad judgment was especially apparent in his choice of John Eaton as secretary of war, and the president's persistent defense in almost total defiance of Washington society of Eaton's wife's honor. The circle of petticoat gossip had branded Peggy Eaton a woman of loose morals and had turned a collective cold shoulder to her. Jackson, perhaps remembering the nasty mess that hastened his own wife's death, defended Mrs. Eaton with a blind vigor and demanded that his cabinet officers and their wives show their loyalty to him by opening up their hearts and homes to the secretary's wife. Only Van Buren was shrewd enough to comply, and his flexibility moved him closer to the general's affections. Calhoun did not follow suit, and soon in Jackson's eyes he was even more suspect for his disloyalty to the president. Later, after the nullification crisis precipitated by South Carolina, the vice president was displaced in the Jackson official family.

Jackson and Union

In his first term, Jackson's slogan became in his own eyes a mandate— "Retrenchment and economy." In foreign policy, he was like his Republican predecessors, a strong nationalist bent on expansion. However, Jackson was at times more aggressive, at least in tone, and he was especially committed to the removal of the tribes and driving the Spanish out of North America—two causes he had been identified with in his earlier public career. In addition, Jackson initially desired to annex Texas, an area excluded from U.S. possession because of the boundaries Jefferson accepted when he took over the Louisiana Territory. Only later in office did Jackson seem to have second thoughts about the timing. For the next several decades, most of the Democratic Party would be committed to bringing the Texas republic into the Union. Jackson told Van Buren he would push for $5 million from Congress to buy the territory in order to keep any foreign power from gaining control of the Mississippi and New Orleans. He concluded that the "god of the universe had intended this great valley to belong to one nation."[10]

Jackson also wanted to move the frontier border in order to acquire more land to relocate Native Americans living east of the Mississippi. His argument was that a natural and accepted boundary would promote amity between the two groups. But his minister to Mexico, Joel Poinsett of South Carolina, was inept and heavy-handed in the way he proposed the purchase, and the Mexican government demanded his recall. In addition, the Creeks and Cherokees did not accept Jackson's logic that relocation was a humane alternative to the inevitable annihilation that would result if they stayed where they were. The policy of the government, he blandly announced, was to introduce to Native Americans the ways of civilization and lead them away from nomadic wanderings to a happy and comfortable life.

Jackson also respected limited government, individual initiative, and states' rights. But his definition of the last excluded any acknowledgment of the right to nullify federal laws or to advocate secession. The president swore that he would rather die in the last ditch than have the Union dismantled. In the Senate the godlike Daniel Webster, as he was called, challenged Robert Y. Hayne of South Carolina in a monumental debate that started with a discussion of public lands and concluded with questions about the very nature of the Union. Webster's words could have been Jackson's, and they were to be Lincoln's sentiments: "I go for the Constitution as it is, and for the Union as it is. It is, Sir, the people's Constitution, the people's government, and answerable to the people."

Then, at a Jefferson Day dinner, the president and Vice President Calhoun headed up the Democratic delegation. The president added to the tension with his toast, "Our Union. *It must be* preserved." Calhoun's response was quick: "The Union. Next to our liberty, the most dear." Neither sentiment was radical, but soon the dinner became the occasion of drawing a line in the dust between Jackson and Calhoun adherents. A delighted Van Buren noted prophetically, "The veil was rent."[11]

Previously, Calhoun and his friends in South Carolina had staked out their position against the Tariff of Abominations of 1828, which had not been repealed after Jackson's election. They asserted the right of states to nullify federal laws if need be and to interpose their state government between the federal government and the citizens of the state. One could trace that tradition to the Kentucky and Virginia resolutions and to the Hartford Convention and the opposition in New England to the War of 1812, and now it became the political theory of the slaveholders' most accomplished theorists.[12]

Jackson's position was clear—there could be no secession from the Union. He warned his friends in South Carolina that if a single drop of blood were shed by those opposing federal laws, he would find out who was responsible and have them hanged. Van Buren, seeking to succeed Calhoun as vice president and to show support for the president, had the New York Democratic Party pass a resolution advocating a second term for Jackson. John Quincy Adams, however, claimed that Van Buren had generally misunderstood the Jefferson dinner confrontation. But Amos Kendall, closer to Jackson than Adams, concluded, "Van Buren glides along as smoothly as oil and as silently as a cat." To add to his ire, Jackson learned that back in the Monroe administration, Calhoun as secretary of war had not supported him in the Florida invasion and had pushed for his arrest and punishment. Consequently, Jackson pronounced Calhoun "the most profound hypocrite he had ever known."[13]

When Congress returned in December 1829, the president was able to make another statement of his political philosophy by vetoing a bill to extend the National Road from Maysville to Lexington, Kentucky. Jackson opposed spending federal funds for obviously local public works projects, even though he was warned that a veto would hurt his party in the West and gain adherents for Clay. But Jackson concluded that the "great body of the people hail the act [his veto], as a preservative of the constitution & the union." Fearful that internal improvement bills would lead to hasty appropriations, corrupt elections, and a general decline of civic virtue, Jackson vetoed the Washington Turnpike bill, measures for building lighthouses and beacons, and a proposal for dredging harbors. He also stopped a bill to purchase stock in the Louisville and Portland Canal Company. His use of the veto restored presidential power and reaffirmed the office as a separate branch of government. In addition, Jackson became the first president to use the pocket veto, whereby the executive kills a bill by simply not signing it when Congress has already adjourned.

Jackson was a soldier and a patriot, but one of his greatest claims to fame was his history as an Indian fighter. He was bold, ferocious, and brutal, and no president, including General Ulysses S. Grant with his terrible campaigns in the Civil War, has been so cavalier in meting out death to his opponents. His philosophy of human liberty and laissez-faire was meant for white men only; as for the Native Americans, he was insistent that they be driven to remote areas west of the Mississippi River. Jefferson had originally proposed removal of tribes unwilling to assimilate. But Jackson did not flinch from the consequences of a policy of confrontation.

In Congress, considerable opposition arose to Jackson's proposal to eject the tribes in the South. But on May 28, 1830, the Indian Removal Act passed the legislative branch, and Jackson assumed he had approval to press on. The president had publicly vowed that no Native American would be forced to leave, but he soon abandoned that guarantee. The apostle of economy and retrenchment proceeded to advocate a removal policy that cost the government an astronomical $68 million and thirty-two million U.S.-controlled acres west of the Mississippi in order to gain one hundred million acres of coveted Native American lands.

Friends of the Native Americans, however, went to court to protect their interests, and they hired William Wirt, a constitutional lawyer of national renown. Jackson seemed to be taken aback at the lack of confidence the tribes had in his leadership and protection. He warned that the tribes could refuse to leave, but then they would be subject to the laws and harsh devices of the states. Jackson played the role of solicitous great white father to the hilt, and initially the tribes tried to appeal to his paternalistic instincts, but they soon learned that they would have to resort to other strategies to guard their lands. Jackson stood firm and concluded, "I have exonerated the national character and now leave the poor deluded Creeks and Cherokees to their fate, and then annihilation, which their wicked advisors has [sic] induced."[14]

The Choctaws finally ceded to the United States 10.5 million acres of land east of the Mississippi River. Their removal was a chronicle of corruption, theft, and mismanagement, which led to the near destruction of that tribe. Even Jackson was shocked when he learned of their extensive sufferings, and he sought to establish new policies to govern future removals. In fact, the brutal treatment of the tribes was a logical outcome of Jackson's support for a wholesale removal policy devoid of humanitarian treaty commitments. In 1832, treaties were signed with the Creeks, Seminoles, and Chickasaws. Only the Cherokees refused to join the exodus.

But that tribe finally exhausted all levels of appeal as well. In 1831, Chief Justice Marshall, writing for the Supreme Court, found the Native Americans to be "domestic dependent nations" subject to the authority of the United States but not that of the states. The Court in a second case found the Georgia laws regulating the tribes unconstitutional. Georgia refused to accept the verdict, and Jackson is supposed to have said, "Marshall made the decision, now let him enforce it." Whether the president made that statement is unclear, but it surely expressed his general views that Georgia could not be forced to obey this particular decision. Also at that time Jackson had taken on one state, South Carolina, in the nullification controversy, and did not need a second confrontation. In December 1835, the Cherokees signed a treaty for the exchange of lands. Jackson's forceful behavior had again prevailed, and the near genocidal consequences of his policies remain a commentary on the darker side of his presidency.

As Jackson faced increasing difficulties, he began to take steps to tighten his control over the Democratic Party and the cabinet. He replaced *United States Telegraph* editor Duff Green with Francis P. Blair, who would head up a new party organ. Blair's *The Globe* was clearly a Jacksonian paper, and its motto reflected those laissez-faire economic views: "The world is governed too much." The president also began to focus on the abolition of the Bank of the United States, and his newspaper organ followed suit. Jackson and some of his closest advisers had come to see the bank as a monopolistic threat to liberty, a monster lined up against decent working people. In his private letters and communications and in his annual message to Congress, he expressed varying sentiments of disapproval.

In the Senate, Benton presented his views in a sharp debate with bank supporter and senator Daniel Webster. Bank advocates reassured the president of the Bank of the United States that Jackson, after huffing and puffing, would still sign the bank's renewal bill. But Benton knew the general better; Jackson, he wrote, "aims at the destruction of the Bank." The administration's opponents were also startled by Jackson's sudden announcement that he would run for a second term despite his earlier protestations. When attempts at a reconciliation between the president and Calhoun failed, Van Buren's star rose—the heir apparent was coming into view.[15]

In the midst of this controversy, Van Buren offered his resignation as secretary of state; his initiative gave Jackson the opportunity to change other secretaries and thus purge his cabinet of disloyal members. Van Buren probably had not seen his gesture to help Jackson as being some sort of master stroke. But his resignation led to his departure from Washington and his subsequent nomination as minister to London. To humiliate him, his enemies eagerly blocked Senate approval. This action forced him to come back home—back to the vice presidency on Jackson's ticket!

The resignations and terminations in the cabinet startled the nation. Never before had a president engaged in wholesale dismissals. Clay called it a revolution and wondered, "Who could have imagined such a cleansing of the Augean stable in Washington . . . a change, almost total, of the Cabinet." As Remini has noted, the controversy reduced Democratic Party loyalty to one question—are you for or against Andy Jackson? In that perspective, the party promoted freedom and the will of the majority, and Jackson alone represented the people. It was a giant step in transforming the limited republic of the Founding Fathers into a nineteenth-century plebiscite democracy.

Critics attacked this "executive tyranny," as they called it, and they denounced the growth of a personal coterie of advisers, which was tagged the "kitchen cabinet." Outside advisers such as Amos Kendall, William B. Lewis, Andrew Donelson, and Van Buren were seen as the real power behind Jackson. The president had heard the accusations and dismissed them out of hand. He was, as his closest supporters knew, a strong executive who surrounded himself with a wide network of advisers, editors, friends, members of Congress, and regional party leaders.

The Monster Bank

Jackson's strong-willed determination, however, is best seen in his epic battle against the Bank of the United States. Secretary of Treasury Louis McLane at first tried to push Jackson toward renewal of the bank's charter.

Meanwhile, Clay garnered the Whig Party's nomination for the presidency and sought to use the bank issue in his coming campaign. He urged Nicholas Biddle, the bank's politically assertive president, to insist on a recharter earlier than necessary in order to make it a campaign issue. Daniel Webster apparently concurred, and Biddle, fearing he would alienate his friends in Congress, agreed.

The president and his allies argued that the bank was "a monster"—a threat to liberty—and that it corrupted congressmen with easy loans and regular retainer fees. Jackson concluded that the bank's friends were attempting to kill him politically, but he instead would kill the monster. When he heard about the Senate vote supporting renewal, he roared, "By the Eternal! I'll smash them!" and smash them he did. Van Buren had counseled caution, as did other prominent Democrats, but Van Buren realized that his fate was tied irrevocably to Old Hickory's moods.

Despite the popular presumption that Van Buren was the main adviser on the bank veto, Jackson mainly consulted Attorney General Roger B. Taney, who had a long history of distrust of the national bank. When Biddle increased his public appearances and put political pressure on Congress, Jackson's darkest suspicions about the bank were confirmed. On June 1, 1832, the bill for recharter passed the Senate 28–20, and on July 3, the House of Representatives concurred, 107–85. Like many Democrats from Jefferson on down, Jackson had reservations about the bank. But he saw the battle in a more passionate and personal way—as a direct threat to liberty and as a concentration of power in the hands of a few. "It is to be regretted that the rich and powerful too often bend the acts of the government to their selfish purposes," Jackson argued.[16]

With his veto, Jackson not only ended the so-called hydra-headed bank but also reasserted a presidency that had been dormant in many ways since Jefferson. In the past, presidents had used the veto only nine times total and usually for constitutional scruples. Jackson clearly was dealing with social and economic policy questions, and his veto was grounded in the laissez-faire tradition of a minimal state and its fear of concentrated power.

In July, Webster openly attacked the president, arguing that "no president and no public man ever before advanced such doctrines in the face of the nation. There never was a moment in which any president would have been tolerated in asserting such a claim to despotic power." Clay added his own observation that Jackson's action was "a perversion of the veto power." But when the pyrotechnics were over, Congress could not override it, and the veto stood.[17]

Thus, the election of 1832 revolved around Jackson and the bank controversy. Amos Kendall became a sort of national campaign manager, and Francis Blair used his newspaper as an effective propaganda tool for the party. Biddle, for reasons known only to himself, not only reprinted Clay and Webster's attacks but also paid for thirty thousand copies of Jackson's original veto message. The bank president's activities only reaffirmed the Democrats' fears as to how the Bank of the United States could be used for partisan purposes.

Jackson's positions on executive power, patronage, the tariff, and internal improvements were all attacked by the Whigs. He had supported a more moderate tariff schedule, but not one that would satisfy the deep discontent in the South, especially in Calhoun's home state of South Carolina. The president was in many ways a states' rights and limited government man, but he despised the "nullifiers," as he called them. He believed that such people were simple traitors and should be hanged. The president hoped that the dissension would quiet down, but he prepared for any emergency. He ordered that steps be taken to protect forts near Charleston, South Carolina. It was the beginning of what was to be a long war of nerves between Jackson and nullifiers.

Armed with hickory sticks and Jackson's popularity, the Democrats prevailed in the election. The Whigs charged that the republic was being undone by "King Andrew I," but the masses did not seem to be swayed. The president won reelection by carrying the electorate 688,242 votes to Clay's 473,462, with the anti-Mason candidate William Wirt and Independent Democrat John Floyd getting some scattered support. Jackson thus carried 55 percent of the popular vote and took 219 electoral votes to Clay's 49, Floyd's 11, and Wirt's 7. His base was the South (except South Carolina) and the West, although he did well in the Mid-Atlantic states and carried Maine and New Hampshire in New England. Even though the election registered a clear Democratic triumph, the president's popular margin dropped by more than 1.5 percent—a rare occurrence for a second-term president. Still, his contemporaries saw his victory as a personal triumph over great, entrenched forces. It was a victory for "Jackson and Democracy," and Wirt concluded that the general might be "president for life if he chooses."[18]

The Progression of Battles

In his second term, Jackson had to confront directly the consequences of his bank veto and also the threat of secession. First, he moved to isolate South Carolina from Georgia, whose leaders were prepared to defy the Supreme Court decision in the *Worcester* case, which dealt with the Cherokees. As noted, Jackson and his supporters decided not to take on two recalcitrant states at once, and the Cherokees were told that they would have no support in federal quarters to fight removal, a policy Jackson supported anyway.

Calhoun, with his brilliant conceptual mind and uneasy commitment to the Union, had proposed a full-blown theory of state nullification against federal legislation. To Jackson it was clear and unvarnished treason, but he was shrewd and bold in his handling of the crisis. In the process he won the support of many of his previous Whig enemies and lost the allegiance of some of the Southern wing of the Democratic Party.

The South Carolina legislature authorized a special convention, which passed an Ordinance of Nullification on November 24 that denounced the tariff laws of 1828 and 1832 as "null, void, and no law, nor binding" on that state. Jackson's public statements were strong, but he proceeded remarkably cautiously. First, he concentrated his forces on the harbor forts and avoided confronting the South Carolinians in installations on the mainland. He appealed to the people of South Carolina and to the moderates in the South, citing the advantages of Union. Jackson was clear: Nullification was "incompatible with the existence of the Union, contradicted expressly by the letter of the Constitution, unauthorized by its spirit, inconsistent with every principle on which it was grounded, and destructive of the great object for which it was formed." In language that Lincoln would echo a generation later, he argued, "I have no discretionary power on the subject; my duty is emphatically pronounced in the Constitution." Nullifiers and Unionists in South Carolina took up arms, but no abrupt actions were taken, although it was clear that tensions were rising in Charleston.[19]

Meanwhile, the president pushed for a revision of tariff schedules, which was introduced in the House of Representatives on June 8, 1833. Jackson also insisted on a Force Bill, which would give him the power to close any port of entry and open others. Brilliantly, the president would force the nullifiers to go out of their way to resist the government if they so dared. Jackson noted that the federal government's law of 1792 (amended in 1795) already gave the president the right to call up the state militia and to use federal ships and troops when its authority was challenged.[20]

Unlike in the secession movement in 1860–1861, slavery was not an issue, and many Southern moderates were willing to support the Unionist sentiments of Jackson. The progress of the tariff reform bill also helped cut the ground from under the nullifiers when Clay and Calhoun agreed on a compromise. Webster challenged Calhoun's arguments and defended the president and the Union, as the Senate supported the Force Bill 32–1 with some nullifiers walking out. The president was obviously less concerned with the tariff rates than with the turmoil in South Carolina, but he did insist that the Force Bill had to pass before the tariff bill. It was a matter of principle to him. South Carolina nullifiers repealed their ordinance in part because of Jackson's stand and also because of the tariff reductions. In addition, the support they expected in the Southern states did not materialize. Prophetically, Jackson warned, "The next pretext will be the negro, or slavery question."

Wherever he went, Jackson generated intense emotions. On one occasion, he was struck by a naval lieutenant, Robert B. Randolph, who on Jackson's orders was dismissed from service for theft; later the president was fired on by a would-be assassin who missed his target and was nearly caned by an angry Jackson. In 1833, the president decided to emulate his successors and undertake a tour of New England. Remarkably, he was greeted with generally enthusiastic crowds, and he was seen as a true nationalist— which indeed he was. He acknowledged the cheers, charmed the ladies, and kissed some babies. One critic described it as "the degeneracy of the age in taste, feelings and principles." Jackson mixed freely with the crowds, and in New York City, he bluntly declared, "Nullification will never take root *here*." One newspaper in Connecticut concluded that he seemed like a father surrounded by his happy children, the type of image Jackson loved.[21]

To the chagrin of the Brahmin caste, he received an honorary degree from Harvard College. Alumnus John Quincy Adams called it a disgrace to confer such honors "upon a barbarian who could not write a sentence of grammar and hardly could spell his own name." Legend has it that the president accepted the degree, which was conferred in Latin, responding, "Ex post facto; e pluribus unum; sic semper tyrannis; quid pro quo." Whether he did string together such common expressions mattered little. He had conquered New England without firing a shot. Even a disgusted Adams had to conclude, "And so ends this magnificent tour."[22]

Jackson was rather ill at the end of his grand tour, but he once again recovered, ready to do battle with his enemies. Uppermost in his mind was the need to finish off the hydra-headed monster bank. After some hesitation, he dismissed his secretary of treasury, William J. Duane, who refused to cooperate in removing the government's deposits from Biddle's institution. This firing marked the first time a president had dismissed a Senate-confirmed cabinet officer, and the question came up whether the president had the right to remove him unilaterally. Replacing Duane with Roger Taney of Maryland, Jackson prepared to sign an order on October 1 that would place all future government deposits in selected state banks and use the remaining funds in the Bank of the United States to pay operating expenses. Originally, there were to be twenty-two selected banks in 1833; by 1836, over ninety were added to the system, all friendly to the Democratic Party and the Jacksonian ideology, causing them to be labeled by critics as "pet banks."

Biddle moved to curtail loans throughout the system and squeeze especially the Western banks and economy. His conclusion was simple: "This worthy president thinks that because he had scalped the Indians and imprisoned Judges, he is to have his way with the Bank. He is mistaken." Some Democrats who had supported Jackson on the veto now bucked on removing the deposits, but Jackson, with a single-minded determination that is rare in politics, pushed ahead fully confident in his cause and in popular sentiment.

The curtailment of credit led to a sharp recession and a new public outcry. Biddle's strategy was "Nothing but the evidence of suffering abroad will produce any effect in Congress." If there were any doubt about the dangers of a centralized bank and the political arrogance of its operating officer, Biddle's very reactions proved the Jacksonians right.[23]

The president's major opposition, however, lay in the Senate, where the forces of Webster, Clay, and Calhoun mobilized to check what they saw as executive usurpation. Jackson feared that Congress would pass a joint resolution ordering that public deposits must stay in the Bank of the United States. In the House, Jackson forces, led by James K. Polk, fought a more evenhanded battle against the bank forces. In the Senate, Clay introduced a resolution asking for a copy of Jackson's statement that he had read to his cabinet members when he discussed the removal question with them. The resolution passed, and Jackson dismissed it out of hand as an inappropriate intrusion in the business of the executive branch. But Clay persisted and offered two resolutions: the first censured Jackson for his dismissal of Duane and the removal of deposits, and the second concluded that Taney's explanation for the removal action was unsatisfactory. In the debates, Clay argued at length against Jackson's view that he was the real spokesman of the people. Webster and Calhoun followed with their own denunciations. It was at this time that Webster privately wrote Biddle asking that his customary "retainer" be "renewed or *refreshed* as usual."[24] As this controversy was occurring, labor violence broke out in Maryland on the Chesapeake and Ohio canal in January 1834. Jackson, in response to the appeals of state officials, sent the military to stop civil disorders, another precedent for this strong president. This was the first time troops were used where defiance of the federal government was not directly involved, and further charges were leveled against "King Andrew."

In his major preoccupation, Jackson and his closest followers not only sought to destroy the bank and remove U.S. deposits but also demanded a return to specie money only. They wanted the deposit banks to stop issuing or receiving bank notes under $5. Thus silver and gold would flow. Jackson believed that specie would protect the laboring classes and end economic exploitation by the rich. The epic battle brought life back to the ailing general. One of his associates approvingly observed, "You would be surprised to see the General. This Bank excitement has restored his former energy, and gives him the appearance he had ten years ago." Senator Benton also noted that he "never saw him appear more truly heroic and grand than at this time. He was perfectly mild in his language, cheerful in his temper, firm in his conviction."[25]

The opposition to Jackson began calling itself the Whigs, after the English coterie that had opposed the abuses of the king and his ministers. For the American Whigs, Jackson had abandoned the careful republican balance of the Founding Fathers for an increasingly plebiscite democracy. In the House, one congressman proposed a resolution of impeachment against the president. In the Senate, the Taney nomination was rejected 28–18, and on March 28, 1834, that body voted 26–20 to censure the president for having "assumed upon himself authority and power not conferred by the constitution and laws, but in derogation of both." Jackson responded with a formal protest reasserting the powers of the presidency and the sanctity of democracy. The resolution had stopped short of impeachment.

The Whigs attacked the idea of even accepting Jackson's statement for the record. Years later, Benton would move that the censure be wiped off the records of the Senate, and a more mellow upper body agreed to do so before Jackson's retirement from the White House. As for the Whigs, they were in the peculiar situation of denouncing Jackson's democratic theories while at the same time appealing to the very people Jackson so praised.

As the bank controversy mounted, the president called for mass meetings and conventions by which the public's views could be directed at Congress. One senator, Hugh Lawson White of Tennessee, concluded that as the years passed, Jackson "became more and more open and undisguised in his interference to influence and control public opinion." Meanwhile, as economic problems mounted, criticism of the bank was heard even in business quarters.

On April 4, 1834, the House voted not to recharter the bank or restore deposits in it, and to support instead the pet banks. When the House sent an investigating committee to Philadelphia to examine Biddle's books, he arrogantly refused to provide the information requested or even to testify before Congress. Jackson had won. Taney followed up with a reevaluation of gold and the establishment of a full deposit system throughout the nation.

Jackson had delayed Taney's nomination as secretary of treasury fearing it would be defeated, which it eventually was. By the time congressional adjournment came, the president had a long list of appointees who were not confirmed, and he continued to have problems with the Senate. The Whigs denounced his "spoils system" and saw it as a mechanism to bring in the newly enfranchised masses. Jackson's views were simply that frequent rotation in office promoted democracy and that no person had a special right to hold office—tenets that added to this leveling impression.

Despite his own passionate expressions in favor of states' rights, Jackson strengthened the presidency and consequently the central government. To continue his policies, he anointed Van Buren as his successor, and the party named Richard Johnson of Kentucky as its nominee for vice president. Johnson was a controversial choice, but his supposed killing of the chief Tecumseh added to his appeal.

To Jackson, the great issues in the campaign should be the issues of economics and democracy. But increasingly the matter of slavery was becoming important. As the American Anti-Slavery Society started sending its abolitionist tracts across the nation and especially into the South, slaveholding apologists in Washington, D.C., tried to censure the mails. Jackson stayed away from the controversy at first, but in December 7, 1835, he asked Congress to enact legislation to prohibit the sending of "incendiary publications" to the South. Calhoun and his allies in Congress went further and demanded a law forbidding abolitionist material in any state or territory where local law prohibited it.

Jackson's second term also saw more successes. The Cherokees finally accepted $5 million for all their lands east of the Mississippi, which totaled approximately seven million acres. The president turned a deaf ear to the pleas of his "red children" and warned that without removal, the Indians would be extinguished. They could not live side by side with "a civilized community." The treaty was approved by a Cherokee vote of 79–7, showing how few Natives chose to vote. Later, fourteen thousand Cherokees signed a petition opposing the treaty, but after a long debate in the Senate, the treaty was ratified there by a single vote. Removal was to take place within two years of the ratification date, May 23, 1838. The Cherokees were finally rounded up, forced into prison camps, and removed in what was to be called "The Trail of Tears." Some eighteen thousand Cherokees were displaced, of whom four thousand died in the process.

The Creeks were not treated much better. Their lands were taken so fraudulently that even Jackson was angry, and he ordered an investigation. But when the tribe took up arms in protest, the government sent in over ten thousand troops, and blood flowed on the frontier once again. Over 14,609 Creeks were removed in the summer and fall of 1836. The same strategies were used against the Seminoles, and the president, an old Indian fighter in the First Seminole War, entered into the conflict with renewed zest when violence resulted. Jackson watched closely as the war continued, and his greatest regret was that the conflict was not won sooner. He was disgusted at the performance of the Floridians, hoping the Native Americans would kill them so that their "women might get husbands of courage, and breed up men who would defend the country." The war continued until 1842 and cost the government $10 million.

In the end, the five major Native American nations of the South—the Choctaw, Chickasaw, Creek, Cherokee, and Seminole—had been removed to the West. Elsewhere, tribes had been pushed from parts of Illinois, Michigan, Wisconsin, Iowa, Arkansas, Louisiana, Kentucky, Indiana, Ohio, Kansas, Minnesota, and Nebraska. After eight years, over forty-five thousand Native Americans had been expelled beyond the Mississippi River. As noted, for $68 million and thirty-two million acres of western land, the United States gained control over one hundred million acres of land—another massive expansion of the white democratic empire. Jackson's justification was that he had saved the Native Americans from extinction.[26]

Old Hickory's Foreign Policy

While Jackson may have seemed embroiled in domestic controversy, he was also interested in the role of the United States in the world. His primary concerns were to further American commercial interests and to vigorously assert national honor and pride. In general, Jackson's foreign policy was similar to his predecessor's policies, but unlike John Quincy Adams, he combined bluster, unaccustomed patience, and often good timing to further American causes rather successfully. As the historian John M. Belohlavek has concluded, Jackson "eagerly pursued a policy of promoting commercial expansion, demanded worldwide respect for the American

flag, restoring American prestige and national honor, and fostering territorial growth." Jackson believed in "Manifest Destiny" long before the term
was coined, and he championed U.S. control of the continent from the
Atlantic to the Pacific Ocean.[27]

His foreign policy was plagued, however, by the uneven quality of his
diplomatic personnel and by the quick rotation of public officials in and
out of government. In two terms in office, Jackson had four secretaries of
state and five secretaries of treasury. He reduced the once powerful cabinet
to a group he rarely consulted, meeting with them only sixteen times in
eight years and discussing foreign affairs at only six of those meetings. In
its place grew up the kitchen cabinet, a group of friends, confidants, and
obscure partisan officeholders who advised the headstrong president. Jackson rode his subordinates on a tight rein, delegating little authority, and
on one occasion he even chastised a cabinet officer for appointing a clerk
without his prior approval. As he once said, a cabinet officer was "merely
an executive agent, a subordinate, and you may say so in self defense."[28]

The president and his various secretaries of state did agree on the need
to reform the State Department and the consular service. Too few Washington officials supervised the nearly 140 consular posts, and incompetence
and corruption were rampant in the consular service. But while the State
Department was being reorganized, Congress neglected to increase its staff
or its salary levels. Jackson worsened matters by some of his appointments.
Most consuls were really commercial agents, and the president often appointed individuals whose skills revolved around party loyalty more than
demonstrated competence.

In dealing with Europe, Jackson accepted the primary importance of
maintaining good relations with England, despite his youthful conflicts
with British officials. The president's policy objectives in Europe were to
settle American claims against various nations for allegedly violating U.S.
shipping rights during the Napoleonic wars and to encourage commercial
relations in the region. By 1836, U.S. exports increased by more than
75 percent and imports by 250 percent over the first year Jackson was in
the White House. In the import-export balance, Britain was central to
American commercial and shipping interests, and Jackson at times would
overlook its policies and even bend the Monroe Doctrine a bit to accommodate that nation.

The administration focused on restoring the lucrative trade with the
British West Indies. As talks on this subject moved slowly, a patient Jackson publicly saluted, "With Great Britain, distinguished alike in peace and
war, we may look forward to years of peaceful, honorable, and elevated

competition." After much deliberation, the nations agreed on a reciprocity agreement in 1830 that revoked the British Orders in Council of 1826 and allowed U.S. vessels to enter Canadian and West Indian ports, provided they were trading only American goods. The president also agreed to arbitration on the Maine boundary question; however, intense opposition from that state and partisan attacks led to the issue being unresolved until 1842, when the state of Maine accepted a much less advantageous settlement. Overall, Jackson exhibited a remarkable ability to compromise with the British, despite his reputation as an Anglophobe over the years.

In his dealings with Spain, the president was less successful, especially in his primary objective—the reduction of duties with Cuba. The weakness of the Spanish government and upheaval in neighboring Portugal led to little progress as far as American interests were concerned. Elsewhere, the administration also attempted to work out stronger commercial ties, especially in the Black Sea with the czarist regime. Unfortunately, the president sent to Russia John Randolph of Roanoke, the erratic former congressman who on one occasion referred to the czar as "a genuine Cossack, implacable, remorseless and blood-thirsty." He left his post soon after being appointed and was replaced by James Buchanan, who proved to be a superb minister and concluded a favorable treaty in 1832.

Far more difficult was the administration's attempt to get the French government to pay millions of dollars owed to American ship owners and captains for violations of neutral rights during the Napoleonic wars. During the pre-1812 period, Napoleon seized more than three hundred U.S. ships and cargo valued at over $7 million. Previous administrations had made little progress on the reparations issue, and Jackson had hoped that by settling with Denmark on similar claims, he might set a useful precedent for negotiations with the French and with the Kingdom of the Two Sicilies (southern Italy and Sicily). Some of Jackson's advisers urged him to resort to trade reprisals, but the president rejected that approach, concluding, "I cannot recommend a war thro' the Customs House." But he did promise that if the French continued their recalcitrance, "you will find me speaking to Congress as I ought."[29]

As negotiations bogged down because of the continuing instability of French politics, the president got irritated and told his advisers, "I know them French. They won't pay unless they have to." Finally, the president decided that if the Chamber of Deputies did not authorize the funds to implement the treaty, he wanted congressional authorization to confiscate French ships and property in the United States.

In the Senate, the Whigs led by Clay had a field day thrashing the president for another manifestation of his autocratic inclinations when he asked for more money for fortifications. Most trying to Jackson, their ranks were augmented by many regular Democrats who resented his aggressive leadership. When the House approved a special fortifications bill, the Senate checked the proposal after massive rhetorical assaults by Webster and Clay. Clay argued that it was a blank check for the executive; Webster called it an excuse for seizing more power; another senator, Benjamin Leigh of Virginia, concluded that the nation would become a military monarchy: "They might as well say that the president should be made consul for life or Emperor of the American people." The measure was defeated by a margin of two to one.[30]

The French Chamber did approve the appropriations but insisted on an amendment that demanded that Jackson explain the purpose of his critical remarks to Congress on the negotiations. The president, with some justification, regarded the request as insulting and a violation of his right to address a separate branch of his nation's government. France should pay "without apology or explanation," the president demanded. Yet Jackson resorted to moderation on the matter. He refused to apologize but indicated that he did not intend to "menace or insult the Government of France." The treaty resulted in $7 million in claims payments and led to other agreements with Naples, Spain, and Portugal. With a mixture of patience and bluster, the administration had achieved an enviable record of success where others had reaped only failure.

The president also submitted a commercial treaty with the Ottoman Empire, which included a provision that would have had the United States help rebuild the sultan's navy. The Senate rejected the shipbuilding article, and several senators attacked the president for appointing commissioners without that body's consent in the first place. The administration also ran into delays in its negotiations with the Kingdom of the Two Sicilies. The Neapolitan diplomats insisted that their nation was too poor to pay reparations for American losses during the Napoleonic period. Consequently, the Americans moved more ships into its naval fleet contingent in the Naples harbor to underscore U.S. determination. A treaty was finally signed, and even Jackson's long-standing critics were compelled to support ratification.

On the other side of the globe, the administration sent its agents to the Orient to further American commercial designs. However, when the president dispatched naval forces to Malay to investigate an attack on Americans, he was subject to considerable criticism in Congress and the

Whig press. An overanxious commander attacked the suspected assailants, and the reports coming back led to controversy. The president, in the midst of his battle over the bank, was hit by more charges of abuse of executive power. In the House, a resolution demanding that the president turn over his instructions to the naval captain was pressed, and Jackson complied with the request the next day. Then it became clear that the captain had overstepped the president's orders, and criticism of Jackson on that score died down. In other regions of the world, the president had instructed an agent to visit Cochin China (Vietnam), Siam (Thailand), Muscat (a sultanate on the Gulf of Oman), and Japan—travels that led to minor and mixed results.

The main area of interest for the administration was South America. By the time of Jackson's election, the British had created a network of agreements and understandings in that region that resulted in investments totaling $40 million, loans to new nations there of over $110 million, and overall trade of $32 million. In comparison, U.S. commerce with South America, excluding Cuba, was less than $10 million. In setting out its overall policies toward that region, the administration uncharacteristically accepted a very limited interpretation of the Monroe Doctrine that accentuated British power there. The president, for example, generally ignored the British takeover of the Falkland Islands off the coast of Argentina, and when Brazil asked what the U.S. position would be in case of a Portuguese takeover of that former colony, the administration vaguely supported independence but shied away from any tough reaffirmation of the Monroe Doctrine. Jackson even refused to mediate a conflict between Peru and Colombia, fearing it would lead to interference in the internal affairs of those nations.

The most difficult challenge to that expressed policy of nonintervention arose over the Mexican situation. The United States desired to add Texas to its enlarging destiny, and John Quincy Adams had tried to purchase the territory for $1 million, an offer Jackson upped to $5 million in 1829. Jackson saw the acquisition of Texas as helping secure U.S. control over New Orleans and the Mississippi and firming up a clearer boundary with Mexico. At that time, Spain was threatening to invade Mexico, and the government there was clearly unstable.

However, the president oddly refused to encourage the strong Texan sentiments for self-government. Despite the fact that Sam Houston was an old Jackson lieutenant in the War of 1812, the president opposed any drastic action likely to lead to war there—believing that diplomacy would still work. There is some disagreement among historians as to whether Jackson was willing to resort to bribery to get Texas. If part of the $5 million ended up being used in that way, he did not care, but Jackson insisted he would not employ "means of an equivocal character" to deal with the issue. When the Mexican government tried to tighten its control over Texas, a war erupted, which led the president of the Mexican Republic, General Santa Anna, to move his army into Texas, where he was defeated by Sam Houston in the battle of San Jacinto on April 21, 1836. Santa Anna, who was captured, signed a treaty acknowledging Texan independence, which he later repudiated. The Mexican government then and historians since have insisted that Jackson encouraged the Texans, but in fact he refused Stephen Austin's appeal in 1836 for U.S. aid to defeat Santa Anna. He even labeled the rebellion "rash and premature." Citing the Neutrality Act of 1818, he stayed out of the conflict, but the opinion of Americans in general was clearly supportive of the new republic. Tensions between the United States and Mexico increased, and the Texans openly lobbied in the American capital for their cause and eventual annexation.

The president remained cautious, arguing that the United States had a treaty with Mexico and that he did not want to seem to have violated it by openly supporting the ambitions of the Texans. He also worried about abolitionist charges that any recognition of slaveholding Texas would open up the sectional question again. Uncharacteristically, Jackson observed that Congress was the "proper power" to advise on the propriety of acknowledging the independence of Texas. A resolution to recognize Texas, however, resulted in a deadlock in Congress, and the issue was bucked back to the president as he publicly sought to find out if the Texans were really interested in being annexed to the United States—which he knew they were. He continued to urge prudence on the recognition issue and even saw Santa Anna on January 19. He and the Mexican leader went on to discuss $3.5 million in compensation for Texas and for lands west to California. No agreement ultimately resulted, however. The administration with the support of Congress finally recognized the independence of the Texas nation, but it would take President John Tyler and later President James K. Polk to fully integrate that republic into the United States with its present borders and the addition of some lands west of Texas.[31]

Thus, although Jackson had no real experience in foreign policy except as a military conqueror and had acquired a reputation for undiplomatic brashness rather than patience, his administration gained some major triumphs in commercial treaties and reparations. Some of his appointees were poor choices and hurt his efforts and caused embarrassment, but overall Jackson proved to be flexible and rather understanding. His foreign policy was aggressive and self-confident, like the very executive he was. Jackson became a war hero who eschewed war and concentrated on promoting American interests and zealously guarding her republican virtue in a setting of Old World diplomats, cynical adventurers, and despotic regimes.

As Jackson's second term came to an end, his political strength in the Senate grew to the extent that not only was Benton successful in removing the earlier censure, but some of the president's nominations were also approved: Taney as chief justice of the Supreme Court, Barbour of Virginia as associate justice, Kendall as postmaster general, and Andrew Stevenson as minister to Great Britain. Jackson also continued to stand in the way of Clay's attempts to sell public lands and funnel the proceeds to the states. To the president, such largess would only encourage the states to depend on the federal government and enlarge the scope of the limited polity he so envisioned. "Money is power, and in that Government which pays all the public offices of the States all political power will be substantially concentrated," Jackson thundered.

Democrats in Congress, though, tried to propose a compromise that would link a distribution scheme for federal revenues with a proposal to regulate deposit banks. The party leaders also tried to quiet the charges that the executive had usurped powers in his unilateral actions on deposit—a favorite Whig charge. The new law sought to recognize the deposit banks, curtail Taney's discretion in the selection of them, and require specie in major transactions, a favorite theme of the president.

Jackson decided to sign the bill, probably because he feared that a veto might hurt Van Buren's election chances. The president received some criticism from his own ranks, but he was especially pleased by the increasing prominence of specie. Also, he was concerned about speculation in land sales and wanted to insist that only gold and silver could be accepted for the purchase of public lands. The majority of his cabinet initially opposed the president's policy, but once again he prevailed. Congress had adjourned when the secretary of treasury issued the Specie Circular on July 11, 1836. His critics were to see this stand as another example of executive abuse of power. The reaction was swift and vociferous, but Jackson stood firm again.

As Jackson aged, he became even more of a voice for democracy, advocating more popular control of government, the abolition of the Electoral College, more rotation in office, popular election of senators, and even the election of federal judges. When a laborer from Brooklyn, New York, sent him a hat he had made, Jackson responded characteristically, "I shall wear [it] with prouder feelings than I would a crown."[32]

As no president in the nineteenth century, Jackson created a public persona that appealed to the populace in a directly emotional way. This aloof warrior, wealthy slaveholding planter, and irascible politician had become a living symbol of the democratic impulse, despite the fact that the men who served in his administration were well-to-do, recognized leaders in their home communities. Jacksonian democracy, as it was later called, seems at times to have little to do with the Jackson administration's practices or even many of its battles. But the president clearly transformed the debates into democratic terms and changed the nature of the presidency itself in the process. He restored the office by making it the focal point of action within the limited context of nineteenth-century politics and gave his successors, in various ways, a model that was more direct and passionate than the Federalists and more active and involved than the Jeffersonians.

James K. Polk: The Arts of Waging Conflict

4

I F IT IS THE OBJECTIVE OF NATIONS to increase their power and influence in the world, then the United States in the period between Jefferson and Polk is surely a candidate for the honors of expansionism. And if the standard of presidential success is the ability to extend the republic's boundaries, then Polk's conquests must rank with Jefferson's Louisiana Purchase as major triumphs in acquisition and imperialism. The Polk administration is the high-water mark of U.S. expansion, of what became known in the 1840s as "Manifest Destiny," that constellation of ideology, self-interest, religious fervor, and economic lust that sought to project the United States as a continental power that would establish its hegemony in the Western Hemisphere.

James Knox Polk was born in 1795 in Mecklenburg County, North Carolina, and attended the state university there, although his family had moved in 1806 to Tennessee. Polk was a congressman from 1825 to 1839, serving the last four years as speaker of the House of Representatives. He was identified as a serious, hardworking Democrat who supported the policies of fellow Tennessean Andrew Jackson and was the floor manager in the titanic bank battle. From 1839 to 1841, he was his state's governor, and three years later he was encouraged to run for president by Jackson, who had given up on Van Buren because of his reservations on taking Texas. At the 1844 convention, Polk was nominated on the eighth ballot. Whigs generally attacked his low profile by asking, "Who is James K. Polk?" But fortified with Democratic Party support and General Jackson's blessings, and standing tall on annexing Texas and claiming Oregon up to the fifty-second parallel, Polk narrowly defeated the better-known Clay.

James G. Birney, running on the Liberty abolitionist ticket, which opposed the extension of slavery, drew off 62,300 votes, which may have cost Clay New York and possibly Michigan, and thus the White House.[1]

Probably no president worked harder at the job than Polk, and surely no president was better able to articulate his objectives and achieve them. On inauguration day, Polk told the historian George Bancroft that his four great objectives would be the reduction of the tariff, the reestablishment of the independent treasury, the settlement of the Oregon question, and the acquisition of California. Polk was to prove to be a determined executive, a strong civilian commander in chief, and a man immersed in detailed control of the government. But he was also a leader who lacked charisma, had no personal following, and had few close friends. He once observed, "I prefer to supervise the whole operations of the Government myself rather than entrust the public business to subordinates, and this makes my duties very great." No wonder he concluded, "With me it is emphatically true that the Presidency is 'no bed of roses.'"[2]

He tried to maintain balance between the wings of the party, curtailed the Van Buren faction, and exercised control over congressional Democrats on the major issues he faced. Polk pushed for cabinet responsibility, but he insisted that cabinet members were his appointees and subject to his oversight and control. As his diary shows, he was continually concerned about disloyalty in the cabinet, especially on the part of Secretary of State James Buchanan, who intended to run for the presidency in 1848 since Polk was committed to serving only one term. One major innovation in the administration was the handling of the budget. Before Polk, the president really had no responsibility over department estimates, which were sent directly to Congress. Polk insisted that all budget requests had to be submitted first to him for his review; an executive budget was then sent on to Congress. Polk did more than collate budget requests; at times he insisted on cuts in those proposals.

He ran a tight administration, in general, and mandated that neither he nor his wife would accept gifts from well-wishers. At one point, he even refused to accept the profits due on bonds he owned for fear of being called a war profiteer. Unlike Jackson, Polk was involved in policymaking and in detail on a day-to-day basis, not just sporadically in particular and singular controversies. Polk's strongest achievements came from his foreign policy and from the territorial fruits of the war he waged. Three days before his inauguration, Polk witnessed the success of President John Tyler's joint resolution inviting Texas into statehood. The bill was passed in the House by a vote of 120–98 and in the Senate by 27–25, and the outgoing president was able to bypass the treaty-ratifying process in the Senate. Polk's electoral victory was a sign to Congress that popular sentiment favored Texas's admission. In fact, Polk may have also helped move the resolution along through his personal influence and quiet lobbying just before his inauguration, thus eliminating the need to have to face the problem of Texas right after taking office.[3]

On another controversial expansion issue, Polk had taken, during the campaign, a hard line in dealing with the British in settling the boundary of the Oregon Territory. Expansionists had coined the slogan "54°40' or fight," referring to the map coordinates of the fifty-fourth parallel, fortieth degree, which embraced all of Oregon. Actually, though, American administrations and diplomats before Polk had pretty much accepted the boundary line as the forty-ninth parallel, which was the old division between British Rupert's Land and French Louisiana west of the Lake of the Woods.[4]

Polk's response was rather ingenious. In his first annual message to Congress on December 2, 1845, he reported that British-American negotiations had broken down, and he recommended that Congress give notice to the British of the end of their convention of joint occupancy. The tone of his message was bellicose, to the delight of Democrats, who believed that the British had no rights in that area in the first place and were in violation of the Monroe Doctrine. Actually, though, while Polk was forcing the issue, he also pushed for a diplomatic settlement at the forty-ninth parallel, arguing that he was simply following that line out of deference to his predecessors.

While the Democrats controlled both houses of Congress, there were strong feelings among the Southern wing that the Oregon issue should be settled peacefully, and they were joined by a cohesive Whig sentiment. Led by a Southern Whig, Senator John J. Crittenden of Kentucky, the Senate adopted a rather conciliatory posture toward Britain, and the House followed suit. As for the British, they also favored a settlement. Faced with the prospect of famine in Ireland and a revolt in his own party on the issue of protectionism, the great British Prime Minister Robert Peel preferred to find a way to reduce tensions with the Americans. In the end, the settlement was at the forty-ninth parallel, and the Senate, on June 12, 1846, accepted the treaty 38–12.[5]

Polk's compromise with Britain was wise and easy compared to his policies toward Mexico, which ended in war and exhibited his talents as a powerful civilian chief executive. Relations between the United States and Mexico had not gone well since the former recognized the Republic of Texas as an independent nation, and matters obviously worsened when nine years later the United States annexed Texas with its consent. Also, there remained a series of claims by U.S. citizens against the Mexican state and a long-standing dispute over whether the Texas border ended at the Nueces River or at the Rio Grande. Polk adopted an aggressive and confrontational position, hoping to get the land between the Nueces and the more southern Rio Grande and also adding California and New Mexico to the Union.

The president sent a special agent to urge the Mexicans to sell California and New Mexico to the United States, using in the process American claims as leverage in the bargain. When the Mexican government refused to negotiate, the president moved American troops into the areas between the two rivers. Polk called the cabinet together on May 9, 1846, to consider his request for a declaration of war, which would be forwarded to Congress; he argued, "In my opinion we had ample cause of war, and . . . it was impossible that we could stand in *status quo*, or that I could remain silent much longer."[6] Four hours later, Polk received news from General Zachary Taylor that the Mexicans had attacked U.S. forces. It is not unfair to conclude that the president's strategy was designed to foster a belligerent act and thus pave the way for a declaration of war. A young Whig congressman, Abraham Lincoln, introduced a series of resolutions demanding to know on what spot the attack took place. The implication was clear that the U.S. forces had provoked the attack. Polk did not even record Lincoln's inquiries in his extensive diary reflections of the period. And Lincoln would not hold office again until elected president himself in 1861.

On May 13, Congress declared war. When Secretary of State Buchanan pushed in a cabinet session for a statement from the president to assure Britain and France that the United States really had no territorial designs on Mexico, Polk bristled. While the United States had not gone to war for conquest, "it was clear that in making war we would if practicable obtain California and such other portions of the Mexican territory as would be sufficient to indemnify our claimants on Mexico, and to defray the expenses of the war which that power by her long continued wrongs and injuries had forced on us." The president went on to explain that he would go to war with Britain, France, or any other nation that sought to interfere with his policies. At a minimum, he insisted that any peace treaty had to include U.S. control of upper California and New Mexico.

To promote a favorable settlement with Mexico, Polk allowed private negotiations with Santa Anna, who promised the Americans that if he were allowed to return to Mexico he would conclude all boundary questions with the United States for a sum of $30 million. The Mexican leader living in exile was allowed to pass from Cuba through U.S. lines in the Gulf and permitted to return to his homeland. Once Santa Anna controlled the country, Buchanan was ready to begin peace negotiations, but the general promptly refused. Thus, through American intervention, an able and astute military commander was allowed to take over the war against the United States.

The president was also hindered by his decision to dismiss his own agent, Nicholas P. Trist, who was genuinely trying to negotiate a settlement, and by Polk's distrust of his military commanders, especially Taylor and Winfield Scott, who were both Whigs and prospective candidates for the 1848 presidential election. While Polk was upset with Trist's apparent arrogance, the administration accepted the Treaty of Guadalupe Hidalgo, which he negotiated. With the cabinet divided on the issue, the president forwarded the treaty to the Senate, and he observed blithely that it had never been his objective to conquer the Republic of Mexico or destroy her separate existence. Privately, he accepted the treaty because of growing opposition to his war policies in Congress, increasing problems with the U.S. Army in Mexico, and the prospect of losing control of New Mexico and upper California. On March 10, the Senate approved the treaty 38–14.[7]

Polk's war had several major consequences: It further antagonized Mexico, created several visible Whig military heroes out of mediocre military men, and added more territory in the South. In the end, the Mexican War laid down straw on the tinderbox of slavery and helped lead to the Civil War. As for Polk himself, his aggressive foreign policies had added so much land that it rivaled the purchase of the Louisiana Territory. The apostle of Manifest Destiny became the father of the states of Oregon, Washington, Idaho, California, New Mexico, Arizona, Nevada, Utah, and parts of Colorado, Montana, and Wyoming.

Polk proved to be a strong and decisive commander in chief, unconcerned with the debate on inherent powers that would figure so prominently in the Civil War. Ironically, while Lincoln opposed the administration's policies in the Mexican War, there is considerable evidence that he emulated Polk in taking an even broader view of the wartime powers of the presidency, one at variance with the Whig philosophy Lincoln held throughout most of his adult life. Whether Polk was a role model for Lincoln is unclear, but there are great areas of resemblance in their vigorous and personal prosecution of the war.

As with Polk's decision to send the troops into disputed territory, Lincoln would be criticized for allegedly having provoked the Confederate states into attacking Fort Sumter. Polk refused to call Congress into session when it appeared likely that Mexico would move against the U.S. Army. Lincoln also did not call Congress back into session for three months as the Civil War was beginning, apparently fearing legislative interference. Later, each Congress declared that a state of war had already existed and gave legislative approval for a president's actions as commander in chief at the time.

Polk, however, in fighting his war, did not ask for an immediate increase in the regular army, preferring at first to rely on volunteer regiments of state militia. When he finally changed his policy and asked Congress for ten regiments, he had to wait from December 1846 to February 1847 for approval. The administration's strategy in the war was to seize the northern provinces of Mexico, capture New Mexico and its critical commercial gateway Santa Fe, move its naval forces toward California, and conquer Mexico City by landing at Vera Cruz and conducting a forced march to the capital city. Unfortunately for Polk, General Taylor on September 25 captured Monterey and later granted the Mexican forces an armistice. Polk ordered an end to the truce and commanded General Taylor to continue the fight. Then, fearing that Santa Anna would send reinforcements to the Mexican forces, Polk ordered Taylor to halt. The general, however, ignored the command and moved on toward Buena Vista, where he won a widely renowned victory. The president was incensed at Taylor and concluded, "He is evidently a weak man and has been made giddy with the idea of the Presidency." Polk had the same disdain and suspicion of General Scott, who was in charge of the march from Vera Cruz to Mexico City. In his diary, Polk confided, "The truth is that I have been compelled from the beginning to conduct the war against Mexico though the agency of two Gen'ls highest in rank who have not only no sympathies with the Government, but are hostile to my administration."[8] Finally, he replaced Scott after a controversial move by the general to court-martial three other officers. Like Lincoln, Polk grew weary of the inactivity of professional soldiers, and he even got involved in supply problems and purchasing decisions. But unlike Lincoln, Woodrow Wilson, and Franklin D. Roosevelt, Polk consistently remained involved in tactics and details while overseeing the strategies of the conflict.

Having been a leader in Congress in a way that no president before him had, except Madison in the 1790s, Polk had a real understanding of the legislative process and the personalities in the legislative branch. Jackson had been able to assert the primacy of the presidency by stressing polarizing issues and by the sheer force of his magnetic personality. Polk had no such personal appeal for the mass of the citizenry, but he was fairly successful in dealing with congressional leaders by stressing the ties of party. He insisted that it was the president and not Congress who represented the national will of the people, and he acted accordingly.

The major domestic piece of legislation the president pushed was the passage of a lower tariff schedule. As a congressional leader and as governor of Tennessee, he had been an advocate of a lower tariff and supported Jackson and Van Buren in their positions. Most of the Democratic Party, except in Pennsylvania and in some other industrial areas, had adopted a low tariff plank. Polk appealed to party loyalty to sway wavering Democrats in the Senate, and the new tariff schedule passed that body by only a one-vote margin before it was approved by the House.[9]

Like any good party leader, Polk counted noses and let wayward Democrats know of his disappointment at deviations. His ire was especially fueled by Calhoun and his followers, who seemed to take pleasure in joining with the Whigs in opposition. As noted, there was increasing criticism of his war policies, especially in the House, which went Whig in the 1848 elections. On January 3, 1847, that body voted 85 to 81 that the war had been "unnecessarily and unconstitutionality begun by the president of the United States." The year before, a Democrat-controlled House had voted for war by a count of 174–14.[10]

New territory raised again the issue of sectional balance and slavery. Polk used his persuasive powers to convince Representative David Wilmot of Pennsylvania not to push his resolution banning slavery in the territories to be acquired from Mexico. He assured him that he did not wish to extend slavery, and that the provinces of New Mexico and California were not suitable for slavery. Wilmot held back on introducing his proviso, but eventually it became part of the congressional debate. Prophetically Polk warned, "The movement . . . will be attended with terrible consequences to the country, and cannot fail to destroy the Democratic party, if it does not ultimately threaten the Union itself."

As with the Louisiana Purchase, there were questions of territorial governments that had to be addressed in those newly acquired areas. Polk supported the extension of the Missouri Compromise, fearing that leaving the slavery question undecided would encourage "ambitious political aspirants & gamblers" to establish parties based on geographical divisions that would imperil the Union. By August, though, the subject of a territorial government for Oregon was separated from the fate of California and New Mexico. Since the president had accepted the Missouri Compromise line, he had no problem with the bill, even though it prohibited slavery in Oregon. Southern opposition, led by Calhoun, mobilized to stop the bill before adjournment. Polk, in response, threatened to reconvene Congress the next day, and eventually the Oregon Bill was passed and Polk signed it.

Polk, though, remained concerned about the problem of territorial governments for New Mexico and California. Senator Benton had issued a public letter to Californians that implied they should form a government with his son-in-law Colonel John C. Frémont as governor. Polk wanted to counter that letter with one of his own, but he was uncertain at first if legally the president and the military could govern the area before Congress passed appropriate legislation. His own attorney general had upheld the right of the people to choose their own government in the absence of congressional legislation.

Finally, after a long cabinet session, the president concluded that the inhabitants should obey the existing government there, and Polk opposed any convention being called to form a new government. He was concerned that a Whig victory in the 1848 election would mean that California would simply go its own way. Polk then decided to throw his support behind Senator Stephen Douglas's bill to admit California into the Union and allow the people in that territory to decide if slavery should be permitted. When Calhoun sought to mobilize the Southerners of both parties in opposition, Polk, himself a Southerner and a slaveholder, used the powers of his office to oppose what he saw as growing agitation. He then even courted Whigs to support the Douglas bill. Concerned about sectionalism, he explained, "I regarded the subject above mere party considerations, and wished it settled, I cared not by whose votes."[11] But the bill did not pass in his term.

Polk was clearly a party leader who was sensitive to the legacy of Jefferson and Jackson and astute enough to press the case for loyalty and regularity. He insisted on establishing a new newspaper that would carry his message and curtail the admirers of Van Buren, and he was the last president to have an effective administration-controlled newspaper. After his term, individual entrepreneurs established their own papers, which were more critical and later sensationalist in spreading the word to a more literate citizenry.

He also tried to use his patronage powers to satisfy the various wings of the party but concluded that the demands were insatiable. Still, he removed in one year more than seven hundred individuals in the Post Office alone. In four years, over 13,500 postmasters were replaced out of a total of 16,000 such positions available. When some New Yorkers and others joined the Free Soil Party with Van Buren, those former Democrats were cut off from the public trough. The loss of this so-called Barnburner element of the Democratic Party was to prove most significant to the outcome of the next presidential election.[12]

Polk was also conscientious about avoiding congressional intrusion with its use of investigative powers into the workings of the executive branch. Several times he refused to respond to requests for information, calling it a dangerous precedent. In other instances, such as a diplomatic incident concerning Ireland, he edited the correspondence he had on the matter. These claims of executive privilege, as they came to be called in the 1950s, were seen by Polk as based on his predecessors' actions and on his constitutional duty and sense of public interest.[13]

Although Polk remains a little-known president today, he emerges by the sheer force of his will and determination as one of the nation's strongest chief executives. Except for Lincoln, he is surely the most able of the nineteenth-century executives, and as with Jefferson, he left an incredible record of territorial gain and expansion. Less than a year after he left office, Polk died at the early age of fifty-three, burned out from the pace and intensity of his duties.

What makes Polk's accomplishments all the more arresting is that he lacked a broad personal following or strong public support that he could count on. He was the first "dark horse" candidate, underestimated and little known—a Harry Truman of his time. In terms of his administration's stated objectives, it is clear that he was an ardent expansionist who would counsel peace, wage war, and tolerate negotiations to spread the eagle across the North American continent. James K. Polk was the greatest and most successful American imperialist of them all.

Abraham Lincoln: The Commander in Chief Goes to War   5

T HE ACRIMONIOUS NATIONAL DISPUTES of the 1850s over states' rights, territorial expansion, the status of slavery, and the right of secession took their toll on the ties that bound the North and South. By the election of 1860, the heterogeneous Democratic Party could no longer bridge the gap across the Mason-Dixon line, and it was rent into three factions. The mainstream Democrats, after a confusing and divided convention, nominated Stephen Douglas of Illinois; the Southern states' rights adherents put forth John Breckinridge of Kentucky; and a group of moderate constitutional Democrats rallied around John Bell of Tennessee.

In the Republican councils, it became obvious that this division might lead their party to victory, and the powerful bosses and state chairmen looked for a probable winner. Going into the Chicago convention, the Republicans had only a single presidential contest behind them with the 1856 campaign of explorer John C. Frémont. In May 1860, they came together to debate the merits of the major contenders, one of whom might very well end up in the White House. The frontrunner was William Seward, nationally known senator, former governor of New York, and the candidate of the powerful machine run by Thurlow Weed. Seward had considerable strength in Maine, Michigan, Wisconsin, Minnesota, California, and Massachusetts, as well as in New York. He was profoundly conservative and yet was identified with his radical remark that there was a higher law than the Constitution—the moral law that prohibited slavery. He had argued that the battle between the forces of freedom and those of black bondage would lead to an "irrepressible conflict."

Posed against Seward were a variety of opponents. From Pennsylvania came Simon Cameron, a longtime Democratic leader who changed his party affiliation and became a Republican U.S. senator. Cameron had established a record as a shrewd political operator and as a rich and successful industrialist. His name was associated with partisan intrigue and backroom deals, but his role as a major figure in the important Pennsylvania delegation gave him considerable leverage in the national convention. However, in his circuitous route to the Chicago convention, Cameron had welcomed Know-Nothing support and thus alienated the powerful German American element that was strong in the Republican Party of that period.

A third principal was Salmon P. Chase of Ohio, a fierce antislavery advocate who had been associated in the 1840s with the Liberty and then the Free Soil parties. Elected governor of Ohio in 1855, he had strong local support for the nomination but little national visibility. A respected and responsible public official, he had distinguished himself during his period of public service in his home state.

An additional contender was Edward Bates, a sixty-eight-year-old Missouri Whig. Bates was a Southern planter, a sensible conservative, a man of conscience who had freed his slaves and provided for them later. Horace Greeley called him a fine candidate, and the powerful Blair clan in Maryland had declared their support for his candidacy.

And last, there was Abraham Lincoln of Illinois, a highly regarded local lawyer who had run for the Senate in his state twice and had been defeated both times, but whose name was prominently mentioned in early 1860 as a possible vice presidential candidate. Many delegates at the convention were seeking a Westerner, one who opposed the extension of slavery in the new territories, who was conservative in speech and in bearing, a candidate who was not associated with the Know-Nothings and could command German American support. On the third ballot, the Republican convention stopped Seward's bid and turned to an available alternative, Lincoln.

Out of the Wilderness

No American political figure is as complex as Lincoln; none has been elevated to legend so firmly. In all popular polls and in nearly all historical judgments, he has assumed the designation of America's greatest president. Such a conclusion would have been greeted with disbelief by his colleagues and contemporaries, and probably even by Lincoln himself. His background is the American dream come true.[1] A dirt-poor boy, with no more than one year of formal education in total, knowing no influential patrons, Lincoln had moved aimlessly across the lonely farms and desolate plains of Kentucky, Indiana, and Illinois. After several years in the state legislature of Illinois, Lincoln got his turn to go to the U.S. Congress—the very term that marked Polk's entry into the Mexican War, a war Lincoln opposed. He was a strong supporter of economic development and insisted for years after the Mexican War that his basic political concern was internal improvements and not the expansion of slavery. As a good Whig and an old admirer of Clay, Lincoln worked hard for the party and waited for some reward, only to find that it was usually denied. He practiced law, met people, and gave speeches filled with cracker-barrel humor and shopworn adages. Over the years, he established himself as an early opponent of slavery but not a New England abolitionist. Disappointed by politics, Lincoln turned more toward building a lucrative law practice and was a corporate counsel for some railroads and the McCormick Reaper Company. Then in the 1850s, Lincoln's attention was refixed on the issues of slavery and its expansion into the territories of the Kansas–Nebraska region and the newly obtained Southwest.

Indeed, as noted, he twice ran for the Senate and twice he was defeated. But in the second race, he won national attention in a series of debates with Stephen Douglas in 1858. Although there were fewer differences between the two candidates than is generally supposed, those debates cast Lincoln into the forefront of Republican leaders. In 1859, he made a lecture swing through New England and New York City and was well received. Despite the fact that he was to retreat from the logic of his position, Lincoln, like Seward, gave the nation a phrase that would be used to identify the magnitude of the new conflict.

In an address at the Republican state convention that nominated him for the Senate in 1858, Lincoln delivered a riveting address, attacking the Dred Scott decision, Douglas's doctrine of popular sovereignty, and Buchanan's policies. He argued that slavery agitation had increased and would increase even more until the crisis had been resolved. Then, in words that would cause Southerners to shudder, he warned, "A house divided against itself cannot stand. I believe that this government cannot endure permanently half slave and half free. I do not expect this Union to be dissolved— I don't expect the house to fall—but I expect it will cease to be divided. It will become all one thing, or all the other."

Under attack by Douglas, Lincoln maintained that he did not support racial equality, and that he believed that the white race should be in ascendancy. He was insistent, especially campaigning in southern Illinois, that he was not in favor of African American citizenship, and he concluded that the federal government lacked the constitutional authority to touch slavery in those states where it was recognized and supported. He even upheld the enforcement of the controversial Fugitive Slave Law passed by Congress. The Lincoln of the 1858 debates has disturbed many modern-day liberals and lent some credence to the view that he was simply—by today's standards—another white racist politician.[2]

Such a characterization is understandable, but it is incorrect. Lincoln all his life opposed slavery and hated what it did to the dignity of the slaves and the character of the masters. Legend has it that he first saw slaves being bought and sold when as a young boy he ventured down the Mississippi River to New Orleans, and he never overcame that sense of horror. In Congress, he introduced a bill to end slavery in the federal capital—an act in advance of his times and one of singular courage. He favored white ascendancy but warned that he did not believe that the "negro should be denied *everything*." He opposed the "tendency to dehumanize the negro, to take away from him the right of ever striving to be a man."[3] Lincoln, the poor boy who made good, looked upon the United States as the last best hope of mankind. He welcomed the upwardly mobile and ambitious, and he denounced the view that every society had to have a "mud-sill," a lower class confined forever to a place on the bottom of the heap. But in the end, the Union he so celebrated was a white man's world. Lincoln was a practical politician, not an abolitionist, although he genuinely hated slavery more intensely and more consistently than almost any other mainstream political leader. As a boy who grew up in states characterized in part by Southern culture and a man who married into a slaveholding family, Lincoln retained many of the racial attitudes of his youth even as president. What made him different from the average politician on the race issue was, first, his genuine hatred of the institution of slavery and his deep personal sensitivity toward human suffering, and second, the unique cataclysmic events that turned a conservative Whig into the Great Emancipator. Thus it was that Abraham Lincoln, who once claimed he was more controlled by events than the master of them, became the greatest revolutionary of them all—the commander in chief who brought about the demise of slavery forever in a land where it had seemed firmly entrenched.

Lincoln was nominated for the presidency for several reasons that are quite different from what would become his destiny. He was seen by the convention delegates as more moderate than Seward and as more acceptable to the South and border states. With his Western background, he was the epitome of the "new man"—the embodiment of the frontier spirit.

His supporters regaled the nation with the legend of the log cabin (that had helped Harrison in 1840) and passed around rails supposedly split by Honest Abe himself. Lincoln, while not ashamed of his frontier past, never really exploited it. He was, he said, of undistinguished background; the story of his family was "the short and simple annals of the poor," he told an early biographer. In the campaign of 1860, he said little, stayed at home as was the custom, and bided his time as the Democrats divided up the vote. The results gave Lincoln 1,866,452 votes to Douglas's 1,376,957, Breckinridge's 849,781, and Bell's 588,879. While Lincoln received only about 39 percent of the popular tally, he polled 180 electoral votes to Breckinridge's 72, Bell's 39, and Douglas's 12. Douglas's popular support, while extensive, was spread across the nation and not concentrated in the major states. Lincoln carried all of the free states except New Jersey, which he split with Douglas. Breckinridge captured the lower South, plus Arkansas, Delaware, Maryland, and North Carolina. Bell also did well in some of those states and carried the border states of Kentucky, Tennessee, and Virginia. Douglas received all the electoral votes of Missouri and three in New Jersey.

Lincoln thus won a large electoral vote victory with less than 40 percent of the popular vote. But his victory was somewhat troubling; it was a clear sectional victory, one likely to further fuel the forces of alienation and secession in the lower South. In the area later to become the Confederacy, Lincoln received not one popular ballot except in Virginia, where he polled some 1,929 votes, most of them in the northern panhandle area around Wheeling. Even Breckinridge, the candidate of the Southern states' rights forces, received over 278,000 votes in the Northern states. Clearly, the Republicans had not moved much beyond Frémont's level of support in 1856, except that under new circumstances victory emerged.

The usual explanation was that the Democrats, by dividing up the vote, allowed Lincoln to creep in. But in fact if there had been a common anti-Lincoln ticket, he still would have won the presidency because the Republicans would have held onto enough of the electoral vote. Unlike Douglas's wide national support, Lincoln's votes were concentrated, and he wasted no votes in futile states. He had no popular support in the South at all and very little in Kentucky, Virginia, and Maryland. Thus, where he did garner popular support, he usually won, and therefore carried the total state electoral vote, except in Missouri and New Jersey. Although voting statistics are confusing and incomplete for this period of history, it appears that Lincoln's victory was due to his ability to join New England with the free states of the Midwest, California, and Oregon. Despite the popular view that it was the German American Republicans who brought victory, it appears that Lincoln's success, in at least the Great Lakes states, was due more to the old Yankee stock that had migrated from New England rather than to foreign-born voters; the only exception was in Illinois, where the German American vote was indeed critical to the Republican ticket.[4]

The election of Lincoln on November 6, 1860, then, was a clear-cut sectional victory, one likely to infuriate Deep South secessionist supporters. To those agitators, the presidential election marked the final insult, even though the Democrats still controlled Congress and the Supreme Court had supported slavery without restriction. As Lincoln celebrated his unique personal triumph and his party marked its first great campaign success, the forces of dissolution were unleashed once again, this time not to be contained.

Early Secession Moves

The election of Lincoln led to Southern cries in more radical quarters for secession from the Union. The moderates in Virginia and Kentucky, however, pushed for a border state convention to slow down the disunion movement. President Buchanan and Lincoln both favored the idea, but hotter heads in the Deep South, especially in South Carolina, wanted to end the Union altogether. Some Northerners, such as Horace Greeley of the *New York Tribune*, urged that they be allowed to leave in peace. As Greeley editorialized, "We hope never to live in a republic whereof one section is pinned to the residue by bayonets." Even Winfield Scott, the head of the U.S. Army, proposed four unions of the states, a rearrangement whereby the slave states would be trustees of the territory south of 36°30'.[5]

Others suggested that the Lincoln electors should vote instead for Breckinridge and support a statesmanlike compromise with the South. Breckinridge's selection would save the Union, it was argued, while Lincoln's formal election by the Electoral College in February 1861 would end it. But as so often happens in political crises, events flow from the actions of the extremists. On December 20, 1860, South Carolina passed an ordinance of secession—it was now a separate nation, at least in the eyes of its own partisans. The impetus for disunion swept through the lower South and by early 1861, South Carolina was joined by Alabama, Florida, Georgia, Louisiana, and Mississippi. Gathering in Montgomery, Alabama, the delegates from those states met to form the Southern States of North America. In February, the secessionists elected Jefferson Davis of Mississippi and Alexander H. Stephens of Georgia as provisional president and vice president, respectively. In March, the forces of secession banded together to depose the Union-oriented governor of Texas, Sam Houston, and consequently that important state entered the Confederacy. Among the states of the Deep South, only in Texas was the ordinance of secession submitted to a popular vote, and there only after its adoption by the state's delegates.

As for the Buchanan administration, it permitted this new government to be established without any interference. The border states, especially Virginia, were not a part of the early secession movement, and it was unclear what type of support the Confederacy would have there. The crisis atmosphere was accelerated by the seizure of federal military establishments in the South; once again South Carolina took the lead. By the end of December 1860, secession leaders controlled post offices, customhouses, the federal courts in Charleston, and Castle Pinckney and Fort Moultrie in the harbor region. Elsewhere, this step was repeated as federal arsenals, forts, and customhouses changed hands. By the middle of January 1861, forts in Savannah, Mobile, and Pensacola were seized, and Southern agents were in the North buying munitions and war matériel.[6]

Yet in the border states, and even among large segments of the Deep South, secession was not greeted with uniform support. Stephens, who knew the president-elect, praised Lincoln as a "good, sound and safe man" and argued that slavery would be protected under his administration. In December 1860, President Buchanan had denounced secession and advocated "peaceful constitutional remedies" to deal with the problem. Congress in response had created a broad-based committee in both houses to deal with the mounting crisis. But the Senate, a body once marked by the great compromises of Clay, Webster, and Calhoun, failed after eleven days to come up with a formula for peace. In the House of Representatives, the same fate resulted, as Republicans refused to agree to Southern demands to protect and extend slavery. Yet both houses passed a proposed constitutional amendment by two-thirds majorities, which would guarantee that Congress would never amend the Constitution to abolish or interfere with slavery. And in the House, John Sherman of Ohio introduced a resolution that neither Congress nor the nonslaveholding states had a right under the Constitution to interfere with or regulate slavery in any state. That resolution passed 161–0. Another compromise came from John J. Crittenden of Kentucky, the successor to Clay's mantle in the Senate, who favored extending the Missouri Compromise line (36°30') to the Pacific coast—thus creating a national Mason-Dixon line protecting slavery below it and prohibiting it in the territories and states above. Republicans attacked his proposal, but in fact it was more restrictive than the Supreme Court's policy in the *Dred Scott* case, which made slavery an unregulated national institution.[7]

Part of the confusion of the period was due to the internal disorganization of the new Republican Party. Many prominent Republicans, including Seward and Weed, were given to compromise. Despite Seward's popular reputation as a radical, he was quite willing to enact a stricter fugitive slave law and to allow the admission of still more slave states. Even when the Southern representatives were absent from Congress in February and March, the majority of Republicans in that body supported the admission of the territories of Colorado, Dakota, and Nevada without having them prohibit slavery, a provision they had previously insisted on when they attacked Douglas. It was, as Douglas pointed out sarcastically in 1861, the exact principle he had proposed in 1854—popular sovereignty.

And what of Lincoln himself? As we have seen, in this period, the president-elect watched carefully what was happening, kept his own counsel, wrote confidentially to a few trusted colleagues, and was preoccupied with the demands of patronage seekers. He felt it would do no good to speak out publicly and might even encourage the secessionist elements. Privately, he favored a fugitive slave law moderately enforced, promised not to recommend the abolition of slavery in the District of Columbia, indicated that he would not support the end of the slave trade in the United States, and said he did not care if slavery were extended into New Mexico (where it was thought the institution would not be economically viable). To his old acquaintance, Georgia politician Alexander Stephens, he promised no interference with slavery where it existed, assuring him that "the South would be in no more danger in this respect than . . . in the days of Washington." He even asserted that he would not discriminate against the South in terms of patronage appointments in its region, or allow Northerners to come in and take over administrative posts there. But on one point, Lincoln refused to yield—he would not accept the expansion of slavery into the new territories. This step, he concluded, would "lose us everything we gain by the election."[8]

On secession he had said little, but he expressed the view that no one state could leave without the consent of the others, and he thought the federal officials should "run the machine as it is." He would support a constitutional amendment to reassure those who feared that slavery would be interfered with, but on the territorial question, he wrote to Republican leaders: no compromise; it would lead to "a slave empire." His position was clear, but it by no means commanded universal support in his own party. Even in Massachusetts, probably the most antislavery state in the Union, twenty-two thousand citizens signed a petition to Congress urging the adoption of the Crittenden compromise.

In terms of the economic realities, it is doubtful that there would have been much migration of slaveholders into the new territories. There were twenty-two slaves in New Mexico (which included present-day Arizona), and even in "bleeding Kansas" in 1860 there were fewer than two hundred slaves out of a population of a hundred thousand people. The Republicans had already let Dakota, Colorado, and Nevada into the Union with no preconditions. In terms of fugitive slaves, which so upset the Southern planter class, the 1860 census numbered them at 803, or about 0.02 percent of the total slave population. These two great issues—territorial expansion and fugitive slave laws—were symbolic concerns far out of proportion to the actual conditions of the time.

But those issues were not unimportant, for they became litmus tests concerning how one felt about the peculiar institution. The South demanded not just protection but also a vote of approval for its way of life. Lincoln's election did not threaten its domestic institutions, but it did signify that the South would no longer be able to check the growing dominance of free-soil northern and western America. It must be remembered that Lincoln was one of the few presidents who was not a slaveholder or a Northerner somewhat sympathetic to the Southern planter class. Lincoln's stand on the territories was clear, and it enabled his party to define itself in contrast to both the Douglas Democrats and the slaveholding interests.

Between the election and the inaugural, Lincoln stayed in Springfield, listening and watching. He realized that some Southern leaders had begun preparations for military operations, and he was concerned about the loss of federal installations. On December 21, 1860, the day after South Carolina's secession, he confidentially wrote General Winfield Scott that he should be prepared "to either hold or retake the forts, as the case may require."

Lincoln carefully worked on naming his cabinet, dealing with the major party leaders and fulfilling agreements made by his managers at the party convention. As his inauguration approached, he bade farewell to his neighbors in a touching tribute:

> My friends. No one, not in my situation, can appreciate my feeling of sadness at this parting. To this place, and the kindness of these people I owe everything. Here I have lived a quarter of a century, and have passed from a young man to an old man. Here my children have been born, and one

is buried. I now leave, not knowing when or whether I may return, with
a task greater than that which rested upon Washington.

As he left Springfield, he traveled by train through Illinois and western
Pennsylvania to the upstate cities of New York, down to New Jersey,
Philadelphia and Harrisburg in Pennsylvania, Maryland, and on to Washington, D.C. His speeches were frequently somber and often melancholy.
He characterized himself as "the humblest of all individuals that have ever
been elevated to the presidency," and he reassured the South of his conservative tendencies and moderate inclinations. The crisis was artificial, he
concluded.

On reaching the capital on February 23, Lincoln was warned of possible assassination attempts and, at the insistence of the authorities, he
arrived early in the morning. His enemies quickly spread the rumor that
Lincoln came into town in a long military cloak and a Scotch plaid cap,
and cartoonists spread the tale of his allegedly sneaking into the capital.
Soon a barrage of criticism would be hurled at this man: they called him
a simple Susan, a gorilla, the ape from Illinois. They insisted that Lincoln
spoke in a crude way, had grown a shaggy beard at some girl's insistence,
and was unused to the social graces of the capital. He was simple, stupid,
and quite homely.

In his inaugural address on March 4, Lincoln struck two themes: his
guarantee that the South should not feel threatened by his election and his
devotion to maintain the Union. Yet he promised that where there was
hostility to the United States in a locality, "there will be no attempt to
force obnoxious strangers among the people," and that while the government had the strict legal right to control its federal officers, he deemed it
"better to forego for the time the use of such offices." Thus, despite his
policy of firmness and fraternity, the new president spoke of temporizing
rather than of asserting forcefully the federal government's authority. The
speech was generally not well received in the South, and the new administration entered office facing the same problems that the previous one had
faced.

Fort Sumter

The first order of business for the new president was patronage. For a
party out of power, the acrimonious election of Lincoln still meant offices,
positions, and newly found opportunities. Much of the public reaction to
Lincoln's balanced cabinet was unfavorable, and Republican stalwart James

G. Blaine recorded that Buchanan's final cabinet had more strong defenders of the Union than the new one. The president managed these patronage chores, but he spent most of his time deciding what to do about the future of federal establishments in the South. As has been noted, Buchanan allowed Southern occupation of many federal installations in the South. He has been strongly criticized for this lack of leadership, but he insisted with some justification that to have replenished the forts in December 1860 would have been "little short of madness . . . with the small force" at his disposal. Lincoln was not unsympathetic to this realistic compromise at first, but compromise was not what he ended up with as the crisis approached.[9]

Once again, the focal point would be South Carolina. There in the harbor, two of the three forts had fallen under secessionist control. Only Fort Sumter remained in federal hands. The fate of Sumter was a subject of early negotiations after the inaugural and, at times, the new administration did not speak with one voice. The federal government had to confront the fact that Major Robert Anderson, the fort's commander, could not remain at Sumter beyond six weeks because of a shortage of food; April 15, 1861, became the day of decision.

Lincoln and his cabinet discussed the matter, and the president found his major advisers nearly unanimous in opposing reprovisioning the fort. At this time, the South sent three commissioners to negotiate with Lincoln on the fate of the fort, and while the president at first refused to see them as representatives of an independent nation, indirect contact was established. The administration's position was confusing as Seward, acting on his own, gave the commissioners the impression that the fort would be given up after all.

The president had seriously pondered the question, fearing that a tough stand would alienate Southern moderates, especially in Virginia, and drive them into the waiting arms of the Confederacy. He had concluded, "If you will guarantee to me the State of Virginia, I shall remove the troops. A state for a fort is no bad business." With the nonsecession delegates at Richmond holding the state in the Union, the president realized that military conflict would force Virginia to choose between its Southern neighbors and its historical attachment to the Union. Fearing the consequences, Lincoln, as late as April 4, was still considering whether to withdraw from Fort Sumter.

As he considered the issue, a conference of Northern governors met at Washington and demanded that Lincoln stand firm on Sumter. In addition, Lincoln's old friend and political confidant, Francis P. Blair, visited him and warned that withdrawal would be treason and would not sit well with the people of the North. Faced with these pressures and increasing secessionist belligerence in Virginia, Lincoln moved toward a tougher line.

Cautiously, he worked out a policy to reinforce the less visible Fort Pickens in Pensacola, Florida, in order to emphasize his overall policy, but also to "better enable the country to accept the evacuation of Fort Sumter as a military necessity" if it came to that. The Buchanan administration had concluded in the last weeks of its term an agreement that it would not reinforce Fort Pickens if Florida promised not to attack it. Lincoln's Pickens expedition ran into problems, however, and his subtle plans were checked as any possibility for a Sumter compromise was ended. The president faced a stark choice: give up Sumter and ignominiously surrender federal authority, or send an expedition knowing it might mean conflict and war.

Lincoln ordered Fort Pickens reinforced, and in a confusing chain of events, he also had the Sumter expedition go ahead. The administration then informed Governor Francis W. Pickens of South Carolina of its intention to send the fort provisions but not men, arms, or ammunition. South Carolina, however, refused to bend and, with Confederate President Davis's approval, attacked the fort. After thirty hours of steady shelling of the fort, Major Anderson surrendered Sumter.

Some critics of Lincoln's policy have argued that he shrewdly maneuvered South Carolina into firing the first shot and thus assuming the blame for starting the war. One of the president's friends recorded that on July 3, 1861, Lincoln said, "The plan succeeded. They attacked Sumter—it fell, and thus, did more service than it otherwise would."[10] Yet even if that remark were faithfully recorded and really reflected his view at the time, Lincoln could not have taken comfort in what he saw happening. The conflict ended the neutrality of several border states and drove an unprepared North into war. Perhaps he misjudged the intensity of Southern feeling about the issue and the results that the fall of Fort Sumter would have on the Southern mentality.

Historian James G. Randall has summarized the Sumter crisis in a balanced judgment:

> When war came it turned out that he had kept the non aggressive record of his government clear, which assuredly is not to his discredit; but to say that Lincoln meant that the first shot would be fired by the other side *if a first shot was fired*, is not to say that he maneuvered to have the shot fired. That distinction is fundamental.[11]

The Sumter crisis showed the extent of the South's alienation from the Union, and the power of the secessionists increased as confrontation led to full-scale war. Whether Lincoln knew what the consequences would be is unclear, but his government's handling of the problem was muddled and indicated that the new president lacked control over members of his own administration, especially Secretary of State Seward. Concerned about saving the Union, pledged to nonviolence against the slave states, and faced with a politically balanced but unstable cabinet, the president began to mobilize the country for a war he kept saying need not have come.

The Eighty-Day Dictatorship

To many of his colleagues at the time, Lincoln seemed vacillating and indecisive during his early weeks in office. It may be that he was moving cautiously through a minefield of hazards, any one of which would have stymied even a more experienced executive. Some of his biographers find that he exhibited many of the symptoms of a nervous breakdown, a diagnosis not out of the question for a man who faced a very stressful situation and had a history of melancholia and some unstable emotional periods.[12]

But if Lincoln did seem unsure of his way and was suffering from doubts at the time, he retained a certain surety of purpose that was often lacking in those who at first questioned his capabilities. He weighed compromise at Sumter but insisted on asserting federal authority in the most nonbelligerent way possible. Oftentimes, caution and prudence are seen as vacillation, just as action and movement seem impulsive to the fainthearted.

Once South Carolina fired on Fort Sumter and the Confederacy lined up behind it, war was inevitable. That development was not remarkable, but the metamorphosis of the man in the White House was. In weeks, a new Lincoln emerged, one fortified with such determination that his strengths were unexpected and mystifying. How did it happen that Lincoln almost immediately began asserting an interpretation of the presidency that rested on no previous example? How did it happen that this conservative Whig, this corporation and neighborhood lawyer, came to assume near dictatorial powers in the nearly three months when he mobilized the nation for war?[13]

The presidents under whom Lincoln grew up were modest men with much to be modest about, to paraphrase Winston Churchill. Some were competent; most were weak; all suffered, except for Jackson and perhaps Polk, from the consequences of the ascendancy of Congress in the 1815 to

1850 era. Many of the most successful presidents of the late eighteenth and early nineteenth centuries, especially Washington, Jefferson, and Monroe, worked through indirection and not by asserting their powers vis-à-vis Congress. Only Jackson and his protégé Polk, neither of whom was Lincoln attracted to, were exceptions. Lincoln, as president, is clearly outside of that dominant tradition, and it is especially strange since his lifelong political allegiance was to the Whig philosophy of limited executive power, constitutional rights, and balanced government. That he would assert such a different view after years in the crucible of war would be explainable; that he did so after only weeks in office is truly baffling.

Perhaps one explanation is that his deep affection for the Union as an almost religious ideal was the driving force. He seized power to save what had been given to him, and all his forceful initiatives were somehow infused with a passion that only responsibility could compel. But he surely disproves the adage that great presidents must be men experienced by years in public office, for though he was good politician, he was not a regular in the public eye. And Lincoln disproves also the supposition that strong presidents pattern themselves on strong predecessors. There were no Roosevelts before him; indeed, they built on his foundation. The Whig Lincoln was by no means a Jackson admirer, and he surely respected Jefferson but did not think him a strong executive; he revered Washington as the premier Founding Father, but the patriarch's problems were not similar to his own. Lincoln, the epitome of the self-made man in so many mythic American ways, is also the self-made president. Before him was little in the way of example; after him would be the severest reaction in American history to the use of executive power. Lincoln stands out in the nineteenth-century American landscape as an anomaly as an executive, a stranger in what was up to then a rather familiar and untroubling political scene.

What made him so different in the early period? From April 12, 1861, to July 4, 1861, the president assumed far-reaching powers, some in violation of the Constitution. The political scientist Clinton Rossiter has called it a "constitutional dictatorship" and concluded that the unusual powers Lincoln assumed in those early months were fairly established by the time Congress reconvened, and that despite congressional attempts to pare them down, Lincoln's powers were virtually intact throughout the war. Thus, he set the pattern that would characterize his behavior for the next four years.[14]

Just what Lincoln believed in April 1861 about those extraordinary powers he assumed is unclear. He said that he had sworn an oath registered in heaven to defend the Constitution. As a young man and as president, he was deeply committed to the Union as a historical entity and as "the last best hope on earth," as he phrased it. On April 15, 1861, he issued an executive proclamation in which he announced that since the laws were being obstructed in the seven states of the Deep South, he would use constitutional and statutory powers to call up seventy-five thousand men in the state militias to put down the insurrection. The Militia Act of 1795 gave the president the authority to call up those units if he found "combinations too powerful to be suppressed by the ordinary course of judicial proceedings or by the powers vested in the marshalls." The president also called Congress into special session, but he set the date on July 4. Probably Lincoln thought that the war would be short and that he could avoid congressional meddling by setting the date three months into the future.

On April 19, the president ordered a blockade on the coastlines of the seceded states, and the next day he ordered nineteen vessels to be added to the navy. By May 3, Lincoln took the extraordinary step of adding over forty-two thousand volunteers to the military and enlarging the regular army by twenty-three thousand and the navy by eighteen thousand. He had already instructed Secretary of Treasury Samuel Chase to furnish $2 million to pay private citizens in New York for military acquisitions. Thus, in contradiction to the Constitution, the executive branch of government and not the legislative had raised up armies and appropriated public funds.

On April 27, the president went further. He ordered the commanding general of the U.S. Army to suspend the writ of habeas corpus in the Philadelphia-Washington corridor in order to contend with mob violence and sabotage on the railroads, and by July 2, Lincoln extended the order from Philadelphia to New York as well. When Chief Justice Taney, sitting in a circuit court case, protested the order, the president ignored the decision. Lincoln went on to close the post offices to treasonable correspondence and ordered those suspected of disloyal and treasonable practices to be arrested and detained in military custody.

When Congress convened on July 4, Lincoln's message laid out the steps he had taken and justified them in terms of "the war powers of the Government"—a novel phrase for that time. He maintained that no government should be asked to forego the right of self-preservation and concluded that this right was centered in the presidency. He argued that his actions, whether strictly legal or not, were necessary and that none of these steps were beyond the "constitutional competence of Congress." Thus, he concluded that Congress should ratify after the fact what he had done and that, under circumstances of grave emergency, the government, headed by the executive, could commit actions outside of the law to preserve the greater fabric of government. In his defense, Lincoln asked, "Are all the laws *but one* to go unexecuted, and the Government itself go to pieces lest that one be violated? Even in such a case, would not the official oath be broken if the Government should be overthrown when it was believed that disregarding the single law would tend to preserve it?"[15]

On August 6, 1861, the Congress retroactively approved all acts, proclamations, and orders of the president concerning the army, navy, and militia call-ups. Later, in 1863, the Supreme Court in the *Prize Cases* upheld the blockade and concluded that the president was the true judge of the type of response the crises demanded in dealing with domestic insurrection.

Early War Moves

In issuing these proclamations after Sumter, Lincoln was faced with some major practical difficulties in a nation of decentralized military power. For example, how should he use those regiments—as a national army or organized by state? Who paid the costs for the war effort? Were the Confederate privateers to be treated as pirates? Were their soldiers traitors rather than belligerents because they were in rebellion?[16] With all of this uncertainty, the president also was faced with demands from the various states to promote their own local sons to major military positions. And in the capital, the War Department was not able to handle the first wave of enthusiastic volunteers, who had to be fed, clothed, and armed before they could fight.

To add to Lincoln's burdens, the Southern states that had tried to stay neutral began to secede after Sumter. On April 17, 1861, Virginia started its movement, and on May 7, Arkansas and Tennessee followed, even though in the latter an initial popular referendum went three to one against secession. A second referendum in June yielded the desired results for the Confederate sympathizers, and Tennessee left the Union. North Carolina soon followed Tennessee, and even those border states that stayed in the Union, except for Delaware, refused to send any regiments to defend the U.S. government until after July 4.

Meanwhile, pro-secession mobs prohibited Northern troops from passing through Baltimore toward Washington. Lincoln at first had to agree with Maryland officials to send the troops around the city; finally Brigadier General Ben Butler moved in and established military control over the city.

Northern newspapers continued their criticism of the weak administration, and patronage pressures mounted on the beleaguered president. Indeed, in the critical months of 1861, half of Lincoln's letters dealt with patronage requests. One old acquaintance, Lyman Trumbull, concluded that "there is a lack of . . . positive action & business talent in the cabinet. Lincoln though a most excellent & honest man lacks these qualities." That impression of general incompetence was only confirmed by the outcome of the first major battle of the war, the confusion called Bull Run. Washington society drove out to the battlefield to watch the event, and at first it seemed that the Union commander, Irvin McDowell, had defeated the Confederate forces of P. G. T. Beauregard. But by evening, Lincoln received the discouraging news: McDowell was in retreat, and a disorganized army was beating its way back to the capital, leaving Washington exposed and vulnerable to a Confederate attack.

Although he did not force McDowell to confront the Confederate armies, Lincoln and his cabinet had rejected General Scott's request for a delay until August. Political considerations required a quick victory, and one that would make use of the ninety-day volunteers whose enlistments would soon be up. Faced with this debacle, Lincoln sat down on the night after Bull Run and wrote out a military plan. He wanted a tighter blockade; a strong force at Fort Monroe and its vicinity; control over Baltimore; a strengthening of the Union position in the Winchester, Virginia, area; movement in Missouri; a reorganization of forces in the District of Columbia; a discharge of the three-month volunteers; and a raising of more forces with longer terms of service. Lincoln insisted that the strategic ports in Virginia be taken, and he wanted a coordinated attack in the West. In July, after the Union debacle at Bull Run, the president named George B. McClellan, the victor in a modest campaign in western Virginia, to be commander of the Union army. The dream of a short, happy war was dashed at Bull Run. McClellan came in with plans for extensive retraining and strategic planning—a prelude, he said, to the major campaigns ahead.

At first, not all the states were anxious to enter the fray. The state of Lincoln's birth, Kentucky, initially worked out a policy of neutrality between the two major armies and promised to respect federal authority and ban Confederate troops in the state if the Union pledged not to move troops through Kentucky. Lincoln dealt with the situation rather gingerly at first, remarking, "I think to lose Kentucky is nearly . . . to lose the whole game. Kentucky gone, we cannot hold Missouri, nor, as I think, Maryland. These all against us, and the job on our hands is too large for us. We would as well consent to separation at once, including the surrender of the capital." His cautious policy seemed to pay off as the Unionists carried nine out of ten of the congressional districts in the June 1861 elections. By the fall, the state was still tenuously in the Union camp.[17]

A very different development took place later in Virginia, as the forty-eight counties in the western part of the state opposed secession and ultimately reorganized in 1863 as a separate state. In Tennessee, the eastern part of that state stayed pro-Union despite the decision of the governor and the legislature to enter into a military agreement with the Confederacy. Farther west, Missouri was also bitterly divided on the issue of secession. Lincoln inadvertently added to the volatility of the situation by sending General John C. Frémont into the region. Frémont immediately generated controversy by issuing a proclamation assuming all administrative powers in the state, ordering persons found with arms to be court-martialed and shot, and confiscating all property held by those in rebellion. In the process, he declared that their slaves were free from then on.

To Lincoln, Frémont's abrupt actions challenged his own executive control of the war and created a hornets' nest on the emancipation issue. Fearful of the reactions of the pro-Union, slaveholding border states, Lincoln refused to upset the delicate balance of sentiments by emancipation. He informed Frémont as politely as possible that no one should be shot without the president's consent, and that no confiscation should proceed outside of the confines set by the Confiscation Act of 1861. That act provided that seizures of assets should be done through the courts and would involve only property used in aiding rebellion. However, Frémont generally ignored Lincoln's orders and proceeded on his own, until finally he was brought down by publicized charges of favoritism, corruption, incompetence, and graft. Lincoln eventually removed Frémont as commander of the Department of the West and consequently incurred the wrath of the abolitionists who approved of the general's order.

By the end of the year, the president faced a difficult balancing act in the border states and had given conservative General McClellan his public support in revamping the newly named Army of the Potomac. To the abolitionists, Lincoln was definitely not a kindred spirit, and to conservative critics he seemed a less-than-imposing executive. Even his own attorney general, Edward Bates, confided to his diary, "The Prest. . . . is an excellent man . . . but he lacks *will* and *purpose*, and I greatly fear he had not *the power to command.*"[18]

Beginning a Foreign Policy

Lincoln's first priority in office was the prosecution of the war, and he was involved in foreign affairs only as they might affect that effort. Observing the new president's displays of caution, his secretary of state, William

Seward, thought he saw a vacuum and attempted early to move in and fill in. In an April 1, 1861, memorandum, the secretary laid out a foreign policy that included evacuating Sumter, defending the Gulf of Mexico ports, and demanding explanations from Spain and France on disputed issues with the United States. If their responses were not satisfactory, Seward wanted to call Congress back into session for a declaration of war. Supposedly, this foreign threat would rally the discordant parts of the Union together and thus avert the possibility of civil war. Seward also proposed that the United States toughen its position toward Great Britain and czarist Russia. He bluntly concluded that the president should either take control of foreign policy or assign a cabinet minister (that is, Seward) to do it. "I neither seek to evade nor assume responsibility," Seward pronounced.[19]

Lincoln, with characteristic patience, simply informed Seward that he saw no drift in his policy and that he had already communicated publicly his objectives in a variety of messages. In terms of establishing foreign policy, the president firmly concluded that such responsibilities were his alone. Working with Seward and some rather capable American ministers abroad, Lincoln from the beginning steered clear of confrontations that might divert resources and attention from the war effort. Some major obstacles were quickly apparent, however. Segments of the British upper class were talking in approving terms of the Southern cause, and Prime Minister Palmerston did not seem friendly to the Union. In fact, except for the Russian minister to the United States, nearly all of the major foreign ambassadors and ministers were favorably disposed to the South.

The Confederates tried hard to push for foreign recognition of their new government, and Jefferson Davis devoted a considerable amount of effort to that cause. Consequently, he also vigorously objected to Lincoln's April proclamations establishing a naval blockade. By that step, though, Lincoln had in fact complicated matters by deciding not to treat the secessionists as pirates or traitors, thus lending support to the view that the Confederacy was a belligerent power. The British insisted on remaining neutral in the dispute for the time being—a step that drew complaints from the Lincoln administration but in the long run worked against the Confederacy.

The Lincoln government and the British had several major disputes with which the president had to deal. In late 1861, an American captain stopped the British steamer *Trent* and arrested two Confederate leaders on board. The British, quite correctly, regarded that seizure as an insult and demanded the release of the prisoners. While many Union leaders saluted

the captain's daring, the administration was more prudent. Lincoln's attitude was consistent: he did not want two wars on his hands. The president
received unexpected help when the queen and her husband modified a
tough note that Palmerston had originally intended to send, thus giving
the Americans a face-saving opportunity to settle the controversy. Finally,
the envoys were released and the administration closed the book on a
particularly difficult episode. Lincoln overall insisted on not becoming
preoccupied with foreign affairs. In late 1861 and early 1862, his primary
concerns were the weaknesses in the Union war effort and problems in his
own cabinet.[20]

The Potomac Command

Lincoln had serious reservations when he appointed Simon Cameron to
be secretary of war, but commitments made by his convention managers
and the need for a broad coalition cabinet led him to bow to pressure. It
was a bad decision, as became all the more obvious as the early phases of
the war ended. Congressional oversight and public opinion became more
critical of the inefficiency, graft, and corruption in the War Department.
By the beginning of 1862, the president offered Cameron a way out: the
U.S. ministership to Russia. Like Frémont, Cameron had embarrassed the
president by advocating in a report that slaves be employed as soldiers—a
difficult issue that Lincoln had tried to sidestep. With characteristic magnanimity, Lincoln defended Cameron against some of the congressional
criticism of mismanagement and pointed out that the early phases of the
crisis required quick action in order to protect the integrity of the Union.
Lincoln insisted that he and other members of the administration were at
least equally responsible for whatever errors or wrongs had occurred.

In Cameron's place, Lincoln named Edwin M. Stanton of Pennsylvania, a Democrat and prominent lawyer whom Lincoln had met on less than
favorable terms before the war. Stanton had served briefly as attorney general in the Buchanan cabinet and had privately been critical of Lincoln and
his abilities. The president's nomination for that post came without much
consultation and apparently was due to his sense that Stanton, as abrasive
as he was, could rein in the chaos of the War Department.

Stanton immediately indicated his sympathy for the newly created
Congressional Committee on the Conduct of the War—a joint House–
Senate group that was to plague the president during his term in office.
The committee conducted lurid investigations of the war effort, attacked
Democratic generals such as McClellan, and pushed the radical Republican

cause and its military partisans—Frémont, Ambrose Burnside, John Pope, Joseph Hooker, and Irvin McDowell. Since Lincoln was committed to McClellan at this time, he too incurred the committee's wrath.

When McClellan was called to take command of the Army of the Potomac in late July 1861, he found a military mess. Even Stanton said that after Bull Run the overall situation was a national disgrace and attributed that plight to Lincoln's running the war effort for five months. Washington was unguarded, and McClellan had before him an ill-equipped, demoralized, and disorganized force. Rather remarkably, McClellan reorganized the troops, improved discipline, moved to protect the capital, constructed a communications system, and won the admiration of his troops, who called him "Mac" and "the American Napoleon."

But McClellan was not as well thought of by radical Republicans and by some of the more moderate cabinet secretaries. He could be rude to congressmen, inflated in his self-estimation, curt to the president, and often too slow in his responses to situations that required decisive leadership without long-drawn-out planning. When on one occasion McClellan, having gone to bed, refused to receive Lincoln and Seward, the president simply passed it off by observing it "was better at this time not to be making points of etiquette & personal dignity." As he observed, one bad general was preferable to two good ones; unity of command, he thought at that period, was crucial to victory. Not everyone was as magnanimous.

But as summer passed and the days moved on, McClellan had not begun the campaign that he had promised. Pressure was building on the administration for a Union offensive. Even Attorney General Bates urged Lincoln to become the actual commander in chief of the armed forces, and when McClellan fell ill of typhoid fever, Lincoln actually considered taking to the field himself to lead the troops. The president began to give closer scrutiny to the operations in the West and became involved in military affairs in Columbus and east Tennessee. He read Henry Halleck's *Science of War* and studied strategic works for military advice. On January 10, 1862, Lincoln seemed especially agitated over the lack of movement, and two days later he called together a council of several generals and some cabinet officials to discuss the war effort. An ill McClellan made plans to leave his sickbed and defend his strategy before the council. But at the meeting, he pointedly refused to discuss his strategy, citing the possibility of someone disclosing his plans.

On January 27, a weary Lincoln issued General Order No. 1, which mandated a forward movement by February 22. Four days later, the president followed up with another order that an expedition should seize a railroad point southwest near Manassas Junction. McClellan formally requested permission to debate the order, and consequently, it was not put into effect. Lincoln was a man gifted with intense powers of concentration, but he was no military strategist and his military experience in the Indian Wars was a minimal duty of which even he made light. Under intense pressure from Congress and public opinion leaders, he pushed for, demanded, insisted on, and pleaded for action. McClellan's caution frustrated even the normally cautious Lincoln. The president admitted that no Union general was better able to organize and train an army, but he complained that McClellan suffered from "the slows." In his cabinet, Chase and Edwin Stanton were consistently opposed to McClellan, and Lincoln was exposed to stories of the general's alleged disloyalty toward him and of his own political ambitions.

In frustration, Lincoln apparently did take to the field himself in May 1862. While on a visit to Fort Monroe, the president, with Stanton and Chase, conferred with naval and military leaders. There is evidence that the president actually led some troops in the capture of Norfolk and sent three gunboats up the James River. Thus Lincoln became for a brief moment the commander in chief on the battlefield that Bates had counseled.

Historians favorable to the legendary Lincoln have generally agreed with his decision to transfer part of McClellan's command to John Pope in June 1862, and then in November 1862 to remove McClellan altogether. They have indeed accepted, almost on faith, the president's judgment that while the general was a great organizer, he lacked the will to fight decisively. Yet it is quite possible to argue that Lincoln, inexperienced in military matters and unsure of his political position, overreacted by curtailing McClellan the first time, overruling his military strategy and interfering with the timetable the general created. McClellan was the best general in the Union army in 1861, and his replacements stumbled from one defeat to another.[21]

McClellan needs to be judged in a broader perspective. He turned a ragtag mob into a fighting force after the debacle of Bull Run. His military objective was to move down the peninsula, while Lincoln and his cabinet insisted on establishing a buffer between the capital and the Confederate forces. McClellan argued, quite rightly, that it was his army and the threat that it posed to Richmond served as the real focus of Confederate attention. In the time he had control of the Army of the Potomac, McClellan never suffered a major defeat, and he prevailed in what may have been the most important battle of the war—the checking of Robert E. Lee's invasion at Antietam, though he did not defeat the Confederate forces. That victory, although too limited in the eyes of Lincoln and his cabinet secretaries, enabled the president to issue the Emancipation Proclamation, and it proved to interested European nations that the South could not win the protracted conflict. One of Lincoln's most able and balanced biographers, James G. Randall, has concluded, "Had McClellan collapsed at Antietam as Pope had done at Second Bull Run, it is hard to see how the Lincoln government and the Union cause could possibly have survived, to say nothing of launching an ambitious emancipation policy, which occurred directly after Antietam." In retirement after the war, Lee remarked that McClellan was the most formidable foe he had faced, a telling compliment in and of itself.[22]

But in early 1862, Antietam was still far away, and McClellan lay ill and buffeted by radical Republican pressures. The general's plan was to move the army down the Chesapeake, up the Rappahannock to Urbana, Virginia, and then across land to the Manassas line above Richmond. The president, who supported a land invasion instead, indicated his disapproval. While McClellan began to modify his plan, the Radical Republicans continued their attacks in public and their character assassination in private against the general. Radical congressmen met with Lincoln and demanded a "reorganization" of the Army of the Potomac—in effect, a move to strip McClellan of his authority as general in chief. On March 8, 1862, Lincoln capitulated to the political pressure, and McClellan lost vital authority just before his major offensive was to begin.

To achieve his objectives, McClellan needed a large, unified army, assets he was denied by the time he began his movement south. As McClellan confronted Lee and Johnston in the Peninsula campaign, General Irvin McDowell was slow in moving his First Army Corps Union forces to assist him. The Confederates at the same time sent Thomas "Stonewall" Jackson through the Shenandoah Valley, inciting fear in Washington that the Confederates would take the capital. Lincoln asserted military control over the railroads, and Stanton demanded that the governors send all the militia and volunteers they had to protect the area. A worried Lincoln wanted McClellan to give up his campaign and come back to Washington.[23]

The president, in fact, tried at times to run the war from the White House. He commanded Frémont, for example, to move against Jackson at Harrisonburg immediately. But Frémont, after promising to go ahead, did not do so, leaving Lincoln to ask, "I see that you are at Moorefield. You were expressly ordered to march to Harrisonburg. What does this mean?"[24] By June 1862, Lincoln was still concerned about McClellan's concentration of forces on the Peninsula and Jackson's presence in the Shenandoah

Valley, even though the latter had actually left. Under increasing attacks from the Radical Republicans in Congress and pressure from Stanton and Chase, Lincoln made Pope commander of the army in Virginia; McClellan was demoted and his title was changed to commander of the Army of the Potomac.

On July 8, Lincoln visited McClellan in the field at Harrison's Landing. The president was clearly thinking about moving the army instead of allowing it to advance on Richmond. McClellan opposed that step and took the occasion to hand the president a letter in which he laid out his own policy about how the war should be run. He had picked the wrong time to be audacious, and the president read the letter and handed it back to him with no comment. In the letter, the general had argued that the war was a battle between armies, and that confiscation, the abolishing of slavery, and other punitive actions on civilians were unnecessary. He concluded with a personal pledge to serve Lincoln forthrightly as his position might require.

The president, returning to the capital, found even more anti-McClellan intrigue, and on July 11, he ordered Henry Halleck to become general in chief, head of all the land forces of the United States. On August 3, Halleck took the step that the president had contemplated; he ordered McClellan to move his troops closer to the capital. McClellan, with his army only twenty-five miles from Richmond, protested that the order would result in a disaster. But Halleck prevailed, and Lincoln had proved himself to be a mediator rather than a leader in what was the most important military decision he had made up to that time.

In late August, Lee and Jackson did with Pope's army what they could not do with McClellan's. They soundly defeated the Union forces at the Second Battle of Bull Run. Pope was soon relieved of his command and returned to the army in the West. Then, two days after the defeat, McClellan was asked by Halleck to command the defenses of Washington, a position with no real control over the armed forces. Lincoln, desperately fearful about the capital, met with McClellan and, according to the general, asked him as a personal favor to take command of the city's defenses. In his diary, Secretary of the Navy Gideon Welles recorded that the president was "greatly distressed" and turned to McClellan because of the confidence the army itself had in him. Welles added that the War Department was bewildered and proposed nothing and did nothing.

It was at this point that Lee made his major move. He advanced toward Maryland, directly threatening Baltimore, Philadelphia, and, as Lincoln feared all along, Washington. At Antietam, on September 17, 1862, the two forces met in the most ferocious battle of the war. It was, McClellan wrote, "the most serious ever fought on this continent." For over fourteen hours, the battle waged; in the end, there were over twenty-three thousand casualties. McClellan did not definitively defeat Lee, but he stopped the latter's advance and proved that the Union army was the match of the Confederate forces. Lee moved back to the lower side of the Potomac. McClellan had saved the capital and probably Lincoln's ability to continue effectively as president and commander in chief.

Instead of giving McClellan his due credit, his critics pressed on. He should have pursued Lee and brought the war to a quick end, they insisted. The president again visited McClellan, calling him his best general and then counseling him to move against Lee quickly. Finally, Lincoln ordered McClellan to cross the Potomac and seek out the Confederates, hoping to beat them to Richmond. But McClellan insisted on regrouping and reworking his strategy.

On October 26, 1862, McClellan crossed the Potomac and slowly mobilized his army for an offensive. Then on November 7, he received notice that he had been replaced, this time by Ambrose Burnside. Again Lincoln had bowed to Chase and Stanton and the Radical Republicans. Later in 1864, the president defended his decision by saying that he had repeatedly tried to get McClellan to move but to no avail. The general had waited nineteen days after Antietam before he decided to cross the river and another nine days before the actual move took place, and made very slow progress even after that. The president concluded, "I began to fear he was playing false—that he did not want to hurt the army. I saw how he could intercept the enemy on the way to Richmond. I determined to make that the test. If he let them get away, I would remove him. He did so & I relieved him." Lincoln had also received a torrent of rumors and false accusations about McClellan's loyalty, patriotism, and political aspirations. The Radicals in Congress and in the cabinet had their way—McClellan was forced out again.[25]

Emancipation . . . in a Way

Lincoln had also incurred the animus of the abolitionists by his cautious handling of the slavery question. They attributed his lack of leadership to a misguided fixation with keeping the border states in the Union and to the unfortunate influence of Seward. Lincoln's attitude toward slavery, as has been seen, was a consistent policy of personal detestation and political conservatism. In his inaugural address in 1861, he had pledged not to touch slavery where it existed and to recognize that the Constitution, which he swore to uphold, sanctioned the institution in oblique language. When the war came and Unionist generals such as Frémont and Ben Butler attempted to free those slaves held by owners in rebellion, the president at first demurred. The decision on emancipation, any form of emancipation, was one he would face in his own time.

But events progressed quickly as runaway slaves moved toward Union army encampments. Partially in response, Congress passed a series of measures that provided for the confiscation and emancipation of slaves under various provisions of law. The first Confiscation Act, approved on August 6, 1861, provided that when slaves were engaged in hostile military service, the claims of owners to such labor were forfeited. A second act, passed on July 17, 1862, declared that the slaves of anyone who committed treason or was supporting the rebellion were "forever free." Another act, passed on the same day, freed slave soldiers and their families held by the enemy, and later in the war, freedom was extended to include slave soldiers of loyal owners who were to be granted bounties. In addition, on April 16, 1862, Congress abolished slavery in the District of Columbia and provided for compensation to the owners; by June 19, emancipation came to the territories, but compensation was not provided. Thus, in some ways the legislative branch had enacted a more extensive policy of emancipation than the president's controversial proclamation did.

Lincoln's attitude toward emancipation was strongly influenced by his pessimistic view about racial harmony. At one meeting, the president told a committee of African Americans that both races had suffered from slavery and that equality was impossible. He bluntly concluded that "on this broad continent not a single man of your race is made the equal of a single man of ours. . . . I cannot alter it if I could. It is a fact." He felt that without the presence of African Americans in the United States, there would have been no war, even though he acknowledged that "many men engaged on either side do not care for you one way or the other." Only the physical removal of the African American race and its colonization in some spot like Chiriqui on the Panama isthmus or Liberia in Africa would bring peace. In addition, the president remained committed throughout his term to compensation for the owners. In March 1862, Lincoln asked Congress to support gradual emancipation to be completed sometime before 1900. This gradual process would be voluntary and controlled by the states, rather than by the federal government. Compensation to the slaveholders, however, would be paid by the federal government. Lincoln's plan angered abolitionists, convinced few border state leaders, and left him without a realistic policy on an issue of increasing importance.

By the summer of 1862, Lincoln apparently moved sharply on the slavery question. Senator Charles Sumner of Massachusetts had tried to persuade Lincoln in December 1861 that emancipation must come, but the president put him off, promising action in a month to six weeks. By July 1862, Sumner pushed again, warning that the Union needed the freed slaves to augment its own armed forces. Lincoln listened, but he concluded that he was afraid that half of the Union officers would leave the army and three more states would join the Confederacy if he heeded Sumner's advice. Finally, as he described it, he had to act. Lincoln concluded, "Things had gone . . . from bad to worse, until I felt that we had reached the end of our rope. . . . We . . . must change our tactics, or lose the game." He quietly worked on an emancipation proclamation, and on July 22, he presented it to the cabinet, not asking their advice on the matter but simply informing them of his intentions. Seward suggested that the president postpone his proclamation until some military victory was secured, and Lincoln saw the wisdom in such a postponement.

As he waited, Lincoln listened as advocates of emancipation called for action, a step he had already decided upon. His general attitude toward slavery was publicly aired in a letter on August 22, 1862, to the editor of the *New York Tribune*, Horace Greeley:

> My paramount object in this struggle is to save the Union, and not either to save or to destroy slavery. If I could save the Union without freeing any slave, I would do it; and if I could save it by freeing all the slaves, I would do it; and if I could save it by freeing some and leaving others alone, I would also do that. What I do about slavery and the colored race, I do because I believe it helps to save the Union; and what I forebear, I forebear because I do not believe it would help to save the Union. . . . I have here stated my purpose according to my view of official duty; and I intend no modification of my oft-expressed personal wish that all men everywhere could be free.

Finally, the president met with his cabinet on September 22, 1862, and after some preliminary levity, announced that he had made a promise to himself and to his Maker to issue the proclamation. He then went on to observe that there might be others who would do better as president, but "I must do the best I can, and bear the responsibility of taking the course which I feel I ought to take." The proclamation, issued by Lincoln as commander in chief of the armed forces, notified the nation that on January 1, 1863, all slaves held in rebellious areas would be free. As a conciliatory gesture, the president indicated that after the war, he would recommend to Congress that all loyal citizens should be compensated for losses incurred by acts of the United States, including the loss of slaves.

A charge frequently made is that Lincoln freed the slaves in states where he had no power to do so and did not touch them in states where he could have. The statement is factually correct but totally misleading. The proclamation was an important step in the destruction of slavery on this continent. In terms of the loyal border states, the president warned that they should accept compensation while it was still an option, but their leaders refused to heed his advice.

Although the moral issue of bondage reverberated throughout the nation, especially in the rhetoric of the abolitionists, Lincoln avoided that approach. He insisted that his decision was based on grounds of military necessity. The president argued that action normally forbidden or deemed unconstitutional could become lawful in emergency times, and that the Constitution invested the executive as commander in chief with the law of war.

Between September and January, Lincoln talked of compensated emancipation so often that some felt that he was backing off from the radical consequences of true freedom. Lincoln's Emancipation Proclamation became confused, in part, because of his own personal ambivalences. In December 1862, a month before the proclamation was to provide for immediate freedom in rebel states, Lincoln was still advocating that each slave state be given the chance to develop its own plan of gradual, compensated emancipation, which did not have to be completed until January 1, 1900. Those states would get federal assistance in the form of interest-bearing government bonds. If a state decided to restore slavery, the only penalty Lincoln would levy would be that the state had to refund the bonds. As late as August 1864, he seemed to depart from his early insistence that rebel states had to recognize emancipation. He told conservative critics, "To me it seems plain that saying re-union and the abandonment of slavery would be considered, if offered, is not saying that nothing *else* or *less* would be considered, if offered. . . . If Jefferson Davis wishes . . . to know what I would do if he were to offer peace and reunion, saying nothing about slavery, let him try me." Thus, if at times Radical Republicans in Congress and abolitionists outside of it questioned the president's commitment to the cause, they could hardly be called men of little faith.[26]

But when the new year 1863 came, Lincoln went ahead proclaiming emancipation throughout the rebel states, except in Tennessee and certain parts of Virginia and Louisiana, which were occupied by Union troops. He cautiously urged the freed slaves to avoid violence and "labor faithfully for reasonable wages." Newly freed male slaves were inducted into the armed services, and the president characterized his policy as "an act of justice, warranted by the Constitution upon military necessity."

The response was mixed, even among abolitionists. Wendell Phillips called for greater support for these newly freed people, and William Lloyd Garrison demanded emancipation in all the states. In the South, the response was, of course, hostile; Davis saw the move as leading to gruesome racial warfare and the old fears of slave insurrections were revived. In segments of the North, the idea of a future containing millions of freed African Americans was not well received either. Yet all knew that something significant had happened through Lincoln's dry and formal declaration.

In Britain, demonstrations of support took place across the island. At Birmingham, over ten thousand people signed a scroll vowing their support to the president on behalf of "all Men who love liberty." In Manchester, a similarly warm address was sent to the president hailing his action. In a touching response, Lincoln reciprocated their sentiments, and in another letter to the working people of London, he cited the glory of free institutions throughout the world. Diplomats reported favorable responses toward the Proclamation in France, and even in Spain among the clergy and conservative leaders.

Lincoln was to say later, "I admit I have been more controlled by events, than I have controlled them." Events had certainly controlled much of Lincoln's response to the monumental tragedy before him. He made war to save the Union, to restore a nation of opportunity for the white race. But by the turn of the wheel of fire, he had transformed the very nature of the war and then the character of the Union. Lincoln would be remembered not for his hesitations, his uncertain displays of leadership, or his delicate balancing acts. By 1863, he was in deep trouble, politically and militarily. He announced emancipation as a way of tipping the scales in what was becoming a long and bloody war. Freed slaves would fight for the Union, would leave the plantation system feeding the rebels, would prove to foreign nations that the South could not win and should not win, and would keep the abolitionists and Radicals in Congress at bay for a while. But by ending slavery, first in the South and later in the rest of the United States, Lincoln changed the moral complexion of the war. He became the Great Emancipator and not the great equivocator; the liberal world statesman, not the perennial candidate for public office. Watching the events unfold, his personal secretary John Hay concluded, "While the rest are grinding their . . . organs for their own glorification, the old man is working with the strength of a giant . . . to this great work."

Yet despite the proclamation, the emancipation of millions did not happen with the stroke of the pen. These African Americans had no income, no clear legal status, no protection on the plantations where the overwhelming majority resided. Because they were declared politically free did not mean that they were economically independent or citizens of the Union. Even in the army, black troops found themselves commanded by whites, subject to prejudice in the Union army, and plagued by late-arriving and unequal pay. Lincoln himself at first was leery of arming ex-slaves and postponed the systematic use of black troops. But the impetus of war rushed ahead, and by the end of the conflict nearly 180,000 African Americans had served in the Union ranks.

Still, in 1864, a committee of inquiry established by the War Department found that emancipation had not come, that the proclamation "cannot free a single slave." The committee wondered whether there would be sufficient guarantees to protect the freedom of the former slaves and urged that emancipation be extended throughout the United States. While some slaves filled the camps of the Union armies, the vast bulk of them did not experience emancipation until the demise of the Confederacy and the eventual occupation of the South by the Union armies. There is little evidence of black riots or violent upheavals on the plantations, yet contemporary observers recorded that Lincoln's proclamation was well known and well received within slave quarters throughout the Confederacy. Nevertheless, slaves must have asked what many whites asked at the time: What would it mean after all?[27]

Assaults on the President

To many of his contemporaries in 1862, Lincoln did not appear to be a great president, nor even a competent one. In Congress, many of his troubles came from a group of senators and representatives that history has labeled "the Radical Republicans." This loosely drawn coalition pushed for emancipation and demanded severe punishment for the secessionists. Some were influenced by that brand of American Protestantism that revels in retribution and casts political events into moral crusades. Others were truly horrified by slavery and lent their might to advancing the cause of freedom. Still more were concerned with the future of their party, the continued cohesion of their political alliances, and the availability of federal patronage. They recognized that a reunited America would bring back Democratic congressmen who would join with their Northern allies and reestablish control of the national government by their party. And friends of the Union army feared prosecutions for some of their actions after the war was over. The Republicans could lose the peace, even after they had led the nation through a successful war. To prevent this restoration, the Radicals wanted to change the nation, to destroy slavery, to cripple the Southern aristocracy, and to enfranchise eventually the only new voters they could count on to vote Republican: the freed slaves. These Radical Republicans had different views on many aspects of these issues, but together they made Lincoln the focal point of much of their animosity. The Committee on the Conduct of the War became one of their tools for extracting retribution, and that group plagued the moderate generals, especially McClellan and his chief subordinates Fitz-John Porter and William B. Franklin, and harassed the wartime president in a way no other legislative committee has ever dared.

In the Senate, the Radicals included Zachariah Chandler of Michigan, Benjamin F. Wade and John Sherman of Ohio, Charles Sumner of Massachusetts, Lyman Trumbull of Illinois, Henry Lane of Indiana, and James Lane and Samuel Pomeroy of Kansas. In the House, the most prominent Radicals were Thaddeus Stevens of Pennsylvania, Owen Lovejoy of Illinois, Schuyler Colfax and George Julian of Indiana, James Ashley and John A. Bingham of Ohio, Roscoe Conkling of New York, Henry Winter Davis of Maryland, and John Covode of Pennsylvania.

On the other side of the aisle, the Democrats were generally in opposition to what they perceived as the abuse of civil liberties by the administration. Some prominent Democrats, especially Stephen Douglas before his premature death in 1861, strongly supported the Union and Lincoln. A second segment was committed to the Union but critical of the government's war policies. A third group did not support the war, advocated a compromised peace with the South, and was soon tagged by their enemies as "Copperheads"—that is, Southern sympathizers.[28]

No major American president has been less successful in leading his party than Lincoln. One reason was that the Republicans were still not a cohesive group but rather an unstable coalition that had just won its first national victory. American parties are by their very nature loose coalitions, but in Lincoln's time, this lack of cohesiveness was even more apparent than before or after his era, such as in the periods of Jefferson and Jackson or the Reconstruction and the New Deal. Lincoln used patronage to build a personal faction, but he still lacked a broad base throughout his term.[29] Second, Lincoln had little experience on the national level and had no background in leading Congress. He strongly exerted his executive powers, but he did so outside of congressional guidelines and not in league with the legislature. Unlike Woodrow Wilson, who saw himself as a "prime minister," or FDR, who redefined his party as the vehicle of the liberal New Deal, Lincoln did not take Congress into his confidence; perhaps he realized he could not do so reasonably. Third, the presidency was cast in a different light in the nineteenth century, especially for old Whigs such as Lincoln. They had not learned the art of subtle and invisible leadership that Jefferson, Madison, and Monroe exercised on Congress through their cabinet and close acquaintances. They did not understand the strong executive model used by Washington and Hamilton and later by Jackson. Whigs respected balanced, efficient, and orderly government. Such a prescription did not lend itself to managing a civil war. Lincoln ran the war with as little congressional support as he could get away with without causing a rupture. In dealing with its leaders, he was polite, patient, and even deferential at times. Then he usually did what he wanted to when he could and prayed for an early adjournment.

Political scientist and presidential expert Richard Neustadt has argued that presidential power is a product of professional reputation and personal popularity. In the grim days of 1861–1863, the president was not seen as a shrewd political operator; alleged inadequacies were frequently commented on, cursed, admonished, and reported. His popularity was low, as best one can tell. The war was going poorly, with the controversial draft, high taxes, and political imprisonments, and the allies of Lincoln were hurt by the performance of the Union armies. Lincoln was the leader of the war effort; he never chose to disassociate himself from it.

Lincoln's stock, then, was not high in 1862. When he informed Congress of his quite legitimate objections to the Confiscation Bill of 1862, his message was greeted with hoots and laughter from Radical elements. Then in September 1862, a group of Northern governors met and decided to force changes in the administration's war policy. Some indicated that, in fact, they wanted the president's resignation, and even a few demanded that Frémont head up a military dictatorship instead. Lincoln allowed the governors to visit the Executive Mansion, but he turned the tables on them by praising their advice. He had them sit with his cabinet, while he monopolized the conversation, and later escorted them out.

A second, more serious challenge that threatened Lincoln's control over his own cabinet took place in December. A group of senators demanded Seward's resignation and forced the president into an untenable position. In a masterly display of adroitness, Lincoln called the cabinet together and indicated that Seward had offered his resignation. He reported the Senate group's remarks and then expressed shock and dismay, noting that he was not aware of any serious disagreements in the cabinet. Having stressed the theme of unity, the president invited the Senate group in later, and before the cabinet (minus Seward), the secretaries supported the president's conclusions.

Rumors spread that the whole cabinet had resigned. Actually, Chase, the favorite of the Radical element, had been embarrassed by the public confrontation and offered his resignation. Lincoln then had Chase's and Seward's letters of resignation—a balanced victory and a net loss for the congressional Radicals. As he phrased it with some glee, "I have got a pumpkin in each end of my bag." Then he sent both men identical statements requesting them to stay. For the first time in his administration, it was clear to all that the president was the master in his own house. Radical attacks continued, but they never again came as close to the heart of the presidency.[30]

The Fierceness of Battle—1863

In the West, Union forces had been on the move in 1862. Military and naval leaders coordinated a series of inland river battles as the Union took Fort Henry and Fort Donelson and occupied Nashville and the railroad terminus at Columbus, Kentucky. But during April 6–7, 1862, the armies of Pierre Beauregard and Albert Sidney Johnston nearly defeated Ulysses S. Grant's troops; with reinforcements, the Union won a major battle and drove the Confederates toward Corinth, Mississippi. Lincoln's spirits were also refreshed when the navy under admirals David Farragut and David Porter prevailed in New Orleans in April. Soon Ben Butler began his controversial occupation of that city, and once again the president had to intervene, finally removing him in December 1862. After the victory of New Orleans, the Union forces went on to seize Memphis, Tennessee, and by the spring of 1863, Grant had decided to move against well-fortified Vicksburg, Mississippi, a Confederate stronghold.

But in the major theaters of action, the picture was dismal. As noted, Lincoln had bowed to Radical pressure and his own misgivings about McClellan and appointed Ambrose Burnside, who led the Union forces on December 13 at Fredericksburg, Virginia, to one of its worst defeats. Confederate artillery and infantry ripped the Union lines to shreds and filled the field hospitals to capacity. The outcome, as expected, was blamed on the president, and more than one critic agreed with the abolitionist James Sloan Gibbons, who implored, "May the Lord hold to rigid account the fool that is set over us. . . . What suicide the administration is guilty of! What a weak pattern of Old Pharaoh! What a goose!"[31]

After more controversy within the War Department circle, Lincoln named "Fighting Joe" Hooker to be the head of the new Army of the Potomac. Still, the president was uncertain about Hooker and wrote him a letter that contained a rather blunt warning, "I have heard . . . of your . . . saying that both the Army and the Government needed a Dictator. . . . What I now ask of you is military success, and I will risk the dictatorship. . . . Beware of rashness, but with energy, and sleepless vigilance, go forward, and give us victories."[32]

Hooker prepared for his much awaited battle against Lee and mobilized a force twice the size of his Confederate opponent's. However, under Lee's superb strategy and Stonewall Jackson's maneuvering, the Confederates dealt Hooker a sharp setback at Chancellorsville, just west of Fredericksburg. Unfortunately for the South, Jackson was mortally wounded in the confusion of battle by some of his own men. Lincoln, dismayed once again by his generals, ordered Hooker to move quickly against Lee. Lee, however, had ambitions of his own; concerned about the uncertain forces of the war and the fate of the Confederacy, he decided to bring the war northward again and strike close to the Union capital.

Meanwhile, Hooker and Halleck had an altercation, and the administration used that incident as an occasion to remove Hooker from his command. Once again, Lincoln had to reach into his bag of officers and come up with a replacement for the hapless Potomac army: George Gordon Meade. The president concluded that the native Pennsylvanian Meade would fight well on his own dung hill, as he put it. At this point, support was building to recall McClellan, and rumors spread that the New York State Democratic Party leaders would raise an army under his command, which would advance on Washington and remove Lincoln and his administration. However, the president had seen enough of McClellan and the opposition fires that he attracted.

In early July 1863, the two great armies in the East met in combat at the little-known town of Gettysburg, Pennsylvania. The result was one of the most costly and clear-cut victories for the Union in the East during the war. At the same time in the West, on July 4, 1863, Grant finally had captured Vicksburg. The Confederacy had seemingly reached its zenith, and the collapse was beginning. To Lincoln, the excitement was tempered when he found that Meade actually did not pursue Lee's army following the battle of Gettysburg and destroy it before it recrossed the Potomac. Lee's forces thus were able to reenter Virginia on July 13 and 14. Once again, the president lamented the generals destiny had willed him.

A disgruntled Lincoln chastised Meade in a letter, "He [Lee] was within your easy grasp, and to have closed upon him would . . . have ended the war. . . . Your golden opportunity is gone, and I am distressed immeasurably because of it." And then, thinking twice on the matter, the president folded up the letter and left it unsent. As expected, the Radicals quickly added Meade—another Democrat—to their enemies list; his important victory at Gettysburg was due to the corps commanders and not his leadership, they argued.[33]

Chancellorsville, Gettysburg, and Vicksburg were marked by high casualties that taxed the crazy quilt of conscription measures that Congress and the president had put into place. In July 1862, a group of governors had urged Lincoln to call for more men and crush the Confederacy once and for all. The president then called for three hundred thousand men to volunteer for up to three years. By July 17, 1862, Congress approved a militia act, which granted to the executive additional powers of conscription for the federal militia but used the administrative agencies of the states. Lincoln followed that step with a draft of three hundred thousand men for nine-month service. By March 3, 1863, Congress finally had approved a centralized conscription system with a large national network put in place. The act, however, allowed a draftee to provide a substitute in his place or to contribute $300 in commutation money. These calls to arms were not well received in many of the loyal states; the manpower shortage was compounded by the fact that over two hundred thousand men eventually deserted from the Union army during the war. In major cities such as Troy, Albany, Newark, and areas in Ohio, Wisconsin, Indiana, Kentucky, Pennsylvania, and Missouri, dissatisfaction spilled over into violence against the draft.

The worst disturbance was in New York City during July 13–16, 1863, where thousands rioted to protest the draft and Lincoln's war policies and hundreds were killed. Many less belligerent citizens questioned the constitutionality of the 1863 Conscription Act, and the Supreme Court stayed away from reviewing the legislation. The confusing and unfair administration of the draft also made it susceptible to severe criticism; learning those lessons, the federal government in World Wars I and II would abandon any initial hope of voluntary enlistments and go to a national draft run by the War Department, using regulations that the military, and not the Congress, would establish.

As he struggled with the musical chairs of command and put patches on the inefficient war machine in Washington, the president received an invitation to commemorate the fallen patriots at Gettysburg on November 19, 1863. By doing so, he took a simple occasion and consecrated the confusing war into a national sacrifice for expiation. In the process, Lincoln imprinted his mark on the nation in a strong symbolic sense, and he became immortal. Legend has it that the president wrote his famous address on the back of an envelope on the trip to the cemetery and that his remarks were poorly received by the audience. In fact, Lincoln worked on his address several times before it was delivered, and it was well received by those who could hear him. His words were recognized once they were printed as an eloquent statement on the war aims and the demands of democratic patriotism.

Lincoln's presentation followed a long, classically eloquent speech by Edward Everett of Massachusetts, the chief speaker for the occasion. The president spoke in a high-pitched voice in the characteristic Midwest twang of the time. Those words invoked the work of the Founding Fathers, respectfully praised the glorious dead soldiers, then rededicated the nation to a new birth of freedom under God, and concluded with the prophecy that "that government of the people, by the people, for the people shall not perish from the earth." Lincoln had been criticized throughout his term for banal utterances and undistinguished oratorical performances, but this time he captured the public mood in a way no statement had since the Declaration of Independence. Moving through the chaos of war, the mishaps of uncoordinated military strategy, the collapse of a train of generals, and the hesitations of emancipation, Lincoln had by late 1863 come to etch himself on the Union imagination.

Unlike the Emancipation Proclamation, with its cool appeal to military necessity, the Gettysburg Address provided the passion and the vision that seemed to animate the harried commander in chief. The issue was not just war but also the very future of self-government on earth. Later, Lincoln began to extend the real meaning of the conflict: "This is essentially a people's contest. On the side of the Union it is a struggle for maintaining in the world that form and substance of government whose leading object is to elevate the condition of men—to lift artificial weights from all shoulders; to clear a path of laudable pursuit for all; to afford all an unfettered start, and a fair chance in the race of life."

The Other President

While Lincoln was struggling with the burdens of war and defining anew the meaning of the gruesome, costly conflict, he had a counterpart who was also facing similar problems: Jefferson Davis. By comparing those two men one can get a better understanding of presidential leadership in this period. Davis was born a year before Lincoln, less than a hundred miles away, in a log cabin not much better than the one Lincoln knew as a boy. Unlike Lincoln, Davis was sent by his family to a Catholic school in Kentucky, even though his family was Baptist, and then on to Transylvania University. Through the influence of his father and an older brother, Davis received an appointment to the U.S. Military Academy. After a successful stint as a soldier, which included distinguished service in the Mexican War, Davis entered politics from the state of Mississippi and became a congressman and later a senator. He also served with distinction in Pierce's cabinet as secretary of war, and when the secession movement gained full strength in early 1861, Davis looked forward to a military appointment, instead of the singular honor of being the first and, as it turned out, the last president of the Confederacy.

There have been many reasons given for the South's defeat in the Civil War: the far-reaching economic superiority of the North, the willingness in the latter part of the war for Union generals to abandon old nineteenth-century European military strategies, the ability of the North to prevent Britain and France from recognizing the Confederacy, the lack of Southern civilian discipline during the war, and a host of accidents and strokes of misfortune in battle or in intelligence gathering. The respected historian David Potter has argued, however, that Davis's deficiencies as a military and civil leader, as compared to Lincoln, really made the difference.[34] And because the South lacked, and discouraged overall, the rise of a well-organized opposition party, there was no real challenge to this mediocre performance. Davis failed in three critical ways. First, he was a proud (at times haughty) individual, rather sensitive to slights and put off by the give and take of politics. Even his wife, Varina, concluded, "I thought his genius was military, but that as a party manager, he would not succeed. He did not know the arts of the politician and would not practice them if understood, and he did know that of war." Second, Davis had a fundamental misconception of his job as president, spending an incredible amount of time on details to the neglect of the larger picture and the need to mobilize his people for a protracted war. Also, he was deficient in handling the political and military role of commander in chief, placed too much emphasis on personal friendship, and did not have the foresight to appoint a general in chief early in the war.[35]

Davis's position, though, was somewhat different from Lincoln's, and the war strategies he supported necessarily reflected that reality. Interestingly, both faced many of the same situations—a reflection of the decentralization of American life; the relatively low level of experience among professional military men; and the pressures for patronage, status, and recognition—the true engines of duty and patriotism.

When the Confederacy drew up a constitution, it retained most of the basic elements of the U.S. Constitution, with certain provisions to protect more explicitly states' rights and slavery. There were some other changes as well: the president was elected for a single six-year term, the president had the item veto over appropriations, cabinet members could be given seats in Congress (though this was not implemented), a budget system was created, and two-thirds instead of three-quarters of the states had to concur for an amendment to pass. At his inaugural on February 18, 1861, Davis compared the South's secession to the Declaration of Independence and cited the "right of the people to alter or abolish them [their governments] at will whenever they became destructive of the compact for which they were established."

Like Lincoln, Davis was a loose administrator, and some of the criticism of his term in office rested on what one of his cabinet members called his lack of prompt business habits. In addition, Davis was a poor judge of character, and he frequently appointed and held on to weak individuals. One of his closest friends, General Josiah Gorgas, wrote, "The President seems determined to respect the opinions of no one; and has, I fear little appreciation of services rendered, unless the party enjoys his good opinion. He seems to be an indifferent judge of men, and is guided more by prejudice than by sound discriminating judgment."

Yet in the crucial first decision that led to the beginning of the war, it was Davis, for better or worse, who made the judgment not to let the North send supplies to Major Anderson at Fort Sumter. The second important event in which he was involved concerned dictating the strategy that ordered General Joseph E. Johnston's army to join Beauregard's forces at the Battle of Bull Run. When Beauregard took credit for the victory, an angry Davis wrote the general that his report seemed "an attempt to exalt yourself at my expense."[36] Unlike Lincoln, who was willing to give his generals even undeserved credit if they would only advance, Davis maintained at times a less than magnanimous attitude in dealing with his subordinates, and he seemed preoccupied by some need to gain on the political front what had been denied him on the battlefield.

But like his counterpart in the North, Davis spent much of his time on the draft and command problems. He saw that after the first enthusiasm of volunteering, even the South experienced a decline in the willingness of young men to enter military service. The Confederate president also went before his Congress and advocated longer enlistments: three years or the duration of the war, not the sixty days that the legislature had enacted. Pushed by generals Lee and Jackson, Davis on March 29, 1862, recommended the passage of the first conscription act in American history, and on April 16, the Confederate Congress approved it.

Able-bodied white males between the ages of eighteen and thirty-five were called up for three years' service, but the act allowed substitutes, as the North's would, and permitted draftees to elect their own officers in the ranks below colonel. Fearing slave insurrections, the Confederate Congress approved an exemption for overseers of twenty slaves or more—a step that was much criticized. As the war progressed, the draft was extended to those men under eighteen years of age and those between thirty-five and forty-five in 1862, and by 1864 to ages seventeen to fifty, although those in the forty-five to fifty category and those seventeen years old were to be confined to the reserves or home guards. Critics such as Governor Joe Brown charged that Davis overmobilized the states, stripping them of manpower to produce food and denying expertise to the industrial and transportation sectors.

Davis did insist on maintaining the code of war in dealing with prisoners and noncombatants. He wrote to Lincoln on July 6, 1861, that if captured crewmen were treated by the North as pirates and thus executed, he would order similar penalties. He also denounced Ben Butler's treatment of the women of New Orleans and proclaimed that Butler would be shot upon capture. Davis seemed especially outraged at the Emancipation Proclamation, arguing that it was meant to encourage slave insurrections; he therefore threatened death to any ex-slave soldiers and their white officers; yet within fifteen months, the Confederacy would be seriously considering the enlistment of black soldiers also.[37] Like Lincoln, Davis was reluctant to approve the death sentence for deserters. Lee had some deserters shot before the cases went to Davis for review, knowing of the president's leniency.

With pride, Davis also pointed out that the Confederate government was not engaged in the suppression of liberty the way the Lincoln administration was, although the Confederate Congress also suspended the writ of habeas corpus. Davis, too, was plagued by military rivalries, personality conflicts, and legislative intrusion. Although he did not have a Committee on the Conduct of the War with which to deal or a real opposition party, the Confederate Congress still contained strong critics of Davis, and when New Orleans fell in August 1862, there was an inquiry into the loss.

In managing the war, Davis, in general, was less interested in naval operations and not convinced of their importance—an unfortunate attitude
in a rebellious nation divided by the Mississippi, surrounded by an ocean
and gulf, and heavily dependent in its foreign policy on using cotton exports as a lever on Britain to gain recognition. Like Lincoln, Davis at times
seemed overly preoccupied with the defense of the capital city, often at
the expense of major strategic war aims. The symbolic value of losing the
capital was extremely important to both men, but, unlike the North, the
South chose to move its capital closer to the enemy lines. Lincoln could
not move Washington, D.C., without admitting defeat, but early on, the
South decided to acknowledge Virginia's importance by transferring its
seat from Montgomery, Alabama, to Richmond.

When McClellan began his first march toward Richmond, Davis took
to the field, visiting the Southern generals, rallying the troops in the rain,
and inspecting defensive works. It was by all accounts a most impressive
and heroic display of leadership. While Lincoln searched for a fighting
general in the East, Davis had wisely decided to release his military adviser,
Robert E. Lee, for field action some fourteen months into the war, after
Joe Johnston's wounding at Fair Oaks.

Lee has become so canonized in the South and so respected in the
North that it is sometimes difficult to realize that in the early months of
his command, he too was learning his craft. He had never commanded a
large body of troops—in fact, none of the leading generals on either side
had ever commanded a division or even a brigade. Americans had not been
to war except in the Mexican conflict some twenty years before and in
occasional campaigns against the tribes. At the time of his resignation from
the U.S. Army, Lee was only a lieutenant colonel. In his early battles, he
left too much to his subordinates and often gave imprecise orders. Indeed,
over one-third of his army was lost in the battles to defend Richmond,
and Lee suffered from shortages of men and matériel throughout most of
his campaigns.

Still, Davis had what Lincoln lacked—two generals, Lee and Stonewall
Jackson, who were a powerful combination in the eastern theater. After
the Second Battle of Bull Run, Lee asked Davis's approval for an invasion
of Maryland and then Pennsylvania. If he were successful, he would be in
a position to threaten Washington and Baltimore, which would encourage
peace sentiment in the North. He urged Davis to follow up military successes with a call for peace that might in turn affect the 1862 elections in
the North. But that victory never came; faced with a restored McClellan
and some bad luck, Lee was stopped at Antietam in Maryland.

For Davis, the war required that he turn his attention to foreign diplomacy as well. His strategy and that of his secretary of state, Judah P. Benjamin, was to induce Britain and possibly France to recognize the Confederacy. Their central assumption was that European mills would grow desperate for cotton, and this would force those nations to come to the aid of the South. But like most economic sanctions and international trade strategies, it was unsuccessful. Cotton was not king, and in fact, Europe began to import cotton from other sources, especially India and Egypt. The United States furthermore threatened to break off relations with Britain if it recognized the South, and despite the predictions of leaders like William Gladstone, Confederate military victories did not come with any regularity. After Antietam, European sympathy toward the Confederacy, where it had previously existed, generally disappeared.[38]

Later, Davis and his cabinet severely injured the South's chances by approving Lee's march into Pennsylvania. The defeat at Gettysburg, coupled with the fall of Vicksburg, crippled the Confederacy. At Gettysburg, Lee lost twenty-five thousand out of the seventy-five thousand men he had commanded and retreated into the South. At Vicksburg, Davis refused to approve his secretary of war's plea to send reinforcements, arguing it violated his prerogative as commander in chief and would wreak havoc on the military department system. Davis insisted that units be maintained separately and had no chief of staff between himself and the military leaders to manage day-to-day matters.

Again like Lincoln, Davis had to deal with the sensitivities of fighting generals, although he was less willing to listen to their self-serving complaints, a woe even the patient Lincoln tired of. In the case of the contentious General Sterling Price of Missouri, Davis finally said he would accept his resignation and would be happy if he went to Missouri and raised a new army of state forces to support the Confederacy in his own way. The next day, Davis backpedaled, and Price decided not to resign after all.

War brings out strong executive leadership, and Davis also was accused of being too powerful, of being a despot. When he invoked the Impressment Act of 1863 and seized half of the cotton supplies, Davis instigated a stream of protest among the planters. Other criticisms came from his handling of the home front, especially finances and transportation difficulties. The Confederate Congress was unwilling to tax its people, in part because its region of the nation was used to low taxation and was unwilling to meet the demands of mobilization. It has been estimated that the Confederacy raised about 1 percent of its income in taxes; thus, paper money with no backing financed the war. Still, at least until the battle at Gettysburg, the currency system did not collapse, although it was teetering.

In terms of transportation, the South had 104 railroad companies with varying gauges of track and few connecting cities. When in 1861 Davis urged the Congress to connect the Danville-Greensboro gap, delays and a lack of cooperation prevented even that minor adjustment. By May 1863, the Confederate government had passed a railroad control act, but its tough provisions were not used as Davis stressed cooperation instead. He also was reluctant to interfere with speculation and hoarding, adhering to a laissez-faire economic theory much longer than Lincoln.[39]

Although Davis did not have as much organized opposition in Congress as Lincoln had, he did have to be concerned about some discontent in the legislative branch. And like Lincoln, he had problems with some state governors, although in Davis's case, the states' rights ethos of the Confederacy ran counter to his need to centralize some activities in the war. Because the South also stressed the importance of a show of unity, there was no real opposition party during the war. Whigs and Democrats were generally expected to work under a unified government. There were, of course, opposition leaders who demanded more activity, less activity, or more patronage. Still, the Confederate Congress was much less effective and intrusive than the U.S. Congress. In part, many able leaders left the legislature and went to war rather than accommodate themselves to simply debating the war. In addition, alcoholism, absenteeism, and florid old-time rhetoric were prevalent in the Confederate Congress. Like Lincoln, Davis rarely took the legislature into his confidence or exerted much legislative leadership. But unlike Lincoln, Davis was often cool, aloof, and autocratic rather than flexible or even noncommittal. He disliked dealing with people motivated by self-interest rather than by patriotism—a fatal flaw in a political leader, especially in that period of history.[40]

As in the case of Lincoln in the North, there was some sentiment in the Confederacy for dumping Davis and putting Lee in his place as a dictator. Still, Davis retained strong control over the Congress, having his veto overridden only once. His base of support was the more moderate and yet deeply concerned representatives from the border and occupied states, and his major opponents came from the Georgia delegation. As criticism mounted at the end of the war, some 40 percent of the Congress could be counted on to oppose the president on occasion.

As was also true with the U.S. Congress, the Confederate Congress sought to control the president's cabinet selections. In 1864, Davis confronted head-on an attempt to limit the terms of cabinet members to two years, a move intended to increase the influence of the Senate. The bill was never voted on; still, Davis was warned that he had to reorganize the cabinet if he were to keep Congress's confidence. He eventually rejected that advice in the sharpest terms.[41]

With the state governors, Davis ran into some concerted opposition, which was even more contentious than Lincoln experienced. The Northern governors usually pushed their president to be more forceful in his leadership; the Southern governors interposed themselves to object to Davis's attempt to provide such leadership. A confederacy of seceded states was brought into existence to underscore states' rights; much of the institutional weakness of that loose union was due to the exact nature of its birth. Judah P. Benjamin wrote in late 1861, "The difficulty lies with the governors, who are unwilling to trust the common defense to one common head—they therefore refused arms to men who are willing to enlist unconditionally for the war and put their arms in the hands of a mere militia who are not bound to leave home."

The most difficult governor for Davis was Joseph E. Brown of Georgia, a Yale Law School graduate born in the red hills of his state. He protested that conscription was unconstitutional because it violated state sovereignty. Davis's response was a defense of the role of the central government and the "war powers" of the Confederate Constitution. He also cited the strength of the opposing army and the critical nature of conscription. Since there was no Supreme Court, the states' higher courts were relied upon for guidance. Georgia's supreme court declared that the conscription laws were constitutional, and so did other state court judges, while the chief justice in North Carolina found them unconstitutional.

Brown, along with Davis's vice president, Alexander Stephens, and others combined to attack the president on his power to suspend the writ of habeas corpus. Davis had suspended the writ only three times and for limited periods to deal with spies and traitors. Brown called his state legislature into session on March 10, 1864, to protest the law and warned against dictatorship. The governor even tried to bypass Davis's regulations dealing with blockade running.

Davis faced another problem with the young governor of North Carolina, Zebulon B. Vance, who criticized the president's promotions policy and also engaged in blockade-running activities. Vance's uncooperativeness was matched by that of South Carolina governor Andrew Magrath, who complained about the expansion of the central government under Davis.

As the war difficulties mounted, Davis became more eloquent in the defense of the cause and in his concerns over Southern honor and the perils of invasion. Despite the criticisms of his tenure, a series of state legislatures led by South Carolina and followed by Mississippi, Georgia, Virginia, and several military units as well passed resolutions of support for Davis. Yet, like Lincoln with the North's "Knights of the Golden Circle," Davis had to be concerned about secret organizations that were not loyal to the cause, such as the "Heroes of America," with rituals, handshakes, and special passwords. These groups were especially strong in the pro-Union areas of western Virginia, North Carolina, and northern Alabama.

Overall, though, the criticisms of Davis's leadership focused on his penchant for detail, his insistence on appointing West Point graduates to leadership posts, his rigid departmental organization, his zealous concern about the prerogatives of his office, his aloofness and poor judgment of men, his loyalty to personal favorites among the generals, and his defensive strategy. The organizational system of the army left each department reporting to Davis rather than to a general in chief as with Lincoln. The result was inflexibility and an inefficient use of manpower, such that when Lee surrendered on April 9, 1865, and his 27,800 troops laid down arms, there were still another 175,000 men scattered about in other sections of the Confederacy.

A comparison of the war presidents indicates that they faced many of the same problems: a nation without experienced military leadership, a decentralized government with little national infrastructure, a legislative branch that was less than supportive, criticisms of alleged arbitrary exercise of constitutional authority, and often a lack of diplomatic skill in their state departments. The South was a traditional agricultural society, bound to slavery, lacking a strong industrial and financial base. Yet in our own time, such "underdeveloped" nations have defeated better organized and equipped foes in long wars of attrition and endurance. By Antietam, Gettysburg, and Vicksburg, it would seem that the course of the war should have been obvious to the South. But the Confederacy pushed on, and the war once again accelerated in a series of bloody battles that taxed Davis as surely as it taxed the other president across the river.

The Forces of Dissent

One remarkable aspect of Lincoln's personality and presidency was his ability to suffer abuse, criticism, and general nastiness without striking back or turning sour. Despite his genuine sense of humility, Lincoln had the assertiveness and self-confidence of a successful self-made man, without exhibiting the usual slightly veiled defensiveness so often characteristic of such individuals. His attitude toward the presidency was best summarized in a story to which he resorted when asked how it felt to be the chief executive of the nation. Lincoln told the tale of a man who was tarred and feathered and ridden out of town on a rail. When someone asked him how he liked it, he responded, "If it were not for the honor of the thing, I'd much rather walk."

For Lincoln, the presidency was not a pleasant task. He was an enormously ambitious man. Indeed, his one-time law partner, William Herndon, wrote that Lincoln's ambition was an engine that knew no rest. But the presidency and the prolonged war brought with it a lasting disappointment, tempered by a sense of duty and stewardship. In the end, Lincoln would reflect, "I dreamt of power and glory, and all I have are blood and ashes."[42]

The president returned from Gettysburg with a mild form of smallpox; characteristically, he joked that now he had something to give all the office seekers who plagued him. Continuing to deal with a hypercritical Congress, the president showed some resentment toward the Committee on the Conduct of the War and its attacks on his judgment. He argued convincingly that while he never doubted his ability to suppress the rebellion and reunite the Union, the committee, however, was "a marplot, and its greatest purpose seems to be to hamper my action and obstruct the military operations." As with other presidents before and after him, he was reluctant to accede to legislative requests for information. The president on one occasion actually cited George Washington for having established the precedent of withholding documents requested by the legislative branch, arguing it would be "incompatible with the public interest."[43]

As the war continued in 1863, the Supreme Court finally gave the president some support. By a vote of five to four, the Court in the *Prize Cases* upheld the executive's war policies that established procedures for seizing vessels that violated the blockade. The contention of Lincoln's opponents was that those war measures—taken between April 15, 1861, which was the date of the president's proclamation of insurrection, and July 13, 1861, when Congress recognized the existence of the insurrection—were illegal. What was at stake was the president's leadership during the first eighty days of the war. Fortunately, Lincoln had appointed three of the five judges who voted in the affirmative that his action was valid.

The most controversial and disagreeable problem was the president's suspension of the writ of habeas corpus and the use of what can justly be called arbitrary arrest. In Baltimore, for example, the administration had ordered the arrest of the mayor and the police chief; in another case, Chief

Justice Roger Taney challenged the arrest of John Merryman in Maryland, who had allegedly expressed his hostility to the United States while holding a commission as a second lieutenant and possessing arms belonging to the United States.[44] Taney flatly stated that the president did not have the power to suspend the writ of habeas corpus. When Stanton tried to appeal the case to the Supreme Court, Attorney General Bates warned against it. A negative decision would "do more to paralyze the Executive . . . than the worst defeat our armies have yet sustained," he argued.

In September 1862 and then a year later in 1863, Lincoln issued proclamations suspending the writ of habeas corpus during the conflict. By 1863, however, Congress had passed an act that allowed the president to suspend the writ; indemnified officers who engaged in searches, seizures, imprisonments, or arrests; and exempted military officers from having to answer court writs. Lists of prisoners were to be sent to federal courts, and judges could discharge suspects upon grand jury findings after those individuals took a loyalty oath.

Meanwhile, the president extended his sway by issuing a set of regulations dealing with the militia under an act passed on July 17, 1862. Those regulations covered not only routine military matters but also the treatment of prisoners of war, noncombatants, spies, runaway slaves, and a host of other problems. The executive branch of government assumed, especially in occupied areas of the South and in several regions of the North, the functions of the judiciary branch. In addition, special courts were established by presidential order in such occupied areas as Louisiana, and they had unlimited powers. These courts had jurisdiction over both men in the military and civilians accused of military offenses, even those arrested for disloyal acts. It was only after the war was over that the Supreme Court in the *Milligan* case (1866) ruled that military courts could not supersede civilian courts in regions where civilian courts were still operative.[45]

Lincoln faced other sources of dissent within the Northern ranks besides so-called Copperheads, or Southern-sympathizing Northerners. Secret societies, such as the Knights of the Golden Circle with its private army and esoteric rites, were also major opponents of the administration. The Knights of the Golden Circle were eventually absorbed into the Order of American Knights; in New York State, another secret society called itself the Sons of Liberty and chose Clement L. Vallandingham of Ohio as the supreme national commander.

Vallandingham was to be one of Lincoln's most controversial critics, a quixotic Copperhead who directly challenged the Union government during its most trying period. Lincoln's response to his challenge was a characteristic mixture of forbearance, firmness, and later simple neglect. Vallandingham was a well-known lawyer and legislator in the ranks of the Democratic Party in Ohio. He had been an officer in the militia and a congressman, and he was an articulate opponent of the war. He attacked the president for violating civil liberties and refusing to work out a peaceful compromise. On April 13, 1863, General Burnside, without the War Department's approval, ordered an end to agitation in the Ohio region; he stated, "The habit of declaring sympathy for the enemy will not be allowed in this department."

On May 1, Vallandingham defied Burnside and at a mass rally of the Democratic Party in Ohio, he attacked the administration again. Vallandingham was roused from his bed in the middle of the night, arrested, tried before a military commission, and found guilty of expressing disloyal opinions aimed at weakening the government. He asked a federal court to issue a writ of habeas corpus, which it eventually refused to grant because it ostensibly lacked jurisdiction. Realizing the embarrassment he had caused the administration because of the controversy, Burnside offered his resignation. Lincoln's response was to the point: "When I wish to supersede you I will let you know. All the cabinet regretted the necessity of arresting, for instance, Vallandingham—some perhaps, doubting, that there was a real necessity for it—but, being done, all were for seeing you through with it." Refusing to commute the sentence, the president decided to ship Vallandingham off behind military lines in the South.[46]

To continue his strange odyssey, Vallandingham persisted and found his way beyond those areas; he eventually returned to the Union by surreptitiously entering through Canada, disguised with a thick mustache and with a pillow tucked under his coat. He later ran unsuccessfully for governor of Ohio. Although the Vallandingham case is often treated by historians as a sort of comic relief amid the tragedy of the war, the challenge to the administration was of some importance. The controversy has to be seen in the larger context of the extensive criticisms of what were perceived as gross violations of American civil liberties by the administration.

Lincoln had designated first Seward and later Stanton to administer the arrests policy. Initially, Seward set up a passport system for those going abroad, created a network of confidential agents, and pushed for expedited punishments. Stanton used an even more extensive detective bureau and a secret service, which was viewed by some as overzealous. It has been estimated that over 13,500 people—and probably more—were arrested and confined to military prisons between February 1862 and the end of the war. Among those people who were arrested were editors and political leaders who had opposed the war effort, including members of the Maryland state legislature.[47]

Lincoln was aware of the early and continued criticisms of this part of his war policy. He defended it on one occasion, pleading, "I am a patient man—always willing to forgive on the Christian terms of repentance; and also to give ample *time* for repentance. Still I must save this government if possible. What I *cannot* do, of course, I *will* not do; but it may as well be understood, once and for all, that I shall not surrender the game leaving any available card unplayed." Yet he realized that the arrest of innocent people raised the level of opposition, which helped the Confederate cause.[48]

In Congress, the controversial issue of arbitrary arrests also surfaced and attacks on Lincoln continued—even among some Republicans. Lincoln's proclamation of September 24, 1862, on the writ of habeas corpus was probably one factor in the party's losses in several border state elections. Still, the president defended his actions and dealt with the supporters of Vallandingham in a particularly telling response. To a petition from an Albany meeting of pro-Union Democrats who protested the Vallandingham arrest, Lincoln's position was clear. The president described the irony of those enemies of the Constitution who used its protections while they sought to destroy the Union it created. He argued the arrests were preventive and not vindictive, and he informed them that Vallandingham had tried to prevent the enlistment and recruitment of troops. Then the president asked, "Must I shoot a simple-minded soldier boy who deserts, while I must not touch a hair of a wily agitator who induces him to desert?"[49]

By February 1864, the Supreme Court had its chance to rule on the Vallandingham controversy. The majority concluded that since the military commission was not a court within the definition of the law, the high court could not issue a writ of certiorari to review the proceedings. Later, in the *Milligan* case, the Court did insist that "martial rule can never exist where the courts are open." Interestingly, Burnside, who had precipitated the original controversy, decided on June 1, 1863, to suppress the publication of the *Chicago Times* for its support of Vallandingham. Stanton's response was quick: he informed Burnside that the president wanted the order reversed and expected to be notified before "administrative" decisions such as the arrest of civilians or actions against newspapers were taken. To add to the president's problems, General Milo Hascall issued a similar order in Indiana against the *Columbia City News*. His order was revoked, and Hascall was sent elsewhere.

Overall though, despite the firestorm of opposition in 1862, the Republican Party did fairly well in the 1863 elections. On September

15, 1863, the president had issued a tightly drawn proclamation that suspended the writ of habeas corpus throughout the United States. Its basis was a congressional statute that had been passed rather than his own definition of executive power. However, Lincoln faced hostility from other important quarters, especially on the draft. The Democratic governor of New York, Horatio Seymour, who was elected in 1862, became publicly identified with those opposing the draft and was mentioned quickly as a prominent possible candidate for the presidential election in 1864. Fearing more disturbances in his state, Seymour asked for lower draft quotas and complained about the calculations being used by the War Department.

Overall, Lincoln looked at the dissent from all sides, which plagued him day after day, and concluded, "I am president of one part of this divided country . . . but look at me! I wish I had never been born! . . . With a fire in my front and rear; having to contend with the jealousies of the military commanders, and not receiving that cordial cooperation and support from Congress which could reasonably be expected; with an active and formidable enemy—in the field threatening the very life blood of the government—my position is anything but a bed of roses."[50]

But such sentiments were a luxury that Lincoln could ill afford. He was calm, calculating, self-effacing, and above all patient—patient almost beyond human endurance. By mid-1863, the South had suffered crushing defeats in two important theaters, and Union armies were moving toward Chattanooga to gain control of eastern Tennessee. However, the Army of the Cumberland led by Major General William Rosecrans and the Confederate Army of Tennessee under Braxton Bragg reached a stalemate. By September 20, 1863, after two days of concentrated attacks on his left flank at Chickamauga, Rosecrans blundered by redeploying units from his right flank and thus opening the way for the destruction of the right wing of his army. Only Major General George Thomas's forces held the line, earning him the nickname of "Rock of Chickamauga."

Lincoln fretted as his generals moved too slowly and indecisively for him. He avoided, as best he could, trying to dictate strategy, but he surely questioned what was happening to an advance he saw often as being excruciatingly slow, and victories that melted too quickly into delays. His chief of staff, Halleck, at times ignored the president's inquiries, but after Gettysburg, Lincoln insisted that General Meade should attack Lee. Lincoln caustically commented, "The honor will be his if he succeeds, and the blame may be mine if he fails." As for Rosecrans, the president tried to assure him of his support, even though he had discussed removing him from command; on top of that, a weary Lincoln wondered why Burnside had not sent the assistance he had promised to Rosecrans.

Then in September and October 1863, major changes in command were made, probably instigated by Stanton rather than Lincoln. Grant, as commander of the newly created Military Division of the Mississippi, was put in charge over Rosecrans; Grant quickly relieved him and gave Thomas command of the Army of the Cumberland. In an impressive turn-around, the Union forces prevailed at Missionary Ridge near Chattanooga and finally defeated Bragg's army in a major encounter there and at Look-out Mountain. On November 25, a delighted Lincoln wired Grant, "Well done! Many thanks to all." Lincoln had finally found his commander.

Winning Reelection

While the Union was chalking up some notable victories in the West, the campaigns in the East seemed costly stalemates that fed the ranks of the Peace Democrats and called down on Lincoln the wrath of the Radicals. Indeed, in many ways, the string of difficult victories in the West, while the Union armies seemed stalemated in the East, may have saved Lincoln and the Union cause. The president had found a general, but one who incurred incredible losses as he waged his battles of attrition. By midsummer of 1864, the campaigns that Grant instigated had not brought clear-cut victories, only more bloodshed and conscription. Lincoln realized all too well that his reelection depended on the military situation more than anything else.

As the Republicans entered the new year, the party was divided between the Radical elements and the conservative Whig group. The Radicals looked for a candidate to stop Lincoln, and they toyed with the prospects of Frémont, Chase, or General Ben Butler. Horace Greeley in his *Tribune* columns added Grant's name to the list, and anti-Lincoln partisans pushed to have the convention postponed beyond its June date in order to gather more support for a viable alternative. The major figure being considered was Lincoln's secretary of treasury, Salmon P. Chase. Chase claimed that he was at first unaware of the growing movement to replace the president with him. Yet he was unhappy with what he perceived to be Lincoln's poor leadership; the president seemed too often listless, inefficient, indecisive, and generally inadequate to the great burdens of the office. A quickly written Chase biography, based on information supplied by the secretary of war, began to appear in public. In major cities, Chase clubs began to spring up in late 1863, and the secretary's name was now prominently mentioned.

Then in February 1864, a group led by Senator S. C. Pomeroy of Kansas sent out a letter proclaiming that Lincoln could not be reelected and that even if he were, the war effort would continue to languish. As an alternative, the "Pomeroy Circular" suggested Chase as a man who possessed the qualities that a president in this crisis needed. Throughout all of this, Lincoln and his secretary of the treasury worked together without speaking of the campaign. Finally, Chase insisted to Lincoln that he had not encouraged the movement and offered his resignation. The president refused the offer, simply stating that he perceived no need for a change.

The conservative wing of the party, led by the Blairs of Maryland, was not content to let the matter drop. Francis Blair Jr., on the floor of the House of Representatives, launched a series of assaults on Chase and his record, from which Lincoln was quick to dissociate himself. Chase's support came from the large number of patronage appointments the Treasury Department controlled, and some officials claimed that they were being asked to align themselves with the secretary against the president. The situation was especially critical in newly occupied Louisiana. Then, in early March 1865, Chase announced in a letter to an Ohio supporter that he was pulling out of the race. Actually, the week before, Ohio had held a Republican Party caucus in the state's general assembly, and the leaders supported Lincoln's renomination.

But Chase's withdrawal did not mark the end of the challenge to the president. A group of Republicans calling themselves the "radical Democracy" met at Cleveland and nominated John C. Frémont for president and John Cochrane, the attorney general of New York, for vice president. The delegates charged that Lincoln had proved to be untrue to the cause of human freedom and that a new chief executive was essential to the salvation of the nation. Frémont, the Republican standard-bearer in 1856, argued that it was Lincoln and not he who had caused the split in the party. The general attacked the administration for its violations on constitutional liberties, its weaknesses, its disloyalty to its true friends, and its overall incompetence.

Other prominent men criticized Lincoln's record. The great orator and abolitionist Wendell Phillips saw the president's reelection as being disastrous to liberty and to the rights of African Americans. Another group of Republican leaders argued for a postponement of the convention, and the *Cincinnati Daily Gazette* reported that prominent leaders were demanding the president's resignation. While these were important pockets of dissent, the Lincoln forces controlled both the party machinery and many of the state and county committees throughout the nation. Lincoln and his supporters were not reluctant to use the full resources of his presidency, including patronage and government contracts, to solidify his strength.

In early 1864, the president began to receive the support of some of the major delegations. In New Hampshire, the state Republican committee supported him publicly; the Republicans in the Pennsylvania legislature followed suit; so did supporters in New Jersey, Indiana, Maryland, Colorado, California, Rhode Island, Ohio, and Kansas. By June, the party convention followed the Lincoln bandwagon. Seeing the probable outcome, the Radicals pressed, as convention losers often do to shape the platform to their liking. The final draft contained a call for an antislavery amendment to the Constitution, a railroad to the Pacific coast, and renewed support for redemption of the national debt. The platform stressed the need for "harmony" in the government—a code word for getting rid of cabinet conservatives like Seward and Blair. The convention nominated Lincoln and added Andrew Johnson of Tennessee to woo war Democrats to the "Union" ticket, as the Republicans called their party that election.

The president apparently at first opposed dumping Hannibal Hamlin as vice president and even considered Ben Butler as a running mate, a choice the general rejected—unwisely, as it turned out. Some of Lincoln's advisers urged him to move rapidly on introducing new states to the Union in order to increase his Western electoral tally, but the president for some reason chose to proceed slowly, probably desiring a genuine mandate and not simply a stacked electoral decision.[51]

His ambivalences in the election were apparent. On the one hand, he refused to get involved in running the political machine, as he called it. "I have enough on my hands without *that*. It is the *people's* business—the election is in their hands." But Lincoln was too astute a politician to neglect the most important contest of his time. He interfered where he saw problems, as in the critical state of Pennsylvania, where he directly organized speakers for the party's cause and used the patronage powers he had to solidify his base. When it was suggested to Lincoln's secretary, John Hay, that perhaps editor James Gordon Bennett of the *New York Herald* might lessen his criticism if he had a promise of a foreign ministry later, Hay disagreed, saying that Bennett was "too pitchy to touch." But Lincoln did not think so, and he offered him the post in France.

In Missouri, John Nicolay arrived bearing Lincoln's instructions to mediate the factionalism there. And although the president was forbidden by custom to "campaign," he did sit for a long interview in August in which he spelled out how emancipation meant two hundred thousand former slaves for the Union army. To those who attacked his abolitionist policy, the president argued, "No human power can subdue the rebellion without the use of the emancipation policy and every policy calculated to weaken the moral and physical forces of the rebellion." And it was probably Lincoln who came up with, or first used prominently, the words that became the unofficial slogan of the campaign: "No time to swap horses in the middle of the stream," a plea for continuity of leadership during the war.[52]

Lincoln's major opponent, though, would not be Frémont but the Democratic nominee, General George McClellan. It is likely that Lincoln had tried to get McClellan to disavow the nomination by offering him a military command once again, including an adjunct position with Grant, or perhaps the command of the Army of the Potomac. But McClellan sought and received the Democratic nomination and then struggled with his position on the party's platform. Vallandingham and his followers had pushed through a plank that called the war effort a failure and demanded an end to hostilities and a convention of the states or some similar mechanism to restore the Union. After hesitating on the issue, McClellan insisted on a guarantee of union before peace negotiations began—the opposite to the order spelled out by the Peace Democrats. Thus entering the election, McClellan was also faced with internal splits in his party's ranks.

Lincoln said little about McClellan's candidacy either publicly or privately. He knew in one sense that the race was his to win or lose and that his fate depended on the military situation. He had, though, aggravated his problems by vetoing the Wade-Davis bill, the Radical Republican plan for reconstruction of the Southern states. The two Republican sponsors of the bill then issued a statement published in the *New York Tribune* that charged the president was guilty of "grave Executive usurpation" of authority. They attacked his reconstructed governments in Arkansas and Louisiana as "mere creatures of his will." And they labeled his actions as sinister, rash, and a violation of the rights of humanity and republican government. Concerned by the charges from men in his own party, Lincoln observed, "To be wounded in the house of one's friends is perhaps the most grievous affliction that can befall a man." As the president had guessed, the manifesto was the first step in an effort to get him to give up the nomination he had just won. Republican Radical Henry Winter Davis issued a call for a new convention in September, and a group of party leaders met surreptitiously in New York and included some important figures from that state and Massachusetts. Thurlow Weed, who attended, informed Lincoln that his reelection was an impossibility, and the president's campaign manager, Henry J. Raymond, agreed. Raymond advocated a publicized peace offer to Jefferson Davis—an overture that obviously would not please the Radicals, who were the source of Lincoln's opposition.

On August 23, 1864, Lincoln wrote out a long memorandum outlining special overtures that he would make to McClellan if the latter were elected. He would urge McClellan to raise as many troops as he could for the final trial, and Lincoln, in turn, would devote all his efforts to assisting and finishing the war. Then Lincoln sealed up the letter and, strangely, had all his cabinet members sign the outside of the document without telling them what was in it.

Another group of Republicans continued the assault on the president and called for a new convention on September 28 in Cincinnati. Before issuing the statement, they polled the Republican governors to see if the president could win in their states in the coming election. But by the time the statement reached the governors, the tides of war had changed. Major General William T. Sherman, Grant's successor as commander of the Military Division of the Mississippi, had captured Atlanta, and the fate of the Confederacy was clear, even to Lincoln's critics. On September 22, Frémont dropped out of the race, apparently as a result of a less-than-honorable deal on Lincoln's part. In order to soothe the Radicals, the president requested the resignation of his conservative ally and longtime friend, Postmaster General Montgomery Blair. Blair and his family had become a lightning rod of the Radicals' animus. Just before his action, Lincoln assured Blair's father that his son was a good and loyal ally and should not be sacrificed for false friends. The president's lame comment to Blair was, "You very well know that this proceeds from no dissatisfaction of mine with you personally or officially."

As the campaign progressed, the president and his campaign leaders used the full patronage at their disposal to foster his reelection. In New York, Lincoln removed Chase's associate, Horace Binney, from the New York Customs House and replaced him with his own man; later he chose a new surveyor of the port and named a new postmaster in New York City. He threw his full support behind the Seward-Weed machine in order to carry that crucial state, and in Philadelphia, Chicago, and Indiana, the president firmed up his control over the patronage network. When he received word that one official was not supporting a regular party nominee, Lincoln bluntly replied, "Your nomination is as binding on Republicans as mine, and you can rest assured that Mr. Halloway shall support you, openly and unconditionally, or lose his head." One newspaper in Indiana complained that hundreds of government clerks were mailing out Lincoln literature instead of conducting the nation's business.

Federal employees were expected to work for the ticket and also to contribute to the Republican war chest; a 3 percent levy on salary was in many cases standard, and postmasters were expected to contribute personally from $2 to $150 each, depending on the size of the post office, to the congressional campaign. The party also expected and obtained campaign contributions from those who were receiving government contracts during the war, and the quartermasters provided the names of those who were favored with government largesse.

Most importantly, the Republicans counted on the soldier vote. Over one million documents were distributed by the party to soldiers, and the president and his campaign managers insisted that troops from critical states be furloughed in time to go home and vote. It has been estimated that the soldier vote, three-quarters of which went for Lincoln, helped the Republicans win six vital states, without which the president would not have been reelected. On election day, November 8, 1864, Lincoln received 55 percent of the vote and carried the electoral vote 234–21. He swept every state in the remaining Union, except Delaware, New Jersey, and his own birthplace of Kentucky. His victory was strongest in Massachusetts, weakest in New York. He did well among the German American population but poorly in the cities and among Irish Americans. Lincoln had earned the right to characterize his own victory: "It had long been a grave question whether any government, not too strong for the liberties of its own people, can be strong enough to maintain its own existence, in great emergencies." To him, the decision was clear: he had asserted the power of the government and had received in the end a mandate from the people to continue the war.[53]

The Trials of Attrition

Lincoln's electoral victory was mainly due to successes in the field. But he knew all too well that the armies were extracting a terrible toll in life and treasure. In February 1864, the president had promoted Grant to lieutenant general, a rank that only George Washington and Winfield Scott (as brevet) had held. A small, quiet, and sloppily dressed man, Grant became the new American hero. The general had decided on a series of offenses in the East designed to end the war. Lincoln seemed unsure of what was being contemplated, writing as late as August 1864 to Grant, "The particulars of your plans I neither know nor seek to know." In fact, Lincoln had submitted earlier his own strategic plan to Grant, one the general found to be unsatisfactory.

On May 5, 1864, Grant began the bloody forty-day "Overland Campaign" that took his armies from the Battle of the Wilderness, through Spotsylvania, to the North Anna River, on to the slaughter of Cold Harbor, and finally the siege of Petersburg. Each was a bloodbath, and the terrible Union losses gave credence to Grant's nickname, "The Butcher." The total Northern casualties from the Wilderness battle through the harrowing battle at Cold Harbor reached 54,000 men—7,621 of whom were killed. At Cold Harbor alone, there were 12,000 casualties, killed and wounded. Later, Grant was to write, "Without a greater sacrifice of life than I was willing to make, all could not be accomplished that I had designed north of Richmond." Many soldiers pinned their names on their own uniforms for identification of the dead later. Legend has it that following a battle, Grant's army moved on, not even bothering to bury its own men.

Lincoln visited the general in late June and expressed concern about the siege of Petersburg. He had written Grant, "I do hope you may find a way that . . . shall not be desperate in the sense of great loss of life."[54] As the North was registering shock over the course and cost of the war, Horace Greeley floated another peace feeler to the president. He had received word that Jefferson Davis had authorized two emissaries to present peace terms. Lincoln agreed to meet with them if Greeley himself escorted them to Washington from Canada, where they were staying. Lincoln's terms were clear: the restoration of the Union, and the end of slavery; the president sent John Hay in mid-July 1864 to Niagara Falls with that message. The peace initiative fell through, but another would follow.

The war continued through the summer. Lincoln had already called up more troops, and opposition to the draft increased. The administration also faced financial problems by this time. Earlier, in 1862, Congress had issued "U.S. Notes," or "greenbacks," as they were called—government paper not backed by gold, which greatly depreciated in value. Congress, faced with the problem of wartime inflation, had tried in 1863 to set up a national banking system to stabilize the problem. That system, planned by Secretary of Treasury Chase, created federally chartered banks, which would purchase U.S. bonds and could use the bonds as security for issuing banknotes guaranteed by the federal government. The banknotes were accepted at par value and could be exchanged for gold. By June 1864, Congress attempted to control speculation by restricting gold trading. In order to fund the war, Congress had voted on a federal income tax of 3 percent on all incomes over $800, a rate that was graduated in 1864 on a scale that went from 5 to 10 percent. Congressional Republicans were anxious to redeem their campaign promises to important constituencies, so in the president's first term they supported a high tariff, subsidized the railroads, passed a land-grant college bill, and created a homestead policy. Lincoln, preoccupied with the war, simply signed these measures and avoided any more confrontations with his own party. Yet another arduous battle was still in front him—Reconstruction.

Prelude to Reconstruction

Lincoln had pretty much run the war in his own way, despite the obstruction of Congress. He intended to do the same with regard to Reconstruction. That decision, made somewhat abruptly, may have been a mistake on his part; surely, it was disastrous to his successor. The president believed that the necessities of war gave him, as commander in chief, extraordinary powers to wage that war, powers that were superior to those of Congress. He had confronted immense opposition, and still he had mandated measures in his early months that were extraconstitutional at best—and so he had Congress ratify them later. He had usually stymied the legislative branch in its attempts to interfere with his choice of cabinet officials and generals. He had declared slaves to be free in rebellious states, again citing military authority. Civilian courts were ignored or superseded, much to the horror of even conservative Union men. Now the president faced reconstruction, and he recognized two facts: first, his powers to move in such extraordinary ways were due to the circumstances of war, and when the conflict was over, his scope of authority would be surely circumscribed; and second, his objectives and those of the Radicals would lead to very different types of reconstructed governments.

As has been noted, Lincoln was by birth and by family ties a Southerner, and despite his general tolerance, he shared (even during his presidency) many of the racial attitudes of that region. The Union, he had said, was the issue, but slavery was in some way the cause of secession. To save the Union, he became an abolitionist; to live up to his conservative inaugural oath, he took on the mantle of Great Emancipator. Still, by 1864–1865, only about 5 percent of the slave population had been freed. Most slaves were behind Confederate lines in the South and still held in bondage.

The president desired a speedy end to the war and a quick rehabilitation of the secessionist states. If one theme comes out in his correspondence on the issue, it is the need to move fast on restoration. Why the haste? In part, it was probably just a desire to get back to normal, to peace and to harmony. But Lincoln's plans ran into opposition from the Radicals in Congress, and some of their concerns were valid.[55]

The war for secession had been supported by most of the Southern leadership classes, and any restoration would bring them back to power. In addition, those states would return to the national government with their senators, their representatives, and their electoral votes; probably very soon a Democratic president and a Democratic Congress would result. Black freedom had yet to be secured; there were serious constitutional doubts about Congress's Confiscation Acts and even more about Lincoln's Emancipation Proclamation. Lincoln seemed firm on abolition by 1864, but still he insisted on discussing colonization, compensation to slaveholders, and a phased-in plan for emancipation—even after he had "freed" slaves in rebellious territories in January 1863.

The Radicals believed, with some justification, that speedy reconstruction would result in a return to the status quo before the war. What would be the political and economic consequences of millions of freed African Americans without jobs and without civil rights? Would they simply be exchanging their status as slaves for a new nominal wage bondage that left them on plantations still run by overseers? All the sacrifice and energy would have been spent in vain. And incredibly, their party—the party of Union and emancipation—could be cast out of power. At stake were not simply the humanitarian goals that came out of the terrible war but also that network of patronage and privilege that war had brought.[56]

A reconstructed South would not support the same economic interests the Republicans had favored, and a South-West alliance would have dismal consequences, especially for supporters of a high tariff. The Radicals demanded retribution and called it justice. Besides their philosophical concerns were the pragmatic problems that success in the war would bring. Lincoln seemed at first interested primarily in a speedy reconstruction, and he created the nucleus of early "restructured" governments in some Southern states to move the process along. In December 1863, the president established a policy of general pardon and a restoration of state governments. He offered a pardon (except in specific cases) and a full restoration of rights (except for slaveholding) to anyone in a seceded state who took an oath of allegiance to the U.S. Constitution, the Union, and all valid congressional acts and presidential proclamations. For restoration purposes, Lincoln decided that if one-tenth of those voting in 1860 would reestablish a republican form of government loyal to the Union, he would recognize it as the true government of that state.

This 10 percent formula was to be the foundation upon which pro-Union governments were to be built, and Lincoln decided to use this formula in several occupied states in order to create models as to how reconstruction under the executive's control could proceed with minimum dislocation and without lasting bitterness. He strongly opposed bringing in outsiders to run these states—a policy later changed and characterized as "carpetbagger" rule. When Louisiana fell to the Union forces, Lincoln began to use that state as a first test. He pushed for elections of congressmen, and after a fight, the House of Representatives voted to seat Louisiana's two elected representatives in February 1863. But matters moved too slowly for the president, and he feared that disloyal elements might preempt his objectives by creating a government that would refuse to recognize emancipation.

By 1864, a state convention in Louisiana proposed a constitution that accepted emancipation, and elections proceeded normally. The constitution was overwhelmingly approved by the loyal people of Louisiana, and it seemed as if Lincoln's plans were working well. But Radical opposition hardened, and some of the leaders in that state refused to support the new government.

The president had moved quickly in other occupied states as well. In Tennessee, he appointed Andrew Johnson as military governor in 1862, and by 1865, a reorganized government was established—although not recognized by Congress until 1866. In 1863 and 1864, Arkansas, a reluctant secessionist state, was reorganized with Lincoln's approval. Local support was strong for such reconciliation, and the president pushed for immediate elections in March 1864. In Florida, the president by 1864 asked for reconstruction "in the most speedy way possible," and he sent his assistant John Hay to aid in the process. Events did not go well in that state, however, and readmission was slow in coming.

The president's formula was flexible and designed to facilitate easy restoration. Basically, the process included the building of a loyal nucleus, a constitutional convention to revamp the state government, and popular elections for state and congressional offices. Voters had to take a loyalty oath, and eventually federal troops were removed, leaving in charge local people pledged to the Union.

In Congress, opposition to Lincoln's policy grew and an alternative was put forth by the Radicals. In the House of Representatives, Henry Winter Davis introduced a bill to guarantee republican government to states where it had been "usurped or overthrown." Davis's original bill required that a majority of white male citizens had to take an oath and that no person who had voluntarily borne arms against the United States, or given aid to such persons, could participate in the creation of a new constitution. No former civil or military officer of the Confederacy could vote or hold office under the reconstructed state government. The Senate agreed with the House version and passed it on to Lincoln, who was in the capital that day.

Lincoln argued that the bill was too inflexible, and he was unwilling to set aside the Arkansas and Louisiana governments he had, in effect, created. The president disagreed with the Wade-Davis emphasis on past loyalty; the future was his concern. He explained, "On principle I dislike an oath which requires a man to swear he *has* not done wrong. It rejects the Christian principle of forgiveness on terms of repentance. I think it is enough if the man does no wrong hereafter."[57] One of the bill's supporters, Senator Zachariah Chandler, argued that the important objective was to end slavery in the restored states, as Lincoln himself had proposed. But the president responded that Congress had no authority to act and that he alone could do on military grounds what could not be done constitutionally in peacetime.

The president pocket-vetoed the bill and continued to advocate quick and amiable restoration. But other Republicans were strong in their opposition to his actions and to his logic. Thaddeus Stevens argued that the Southern people had to "eat the fruit of foul rebellion" before they could return. He was committed to the "perpetual ascendancy" of the Republican Party, and he saw that its entire economic program of subsidies and privileges was at stake.

The Thirteenth Amendment

By 1864, Lincoln and the Congress had both proclaimed an end to slavery, and yet it remained an institution. As has been noted, the president in his proclamation in 1863 had used what he argued were his war powers and freed the slaves in most of the areas in rebellion. In Congress, support had grown even earlier for some drastic challenge to slavery. As has been seen, in August 1861, Congress passed the first confiscation act, which provided that slave owners forfeit those slaves used in military service against the United States. In July 1862, the second such act declared "forever free" all slaves of owners who supported the rebellion or were guilty of treason, a provision close to Lincoln's later edict. Congress also abolished slavery in the District of Columbia and in the territories, granted freedom to slaves who served in the Union armies (by 1864, even if they were owned by Unionists), and ended the fugitive slave laws. Yet, even though Lincoln's actions were in fact less far reaching on paper, his proclamation still took on great importance in the symbolic and practical world of war and abolitionism. He had acted because of military necessity using his self-proclaimed war powers. His proclamation was enforced by the powerful Union army, while the Confiscation Acts depended on federal courts, which were often not operating.

In 1864, Lincoln was pushing for emancipation and had by that time generally, but not totally, given up on compensation, having seen that gradualism was not possible. The question remained whether the proclamation or even the congressional confiscation acts were constitutional and whether emancipation would continue to be national policy after the war ended. The president had insisted that the Republicans in the election of 1864 support an antislavery amendment to the Constitution, and after his victory, he pushed for its approval.[58] Lincoln spoke to moderate Democrats in Congress, used some patronage to further his case, and was successful in getting the lame-duck Congress to reconsider and pass the proposed amendment in early 1865. It has been speculated that the president persuaded Senator Charles Sumner to postpone consideration of a bill to regulate the Camden and Amboy railroad in New Jersey in return for the company's help in getting several Democratic congressmen to support the amendment. Lincoln probably backed off, knowing Sumner's general attitude to such pressure. For whatever reason, enough Democrats in the last session switched, and the Thirteenth Amendment was approved. Lincoln regarded it as the fulfillment of his work, a great moral victory, a cure for many of the evils he saw before him. By the end of 1865, the Thirteenth Amendment was added to the Constitution, with its provisions that prohibited slavery and involuntary servitude in the nation. William Lloyd Garrison fully credited the president with the amendment; the glory belonged to "the humble railsplitter of Illinois—to the presidential chain-breaker for millions of the oppressed—to Abraham Lincoln!"

The war was coming to an end. As his first term concluded, Lincoln again was approached by a peace commission, and this time he went with Seward to meet the group at Hampton Roads, Virginia, on February 3, 1865. Lincoln greeted Confederate Vice President Alexander Stephens and several others, and once again they explored possibilities for terminating the war. Lincoln's position was reiterated: he insisted on a restoration of the Union and refused to get dragged into a common alliance for a war against the French-controlled Mexico. Stephens, according to his recollections, asked the president if the Emancipation Proclamation would free all the slaves in the South or only those who were actually freed during the war. Lincoln supposedly said the proclamation was a war measure and would become inoperative after the war. Seward informed them of the

Thirteenth Amendment but also viewed it as a war measure that could be defeated if the Confederate states returned to the Union in time. Lincoln instead argued that the South could postpone the adoption of the amendment for a five-year time span and held forth the carrot of compensation.

If Stephens's memoirs are correct, Lincoln was talking once again of graduated emancipation with compensation, arguments that he earlier had indicated to others he had abandoned. And if Stephens's views are faithful summaries of Lincoln's feelings, the president's record on emancipation is even more confusing. For while he was pushing the Thirteenth Amendment clearly and decisively, he was still clinging to a moderate course that he himself had made impossible. In any case, the Confederates rejected Lincoln's plan, a development that probably saved the president from intense attacks by the Radical Republicans if they had known of the alleged conversations at that time. When Lincoln came back to the capital, he presented his cabinet with a proposal resurrecting compensation; to a man they opposed his plan, and he dropped it. The war had ground too deeply for half-measures now.

By March 1865, Lincoln's second inauguration was imminent, and there even was talk of his running again in 1868. In his short inaugural address, the president blamed the war on the development of slavery and ended with those familiar sentiments, "With malice toward none; with charity for all; with firmness in the right, as God gives us to see the right, let us strive to finish the work we are in."

Meanwhile, the war continued. Sherman's armies captured Savannah and marched on the Carolinas, and Grant finally took control of Petersburg on April 3, 1865. The president accepted Grant's invitation and went to visit his army as it reached the Confederate capital. Almost recklessly, the president watched the forces in the city, landed at Richmond, and walked up Main Street to the executive mansion evacuated by Jefferson Davis. Soldiers cheered Lincoln, and African Americans sang and shouted in the presence of the Great Emancipator. Then, in the main parlor, where even today one can feel a sense of eeriness, Lincoln met with Union officers and Richmond citizens. One newspaper writer noted that the president came without pomp or parade, not as a conqueror but as a friend to rebuild what had been destroyed.

In the next few days, Grant continued on, and Sherman wired that "if the thing is pressed, I think Lee will surrender." Lincoln's response to Grant on April 7, 1865, was clear—"Let the *thing* be pressed." On April 9, Lee surrendered at Appomattox Court House. The administration had made it clear to Grant that he was not to discuss any political questions, that such matters "the president holds in his own hands." Even after the capitulation, Lincoln struggled with reconstruction, most especially in Virginia, where leaders had been assured that the president had sanctioned their calling back the Virginia legislature. In another change of policy, Lincoln began to talk of allowing "the very intelligent" African Americans and those African Americans who had served in the Union army to vote. Actually, he had earlier suggested that policy in discussions about reconstruction in Louisiana and now raised it on April 11, 1865. He promised some new announcement concerning the South later, and he had requested, probably as a gesture of reconciliation with Congress, that Senator Sumner accompany him as he delivered some general remarks to a crowd before the White House.

In the cabinet, he admitted that he may have moved too fast in reconstruction, and he instructed Secretary of War Stanton to draft an executive order setting up military governments for former Confederate states. To Stanton, this meant that the president had moved toward the Radical position; although the African American suffrage question was deferred, the secretary concluded that a long cabinet debate was in order on this and other matters. The president also indicated that he did not intend to call Congress back into session, and thus from April to December, he once again would have a free hand. Those were the last decisions the president would make.

Lincoln's Leadership

Lincoln's murder on Good Friday, April 14, 1865, transformed him into a national martyr, and the manner of his end and his own sentiments of clemency made him the Christ symbol of the American dream. Surely, his presidency had been an extraordinary one, not just in the exercise of power, but also in its single-minded devotion to the Union. The "poor boy made good" had become the Great Emancipator; the wavering conservative Whig had been transformed into a man of vision and liberty. At times, Lincoln seemed to be vacillating and unsure to his contemporaries; to history, he became the prudent leader weighing all factors until he could shape events to fit his destiny. His detractors have been debunked themselves by the mainstream interpretations of history—his generals were too slow, just as he said; some of his cabinet too disloyal, just as he feared; the Radicals too vindictive, just as he charged. The Civil War, even in the South today, is seen favorably through Lincoln's eyes.

Yet the Lincoln presidency is a more varied pattern than that. He appointed some very poor cabinet officers and gave them considerable leeway. The quick mobilization in the spring of 1861 led to speculation, mismanagement, and corruption. A few critics have even argued that Lincoln may have prolonged the war by his sacking of McClellan. Lincoln's fluctuations with peace offers are seen now as shrewd efforts to get the Peace Democrats on his side; in fact, they may have been unnecessary confusions, especially toward the end of the war. The administration's dragnet policies of arrests did not have to be so extensively applied and extended throughout the war. The suspension of civil liberties, which Lincoln defended and modified, created immense political problems, some of which would not have been necessary if the army had been more carefully controlled. And once he freed the slaves, Lincoln needed to give more attention to their plight and what would happen to them. It was not enough to say he only freed the slaves to save the Union; once they were freed, what did the president intend to do besides allow them to serve in the Union army?[59]

As Lincoln liked to say, he was confronted by facts and not by a theory; some of the Radicals recognized the facts much earlier than did the president. The greatest problem of his presidency was his inclination to exclude Congress as much as possible from the major decisions of the war. More than Jackson, whom he did not admire, and Polk, whom he criticized, Lincoln ran the government as much as possible without legislative guidance. Perhaps it was necessary considering the quality of that body, or perhaps it was a decision that led to the growth of a cohesive Radical wing. Still, the Civil War is to a great extent the Lincoln presidency writ large. His election was the immediate cause of secession, his early months set the framework of the North's response, his decisions created the war machine, his timing prevailed in emancipation, and he planned the reconstruction. When all is said and done, Lincoln stands like a colossus in that conflict and, by his words, posterity has come to give meaning to the war, the Union, and the terrible sacrifices he extolled. No president in that century, and none except Franklin D. Roosevelt in our history, so expanded the office and transformed it and the republic it serves.

Theodore Roosevelt: The Dynamics of Domestic Reform   **6**

THERE HAVE BEEN MORE IMPORTANT and more accomplished presidencies than Theodore Roosevelt's, but none as interesting and flamboyant. After the long drought of formal and distant executives, Roosevelt reinvented the presidency in time for, or in league with, the growth of the broad popular media. In part, Roosevelt's astonishing political career was formed not by a string of lasting achievements but by a chimera of fleeting but powerfully imposed images. Like John F. Kennedy, another very young president in American history, TR (as he was called) left a legacy of stirring impressions that are still captivating—especially when not looked at too closely.

Roosevelt's early years are almost as well known as Lincoln's. TR was a sickly boy who overcame his youthful illnesses by willpower, determination, and exercise. He was an author, a learned naturalist, and an aristocrat in a profession dominated by extortionists, ethnic vote peddlers, and mossback politicians. He acquired a reputation as a "good government" reformer in the New York legislature and in the U.S. Civil Service Commission, a cowboy in the South Dakota Badlands, an aggressive assistant secretary of the navy, a war hero in the charge up San Juan Hill, and a competent governor of the Empire State. To get the young Roosevelt out of New York, several Republican bosses pushed him onto the McKinley ticket, leaving Senator Mark Hanna of Ohio to exclaim prophetically that they were putting that "damn cowboy" one bullet away from the presidency.

On September 14, 1901, Theodore Roosevelt, at the age of forty-two, became the youngest man ever to assume the presidency. He was, by all accounts, a brilliant, impulsive, and yet calculating politician. And he represented a very different view of politics. For the first time in nearly a century, the United States had a president drawn from the patrician Eastern class, educated by tutors and at Harvard College, and linked to some of the oldest families in the United States. Despite his occasional opposition to the bosses, by 1898 Roosevelt made a deal with Republican boss Tom Platt and New York railroad interests not to upset the state party machine if he were elected governor. Roosevelt won by only eighteen thousand votes and, as the state's chief executive, compiled a very respectable record, which included measures to tax corporate franchises, promote civil service, and encourage conservation. He was both adored and hated, usually for the same reasons. Roosevelt was harsh, arrogant, and the master of a volcano of what seemed uncharted energy. Henry Adams said that he was "pure act," and Henry Demarest Lloyd characterized him as a person with the "same appetite for the spread of ideas by explosion which Napoleon had."[1]

Roosevelt gave the impression of being a man who loved life in its roughest and most concentrated forms, yet his letters to his children are the tender admonitions of a sensitive father. He never fully recovered in some ways from the loss of his first wife and his mother on the same day, and he never revealed his personal anguish to the outside world. Roosevelt's philosophy of life was a gospel of action, which seemed to help him forget the deep pessimism he entertained about human existence. His words reek with obsolete and vulgar nineteenth-century concerns about racial purity and ethnic stereotypes. Only TR could seriously define a man's mission in life as to "work, fight, and breed."[2]

He is frequently quoted as advocating that Americans should speak softly but carry a big stick. In fact, TR did just the opposite: he blustered all over the international stage and rarely used force of arms. In an America of unlimited ambitions and vague imperialist dreams, Roosevelt had to face the world with a modest navy and a decentralized military establishment. He generally despised those who got in his way—for example, regarding the Latin American nations as "banana republics" headed by "Dagos" and "inferior races." Roosevelt joined his assertiveness with a high sense of moral purpose, which seemed to some Americans the spirited essence of progressivism and to others as sheer hypocrisy.

Roosevelt had great practical confidence in the abilities of a strong government to dole out justice; he supported reforms because he hated revolution and agitation, and he saw the presidency as the nerve center of a powerful American nation-state. Roosevelt came out of a tradition that viewed the upper classes and their middle-class allies as the great protectors of the capitalist order. Although he was labeled the "trustbuster," in fact he did not wish to break up many of the great concentrations of wealth but tried instead to force those corporations to acknowledge the regulatory rights of the government. Between those big corporations and organized labor, both of which he was leery of, TR positioned the federal government as an honest umpire, dedicated to conservative change and justice.

The world of the early twentieth century saw considerable agitation as the cities and states sought to regulate, if not destroy, the large corporations that led to monopolies in major industries and fields of commerce. Whether it was railroading, oil, banking, or manufacturing, the pattern was the same. A few corporations were controlling wages, prices, and supplies—destroying the free-enterprise faith in open markets and honest competition. Some of the populists on the farms followed William Jennings Bryan and insisted on the breakup of those new combinations of wealth and power. To their strength was added the progressives—middle-class reformers—who sensed a loss of the old America of family farms, established neighborhoods, village stores, and small law firms. In their eyes, the new America was a world run by crude, uneducated men with no old family ties and little respect for the traditional ways of life. Some progressives agreed with the populists—break up the corporations!—while others, like TR, saw the development of large economic units as inevitable and somewhat advantageous in the long run for society. For the latter group, the government must abandon its laissez-faire policy and take its rightful leadership role in this new economy. The personally conservative Roosevelt, though, saw across the land the rise of large number of men and women, on and off the farms and in the middle-class professions, who made their political fortunes advocating reform.[3]

The reform gospel was spread to cities as diverse as Detroit, Toledo, San Francisco, Cleveland, New York, St. Louis, and many other major urban areas of the nation. In 1902, the journalist Lincoln Steffens wrote a series of articles called "The Shame of the Cities," which rocked the placid elites and spurred on municipal reformers. In the states, a series of reform governors were taking control, the most famous being "Fighting Bob" LaFollette in Wisconsin. Throughout the Midwest and on to the West and the South, populist-progressive governors were winning elections. In New York and later New Jersey, TR and then Woodrow Wilson were riding the crest of that wave of change and unrest. The progressives, especially in the West, wanted democracy above all else. Their tools were the initiative, the referendum, and the recall—each of those devices leaving decision-making in the hands of the citizenry. Now the people, over the heads of the legislatures, could initiate legislation, vote on it in elections, and recall public officials by ballot before their terms were up. In the Rocky Mountain area, women were getting the right to vote—a movement that would sweep the nation in the next ten years. Only in the South was the democratic impulse partially thwarted by the disenfranchisement of African Americans and the inability of the populists to create a lasting poor white– African American alliance.

Several states enacted child welfare legislation and minimum wage laws for women. And five states limited the power of judges to issue injunctions aimed at labor unions and strikers. Thus, by the time Roosevelt assumed the presidency, the republic was in a progressive upheaval, and he was both a participant and a future weather vane in many of its causes. Roosevelt, though, was not a simple opportunist catching which way the wind was blowing; he was in fact a genuine conservative reformer whose national pride and delight in the strengths of the American race led him to counsel justice, demanding what he termed a "square deal" for the American people.

The Conservative Congress

Almost immediately the new president was given conservative advice on the need to continue McKinley's policies—advice that he quickly committed himself to publicly. His brother-in-law Douglas Robinson warned Roosevelt that the financial community was afraid that he might curtail the influence of business and that he should be closemouthed, conservative, and willing to keep McKinley's cabinet intact. Mark Hanna himself took the young president aside, calling him "Teddy" (to Roosevelt's disgust), and asked him to go slow and listen patiently to the right people. Roosevelt's response was instructive: "It would not be possible to get wiser advice and I shall act exactly upon it. I shall go slow."[4]

Even if the president had wanted to quicken the pace and present a strong progressive agenda, he was faced with solidly conservative Republican majorities in both houses of Congress. By 1910, the Senate was in the hands of individuals who saw themselves, and the future of their party, as bound up with the new corporate America. The main leader was Nelson W. Aldrich of Rhode Island, a multimillionaire who appropriately gave his daughter in marriage to John D. Rockefeller Jr. Aldrich believed unabashedly that the government should align itself with big business and finance, and he worked quietly behind the scenes and controlled the goings on of the upper house. His major allies, John C. Spooner of Wisconsin, Orville H. Platt of Connecticut, and William B. Allison of Iowa, were important associates in steering the Senate onto conservative paths.

In the House of Representatives, a weak speaker, David B. Henderson, was succeeded in 1903 by "Uncle Joe" Cannon—a vulgar and effective horse trader who ran that body for seven years with a strong hand. Thus the conservative alliance in Congress had a powerful braking effect on what Roosevelt could do or even chose to propose. Platt had warned his fellow Republican leaders that they had to watch Roosevelt closely—that he had a tendency to wander. They had to keep in touch or the president might work against their interests. In his first message to Congress in December 1901, the president gave a generally comforting agenda. He denounced assassins and anarchists, pushed for educational and means tests for immigrants, characterized as natural the development of large corporations, supported the tariff, and pushed for expanding foreign markets and upgrading the merchant marine. Yet in the long document, TR also wrote of some of the grave evils of many of these corporations, argued that the laws had not kept up with these economic developments, and asked for a stronger Interstate Commerce Act. He mentioned the idea of a canal connecting the Atlantic and Pacific oceans and recommended the creation of a new cabinet-level agency, the Department of Commerce and Labor.

While Congress pondered the message, the public was fed a steady diet of Roosevelt's personality. As no president in memory and probably none up to that time, TR became a "personality"—a politician whose every action seemed newsworthy and exciting. His family, his friends, his guests, his large teeth, his thick glasses, his big game hunting, and his horseback riding—all were sources of media attention and delight. In a way that Washington and Lincoln had not done and that even Jackson had avoided, TR became a very visible tribune of the people, a popular advocate whose personality seemed immediate, direct, and committed to their personal service. He furthered that impression by getting involved in a variety of interests, from patronage politics to simplified spelling, from stamp designs to foreign policy.

Yet in Congress, his support was much weaker than with the public at large. With his proposal to set up a Department of Commerce and Labor, Roosevelt ran into immediate problems, and even after a compromise with Aldrich, the bill still languished. The president then decided to openly attack John D. Rockefeller, claiming that he was masterminding the secret opposition; eventually, the bill was passed by Congress. Roosevelt then turned his attention to land reclamation, and despite Speaker Cannon's criticisms, he was able to come up with a reasonable proposal that was signed into law. With Elihu Root, his secretary of war, the president tried to gather support for a major reorganization of the armed services, but parts of the proposal went against the American tradition of decentralized control.

The main issue that faced Roosevelt was that perennial headache of presidents—the tariff. American corporations wanted to find markets for the products they were turning out in increasingly large numbers, but the Dingley Tariff, in force then, set rates so high that foreign governments were responding with high rates of their own. Farmers, of course, had historically opposed high tariffs and needed open markets for their foodstuffs as well. The major difficulty, however, was that most manufacturers sold in the domestic market and favored high rates, and those corporations were the backbone of the Republican Party.

Roosevelt was not politically committed to lowering the tariff, but he focused his attention on getting specific reductions for goods from Cuba and the Philippines in order to cement their allegiances to American foreign policy. But even those limited proposals drew strong opposition from tobacco, cane, and sugar beet farmers in the South and West. Despite the nominal support of the conservative Senate leaders in 1902, a Cuban import bill failed. After a special session of Congress, TR finally won a 20 percent reduction on Cuban products in return for a 20–40 percent reduction on American products entering Cuba. The Philippines bill, however, was unsuccessful. In general, the president used the threat of tariff reform as a way to force conservative Republican leaders to support his proposals for railroad reform instead—clearly a more important priority for him in the long run.[5]

A Square Deal

Roosevelt, then, started off with a mixed record, and major progressives were concerned about his easy willingness to compromise with the conservative leadership. Characteristically, TR was to make his progressive record, not in Congress, but outside of its corridors in two very different and very dramatic exercises of presidential leadership: the Northern Securities Company case and the anthracite coal strike.

On February 19, 1902, Roosevelt had his attorney general, Philander C. Knox, announce after little consultation or advance notice that he would file a suit under the Sherman Anti-Trust Act to dissolve the Northern Securities Company. Stock market prices tumbled, and TR found himself being pilloried for his incredible audacity, although Hanna privately admitted that even McKinley was considering such a step before his death. Northern Securities was a vast holding company that controlled three large railroads in the Northeast; the major powers behind the merger were J. P. Morgan, E. H. Harriman, James J. Hill, and the Rockefeller group.[6]

A year later, a federal court, and eventually the Supreme Court, upheld the right of the federal government to exercise oversight concerning such mergers. It was a striking victory for Roosevelt and for the progressives. What made the decision all the more remarkable was that in 1895 in a similar case, the Court had overruled the Cleveland administration's attempt to dissolve the American Sugar Refining Company. In retrospect, Roosevelt justifiably bragged, "This decision I caused to be annulled by the court that had rendered it." In the next seven years, his administration would file cases against forty-four corporations, many of them large combinations, including the "beef trusts," Standard Oil, American Tobacco Company, New Haven Railroad, and DuPont.

Although Roosevelt was not in general an advocate of breaking up corporations, his exercise of presidential power in these cases led to a popular, and then historical, image that he was the great "trustbuster." The president probably was motivated by a political need to establish clearly and convincingly his progressive credentials, and this step was one that could be taken quickly and without congressional check. Also, as an Eastern patrician, Roosevelt was genuinely disgusted by the parade of examples of new, tasteless demonstrations of wealth exhibited by the Morgans, the Harrimans, and the Rockefellers. He concluded that of all the "forms of tyranny the least attractive and the most vulgar is the tyranny of mere wealth." To Roosevelt and his class, wealth was to be used in unostentatious displays by men and women devoted to community service and good works. Their ideal was a sense of noblesse oblige, a concern of the well born for the less fortunate. The mere accumulation of wealth to the point of extravagance and, more offensively, vulgar display was simply bad taste. Like most presidents of his time, Roosevelt would have to deal with J. P. Morgan during periods of economic crisis. But he detested the feeling that Morgan treated him—the president of the United States—as an equal. As for his own concept of the office, TR later commented, "I did not usurp power, but I did greatly broaden the use of executive power." And so Roosevelt broke up the trusts, even though he would confess that the issue was federal control over all combinations engaged in interstate commerce, and not "the foolish antitrust law." Thus are legends made.[7]

The second major controversy that solidified his progressive image was the strike in May 1902 of fifty thousand anthracite coal miners in northeastern Pennsylvania. About three-fourths of the anthracite coalfields were owned by six railroads in the region, and the railroad presidents took a tough line on the strike. The strike went on through the summer, and anxious Americans wondered if the winter would see no coal and a danger of freezing in homes, schools, and businesses. A public cry was raised for arbitration, and a Roman Catholic archbishop, John Ireland, offered to mediate the dispute. The answer of the major railroad president, George F. Baer, was succinct and characteristic: "Anthracite mining is a business and not a religious, sentimental, or academic proposition." Later, Baer credited God himself with having delivered the nation's resources to the Christian men who were leading these corporations.[8]

As the situation worsened, the president avoided premature intervention. Finally, on October 3, he called the mine owners and the union to the White House and recommended a joint meeting to try to get them to reach an agreement. The owners, led by Baer, refused to even talk with the union, and Baer insisted that the president use his power to restore order by sending the army in as Cleveland had done in the Pullman strike. The owners concluded by refusing TR's request for arbitration of the issues and insisting on a complete capitulation by the union.

Roosevelt was both angered and insulted by this treatment and by what he called privately the owners' "arrogant stupidity." Bluntly, he fumed about Baer, "If it wasn't for the high office I hold, I would have taken him by the seat of the breeches and the nape of the neck and chucked him out of that window." The president decided on several courses of action. First, he asked the governor of Pennsylvania to request federal troops, which Roosevelt intended to use, not to crush the union, but to run the mines in place of the owners. Presidents had in the past, of course, used federal troops to preserve peace and order but not to actually acquire the mines. Then TR had Secretary of War Root meet with J. P. Morgan to get the financier's approval of a compromise for a five-man arbitration commission. Eventually, an expanded commission was set up and came in with a strike settlement favorable to the miners. Consequently, Roosevelt received credit for his statesmanship and assertive leadership.[9]

TR concluded that he had dealt fairly with both the workers and the owners; later he would argue that he was simply guaranteeing all people "a square deal"—a slogan that stuck to his administration. Roosevelt, of course, was not an ardent sympathizer with organized labor by any means, but he accepted the need for such combinations in the new corporate economy. In other instances, however, he used troops in Colorado and Nevada in labor disputes and was criticized by union supporters. In cases of industrial violence, TR quickly attacked such transgressions, but at the same time, he was willing to meet at the White House with Samuel Gompers and other labor leaders to solicit their views.

He exhibited the same openness when he invited the African American educator Booker T. Washington to the White House. Roosevelt had sought to establish a broader-based Republican Party in the South, and he was openly consulting Washington about patronage matters—a unique honor for an African American leader. However, a firestorm of opposition arose, especially from Southerners, about entertaining African Americans in the executive mansion. TR and Washington both refused comment on the flap, and the president remained ostentatiously warm to Washington, although he did not repeat the invitation during his terms. Personally, Roosevelt was an exponent of racial purity and the destined supremacy of the Anglo-American strain. But beyond the cobwebbed recesses of nineteenth-century thought, he was a good practical politician who liked people and reached out instinctively beyond even the confines of his own prejudices.[10]

The Big Stick

Like many presidents, Roosevelt found that foreign policy offered him greater freedom to exercise his initiative than domestic affairs. He believed, quite correctly, that the United States, like Germany and Japan, was moving toward a greater role in the world. A fervent advocate of national assertiveness and imperialism, before he left office he had shamelessly thrust the United States into new Latin American ventures, into the Pacific region, and even into Morocco. He had built up the navy, intrigued in the Panama Canal affair, and mediated the Russo-Japanese War, winning the Nobel Peace Prize for his efforts.

In his imperialist designs, Roosevelt as usual had a righteous justification for his actions—one in common with many progressives in the United States. Like much of the European ruling class, they saw the great powers as the vanguard of enlightened thought with a special civilizing mission to people of color, who often not so coincidentally lived in colonies rich in raw resources but poor in organized military and political strength. TR's first diplomatic excursion was in Venezuela, dealing with its president Cipriano Castro, whom the president found to be "an unspeakably villainous little monkey." Castro had contracted large debts for public works, and by 1901, Germany and England especially were demanding repayment. Roosevelt decided to use the occasion to reinterpret the Monroe Doctrine in a pronouncement that was termed the Roosevelt Corollary.

In July 1901, he concluded, "If any South American country misbehaves toward any European country let the European country spank it." However, the United States would not permit a European nation to permanently occupy new territory in Central America or South America. In Venezuela, the parties eventually agreed to arbitration. Roosevelt maintained later that he had threatened the Germans with sending Admiral George Dewey and his fleet to Venezuela if the kaiser did not agree to arbitration. It is a colorful story, and quite probably the president had made some such subtle threat, but the German government had already agreed to a peaceful settlement before the Roosevelt meeting.[11]

Interestingly, although TR had so insisted on arbitration in the Venezuela case, he refused to embrace it as willingly in a dispute that involved the United States and Canada. For some time, the two nations had been unable to agree on the southern boundary of Alaska, an issue that became important after the discovery of gold in the Klondike in 1896. The U.S. claim was rather strong; Roosevelt not only insisted on asserting that boundary, but he actually made secret preparations for war with a historically friendly ally. In March 1902, he instructed Root to quietly send additional troops to southern Alaska. By January 1903, Roosevelt had a change of heart and accepted an arbitration panel of six impartial jurists, three from each side. Violating the spirit of the proposal, he then went on to name Secretary of War Root, Senator Henry Cabot Lodge, and former Senator George Turner. The president informed the three Americans that they should be impartial, but they must not compromise on the principle involved—that is, his view of the appropriate boundary line. The final report of the tribunal upheld the U.S. position.

Roosevelt continued his enforcement of the Monroe Doctrine in Santo Domingo's disputes with foreign creditors as well. He had already concluded, in the case of Venezuela, that his policy "will show those Dagos that they will have to behave decently." In Santo Domingo, foreign creditors were owed $18 million, and the president grew concerned again about the possibility of foreign intervention. His solution was that the United States would push for an agreement whereby American agents would supervise customs receipts so that 45 percent of the total would go to the Dominicans and the rest to reduce foreign debts. When the Senate refused to approve the protocol with Santo Domingo, Roosevelt insisted that American agents take charge of the customhouse until the Senate concurred, which it finally did. Privately, Roosevelt concluded that the Senate was incompetent, filled with yahoos, and indifferent to the nation's honor.

In neighboring Cuba, TR's approach was equally high handed. The hero of San Juan Hill supported the American demand that the new Cuban constitution should contain provisions that guaranteed to the United States the right to intervene to protect order and prohibited Cuba from making treaties that granted special privileges to other foreign nations. In addition, Cuba was to lease Guantanamo Bay and Bahia Hondo to the Americans for $2,000 a year.[12]

Across the ocean, the United States still was in conflict with the Philippines, a nation that had been freed of Spanish rule only to find American administration substituted instead. The Filipinos waged a guerrilla war against the United States, which resulted in barbarities on both sides and led TR to conclude that American guilt was somehow balanced against the "far greater atrocity" of the natives.

To deal with the problems, President McKinley had appointed William Howard Taft as civil governor, and Taft was quite successful. At Roosevelt's insistence, he helped settle in 1902 the land claims of the Dominican and Franciscan friars in that country. As noted, TR sought to increase U.S. influence by promoting tariff reductions with the Philippines, although he was unsuccessful. In general, these and other initiatives were aimed at building American power in the world, and in the process they increased TR's visibility at home and abroad. Nowhere was this more apparent than in the Panama Canal dispute.

The Panama Canal

The dream of building a canal across a narrow strait somewhere in Central America was not a new idea that originated with Theodore Roosevelt. Americans had been talking about a canal for decades, and the French had actually tried unsuccessfully to complete the difficult task. Looking back at his behavior, Roosevelt maintained that the proceedings "were taken with the utmost care," and that his action was "carried out with the highest, finest, and nicest standards of public and governmental ethics." Years later, however, he would boast that he himself "had taken Panama."

Interest in the digging of a canal increased, especially because of the long time it took for U.S. battleships to go around Cape Horn to join the fleet near Cuba during the Spanish-American War. By the summer of 1901, in order to move ahead with the project, TR was willing to guarantee the right of neutral passage to all ships, but he insisted that the United States had to control the canal. In November, the British agreed with Roosevelt's demand, and a treaty was approved by the Senate. The major question was where the canal would be built. Two routes were being considered, the Panama region of Colombia and the isthmus in Nicaragua. Through the efforts of a French engineer and a New York lawyer, who generally worked separately, the Panama route was favored by the administration; in the end this decision resulted in endless intrigue and led to Roosevelt's controversial diplomacy.

The main objective of these two agents, Philippe Bunau-Varilla and William Nelson Cromwell, was to garner some $40 million to pay off the claims of the original French investors. Cromwell had been successful in getting the Republican presidential convention's platform in 1900 to avoid endorsing a Nicaraguan canal. Acting on behalf of his New Panama Canal Company clients, he had in fact billed the company for $60,000, which he donated to the Republican National Committee. In 1901, Bunau-Varilla approached Mark Hanna to push for the Panama route and impressed the senator with the merits of his case. In May 1901, however, the McKinley-appointed Isthmian Canal Commission recommended Nicaragua and rejected the high cost of buying out the French stockholders in the Panama venture. The price the French had asked, $109 million, was considered far too high; a $40 million estimate was advanced instead. Bunau-Varilla insisted that the Panama Canal group recognize reality and scale down its demands to the $40 million evaluation. Under Hanna's prodding, Congress passed the Spooner Act, which gave preference to building in the Panama region within a reasonable time. After that period elapsed, if no progress were made in Panama the canal would be built instead through Nicaragua.

To Roosevelt, the building of the canal and sole U.S. possession increased American power and prestige in the world. The negotiations with Colombia, though, added to Roosevelt's problems. The Colombian minister to the United States and Secretary of State Hay had agreed to a treaty, but the Colombian government argued that some duress and misrepresentation were involved. The treaty draft had provided for $10 million in gold and an annual rent to Colombia of $250,000. In addition, the United States would pay $40 million to the stockholders of the original French company. The treaty also contained serious abridgments of Colombia's sovereignty involving its own actions and territorial jurisdiction. To Roosevelt, however, the holdup was simply "those contemptible little creatures in Bogota," those "foolish and homicidal corruptionists," "these cat-rabbits" who wanted more U.S. money.

Despite American pressure and the threat of a Nicaraguan canal deal, the Colombian Congress rejected the treaty on August 12, 1903. To the agents of the French company, $40 million was in the balance. As Americans later found out, many of the old stockholders had sold out entirely their interest in the company to people whose names were never made public; what is known is that J. P. Morgan and Company was the middle-man in the transactions with the canal company. Roosevelt later wrote that the Colombian government was intransigent because it wanted some of the $40 million earmarked for the French investors. Yet one of Roosevelt's biographers, Henry F. Pringle, had concluded, "To save the money of the unidentified stockholders, whose names he did not know, Roosevelt made ready to seize Panama. He was not deterred by possible bloodshed or by the fact that the United States would violate the fundamentals of interna-tional laws. His program was formulated very quietly."

Three days before the Senate approved the treaty in March 1903, Roo-sevelt ordered Secretary of War Root to send two or three military officers to reconnoiter the coastal area in South America in case of a confrontation in the Caribbean or Gulf of Mexico. Roosevelt also received an interesting note from Professor John Bassett Moore, an expert in international relations at Columbia University in New York City, which indicated that a treaty signed in 1846 gave the United States the right of way in the isthmus of Panama.

Meanwhile Panamanians, with little love for the Colombia govern-ment, planned a secession movement, and Roosevelt, despite his early disclaimers, was aware of the plans for revolution. Both Cromwell and Bunau-Varilla were involved in the upheaval, and the Panamanians finally succeeded in pulling away from Colombian control. The Panamanians, however, were alarmed that the Colombians would send more troops to put down the revolt and urged the Americans to prevent reprisals from occurring. The Roosevelt administration conveniently insisted that the newly remembered treaty of 1846 would provide sufficient justification to assist the Panamanians. On November 2, American naval commanders were instructed to "maintain free and uninterrupted transit" in the area. After some confusion, the Panamanian revolution succeeded, and Roos-evelt got the friendly government he wanted and needed.

In his message to Congress on January 4, 1904, the president cited the Treaty of 1846 and insisted the United States was acting to preserve free transit. Actually, in the past the United States had sent troops at the re-quest of Colombia (except in one instance) to put down various uprisings. Years later, Roosevelt concluded, "I took Panama without consulting the Cabinet." And in 1911, he told a college audience, "I took the canal zone and let Congress debate, and while the debate goes on the canal does also."

When President Woodrow Wilson later concluded a treaty with Colombia that provided for an apology and $25 million for the canal,

Roosevelt was furious and his Republican associates prevented the Senate's approval. By the time of the Harding administration, though, the United States was increasingly interested in Colombia's oil reserves, and with TR dead, even his friend Henry Cabot Lodge supported forwarding the $25 million.

In another development, the *New York World* in the 1908 campaign published a series of articles that indicated that part of the $40 million payment went to Americans, including Roosevelt's brother-in-law and Taft's brother. Roosevelt, still president, was upset at the charges, claiming that all the money went to the liquidators appointed by the French government, just as he had been assured. An angry president pushed for state indictments for libel against several newspapers, including the *World*, under an 1898 law based on an earlier 1825 statute. The case rested on absurd grounds, and the government was unsuccessful. In 1908, another footnote appeared in the Panama controversy. Four years before, Cromwell had given $5,000 to the Republican campaign, but in Taft's campaign, he offered $50,000. Taft was markedly uncomfortable with the pledge, but TR admonished him, "If I were in your place, I would accept that contribution of Cromwell's with real gratitude."[13]

As TR traveled through the Midwest to California on a speech-making swing during his first term, he reflected with some melancholy that his popularity was not as high as it seemed to those around him watching the crowds. He argued he would never be reelected on his own. "They don't want it . . . Hanna and that crowd. They've finished me. I have no machine, no faction, no money." Roosevelt maintained that he could not be elected without the support of New York State, which he could not get because of past hostility toward him.

But like so many men in public life, Roosevelt was too removed from what was happening and from the hold he had on the populace. A worried TR decided to trim his sails a bit. The work of his new Bureau of Corporations did not begin until after the election. The president also continued to sidestep the troubling tariff issue. And after some hesitation, he finally dealt with postal frauds that had been uncovered and that involved the secretary of the Republican National Committee.

His 1903 tour of the country had included some public hunting trips designed to further Roosevelt's image as a great outdoorsman. In the past, the president had expressed concern that he not fail in these manly excursions, and he wanted "sure information" about where the game was. In another letter, he insisted on knowing where the mountain lion region was "in advance." And he wrote later in 1905 to a friend that it was essential that *he* kill the first bear: "This sounds selfish, but you know the kind of talk there will be in the newspapers about such a hunt, and if I go it must be a success, and the success must come to me."

In the campaign, though, Roosevelt noted that people came to "see the President as much as they would have come to see a circus." In Butte, Montana, an enthusiastic mayor ordered the waiter to pull up the shades "and let the people see the President eat." Meanwhile, Hanna had decided not to mobilize any opposition to TR's nomination. Then in February 1904, Hanna died of typhoid fever, and Roosevelt's main opponent, if there really was one, disappeared from his mind. Roosevelt easily won the nomination and triumphed over the conservative Democratic candidate, Judge Alton B. Parker, carrying all the states except those in the solid South. For reasons that are not clear, Roosevelt decided right after his victory to affirm that under no conditions would he be a candidate for another term, an honest but impulsive remark he would come to regret.

Despite their misgivings, American big business continued to fund the Republican cause. Later investigations showed that the Republican campaign received large corporate contributions from several insurance companies and that E. H. Harriman collected $200,000 and donated $50,000 himself to the party. J. P. Morgan gave $150,000 in cash, and an associate collected another $165,000. Apparently TR did not know that $125,000 in cash was contributed by Standard Oil. As best as can be estimated, over 70 percent of the more than $2 million Republican war chest had come from corporations.

A clearly delighted Roosevelt on the night before his inaugural pledged, "Tomorrow I shall come into my office in my own right. Then watch out for me." In his annual address in December 1904, the president gave the Congress a fairly conservative message filled with his usual pieties. But then the next month at a dinner of the Union League in Philadelphia, TR lectured the wealthy guests with a warning that no free people would "permanently tolerate the use of the vast power conferred by vast wealth" without some government check. William Jennings Bryan praised the president's speech, and corporate moguls must have wondered why they invested in his campaign in the first place. The Great Commoner urged Democrats to support Roosevelt's new agenda, especially the regulation of the railroads, or lose Bryan's stamp of approval.[14]

The Roosevelt Diplomacy

Roosevelt's reelection also gave him the opportunity to proceed more boldly in international affairs. A great nation required a leader who understood the realpolitik of the world, one who could position the United

States in its proper place in the sun. Before his term was up, the president was involved, to his delight, in the Russo-Japanese War, the Morocco incident, and a series of high-level contacts with the czar, the kaiser, and numerous ambassadors and ministers.

In Roosevelt's worldview, the United States was on the verge of being a major nation, and it had to be sensitive toward the balance of power not only in Europe but in the Far East as well. The great European powers were concerned about commercial opportunities in the China region, as was the United States in the past. In 1899, the United States had insisted on an Open Door policy in that nation, and now the administration wanted the United States to have the same treatment "as the most favored nation" received in China—that is, parity with the major powers engaged in commerce.

In his analysis of the Far East, Roosevelt vacillated between regarding either Russia or Japan as the greatest competitor to the United States. In 1898, he had leaned toward the Japanese as a counterweight to Russia, and he had watched as a weak China was being divided up by the major powers, with Russia curtailing U.S. and other nations' interests in Manchuria. As president, TR lamented the general lack of interest by the American public in the fate of China and his inability to press harder on American claims. Then on February 8, 1904, the Japanese attacked the Russian fleet near Port Arthur. Roosevelt had, in fact, contemplated war with Russia because of her actions in the Far East, and he welcomed Japan's attack on the czarist regime. "I was thoroughly well pleased with the Japanese victory," he confessed, "for Japan is playing our game." He even considered the possibility of aiding the Japanese and told the secretary of state he was inclined to send the Asiatic Squadron northward to bottle up the Vladivostok fleet. But by May 1905, the war was over.[15]

Roosevelt leaned toward some sort of understanding supporting a Japanese sphere of influence, but Secretary of State John Hay warned him that U.S. public opinion would not endorse any action with Britain and Japan against Russia. The president indicated in July 1905 that he had told Germany and France that the United States would side with Japan as far as was necessary to stop an alliance against that nation. Yet, just as quickly, the president wondered if the Japanese would not become "intoxicated by their victory over Russia" and then turn against the United States. He now pushed for a mediated settlement, arguing that the war would end if Japan would abandon her demands for an indemnity from Russia.

Roosevelt served as the mediator of the war, and at the Peace Conference at Portsmouth, New Hampshire, he proposed a set of terms that eventually were accepted. The president was somewhat criticized in Japan, but the international community acknowledged his skill, and he was awarded the Nobel Peace Prize. Thus it happened that one of the most belligerent of modern presidents, one of the most passionate celebrators of the virtues of war, became the advocate of sweet moderation and reasoned diplomacy.

Roosevelt's sights moved toward another troubled spot—the sands of Morocco, a region that drew the European powers into a strained conflict that prefigured the First World War. In 1880, the European powers had agreed to parity of favored treatment in Morocco and a pledge to protect foreigners there; the United States had been a part of that understanding. France, however, with its claim on Algeria, also wanted to control Morocco, and Britain eventually supported this hegemony if it received French approval of its control of Egypt. Meanwhile, Germany, in an increasingly nationalistic mood, also desired to use Morocco to flex its new muscles. The sultan in Morocco, angered by the Anglo-French agreement, turned toward Germany and even invited the kaiser for a state visit at Tangiers.

The kaiser appealed to TR to join him in affirming the principles of the Open Door doctrine in Morocco, but Roosevelt refused to commit himself to a position opposing the British and French governments. Seeing his prestige buffeted on the matter, the kaiser then advocated an international conference to settle the dispute about European interests in that region. Roosevelt, with no real diplomatic establishment in the areas, was somewhat misinformed about the intentions of the parties and was especially ignorant of secret Anglo-French understandings. Still, Roosevelt supported French control over Morocco and instructed the U.S. delegate to the Algeciras Conference, Henry White, to "keep friendly with all" and "help France get what she ought to have." In the end, France and Spain were to control Morocco, with Germany having little to show for its humiliating efforts. The results of this disagreement, though, were far more important than was apparent to the principals at the time, for the circumstances of the dispute led to more tensions among the European powers.[16]

The other foreign policy difficulty TR faced was the hostility of Japan due to the treatment of its nationals in California. Added to those feelings, some elements of Japanese society had felt that Roosevelt himself had been unfair in the Portsmouth Conference. In fact, in September 1905, anti-American riots took place in Tokyo and four U.S. churches were burned. Then, in October 1906, the San Francisco school board ruled that Japanese children were to be excluded from its public schools. The president immediately condemned the action and announced he would use federal troops if necessary to force California to honor U.S. policy. Still, the president was convinced that Japan, fresh from its victory over Russia, might become too puffed up to see his line of reasoning on how to handle this matter. So, in typical fashion, he sent the U.S. fleet halfway around the world, and when there was some talk about Congress not appropriating funds for this grandstand gesture, Roosevelt observed that current funds would not allow the navy to return! Surely, Congress could not leave it out of port in foreign seas.

Roosevelt in this period was also receiving rumors and diplomatic messages warning that Japan was preparing for war and had designs on American Pacific territories and even on California. The kaiser indicated that he had evidence that the Japanese intended to come through Mexico. As for the president, he continued to insist on Japanese rights in California, and in a secret agreement, Roosevelt promised that if San Francisco would remove its educational restrictions, he would ask Japanese leaders to stop immigrants from coming to the United States via Hawaii, Mexico, Canada, and the Canal Zone. But these understandings fell though, and race riots occurred in San Francisco in June 1907.

Arguing that the Japanese were proud and warlike, the president pushed for naval preparedness. Secretary of War Taft reported on the defense of the Philippines, Hawaii, Guam, and the Pacific coast, and the president ruefully judged the Philippines "our heel of Achilles" in case of a Japanese attack. Reviewing his order, Roosevelt wrote of the Japanese, "I am none the less anxious that they should realize that I am not afraid of them." As for the Japanese in California, the issue remained unsettled and continued to fester as a problem in the Taft and Wilson years and beyond.[17]

Thus, Roosevelt devoted his considerable energies to help project American power in a variety of ways on the world stage. But the willingness of his fellow citizens to support such an aggrandized role was limited. While there was some support for imperialist adventures, many Americans felt uncomfortable in that position. Their tradition was a different one from Europe's. Americans fought the Native Americans, annexed land, and created a system of equal states. Empires, colonies, and noncitizenship status were rather alien to most democratic leaders in the United States. Roosevelt was president too soon—he would have relished leading the nation into a war, as opposed to Woodrow Wilson, whom he despised, or his more pleasant and devious cousin, Franklin.

Reforming Society

In the middle of his second term, in 1906, Roosevelt wrote to Taft, "I do not like the social conditions at present." As he had in the past, he found fault with the arrogance and greed of the very rich, and he worried that corruption in business and politics had led to an increase in left-wing propaganda and socialist agitation. Roosevelt preached social reform, but stymied by the conservative leaders in his own party, he ended up with very limited achievements in his time in the presidency. An acute observer of American society, Roosevelt feared the rise of socialism and class unrest; being a true conservative, like Otto von Bismarck in Germany and Benjamin Disraeli in Britain, he knew that the best antidote to the left is social reforms made by the right.

Roosevelt, however, was aware that business people quickly attributed any downturn in the economy to his antitrust policies, and he warned that party divisions would lead to a Democratic victory. He continued to sidestep the tariff issue, arguing for a revision of the rates, but concluded, "It is not an issue upon which I should have any business to break with my party." Blithely in 1907, he praised the conservative Speaker of the House, Joe Cannon, by saying he had accepted for the last two years the Speaker's views on the tariff, and that his advice was "wiser than the course I had intended to follow."[18]

On the issue of the railroads, Roosevelt was more aggressive. For some time, the railroads had been under attack for their preferential treatment of some customers and for varied rate structures. The 1887 Interstate Commerce Act had been passed in response to these objections, but the law proved ineffective. Roosevelt asked Congress to strengthen the act in the area of prohibiting rebating to selected customers—a particularly radical reform, but one that was not matched by proposals from the president in other major areas that also needed regulation. In an address before the Union League Club in 1905, Roosevelt advocated a tribunal to control railroad rates as well. The railroad magnates counterattacked with a major public relations effort, but TR was helped by a report from the federal government's Bureau of Corporations outlining the business practices of Standard Oil. That study concluded that the company had benefited from secret railroad rates, and popular cries for reform soon mounted. The House of Representatives supported Roosevelt's regulation proposal, but the Senate continued to oppose any changes. After considerable jockeying, the president and the Senate agreed to a law that gave the Interstate Commerce Commission considerable oversight over the railroads. The commission was granted greater rate-making authority, but the conservative federal courts had extensive rights to review its decisions.

Roosevelt's rhetoric was more radical than his actions or than even his basic inclinations would admit. He took on the railroads and the great corporate trusts, but the results were limited. Despite his reputation as the "trustbuster," his administration initiated in eight years about half the number of actions to break up these combinations that the conservative Taft did in only one term—though one can argue that Taft would have never started his activity if TR had not come before him and shown the way.

And even though he was a critic of corporate America, Roosevelt was very uncomfortable with the new breed of journalists who were exposing evils in society, labeling them contemptuously as "muckrakers." For example, when he met Upton Sinclair, whose book *The Jungle* exposed the filthy meat-packing houses, Roosevelt cautioned, "Really, Mr. Sinclair, you *must* keep your head." Still, the president himself was not above warning the meat packers that he would release a very damaging government study of meat-packing conditions unless they told their lobbyists to support his reform proposal. Consequently, on July 1, 1906, an inspection bill passed Congress, following on the heels of the Pure Food Act, which TR had signed into law a month before.

Thus, Roosevelt was quite willing to use the forces of dissent in his own crusades, promising moderate reforms but accompanying those initiatives with powerful indictments against whatever miscreants he was taking aim at. And, of course, the president established a genuine record of accomplishment in the area of conservation, not only in his handling of public lands and resources, but also in extending the sway of the federal government as steward and in building a strong coalition to support his efforts. In his enthusiasm, Roosevelt was not afraid to stretch congressional statutes in this area to their farthest boundaries and to use executive orders to do what those statutes had not covered to his satisfaction.[19]

At times, though, Roosevelt's behavior seems mystifying and contradictory, leading to charges from his critics then, and some historians since, that he was simply a hypocrite who clothed his ambition with high-sounding pieties and hollow morality. One episode that brought considerable censure on him was a deal with J. P. Morgan in 1907. At that time, the nation was faced with serious banking problems, which threatened to upset the speculative base that ran through much of the private enterprise system in the East. When the bank crisis significantly worsened, Roosevelt was busy hunting bear in Louisiana. His secretary of treasury, George B. Cortelyou, put $25 million of government funds in national banks to stabilize the situation, and Roosevelt concurred in that step. Unfortunately, the guarantee had only a temporary calming effect, and matters quickly worsened. Especially vulnerable was the Tennessee Coal and Iron Company, whose stock had been used as guarantees for loans made by various brokerage houses. Finally, Morgan once again took a hand in the matter and offered to have U.S. Steel Corporation buy up the threatened company for $45 million. However, the wily Morgan wanted a commitment from the president that the Justice Department would not use the antitrust law to challenge the acquisition. His agents insisted on an early meeting with the president, and Roosevelt pledged, "I do not believe that any one could justly criticize me for saying that I would not feel like objecting to the purchase under the circumstances." Oddly, Roosevelt claimed he never knew nor did he want to know which company was at stake.[20]

Quickly, critics of the deal argued that TR had been duped by the Morgan interests and that the sale was a giveaway to U.S. Steel, leaving it with another $1 billion in assets purchased for only $45 million. But the president insisted then and years later that everyone benefited and that he would have been "a timid and unworthy public officer if . . . I had not acted as I did. I never had any doubt of the wisdom of my action—not a moment." Probably what contributed to the president's decision was the declining economic situation in 1907 and his reluctance to aggravate it, regardless of what benefits may have accrued to the U.S. Steel trust.

The year 1907 also witnessed Roosevelt in a nasty tiff with railroad magnate E. H. Harriman, who was active in New York State Republican Party politics. Harriman charged that Roosevelt had asked him to raise $250,000 to save the state from the Democrats and from publisher William Randolph Hearst. When the two had a falling out, mutual recriminations followed, and Harriman and TR published letters supporting their positions. Unfortunately, in one of his letters, Roosevelt had used the gratuitous remark, "You and I are practical men"—a comment that was seen as implying some special arrangements between the two.

Roosevelt's most unfortunate decision, though, came in the Brownsville incident. In early August, three companies of African American infantry troops were sent to Texas, and local white residents immediately objected to their presence. Several weeks later, one civilian was killed and a policeman wounded in an attack presumably begun by some African American soldiers. The military authorities were convinced that even if they could not find out who was specifically responsible, it had to be true that some of their soldiers were involved. The inspector general warned the men that the president had authorized that the entire battalion would be dismissed if the guilty men were not found. Roosevelt waited until after the election in 1906 and then ordered about 160 men dishonorably discharged, stripping them of their pensions and ending the careers of some individuals who had been cited for conspicuous bravery and heroism in other engagements. Congressional critics attacked Roosevelt for racism and for making an abrupt decision based on faulty information and evidence. Roosevelt, in typical fashion, continued to defend his decision, but it began to ring less and less true as time passed. Tellingly, he omitted the incident totally from his autobiography of accomplishments.[21]

As has been seen, a part of Roosevelt's appeal was his ability to seem spontaneous—a willingness to express an uncontrollable urge to comment on a variety of topics, from birth control, football, simplified spelling, coinage, pseudo-naturalist writers, to whatever else crossed his attention span. Ruefully, he once wrote to a friend in 1907 that a president should probably not go into areas outside those his office was responsible for, but he still did as the spirit moved him.[22]

By the end of his second term, Roosevelt was just approaching fifty years of age and was still filled with enthusiasm and energy. Unlike many of the presidents, he loved the job and commented, "The burdens . . . will be laid aside with a good deal of regret." As a lame duck, he faced increasing resistance in Congress and some vigorous criticism of his views, which ranged from his attacks on the judiciary to his advocacy of simplified phonetic spelling. Almost as if relieved from conventional constraints, Roosevelt turned to the political left and advocated openly a series of reforms that troubled conservative Republican leaders.

In January 1908, the president recommended an employee liability law, workmen's compensation for government employees, limitations on the judiciary's use of injunctions in labor disputes, a strengthened Interstate Commerce Commission, and restrictions on stock market practices. He attacked the "speculative folly and flagrant dishonesty of a few men of great wealth" who threatened the body politic. Then, in late December, Roosevelt unfortunately called into question the integrity of Congress after it moved to restrict the activities of the Secret Service. Rumors in Washington had spread the accusation that the White House was using the agency to collect information about important clients who frequented local brothels. That information would be used allegedly to get recalcitrant congressmen to support the administration's proposals. Whether these fears were well founded or not, Congress decided to make sure that the Secret Service could not be used for any duties except protecting the president and tracking down counterfeiters. Roosevelt angrily reacted that the legislative restrictions would only benefit "the criminal class." A furious House chastised Roosevelt for what was seen as a slur on Congress and passed a formal rebuke, which no president since Jackson had experienced.

Undaunted, Roosevelt, in 1907, nearing the end of his term, came up with a novel idea—a House of Governors—and in May 1908, the state chief executives met to consider the president's various proposals on conservation and public land usage. But it was a Roosevelt-led production, and the meetings were not well received. Thus, having barred himself from a third term, and in the full vigor of middle age, Theodore Roosevelt, surely the most publicly energetic of presidents, faced an early and unwanted retirement. His last legacy was one he would bitterly regret—his handpicked successor, William Howard Taft.

The Bully Pulpit

Evaluations of Theodore Roosevelt have varied widely—from committed progressive to opportunistic conservative, from racist politician to enlightened leader, from ineffectual president to strikingly great executive. One of Roosevelt's biographers, Henry Pringle, concluded his study with the simple observation that TR's achievements were not substantial. Another authority, John Morton Blum, has argued that some people may find that

> much in his career seems in retrospect scarcely worth the strong emotions and heated righteousness with which his speeches and letters are filled. But even when his just causes were narrowly partisan, he felt strongly. Today's insouciant critics, unlike [Stuart] Sherman, censure as quixotic adolescence or dangerous diversion the intensity of act and feeling they no longer share. Even they, however, do not find it dull.[23]

The debate about Theodore Roosevelt, however, has never revolved around the issue of dullness. On that account, he is clearly more fascinating, more varied, more personally colorful than any other man, including Jackson, who has acquired the office. But what of his judgment, his political skill, the vision he bequeathed of his office and his nation? Those are the true criteria of presidential greatness. When TR is compared with Wilson, his cousin FDR, and Lyndon B. Johnson, he is clearly not in their league as a leader of the legislative process. His accomplishments are far more modest, almost to the point of lending some weight to his critics' charge that he talked a good game but rarely delivered. What must be remembered, though, is that TR faced a much more conservative—indeed, stubbornly mossback—leadership with a cohesive tradition of standpattism. There were powerful currents of reform astir in the cities and the states, but Roosevelt, like no one before him, made progressive reform the presidential agenda. None of his predecessors—including Jefferson, Jackson, or Lincoln—so advocated liberal reforms as TR did.

And he was a genuine reformer, one committed to restoring integrity to public life and placing the government in a position as referee between the powerful interests and corporate combinations arising in the new America. Roosevelt was a man guided not by theology but by moral codes; he thought less of God than of character and good works. He was concerned with stability and public order, and he was an advocate of efficiency, the scientific method, expert advice, and good government. TR knew the world of rough-and-tumble politics, mastered its nebulous rules, and bested the lower-class bosses and socialist charmers to become one of the fastest-rising stars in American politics. Roosevelt knew the ambiguities of power, and when he compromised on principles, he still had to convince himself that he was morally justified in some way or another. At one point in his career he observed, "Public men have great temptations. They are always obliged to compromise in order to do anything at all." Yet he disliked the "malicious impracticable visionary" as much as the "vicious and cynical professional politicians," and there were elements of both types in his own personality.[24]

On one level, Roosevelt urged his fellow citizens to "live wise, brave and upright lives," to play one's "part, manfully, as a man among men." On another level, he bluntly extolled them to work, fight, and breed. Roosevelt accepted the nineteenth century's fixation on racial gradations; for him the inferior races were from Southern and Eastern Europe, and he regretted that their waves of immigration flooded the cities, debased his version of middle-class democracy, and diluted superior native American life. And yet he expected that the second and third generations of these immigrants would fit into American society and learn the virtues of self-restraint, courage, and hard work that he so prized. Roosevelt believed in the building of character, as he believed in the building of one's body, and in the enhancement of national self-determination and the aggrandizing of power to face the harshness of the real world. As America came of age, it was time for her to both seek a proper place in the sun and also assume responsibility for the fate of the family of nations.

In terms of the presidency, Roosevelt had the most articulate theory of the office of any of its incumbents. He observed, "There inheres in the Presidency more power than in any other office in any great republic or constitutional monarch of modern times." He advocated, as he said, a strong executive, and he extolled power. Roosevelt, like so many popular leaders, sensed a special bond with average Americans—"people who believed in me and trusted me and followed me." He saw himself as "the man of all others whom they wished to see President" and concluded he "was a steward of the people bound actively and affirmatively to do all he could do for the people." The president could do anything the nation required unless it was specifically forbidden by the Constitution, he insisted. Roosevelt defended his stewardship theory, concluding, "Under this interpretation of executive power I did and caused to be done many things not previously done. . . . I did not usurp power, but I did greatly broaden the use of executive power."[25]

He asserted that the new combinations of wealth and labor required giving "adequate power of control to the one sovereignty capable of exercising such power—the National Government." Many of TR's efforts were concerted and skillful attempts at building up the expertise and administrative control of that government to regulate trusts, conserve public lands, and fulfill major elements of the progressive agenda. Roosevelt did not become popular just because he identified with progressive reform; he genuinely mobilized public opinion into political channels that made such reforms possible. His record even before his ascension to the presidency was dominated by the reform impulse, characteristic of the best sentiments of his class.

It is a mistaken belief in historical inevitability that leads to the simple assumption that progressivism as a movement was so powerful it had to spill over to the presidency. The judiciary and the Congress were controlled by conservative Republicans, and if McKinley had lived, there is no evidence that he would have converted to the reform wing of the party. Why should he? The Democratic Party was not a serious threat and the last "liberal" president, if that term can be used at all, was Jackson. Bryan, with his strong Western and Southern support, was a compelling figure, but one that the Republicans regarded as their best fund-raising asset in that era. Roosevelt, then, was a fateful mistake for the party leadership; as president, he helped unleash the forces of reform, and using his personality and patronage, he put the presidency behind a generation's reform agenda. Without his presence, it is quite likely that the Republican Party would have avoided those sentiments or so compromised them that they would have had no impact on national life. And most important, TR changed the presidency and made it more of a populist, visible, and activist institution. In the end, his unvarnished ambition led Roosevelt to split the Republican Party, which he had been loyal to all his life, and resulted in the election of Woodrow Wilson, who picked up the mantle of progressive leadership. Before TR, the presidency was a national clerkship, curtailed in part as a reaction to Lincoln's wartime ascendancy and also because of the late nineteenth-century bias against using politics as a way of setting priorities in a country of rough and rampant economic development.

When Roosevelt volunteered to step down and told the world he was off to hunt lions, he left an office very different from the one he inherited. Roosevelt created an executive branch that was more visible than Jefferson would have tolerated, more popular than Washington or Grover Cleveland would have wished, and more broadly based than Lincoln's term allowed. Roosevelt was not a figurehead, a patriot king, a national clerk, or a prime minister. His model of the presidency was quite different from what had gone before, and it had an immense influence on his younger cousin, Franklin D. Roosevelt. His years marked the beginning of the Rooseveltian presidency, of an assertive executive advocating a national domestic agenda and a powerfully positioned foreign policy.

Students of history have tried to summarize his views of the office and often become confused in dealing with his complex personality. Yet TR said it best: the presidency was a "bully pulpit"—and like a secular preacher he proclaimed the gospels of good works, decent character, hard work, and social balance. His compromises may seem too easy and frequent, his rhetoric much too belligerent and often demagogic, especially when he was out of office after 1909, but Theodore Roosevelt insisted on using his positions of power to discuss the great issues of his time—as he saw them and in his own way. After all, what good was a pulpit to him if he had no message to justify his stewardship to himself and to the members of his social class, who originally insisted that gentlemen do not enter democratic politics?

Woodrow Wilson: The Progressive Agenda at Home and Across the World 7

THE ELECTION OF 1912 SAW a split in the Republican Party and led the Democrats back to control of the presidency. Freed from the postwar legacy of Reconstruction and willing to accept the mainstream of progressive reform, the Democrats nominated Woodrow Wilson, the governor of New Jersey and former president of Princeton University. In a short eighteen months, Wilson had moved from private life to the White House and, in the process, redefined his own understanding about American society and redirected his once conservative political party. The Wilson presidency was to have a profound impact on the domestic life of the American people and an even more dramatic impact on the Western world. His first term was a sparkling triumph of presidential leadership; his second term led the nation to war and left Wilson and a generation of his fellow citizens broken and disillusioned about America's role in foreign affairs. Except for Lincoln's term in office, no presidency up to that date so jarred the settled ways of Americans and so expanded the powers and potentialities of the presidency.

Born in Staunton, Virginia, into a Presbyterian minister's family, Wilson went on to become first a lawyer and then a college professor. At Princeton, he was recognized as a splendid teacher and was in his prime probably the highest paid college professor in the country. A nationally recognized scholar, Wilson criticized in his books the dominance of Congress and its committee system and pressed for a stronger executive. In this period, the late nineteenth century, the presidency was in a state of obvious decline, and Wilson's plea seemed at best novel and clearly impractical. But in his critiques, Wilson put forth a very different model of the presidency, one based more on the British prime ministership than on the tradition of either strong presidents or the recent record of weak ones.

Wilson loved Great Britain, its land, its history, its culture, and its institutions. He proposed that the American system emphasize the role of party government and make the president the chief spokesman for his party. In place of the traditional American emphasis on the separation of powers and a limited executive, Wilson advocated a fusion of Congress and the president, with the president providing a basic agenda for that party and the nation. The president was obliged, Wilson concluded, to be as big a person as he could be, and the parties had to be more responsible to public opinion and amenable to strong presidential leadership. Looking at the parties of the late nineteenth century, Wilson critically observed that the American system had no parties, no principles, no leaders.[1]

But despite his interest in national affairs and his reputation as an original thinker on the problems of government, Wilson's role remained confined to the fiercely myopic disputes and intrigues so characteristic of faculty politics. Leading a group of "young Turks" at Princeton, Wilson was offered the presidency of that institution in 1902. His objective was to take an insular and somewhat mediocre college and place it into the first rank of higher education. During most of his time in office, he was rather successful in expanding Princeton's programs and attracting splendid young faculty. Then, in a bitter controversy, Wilson proposed breaking up the exclusive undergraduate eating clubs and replacing them with college-run residential houses. Opposition mounted to both his plans and his attempt to control the site of the graduate school. Wilson adroitly transformed the campus controversy into a highly touted battle against privilege and for progressive democracy, and he took his position to the alumni nationally, receiving considerable publicity in the process. There, on a small college campus known for its love of elitism, was a president waging a battle for the principles of democracy and the causes of progressive reform everywhere. Wilson ultimately lost the battle, but he gained so much visibility that when the Democratic Party bosses in New Jersey were searching for a respectable candidate for governor, they turned to Woodrow Wilson. Wilson accepted their offer, won the election, and ungratefully repudiated the bosses. He quickly compiled a model record of progressive legislation, and in the deadlocked convention of 1912, Wilson received the Democratic nomination for president on the forty-third ballot.[2]

Setting the Progressive Course

In the twentieth century, there have been three periods of creative presidential leadership in domestic affairs: Wilson's first term, FDR's first term, and Lyndon Johnson in the 1963–1967 years. The Roosevelt reforms were largely due to the frightening consequences of the Great Depression, and Lyndon Johnson's legacy rested on the aftermath of his predecessor's assassination and his own tremendous victory in the election of 1964. What is extraordinary about Wilson's successes is that he had neither a domestic crisis nor a grandiose electoral triumph as a background. He won the presidency during fairly good economic times, in a tranquil period abroad, and by a thin plurality, having received no more votes than Bryan did in his races when he lost in a two-man contest. Yet Wilson came into office, as no president did before him, with a sense of having a very specific agenda to fulfill.

No task is more difficult for a president than to provide consistent and ongoing leadership of Congress, with that body's own sense of power and history and its organization of vested interests. But Wilson had written convincingly about the importance of providing strong executive leadership, and remarkably, he did just that. There were several factors that assisted him in compiling that record. First, Wilson decided that he would work through the Democratic Party and not try to build an ad hoc coalition of progressives in Congress. He presented a complete program and worked well with the committee chairmen. Second, the Democrats had a majority of 291 members out of 435 seats in the House in the 1913–1915 session, which increased their cohesiveness, and many of the party members were new to that body. Some 102 of the Democrats had been elected for the first time, and they looked to the president of their own party for leadership. Many of the established Democratic leaders agreed with Wilson that the future of the party depended on how well the president performed, and they were anxious to make him in turn look good. And last, the winds of progressive reform had swept through Congress as well, and even among many Southern senators there was a general willingness to use the legislative process to achieve some of the reformers' goals.

Wilson focused his attention on the tariff, and he dramatically appeared before Congress with his message. No president since John Adams had personally gone to Capitol Hill, and Wilson's appearance underscored his commitment to work with the legislative branch. The tariff question had been a perennial source of controversy in America from the beginning of the nineteenth century through this period. Lincoln and the Republicans had erected a high protective tariff, which had stayed high despite the persistent efforts of Democrats and even some Republican presidents to alter the duty schedules. Working closely with the chairman of the House Ways and Means Committee, Oscar W. Underwood, Wilson pushed through a tariff bill that cut rates from over 40 percent to 29 percent and eliminated the tariff for a variety of goods. To compensate for that loss of revenue and from the prohibition of alcohol, the administration and Congress approved an income tax.

In his dealings with the Senate, Wilson faced stiff opposition and a massive public lobbying effort directed against the bill. In another dramatic move, the president openly attacked the lobbyists for interfering with the congressional debates, and he warned that the people, unlike the powerful interests, have no lobby in Washington and were "voiceless in such matters." When several Republicans attempted to embarrass the president by calling for an investigation of his charges, the tactic backfired. The investigation clearly showed that the sugar lobby in particular was a well-heeled force willing to use its considerable influence to thwart reform. In any case, the battle for a new tariff bill, which had so stymied presidents before, showed Wilson at his progressive best. He was indeed the prime minister he had envisioned. As he wrote one recalcitrant senator from Louisiana, J. R. Thornton, "No party can ever for any length of time control the Government or serve the people which can not command the allegiance of its own minority." Wilson's principal biographer, Arthur S. Link, has concluded that "by virtue of this victory Wilson's dominance in the Democratic party was firmly established." But the tariff victory was just the beginning.[3]

Wilson's second major triumph came in a cause he himself understood only in the vaguest sense. For some time, the Senate had debated various proposals to reestablish a national banking structure. The panic of 1907 had shown many people some of the problems associated with immobile reserves and an inelastic money supply. The banking interests, through the good offices of Senator Nelson W. Aldrich, pushed for one central bank with fifteen regional branches and a capital reserve of at least $100 million. The branches would be controlled by the member banks, and the branches would elect thirty of the thirty-nine directors of the central board. It was clearly a national bank of the United States, run by and for the banking community.

But different views were emerging on the issue. In 1912, the House Banking Committee, chaired by Carter Glass of Virginia, supported a more decentralized system, and Secretary of State William Jennings Bryan pushed for government control over the whole enterprise, especially over the issuing of currency. The great populist sentiments rose up again to challenge the powerful banking interests, and critics from the Western states especially seemed to echo the old Jeffersonian fears about Hamilton's First Bank of the United States. Wilson himself cared little about the proposal and frankly admitted that he was not very knowledgeable about banking in general. But he was concerned about the effect the dispute would have on his party and on his ability to lead the nation. To make matters more difficult, his own secretary of treasury, William McAdoo, proposed another alternative—the establishment of a banking system under his department's control.[4]

Wilson was at first sympathetic to Glass's proposal, but after discussions with progressive spokesman Louis D. Brandeis, he agreed that the government must in some way control the banking system. On June 23, the president once again appeared before Congress and presented his case. He stressed public control as a basic principle but urged a common approach in working out the details. However, the populist elements in his own party, especially those in the South, demanded a more radical guarantee: they insisted on a prohibition against interlocking arrangements among banks and strong governmental control over the currency supply.

In response, Wilson pledged himself to the interlocking directorate amendment and the discounting of short-term agriculture paper, while Bryan pushed the agrarian Democrats to support the modified Glass bill. The result was impressive—the Democratic caucus voted to accept the proposal by 116 to 9. After some difficult weeks in the Senate, Wilson's support tipped the scales and the Federal Reserve Act was approved. The bill represented one of the major legislative accomplishments of Wilson's early years, and its central structure is still a part of American life. The final law provided for considerable private control, while it also gave the nation some currency elasticity and loosened the concentration of credit reserves centered in New York City. But as the Great Depression of the 1930s and the Great Recession of 2008 would show, banking and stock exchange practices were dangerously manipulative, overly speculative, and deleterious even to the most ardent free market advocate. Within the perspective of the progressive period, however, Wilson had reasonably protected the public interest and had added another triumph to his increasingly impressive record.

In the early years of his first term, though, Wilson retained many of his conservative views about the limited role of government in American life. He wavered at first on whether to exclude labor unions from the antitrust laws, although he finally agreed to honor the Democratic Party's commitment on the issue in its platform. However, farmers were less fortunate: Wilson refused to approve a special measure to grant rural credits to hard-pressed agricultural areas. And as for women's suffrage, an unsympathetic Wilson stood above the fracas, hoping the bill would die in Congress, which it did.

Wilson did support the Seamen's Bill, which gave U.S. sailors more contractual rights in dealing with shipping companies and mandated improved safety regulations. The most glaring violation of Wilson's progressive record, however, came in the field of civil rights for African Americans. Wilson opposed the appointment of a National Race Commission, watched as his postmaster general suggested resegregating federal agencies, and allowed African Americans in that department to be fired. Wilson himself wrote that he approved of "the segregation that is being attempted in several of the departments."

Under pressure from Brandeis and his progressive allies, Wilson went on to consider the question of unfair trade practices—a matter of considerable importance within the business community, especially the U.S. Chamber of Commerce. Brandeis and his supporters in Congress pushed through legislation to establish an independent regulatory agency, and Wilson, for reasons of his own, approved the legislation. His appointees to the agency were rather weak choices, however, and even Brandeis was to observe, "It was a stupid administration."

By late 1913 and into the winter and later the spring of 1914, a major recession swept through Europe and reached the United States as well. Unemployment increased, production dropped, and the president, under attack for his reform policies, began a concerted campaign to court business support. The Justice Department advised corporations on what combining arrangements or mergers would be acceptable, and the president handed over virtual control of the Federal Reserve Bank to the banking interests and business-oriented appointees.

By late 1914, Wilson was announcing the end of the New Freedom reform agenda, and the progressives were wondering if he was indeed committed to their long-standing causes. One astute progressive, Herbert Croly of the *New Republic*, bitterly concluded that Wilson had "misconceived the meaning and the task of the American progressive." He found the president a "dangerous and unsound thinker on contemporary political and social problems. He deceives himself with these phrases, but he should not be allowed to deceive progressive popular opinion." Actually, Woodrow Wilson was a conservative who adopted portions of the progressive agenda that aimed at fair play, honest business practices, and fair competition at home and abroad. He did not see his role as a social reformer or a radical activist.

His legislative skills, however, were greater than those of any president before him; his philosophy of party leadership was well thought out and highly successful. Wilson was above all a persistent and articulate advocate of his positions and a refreshing change in the seemingly leaderless Democratic Party. By the end of his first term, he had veered sharply to the left, seeking to capture the advanced wing of the progressive movement in time for reelection, and in the process once again established an incredible record of leadership. But after the first burst of domestic reform, he turned his attention to foreign affairs—first to Latin America and then to the unfolding of the Great War in Europe.[5]

Marine Diplomacy

Like so many of his Republican predecessors, Woodrow Wilson was, at first, not concerned with foreign affairs. During his academic career, he was rather uninterested in international relations and not sympathetic to European preoccupations with a balance of power. With his first secretary of state, William Jennings Bryan, Wilson adopted a moralistic view of foreign policy in which America had a special obligation to foster Christian progress and democratic movements in other countries. Wilson and Bryan's sense of commitment was so strong that it often led to crude interference in the affairs of other nations, interference that at times was as blatant as that of the most imperialist nation. Years later, some historians would argue that Wilson and Bryan used the rhetoric of Protestantism and democracy as a smoke screen behind which they promoted American power and safeguarded American corporate interests abroad. While the reforming spirit may have been used by others in such ways at that time and surely later, Wilson and Bryan were Protestant preachers on the world stage, and they seemed to have been especially influenced by the notions of stewardship and public service.

In keeping with his characteristic concerns about international fair play, Bryan was instrumental in 1913 in getting the U.S. government to withdraw from the Six-Power Consortium, which was created to float a $125 million loan to the Chinese regime. Wilson maintained that the United States "ought to help China in some better way." The American government insisted that the loan agreement was a threat to the independence of China and by the spring had pulled out of the arrangement, thus leaving China more at the mercy of European imperialist powers and the overreaching ambitions of the Japanese.

However, while the president and the secretary of state were sincerely solicitous of Chinese interests, they were less sympathetic to Japanese sensitivities. In California, strong pressure arose to prohibit Japanese ownership of land in that state. The Japanese government felt that such a move was another calculated humiliation of its nationals and of its proud heritage. Instead of insisting that California back off its jingoistic policy, Wilson actually encouraged state leaders to find a solution that would offend that foreign nation "as little as possible," while he explained that he still concurred in their general objectives. As might be expected, the California legislature moved ahead with its discriminatory legislation.

On April 19, 1913, Wilson decided to ask the state's citizens to exclude Japanese from owning land in some way that would not embarrass the federal government, and he sent Bryan off to California to reformulate its policies and work out some agreement. The secretary was not successful, and the administration then faced an angry Japanese government. Meanwhile, American military leaders became worried about the vulnerability of the Philippines to a possible Japanese attack if matters grew worse, and Wilson belatedly tried to decrease tensions between the two nations. Prolonged negotiations went on, which in the end led to no real settlement. By then, the Japanese had entered the Great War and had pushed the Germans out of Shantung Province in China, moving to consolidate their interests in Manchuria. Bryan insisted again on a reaffirmation of China's rights and stressed the treaty ties between China and the United States, thus successfully curtailing Japanese advances somewhat and helping foster a history of hostilities that eventually led to the attack on Pearl Harbor.[6]

Much more than in European affairs, Wilson gave Bryan a free hand in Latin America, and the secretary of state negotiated in 1913 and 1914 a series of thirty treaties to underscore his approach of formal conciliation processes to solve disputes. Even Britain, Italy, and France signed such documents, and Bryan regarded those agreements as the major achievement of his long public career. Theodore Roosevelt denounced the whole approach as absurd, but Bryan caught the public imagination in his quixotic search for a better world.[7]

Still, the main legacy of the Wilson years in Latin America, especially in the Caribbean, was one of extensive intrusion, involvement, and military control. In 1909, the secretary of state under Taft, Philander C. Knox, had encouraged the establishment of a conservative government in Nicaragua underwritten by American bankers. The new government there pressed on the American administration an option for a canal route through its nation's isthmus for $3 million. The Senate Democrats defeated the proposed canal treaty, and by the time Wilson came in, the Nicaraguans wanted to renegotiate the failed treaty. American business interests pushed for a draft that would allow for a canal route and also include a provision that allowed the United States to intervene in Nicaragua. Surprisingly, Bryan concurred in the draft, but again Senate Democrats refused to compromise on the intervention principle. It was finally eliminated, although intervention became the U.S. practice in that nation's affairs and left a bitter legacy that helped foster the Sandinista Marxist regime that came to power in the late 1970s. In 1912, a revolt against the conservative government was put down with the aid of twenty-seven hundred American marines, and U.S. forces stayed in that country until 1925.[8]

Some of that same philosophy guided the Wilson administration's approach toward the Dominican Republic. Unfortunately, Bryan had sent James M. Sullivan as minister to that country. Sullivan had used his good offices to further the interests of some banking friends and in the process interfered in that nation's domestic politics. Wilson finally relieved Sullivan and sought to work with the Dominican Republic's leaders to restore stability in the region. After a brief respite, fighting ensued, and Wilson sent in American marines; by 1916, the United States was essentially running that nation also.

Across the border in Haiti, the same set of events seemed to be occurring. Repeated instability in that nation led to the sending of U.S. troops, but unlike the Dominican Republic situation, the Haitian soldiers rose up against the invasion. By September 1915, Haiti became a protectorate of the United States—a step forward in Bryan's drama of putting all of the Central American republics under U.S. aegis.

Historian Arthur S. Link has generously insisted that the United States with all its heavy-handedness was still guided by a general Christian conviction of the need to help the Caribbean countries, whether they wanted to be helped or not. He concluded that Bryan honestly did try to protect the rights and interests of those foreign nations. In Cuba, for example, Bryan told the government there not to sign a loan agreement with Wall Street firms because it was not in that nation's interests. In other instances, Bryan stopped the Nicaraguan government from negotiating a loan that would have given unfair advantages to American bankers. When the Haitian government decided to give unwarranted concessions to American investors to win U.S. favors, Bryan bluntly disagreed and insisted that the American government was willing to protect Haiti from "injustice or exploitation at the hands of Americans." Bryan later went on to try to smooth over bad relations with Colombia, which went back to Theodore Roosevelt's grabbing of the Canal Zone region in 1903. Wilson and his secretary of state negotiated a treaty that constituted an apology for Roosevelt's action; as has been noted, the former president was furious, and his friends prevented ratification in the Senate. In 1921, the Senate approved a treaty that gave Colombia $25 million but no apology.[9]

Mexican Embroglio

The most serious of Wilson's early foreign policy mishaps was his misguided, but probably sincere, attempt to impose his views on what the Mexican revolution should be in that divided nation. The long history of Mexico has been scarred by foreign conquests, domestic exploitation, and the maldistribution of even the most basic necessities. Wilson and Bryan were in sympathy with the aims of the revolution, but their good intentions took little notice of the uncertain realities of that alien way of life and of the differing ways the Mexicans solved their own problems.

By the time Wilson took office, the reform regime of Francisco Madero had been overthrown, and he was murdered by one of his own generals, Victoriano Huerta. Despite considerable pressure from American financial interests to recognize the new regime, Wilson and Bryan once again had a moral litmus test that had to be satisfied. They believed that since the constitutional government had been overthrown, they could not proceed to recognize the military coup d'état. Privately, Wilson concluded to a friend, "I will not recognize a government of butchers." Publicly, he maintained that the United States would not accept the legitimacy of Latin American governments established by fraud and force. While he was reaching for justification for his actions, Wilson also became aware of the rise of anti-Huerta forces in the northern states of Coahula and Chihuahua led by Venustiano Carranza, the governor of the latter region.

As the administration watched carefully, major corporate interests in the United States that had a stake in Mexico pushed for a compromise. They urged the State Department to recognize Huerta, and they insisted that he was pledged to call an election before late October 1913. Wilson agreed and sought to effect a compromise government in Mexico. But almost from the beginning, Wilson's poorly conceived request went unheeded. Huerta saw Wilson's offer as another example of Yanqui interference, and Wilson's agent, John Lind, gave the impression of trying to bribe the Mexican government. After these unsatisfactory developments, Wilson was assured that Huerta would not be a candidate for president in the upcoming election. Just as that matter was settled, Huerta turned around and arrested 110 members of the Chamber of Deputies, thus breaking off the last connection he had with his nation's constitutional government. To Wilson's chagrin, the new British minister to Mexico, Sir Lionel Carden, backed Huerta's precipitous actions.

Wilson took the developments in Mexico as a personal affront, and he tried to get other governments to withhold recognition of the regime. As

Bryan noted, Wilson now came to see that it was "his immediate duty to require Huerta's retirement from the Mexican government and was willing to use any means necessary to do so." From November 1913 to April of the following year, the president made the Mexican question his main preoccupation. Wilson received, at first, support from Germany for his policy, but the British government proved to be the main stumbling block with its concern over Mexican oil imports. For better or worse, Wilson described his own motives—he would "teach the South American republics to elect good men." As the insurgent forces grew stronger against Huerta, Wilson became bolder. He thought about asking Congress to declare war against Mexico and wanted to blockade the ports, shut out European influence, and perhaps even send troops to the northern states in Mexico. Wilson's confidant, Colonel Edward M. House, observed in his diary that the president realized the problems he would have with some of the European powers if he moved, but "he seems ready to throw our gauntlet into the arena and declare all hands must be kept off excepting our own."

While the anti-Huerta forces were making headway, their leader Carranza warned that he did not want American troops or advice. Instead, his side needed recognition of its belligerent status and the right to transport arms from the United States. Wilson desperately wanted Huerta out, but he remained reluctant to use American troops in the civil war. As usual, destiny took a hand, and in April the Mexicans arrested the crew and paymaster of an American ship. The Mexicans quickly apologized, but Wilson used the incident to charge that American honor had been violated. The Huerta government had to salute the American flag as a part of its penance, even though the United States refused to recognize that regime as the legitimate government of Mexico.

Wilson went before Congress to stoke the fires of war, and there was talk of occupying Vera Cruz. The president asked for congressional authority to deploy the armed forces. While the legislative branch was debating the proposal, the United States learned that a German ship carrying ammunition for the Huerta regime was heading for Vera Cruz. Wilson promptly ordered the navy to occupy the port city, and by April 22, the United States controlled Vera Cruz.

Meanwhile, the Senate refused to approve a resolution giving the executive the power to send troops anywhere in Mexico to protect U.S. lives and property. Protests from left-wing and pacifist groups began to mount, and Wilson's actions seemed out of proportion to his stated objectives. Was the United States really going to war to get an apology from a government it did not recognize—or was it going to war to underscore

Wilson's insistence that Huerta was to be removed? Fortunately for the administration, Argentina, Brazil, and Chile offered to mediate the dispute. Wilson agreed with Bryan's decision to accept that offer, but once again he insisted Huerta must leave office.

In Mexico, Carranza refused to accept the mediation offer, and he pushed for a major social revolution in his homeland. In July, Huerta finally stepped down, and a month later, Carranza was in power. Soon his forces were split, and a dissident faction led by Pancho Villa, an admirer of the Americans, fought the new government. From then on, the administration's control over events disintegrated even further. By late 1914, Theodore Roosevelt was charging Wilson with having created the situation in Mexico in the first place, a mess that could only be cleaned up, in his opinion, by the use of American forces. The Catholic Church in the United States, anxious about the Catholic Church's interests in Mexico, pushed through the American hierarchy and expressions of support for American intervention from some groups of influential laypersons.

The president stalled, trying to get the two sides to stop fighting. At the same time, Wilson was faced with the presence elsewhere of German submarines threatening shipping, and he wanted no war now in Mexico. The administration recognized Carranza's government, bowing to the inevitable. Catholic leaders blasted Wilson's decision; for a while the president actually thought of publicly attacking the Church, but he finally abandoned his plan.

Villa, in turn, decided to begin a campaign of terror against U.S. interests in Mexico, hoping to point out the weaknesses of the Carranza regime and to foster a split between that government and the Americans. Wilson responded by getting the Mexican government to approve the U.S. sending the military against Villa, including the right to cross the border in hot pursuit. Led by General John J. Pershing, the Americans pursued Villa's bands some three hundred miles into Mexico. Carranza was soon faced with an uproar about foreign troops being allowed to roam the countryside, and he demanded that the U.S. forces leave. Villa continued his attacks, and Wilson was under pressure to occupy the northern states of Mexico in order to do what the Carranza regime could not: protect U.S. citizens and the state of Texas.

Events seemed to spin out of the president's control once again. The American military prepared for an invasion of Mexico, and Wilson called up one hundred thousand National Guardsmen and sent more warships toward the Mexican coastlines. Carranza insisted that U.S. troops would only be allowed to go directly north on their exit home, and spontaneous clashes between Mexican and American forces broke out as tensions increased markedly. Wilson prepared an account of the history of these events to be delivered to Congress as a spur to requesting congressional authorization to use armed force. Yet the president insisted on controlling the military's plans, and he personally opposed any war efforts, especially with the ominous events in Europe. Carranza, faced with his own internal problems and the shakiness of his regime, was equally wary. Once again, U.S. pacifist groups stirred up the supporters of progressivism against war, and they had a decisive impact on public opinion and on Wilson as well. Finally, the two governments agreed to the creation of a special commission to investigate their problems and outstanding controversies. The commission was unable to secure Carranza's final consent to its recommendations and simply concluded its work in January 1917.

Wilson, faced with a greater challenge in Europe, withdrew U.S. forces from Mexico. Despite his moralistic insistence on supporting the aspirations of the Mexican people and his genuine sympathy for the revolution, Wilson emerged in many eyes as an enemy of Mexico. However, he had courageously resisted pressures to recognize Huerta and remained true to his and Bryan's view of the progress of democratic institutions. But in the process, Wilson gave signs of the inflexibility and ineptitude that would at times characterize his dealings on a larger and more important stage.[10]

Too Proud to Fight

Since the Washington administration, the United States had insisted on freedom of the seas, and its presidents had linked national honor and esteem with the ability to trade without condition even at times of war in Europe. The Democratic Republicans, especially Jefferson and Madison, led the nation through a painful embargo and a devastating war to reassert U.S. commitments to free ships and free trade. Now a century later, another president was to come to grips with the same issue and in the process propel the United States, however reluctantly, into the ranks of the world powers.

The war at first made no sense: an Austrian archduke and his wife were assassinated, and then a series of ultimatums and misjudgments occurred, which led to a terrible, stalemated war. To Americans, it seemed like a typical European war—a continuing reminder of the benefits that the Atlantic Ocean brought with its isolation. Wilson responded by affirming American neutrality and avoiding the heavy-handedness that characterized his attempts to implant his kind of democracy in alien lands.

Both the British and the Germans skillfully employed propaganda efforts to woo the American public, but Wilson reminded his fellow patriots that the United States must be neutral in thought as well as in deed. Most Americans, like their president, probably leaned toward the Allies, but few wanted war. On August 9, 1914, the president issued his neutrality proclamation to general praise at home.

But soon the administration was faced with a quandary about the implications of neutrality. In August 1914, the French government sought a $100 million loan from J. P. Morgan and Company. The administration feared that a denial of the loan would lead foreign nations to demand large amounts of gold as payment for obligations already incurred. But Bryan and Wilson held firm—a loan would be a violation of true neutrality. However, in reality, such a policy did work to the practical disadvantage of the Allies, the main borrowers and customers of American goods before the war.

By early 1915, the United States found itself at loggerheads with the British and its great navy over the issue of the traditional freedom of the seas. The British sought to cut off basic supplies to Germany, even if those supplies came through neutral ports. Wilson countered with a proposition that, in effect, opposed the British attempt to control goods going through neutral ports and would have voided the creation of a contraband list. The British ministry refused to give up one of its major weapons in the war, and Wilson did not push them hard on the principle, as the Jeffersonians had a century before. The two governments also disagreed on whether German ships in American ports could be bought by U.S. citizens, since the British feared the establishment of German-controlled front companies.

But during those difficult times, the really important development was the German submarine. In February 1915, the Germans began a counterblockade of the British Isles, with a policy of shooting on sight suspected enemy vessels in that region. To pacify American opinion, the Germans offered to end their blockade of the British if the British would in turn end theirs and relieve what the German government insisted was "starvation" in their nation.

For Wilson and his new secretary of state, Robert Lansing, the time was ripe for a special offer to mediate the war. Wilson sent his trusted aide, Colonel Edward House, to Europe to lay the groundwork for a new peace initiative. House seemed to make some progress in England until the sinking of the British liner *Lusitania* on May 7, 1915. As the Germans proceeded with submarine attacks, Wilson clearly was disturbed. At home, there were demands from Theodore Roosevelt and his allies for a strong response to the German attacks, but the predominant public opinion was still for peace and noninvolvement. The president captured that sentiment in a speech in Philadelphia when he observed, "There is such a thing as a man being too proud to fight."

Wilson found himself buffeted on both sides, however. With support from leaders in the German American and Irish American communities, a movement to establish a U.S. embargo was gaining support. But the sinking of the *Lusitania* added to tales of German atrocities and the overall disregard by the barbaric "Hun" of human life and liberty. Then, in a peculiar turn of events, the U.S. Secret Service claimed that it had found a briefcase that contained German propaganda plans targeted at the United States.

After several sinkings and mounting American outrage, the German government gave a written pledge that, in the future, ocean liners would not be attacked without warning. For the president, the German commitment represented a substantial diplomatic victory. On the other side of the conflict, the British, who were aware of growing U.S. opposition to the arms embargo, decided to buy up enough cotton to fix the price at ten cents a pound, so as to prevent Southerners from joining with isolationist Midwest representatives in Congress. The secret agreement was officially unknown to Wilson and Lansing, according to Arthur Link. It was a private deal between the British government and several American parties, including W. P. G. Harding of the Federal Reserve Board, to get around the neutrality policy and stabilize cotton prices.

The administration was aware of a public push by the Allies to float a major loan to support the purchase of arms in the United States. In September 1915, the administration reversed itself, abandoned the policy of former secretary of state William Jennings Bryan, and allowed American lenders to underwrite, in effect, part of the Allied war effort. To the Germans, who lacked the British domination of the seas, the movement of supplies and arms from the United States to Europe clearly benefited the Allies. And the decision to lend the French and British substantial funds turned the United States into a very nonneutral neutral.

Faced with the submarine incidents in 1915 and evidence of German diplomatic intrigue, Wilson had to come to grips with a call for more military preparedness. Early in 1914, he had laughed off initial calls for more aggressive responses, and the preparedness campaign was led by major Republican politicians and their associates in influential financial and industrial circles. In July 1915, a wary Wilson asked Secretary of War Lindley Garrison and Secretary of the Navy Josephus Daniels to look at the overall situation and review U.S. military security. As might be expected, the military proposed a major buildup of U.S. naval strength, substantial increases in the regular army, and the introduction of a new Continental army in place of the National Guard. But the president himself had turned toward a more aggressive posture, partially because of the sinking of the *Lusitania* and probably out of a realization that his diplomatic efforts were unlikely to be fruitful. His old progressive coalition bitterly opposed the shift, and major segments of labor and farmer groups in the Midwest joined with traditional left-wing and pacifist organizations to demand a policy of real neutrality and nonintervention. Wilson, preoccupied with his court-ship and remarriage at the time, at first simply overlooked the growing opposition.[11]

Finally sensing the battle he was facing, Wilson took the issue to the people, and in early 1916, he traveled across the country, pleading for a stronger defense and citing the explosive situation. But the pacifist spirit was strong, and while Wilson was well received, Congress did not feel any shift of public opinion. Wilson was forced to compromise on the National Guard, dropping the idea of a Continental army and trimming back his recommendations. In the process of capitulation, his secretary of war re-signed. In the end, though, Wilson was able to double the regular army to over 11,000 officers and over 200,000 men, set up volunteer summer training camps, integrate the National Guard eventually into the federal establishment, and increase its strength within five years to 17,000 officers and 440,000 men. In the Senate, a bill for a large navy prevailed over the more modest House version, and construction was authorized for a sub-stantial increase in the number of battleships, cruisers, and especially de-stroyers and new submarines. The long-range objective, in Wilson's mind, was not simply preparedness but also eventual parity with the British navy. Congress then approved the establishment of a U.S. shipping board that could spend up to $50 million on the development of a merchant marine service, which could be attached to the navy.

Wilson accepted preparedness and made it a part of his own program, but his heart in the 1915–1916 period still lay in the desire for a diplo-matic settlement in which he hoped to play the role of world peacemaker. Colonel House explained to the French that if it appeared the Allies were losing, the United States would intervene on their side, but Wilson and Lansing were in fact working in a very different direction as they dealt with the issue of armed ships. To avoid confrontations between armed ships and German submarines, Wilson and Lansing sought to disarm the ships. The Germans were delighted at first, but Lansing backpedaled and observed that he could not insist on having the Allies accept the proposed change.

In Congress, Wilson's opponents expressed dismay at the president's alleged ineptitude. Even some of his supporters wondered if Wilson was moving the nation inadvertently toward war. The president defensively argued that he had worked for peace more than anyone else, but he still had to put down a revolt among his own usual supporters in the Congress on the issue. Now the president found himself the recipient of Republican support, as anti-German sentiment mounted.

Would Wilson insist that the Germans rescind their orders authorizing attacks against armed merchantmen? Once again, the president refused to take that step. But at the urgings of his advisers, the president demanded an end to German attacks on shipping and threatened to break off diplomatic relations if that did not occur. In April 1916, Wilson went before Congress and repeated his decision. Surprisingly, the German monarch responded by ending submarine activity in the war zone and announcing that his nation's submarines would stop and search merchant vessels before attacking.

The crisis passed, and American scrutiny focused instead on British violations of freedom of the seas and its brutal treatment of the Irish in the 1916 rebellion. Wilson had grown disgusted with the British opposition to his mediation plan, and when the British published a "blacklist" of American and Latin American companies with which their citizens could not do business, the president bitterly but privately characterized the English leaders as "poor boobs." By the fall of 1916, the U.S. ambassador to Great Britain, Walter H. Page, recorded with obvious dismay that Wilson "said to me that when the war began he and all the men he met were in hearty sympathy with the Allies; but that now the sentiment toward England had greatly changed. He saw no one who was not vexed and irritated at the arbitrary English course."[12]

The Election of 1916

Wilson was a smart enough politician to recognize that the Democratic Party was not the majority party going into the 1916 campaign. Theodore Roosevelt had gone back to the Republican fold, and major elements of the progressive and pacifist groups had been offended by the president's conversion to preparedness. Bryan was making noises about opposing Wilson's renomination in order, as he put it, to protect the nation at peace.

Then, in early 1916, Wilson made a brilliant strategic swing to the left and began to spearhead a new cycle of reforms. In the past, the president had been the major voice of conservative progressivism, of a strategy to restore fair play and honest competition in the marketplace instead of advancing the welfare state. In the process, Wilson had put on a dazzling display of presidential leadership for rather limited objectives.

In January 1916, Wilson nominated Louis D. Brandeis—a controversial progressive lawyer and the first Jewish nominee—for the Supreme Court. Senator Robert LaFollette, the symbol of Wisconsin progressivism, praised the nomination, and the president, facing intense opposition, pushed the choice through the Senate after a very tough battle. Meanwhile, Wilson completely reversed himself on extending rural credits to depressed farming areas. For two years, he had held up the proposal, but by 1916, he criticized the bill as too modest and supported a more comprehensive proposal than even the sponsors put forth.

Wilson turned his attention to workmen's compensation and put pressure on Congress to pass the Kern-McGillicuddy bill extending benefits in that area. To that achievement, he added the Keating-Owen child labor law, a proposal curtailing employment of the young that had been buried in the Senate. The president went on to reaffirm his anti-imperialist intentions by pushing for autonomy for the Philippines. For business, he supported a tariff commission and antidumping legislation and urged American corporations to combine in the export trade. For all practical purposes, the old Democratic coalition of urban machines and Southern conservatives had taken over the Progressive Party's reform platform of 1912.

As for the Republicans, they were faced with a growing resurgence of Midwest isolationist support and a repudiation of TR's bellicose foreign policy. Roosevelt sought the nomination again and urged his Progressive Party followers to disband their third party, which many did. But the GOP wanted victory, and it turned to Associate Justice Charles Evans Hughes, a well-regarded but quite independent former governor of New York with a strong record of progressive reform.

Wilson controlled his party's machinery, and at the St. Louis convention he dictated the theme: "Americanism." Flags draped the gathering, and the platform supported peace, preparedness, progressivism, and a League of Nations. Democratic orators fell all over each other to praise the president's refusal to lead the nation to war. The party's publicity directors coined a simple, but effective, slogan for Wilson: "He kept us out of war." Wilson himself never used that statement, but he did not have to. The party sent its partisans out with the message; the most effective was, of course, William Jennings Bryan, who brought his pacifist gospel to great gatherings in the Midwest and the Far West.

Hughes found that he was linked up with TR's bellicose statements, and try as he might, he could not separate his views from the threats of the old bull-moose warrior. Hughes also offended the important progressive

Republican governor Hiram Johnson of California, and he was supported too openly by German American groups and the German-language press. Also, in the middle of the campaign, Wilson confronted a railroad strike, which he was unable to settle by negotiation. The president then went to Congress asking for new authority to end the strike, in the process announcing that he supported the union's demand for an eight-hour day. Hughes at first seemed to have benefited from Wilson's actions, but in the long run, the president's leadership solidified his position with labor and the social work–oriented constituencies. Now it was Woodrow Wilson, and not Theodore Roosevelt, who was becoming the great progressive symbol and a proven leader who had refused the path to war in order to concentrate on domestic reforms.

The election was incredibly close; Wilson went to sleep believing that he had lost. But the West—most importantly, the state of California—surprisingly went Democratic. Wilson received 9,129,606 votes to Hughes's 8,538,221, and an Electoral College victory of 277 to 254. The president had carried the solid South, Maryland, Kentucky, Missouri, Oklahoma, New Hampshire, Ohio, Kansas, Nebraska, North Dakota, Montana, Wyoming, Colorado, New Mexico, Arizona, Utah, Nevada, Idaho, Washington, and California. Even the German American vote went to Wilson in Maryland, Ohio, and parts of Wisconsin; the Democrats, though, lost their traditional allies, the Catholic Irish Americans, probably because of Wilson's refusal to endorse the Easter Rebellion in Ireland and his support of the anticlerical Mexican revolution. However, the appeal of peace and reform had swept beyond the expected boundaries. The Socialist Party strength dropped by nearly half—most of those defections probably going to Wilson. The president also did well with women voters, even among Republican women in certain areas, probably because of their fear of war. In Congress, the Democrats still controlled the Senate, although by a margin of eight, and the House was divided with 213 Democrats, 217 Republicans, 2 Progressives, 1 Prohibitionist, 1 Socialist, and 1 Independent. Wilson biographer Arthur Link has concluded that it was a victory of the South and the West, of the farmers, small businesspeople, and labor elements over the large industrial, transportation, and commercial interests. Wilson won on a peace-and-reform pledge; yet within a year, he would recommend war and then give up the salutary exercises of reform.[13]

A World Made Safe for Democracy

In Europe, the terrible slaughter continued. Each side mounted frightening offensives to bring victory, but victory did not come. The British increased their economic blockade on the seas, and earned more animosity from American shipping interests. The winter of 1916–1917 saw increasing estrangement of the two English-speaking democracies. At the same time, the German government debated whether to end its self-imposed ban and move toward unrestricted submarine warfare. Wilson maintained that the American people wanted neutrality, regardless of what happened to their rights on the open sea. "I do not believe the American people would wish to go to war no matter how many Americans were lost at sea," he explained to Colonel House and Vance McCormick. And he was undoubtedly correct in his judgment of public opinion.[14]

Wilson had decided after the election to keep faith with his campaign pledge, and he insisted on sending House again to Europe to press for peace. The colonel was concerned: What if the Allies refused the offer and the United States thus moved as a consequence closer to Germany? Would France and Britain declare war on America? Wilson was clear: he would then ask the United States to go to war against them. Then, in brilliant analytical fashion, the president sat down and wrote out his views of the war. He found the causes of the war were confused, and he argued that that confusion left the positions of the neutral nations intolerable.

As the war continued, the president considered halting American bank loans to the Allied nations. Indeed, a majority of the members of the Federal Reserve Board had grown worried that the American economy was becoming too dependent on Allied spending. In the midst of these concerns, the German government announced its willingness to end the war, and Wilson followed that announcement with a public peace message. Unfortunately, it was not clear to the Americans that the German government's terms included keeping or even expanding into the important strategic areas Germany had conquered or had designs on. In addition, the German military had decided to push for a new submarine offensive in the hope of final victory, seeing this as its last chance to win a decisive and favorable end. The Allied position hardened, and the Allies informed Wilson that they intended to destroy German attempts at hegemony in Europe and would then demand reparations from the Central Powers.

At the turn of the year, Wilson moved the United States publicly to a position from which he hoped he could influence the peace. He urged a "peace without victory" and a "peace among equals," and he stressed self-determination for all nations, disarmament, and freedom of the seas. The president claimed to speak for the "silent mass of mankind" fed up with death and ruination. But events changed his ambitions, when the German government finally announced that its submarines would sink without warning any ship in a war zone running from Great Britain down the coastline toward the eastern Mediterranean. The Germans had assumed that they could defeat Great Britain before the United States could mobilize its resources and armies on the Allied side. It was a critical error, one that led the United States into war and tipped the scales against the Central Powers.

Wilson, however, still refused to abandon his role as mediator, fearing that America's entrance into the war would mean the end of "white civilization" as the world knew it. The president broke off relations with Germany but chose not to advocate war. He did not ask Congress for additional funds or push any more preparedness plans, fearing it would give the Germans cause for more belligerence. When, on February 23, several members of his own cabinet insisted that the administration protect ocean-bound commerce, the president was sharply critical. Wilson faced two major problems. The Senate Republicans were demanding that he call the new Congress into special session in order to put pressure on the executive for more bellicose action. Then his ambassador to Great Britain, Walter Page, informed him that the German foreign secretary, Arthur Zimmermann, had sent a message to the German minister in Mexico that had been intercepted. The message pledged that if the United States and Germany went to war, the imperial government would be willing to form an alliance with Mexico. If the Mexicans went to war against the Americans, the Germans would guarantee that the "lost" territories of Texas, New Mexico, and Arizona would be returned.

To complicate matters, the Russians in February–March 1917 overthrew the czar and briefly established a parliamentary government, thus reinforcing the idea that the forces of democracy were grouped on one side opposing the Central Powers' militarism and despotism. By mid-March, Wilson was deeply troubled by the choice before him. He stayed in the White House and listened as the awesome debate mounted. It was clear that the Allies were in bad shape and that the submarine campaign had severely cut into Allied and neutral shipping.

In late March, the president authorized conversations with the British admiralty about war operations and joint planning, and he called up units of the National Guard. At a critical meeting with his advisers, all of the major cabinet secretaries pressed for war. Wilson prepared to call Congress together for a declaration of war, while he confided to a friend that war would overturn the world as they knew it. One newspaperman recorded that Wilson had solemnly observed that once he led the people into war,

> they'll forget there even was such a thing as tolerance. To fight you must
> be brutal and ruthless, and the spirit of ruthless brutality will enter into the

very fiber of our national life, infecting Congress, the courts, the policeman on the beat, the man in the street. . . . He thought the Constitution
would not survive it; that free speech and the right to assembly would go.
He said a nation couldn't put its strength into a war and keep its head level;
it had never been done.

He seemed to reach out desperately for an alternative.

In the end, Wilson was not, as his critics later charged, carried away
by his own rhetoric or moved by blind and passionate idealism. Nor did
he fear that U.S. corporate interests were being significantly threatened.
To the progressives and the pacifists, the United States went into war to
save the $2 billion the bankers had lent the Allied governments. Later,
after the war, critics would charge that the American economy had been
tied to those banks and the munitions makers, and that they and the propaganda agents in foreign governments had led the nation into a war no
one wanted. Still others were to say that the American people opposed
German power and stayed out of the war only as long as it was clear that
they would be defeated by the Allies. When it became obvious that that
was not going to happen, the United States entered the war to protect the
democratic West.

Perhaps all these factors played a role in American intervention. But
central to the United States going to war was Woodrow Wilson, his judgment, his sympathies, his sense of history. Despite his pleas for strict neutrality of deed and thought, he personally favored the Allies. He was by
training and by inclination an Anglophile who was deeply concerned about
the brutal German invasion of Belgium and the killings at sea. He surely
was influenced by evidence of German intrigue against U.S. interests. But
he had initially hoped that the combatants would enter into a brokered
settlement, and he moved toward an even stricter posture of neutrality. It
was the Germans who pushed him over the line—unrestricted submarine
warfare confirmed his worst suspicions about their power and intentions
and left the president with the impossible policy of doing nothing while
his own citizens were likely to be killed on the seas.

On the evening of April 2, 1917, Woodrow Wilson went before
Congress and pronounced that there was no alternative but war. And to
explain this step, he reached for a higher moral plane. The German government was a foe of freedom-loving peoples. "The world must be made
safe for democracy," he explained—a slogan that would echo throughout
the nation and the world. In words that would give clear meaning to an
ambiguous cause, the president exclaimed:

The right is more precious than peace, and we shall fight for the things which we have always carried nearest our hearts—for democracy, for the rights of those who submit to authority to have a voice in their own Governments, for the rights and liberties of small nations, for a universal dominion of right by such a concert of free peoples as shall bring peace and safety to all nations and make the world itself at last free. To such a task we can dedicate our lives and our fortunes, everything that we are and everything that we have, with the pride of those who know that the day has come when America is privileged to spend her blood and her might for the principles that gave her birth and happiness and the peace which she has treasured. God helping her, she can do no other.

It was a brilliant statement of American idealism in a world seemingly weary with wars of national interest run by limited politicians who stayed in power by sending other people's sons to war. Now Wilson would join them in their common destiny. But the president remained troubled, troubled even at the moment many of his opponents admitted was his finest hour. Legend has it that as he left the Capitol, he spurned the applause, wondering quietly how people could cheer a speech that would send so many boys to their deaths. And when he arrived back at the White House, he sat and stared out at the darkness and cried. Quickly, Congress approved the resolution, and the nation mobilized for war—the war to end all wars, the war to make the world safe for democracy.[15]

On the Western Front

As the U.S. Congress voted to enter the conflict, the war on the western front was at a stalemate after several years of carnage. The 1914 Battle of the Marne and the resulting "race to the sea" led to the monumental destruction of armies and men on all sides. And a new type of engagement, trench warfare, entered the popular vocabulary—trenches that were sordid, stinking, filthy hovels that became the horrid destiny of the infantry and artillery forces on both sides. In the East, the Russians, who had suffered great casualties in stopping the German Gorlice-Tarnow offensive in 1915 and gained a costly victory in 1916, had finally risen up in desperation after much bloodletting and toppled the czarist government in 1917. A Social Democratic government, headed by Alexander Kerensky, pledged to continue the war, but after its disastrous campaign against the Austro-Hungarian and German forces, a determined Bolshevik regime came to power in October. In the midst of the turmoil and the war, traveling across Europe partially under German auspices, Vladimir Ilyich Lenin and several associates moved toward their destiny. Communism, the diseased ideology of the liberal West, was to be implanted in precapitalist, peasant-dominated Mother Russia, which, following the Bolshevik triumph, was rechristened the Soviet Union.[16]

Several generations of historians and countless other citizens across the globe have struggled then and now with the question of what caused the First World War. It is as if they sensed that it was too gruesome and far reaching to have come about by accident or as a consequence of the killing of the Austrian Archduke Franz Ferdinand and his wife by a Serbian nationalist on June 28, 1914. Authorities on the war still disagree, but in general there are probably four underlying causes that can be identified.

The most important was the development of a web of entangling alliances in the period following the Franco-Prussian War in 1871. As a result of that war, Germany annexed Alsace-Lorraine, and Otto von Bismarck, the Reich chancellor, created a series of alliances in order to isolate France and prevent retaliation for that humiliating loss. In 1879, Bismarck tied Germany to Austria-Hungary, and in 1882, to both Austria-Hungary and Italy. Then, in 1887, Bismarck made an agreement with czarist Russia to guarantee (with some exceptions) each other's neutrality if one of them went to war against a third party. Unfortunately, Bismarck was dismissed from office in 1890, and the kaiser did not choose to renew the so-called Reinsurance Treaty after that year. Thus Russia and France, both fearful of the newly assertive German empire, came together in their own mutual defense pact, or entente, to guard against a German attack on either one of them. Watching Germany's vigorous naval expansion, Great Britain began to be concerned and entered into a pact with its once hated enemy, France. These pacts then created a sense of mutual concern among the great powers of Europe and forced unaligned nations into one orbit or the other.

A second destabilizing factor was the rapid growth of huge national armies and armaments. The success of the Prussian armies made a profound impression throughout Europe, and those developments led to an increase in standing military forces. By 1914, the five major Continental powers had combined forces of about 3.5 million men under arms plus millions of others on reserve. Those mobilized forces led to growing public suspicions about other nations' aggressive intentions, more forceful diplomatic posturings, and a development of powerful general staffs planning for the next war. A. J. P. Taylor concluded that "the terrible time-table [for the mobilization] of the European General Staffs had far more to do with the actual outbreak of the World War than the deliberate decision of any man or Government."

A third factor that led to the outbreak of war was the rapid rise of imperialism as a way of thinking and as a way of life. The great powers coveted colonies for their cheap raw materials and monopolistic markets for manufactured goods. Economic competition grew into passionate debates over national honor, civilizing missions, and a nation's rightful "place in the sun." The result was an increase in tensions in areas of the world where conflicts between the great powers and their surrogates might break out.

Added to these dynamics was the spread of nationalism among various groups, especially in the Balkans. Nationalist unrest was not new to Europe, of course, but in this period, Russia and Austria-Hungary sought to use these destabilizing aspirations to further their own designs. Also, despite attempts by the diplomats to contain these fierce ambitions, periodic crises would break out. The most severe was in 1908, when Austria-Hungary announced that it had unilaterally chosen to annex Bosnia and Herzegovina. Under great pressure from Austria-Hungary's ally Germany, the Russians were forced to accept the annexation. With that humiliation in mind, Russia (with its ally Serbia) made preparations for war. Conflicts in Morocco and in the Balkans in 1912 further accentuated tensions among the great powers, and the size of standing armies grew.

In December 1912, a secret memo of the German general staff predicted that in the coming war with France, it "would be necessary to violate the neutrality of Belgium." By early 1914, the Russians were meeting secretly to plan for action in the straits near Constantinople and laid out plans for a military offense in the west. In general, the European chiefs of staff expected a short war, one that would favor the first nation to strike. Their model was the German wars of unification; a more appropriate model would have been the long, bloody civil war of attrition in the United States. Grant and Sherman would have been better models for military strategists than the European generals Clausewitz or Moltke.

When Archduke Franz Ferdinand, the heir to the Austro-Hungarian (or Habsburg) throne, went to the capital of Bosnia, he was aware of the threat of Serbian assassins in that region. Under the alleged instigation of the head of the intelligence division of the Serbian chief of staff, three Bosnian men volunteered to kill the archduke. To the Habsburgs, the assassinations of the archduke and his wife lent themselves to a reckoning with Serbia, and, with the support of Germany, they prepared for a local war. The Austro-Hungarian regime issued a series of ultimatums, and the Serbians surprisingly agreed to nearly all of them. But the Austrians wanted war and severed diplomatic relations with Serbia as a prelude to military engagement. Concerned about these happenings and preoccupied with the fate of Constantinople and the straits, Russia supported the Serbians. As tensions increased, the British foreign minister, Sir Edward Grey, proposed a peace conference and a mediation of the dispute. To avoid any such mediation, the Austrians declared war on Serbia on July 28 and bombarded Belgrade the next day. Meanwhile, the Russian military had been preparing for war also, and on July 29, it mobilized against the Austrians. Soon France followed Russia and the war began.

Germany's success in the war depended on rapid action, while Russia, because of her vast areas and poor transportation, needed more time for mobilization. Now the system of entangling alliances fueled the fires of war. Great Britain insisted that the neutrality of Belgium and Luxembourg must be respected, but the Germans needed to defeat France quickly, and the corridor through those small countries was the fastest way to accomplish that objective. This "brutal" invasion of Belgium was used by British leaders who wanted war to defend their empire's interests. British public opinion was treated to detailed statements on "the rape of Belgium" by the Huns. In fact, British foreign policy had been historically committed to protecting the narrow seas across from the channel and to stopping any one nation from gaining hegemony on the Continent. The British had gone to war in the past, partially for these reasons, against Louis XIV and Napoleon I. The Germans protested that "necessity knows no law" and expressed shock that Great Britain would go to war over "a scrap of paper"—its treaty obligations with Belgium. But by August, even Japan and Turkey were in the war, and it had indeed become a worldwide conflagration. In his own way, British Foreign Minister Grey correctly summarized what was happening when he grimly prophesied, "The lamps are going out all over Europe. We shall not see them lit again in our lifetimes."

Europe had known war before, but never with the mechanized barbarity that this total war brought. The casualties were so high that their count even today numbs the mind. The official statements indicate that Russian casualties reached 1.7 million men (although the true total is probably double that number); Germany lost 1.8 million, surely another underestimation; France, 1.3 million; the United Kingdom, 744,702, and the British empire, 202,000; Austro–Hungary, 1.2 million; Italy, 460,000; Turkey, 325,000, plus many more unaccounted for; and the late arriving United States, 115,660. Probably not since the Black Plague of the Middle Ages, which killed one out of every three people, had death visited so many households in Europe.

Even more stark were the casualties of the major battles of the war. A few will suffice to give a frightening sense of the carnage. On the eastern front in September 1914, the Austrian chief of staff Conrad von Hotzendorf lost 350,000 of the 900,000 men in his army near the Galicia region. At Tannenberg, the German generals Paul von Hindenberg and Erich Ludendorff in August 1914 defeated Aleksandr Samsonov's Russian armies and took 120,000 prisoners and decimated that fighting force. In September, they defeated the Russian First Army, inflicting 125,000 casualties in the battle of Masurian Lakes alone.

In the west, the first battle of Ypres resulted in the loss of 58,000 British officers and enlisted men—the virtual destruction of its regular volunteer army, which led to conscription to fill the new ranks. On the German side, the battle would be called by some "the slaughter of the children," a lament over the demise of so many young men of promise. In May 1915, at the battle of Ambers Ridge, the French suffered 100,000 casualties and the British lost 27,000, with the military results negligible. In ten days in September, the French lost another 145,000 men, achieving no military objectives at all. By March 1916, the Germans suffered the loss of 81,000 and the French 89,000 at the Battle of Verdun. After ten months, the total on both sides reached an incredible 700,000 killed and wounded. After four months at the Battle of the Somme, even more carnage resulted—415,000 British empire casualties, 195,000 French casualties, and German losses at least equal to the total of the Allied nations they opposed.

In the Balkans, the Serbian army, with thousands of old men, women, and children following, retreated through the mountain snows. Only one-quarter of the 400,000 people survived the march. After eighteen months of war, Serbia had lost over one-sixth of its total population. In June 1916, the Russian general Aleksey Brusilov attacked the Austrians in Galicia, taking 400,000 prisoners. Later in his last desperate offenses, Ludendorff's plans for victory cost the Germans over 350,000 men. And on it continued—staggering casualties for literally yards of disputed territory, incalculable civilian losses, new weapons of frightening efficiency, and the early introduction of gas warfare. It was in the midst of this expensive stalemate, this hopeless vision of death, destruction, and trench warfare, that the Yanks came to save the Old World from itself and guarantee a bright future that promised the triumph of democracy and decency.

Initially, the chiefs of the general staffs of the German and Austro-Hungarian armies had decided to attack France quickly and then turn their forces toward Russia. But in the early weeks of the war, Russian stubbornness and bravery and a series of major miscalculations by the German military leadership prevented a quick triumph and led to an eventual deadlock. After the Russians finally signed a humiliating peace treaty, the Central Powers planned to concentrate their forces and effect a major breakthrough in the west, one that would force the remaining Allies also to sue for an unfavorable peace. When the United States entered the war in April 1917, that last great offensive was not yet in the offing. By 1918, the Americans had somewhat supplemented the Allies' strength and provided supplies and munitions for their desperate war effort. Suddenly, when the Ludendorff offensives in 1918 failed, it was the German high command that contemplated surrender. An easy conclusion would be that the American fighting force made the difference. However, American participation was rather slow in coming, especially in terms of experienced warriors in the field. What the American presence did do was markedly raise the morale of the European leaders and their armed forces. After three long years of indecisive fighting against the Central Powers, the Allies now had another major power on their side—one that seemed fresh and free from much of the fatigue of the terrible trench warfare that had undone the sons of the French and British empires. As Churchill showed so ably in a later war, great campaigns are won by spirit, determination, guile, and baffling surprise, as well as by superior manpower and synchronized movements.[17]

When the United States entered the war, it had little to contribute at first but that sense of common participation. In April 1917, the army comprised 5,791 officers and 121,797 enlisted men—a total that was equal to less than half of the total casualties sustained at the 1916 Battle of the Somme. In addition, there was another semiprepared force of 181,000 men in the National Guard, about 40 percent of whom were called up to federal service.

Wilson had shown little concern initially about the state of the military; as late as 1916, he had abandoned his own secretary of war's proposal to create a Continental army. However, in one brief year, from 1917 to 1918, the American military, buttressed by new civilian agencies, created an incredible war machine of over two million men and laid out a seatrain that carried millions of pounds of foodstuffs and munitions to Europe. No one expected the Americans to mobilize so quickly, and few understood the economic and shipping capacity of that nation. As in World War II, the American contribution was not brilliant strategy or exceptional discipline in the ranks, but rather the creation of an arsenal of democracy. The imperial high command misunderstood the United States' capacities, and so would Hitler a generation later.

In a crucially important decision, the president decided to raise an army using the draft rather than volunteers. Thus, Wilson avoided the mistakes of the British government, which had relied on volunteers and their sense of adventure and glory to fill the ranks—until the debacles of 1916 made that approach unworkable. After an acrimonious debate, Congress passed the draft bill; the president signed it into law on May 18, 1917. Men were drafted by a lottery, and the president drew a capsule with a number in it to start the process. In performing his duty, Wilson wore a blindfold made from a strip of cloth from a chair that was used at the signing of the Declaration of Independence.

The armed forces began a massive building and training program, introducing many young men to a broad range of experiences that they had never seen back home. Optional life insurance made its debut; intelligence, or IQ, tests were introduced; and GIs were given lectures on moral guidance and personal hygiene. Psychologists declared that a third of the soldiers were illiterate, and half of the white and 90 percent of the African Americans were classified as "morons," supposedly having intelligence scores below the mental age of thirteen. The army revised its primitive tests; a new finding emerged as African American Northerners did better than rural whites in many cases. By January 1919, the army abandoned its testing program after complaints from officers and the general public about its efficacy and accuracy. On a lesser issue, when Wilson was asked his opinion about saluting officers, he seemed to be rather unenthusiastic about the elitist practice; his chief of staff, Peyton March, went on to celebrate its virtues and warned that the Bolsheviks had abandoned the salute just before the collapse of the Russian army.[18]

In day-to-day military matters, Wilson relied on his secretary of war, Newton D. Baker. Baker, a slightly built five-footer, had met Wilson when they were at Johns Hopkins University; he had gone on to become a reform mayor of Cleveland, Ohio. Baker was generally a pacifist by inclination and for nearly two years, from March 1916 to 1918, he allowed the War Department's decentralized and inefficient system to continue. The department was organized around a collection of virtually independent bureaus with a very weak general staff. But by the winter of 1917–1918, it became obvious to Congress, the public, and even the military (especially General John "Black Jack" Pershing, then commanding U.S. forces in Europe) that the war effort was going poorly. The mobilization effort was slack and not responsive, production was moving too slowly, and Pershing was unable to build and maintain the type of armed force that he saw as essential.

The president finally moved in and asked the astute financier and Democratic Party adviser Bernard Baruch to take over the War Industries Board, and Baker decided to call Major General Peyton C. March back from France to be chief of staff. Almost immediately, March had to deal with serious problems of shipping, training, censorship, and relations with Russia. The general staff he inherited was used to normal business hours and rarely worked nights or on Sundays. At the start of the war, the number of general staff officers was limited to nineteen; by the end of the conflict, the total personnel had jumped to 1,072. March's first order of business was how to deal with the need for additional shipping and more efficient coordination of the flow of troops and supplies to European ports.

He clashed with Pershing on the promotion appointment list and with the chief of staff's desire to rotate War Department officers with field officers in the European theater. At home, March was brusquely efficient, firing older and ineffectual bureau chiefs and pushing for a stronger centralized staff system. One of his colleagues wrote, "He took the War Department like a dog takes a cat by the neck, and he shook it."

March found himself dealing with powerful civilian boards, especially the War Industries Board headed by Baruch. In order to alleviate shipping and supply problems, March had to work directly with these wartime agencies and civilian authorities. Every Wednesday, March would meet with Baruch and the chairmen of the Shipping Board, the Shipping Control Committee, the War Trade Board, and the chief of Naval Operations to coordinate the critical movements of men and matériel.

In terms of strategy, March insisted that the American forces be concentrated on the western front and not be sent to Siberia to divert German forces on the eastern front as some were proposing. To him, Russia was a vast morass, with great problems for any nation that tried to protect and supply its far-flung troops. The best strategy was to focus U.S. efforts in the western theater. March had also previously seen the Japanese army in Manchuria, and he did not trust that nation as an ally.

Already in the war a year, the United States had yet to engage the enemy in any significant campaigns. In response to urgent Allied pleadings, March stepped up troop shipments, and the flow of men sent to Europe was double the previous highest monthly crossings. In France, General Pershing insisted on maintaining his control over all American troops, and March pushed for the rapid formation of complete divisions to give him some fighting forces overseas.

Pershing began planning to feed, house, and, most importantly, train farm boys and factory workers as soldiers. He pushed March, Baker, and Wilson for more and more troops and faster supply convoys and, on his own, committed the United States to a hundred divisions. The War Department was startled; it responded with a plan for eighty divisions, and in 1918 President Wilson agreed to that commitment. By the time of the armistice, the American Expeditionary Force was at forty-two divisions. With Wilson's support from the beginning, Pershing had insisted that the American Expeditionary Force divisions had to stay together and not be amalgamated into British or French units. The Americans were still used to a war effort that relied on individual marksmen and not machine gun saturation, and their officers had no real understanding of gas warfare. Even Pershing himself retained an affection for the horse cavalry. Adding to March's burdens and Pershing's difficulties was the chaos in French ports as they tried to handle the volume of U.S. matériel coming in and the inability of French railroads to move supplies across that nation.

Pershing's problems were compounded by the increase in venereal disease, a situation the general had confronted in the Mexican campaign where he had led U.S. troops against Pancho Villa. About one-quarter of the British soldiers had contracted variations of the disease, and Pershing found a similar problem in the American ranks. French premier Georges Clemenceau, fearing the reputed ardor of American boys present in his nation, offered to set up houses of prostitution with state-inspected prostitutes to prevent the spread of the dreaded disease. Pershing dutifully passed on the suggestion to Secretary Baker, who promptly responded that Wilson should not see the letter "or he'll stop the war."[19]

Despite their occasional disagreements, Pershing was very dependent on March. In advocating more control and professionalism, March resisted political influences in the appointment of officers, even on one occasion refusing a request from the president. His concern for efficiency and his personal bluntness incensed some congressional opponents, but March's response was clear: "You can not run a war on tact." March, though, was effective; by the summer months of 1918, the United States was sending about 9,500 soldiers a day abroad. Pershing pushed harder still, insisting that the Americans had to have one hundred divisions by July 1919, and he had the Allied leaders—Vittorio Orlando, David Lloyd George, and Georges Clemenceau—endorse that demand in a letter to President Wilson. To March, Pershing's plan was impossible; by American calculations, one hundred U.S. divisions were equivalent to two hundred European divisions, and when support and replacement troops were added, the American Expeditionary Force would reach five million men. That force would be 25 percent larger than the combined Allied armies then on the western front.

For March, it was an extraordinary request, not only in terms of raising and training soldiers, but also shipping them across the ocean and providing supplies to French ports that already could not handle the American influx. Despite Pershing's concerns that the home front was lying down on the job, March was certainly pushing ahead. He advocated that the draft age be expanded from the twenty-one to thirty age group to eighteen to forty-five, and he insisted on universal military service. Still, he argued against Pershing's proposal for one hundred divisions, and he put up strong opposition to any Siberian expedition.

But Wilson and Secretary of State Lansing began to see some military and diplomatic advantages in landing in northern Russia. The Allies apparently felt that a force in the free port of Murmansk could protect that city from the Germans, safeguard Allied war supplies, and guarantee an escape line for Czech troops en route to that region. Baker and March insisted that the United States avoid such a show of force in such a far-away theater of action. At a cabinet meeting, the general continued to oppose the venture, until Wilson recited a summary of his opposition: "You are opposed to this because you do not think Japan will limit herself to 7,000 men, and that this decision will further her schemes for territorial aggrandizement." March agreed and added that he opposed the scheme for military reasons as well. But Wilson had made up his mind and responded, "Well, we will have to take that chance."

As expected, March and Pershing were occasionally at loggerheads due to their differing perspectives. While March insisted on establishing preeminence over other segments of the military, Pershing refused to see March as his superior in any way and resented his curt tone in cables sent to his office. The chief of staff position, as originally conceived, was to be a central office and the focal point through which the president and his secretary of war controlled the army. The position was to involve vast supervisory power over line and staff officers. The trans-Atlantic war complicated matters, and Pershing was granted supreme power in France, subordinate only to the president's general command responsibilities.

Although Wilson left direct military matters to Baker and the officer staff, he was not removed from making important decisions on critical war matters. On one occasion, for example, he pointed out to March that he was disturbed to find that the current proposals "for the supplying of war needs, either directly, or indirectly, are in some instances far in excess of the productive capacity of the country." On another occasion, it was Wilson who refused to support universal military service, and he also told March he wanted American transports stopped during the influenza epidemic in the fall of 1918. March insisted that such a slack would boost German morale, and Wilson finally backed down.

At the Navy Department, Wilson had appointed a Bryan Democrat from South Carolina, Josephus Daniels, who knew little about the navy, and added to his troubles by appointing an ambitious Franklin Delano Roosevelt as his assistant. The navy still lived in the era of large battleship fleets and ignored the world of the submarine. Its leadership was distinctly anti-British, and its proposed new program was to arm merchantmen, build a 110-foot patrol boat, and use blimps to patrol bases in the Atlantic.[20]

At sea, the Germans placed more emphasis on their U-boats (*Unterseebooten*), and in the 1914–1918 period, some 5,700 Allied ships were sunk. In 1914, the Germans had downed about 300,000 tons of shipping; by 1917, it was over 6.2 million tons. To overcome the German assaults, the Allies began to use large convoys to protect shipping and facilitate the movement of men and matériel. The U.S. Navy, with its destroyers, provided the protection necessary to send the boys to Europe.

By the spring of 1918, the period of consolidation and training was over, and at last the American troops were ready for combat. And it was none too soon, as following the collapse of Russia the Germans could afford to move five hundred thousand troops to the west. Matters had worsened especially in the French army, where mutiny had broken out in 1917 and the officers initiated random executions to restore discipline. The new Allied power, Italy, found its army in even worse shape, particularly after the costly Battle of Caporetto in October 1917.

In the spring of 1918, the Germans, headed by General Ludendorff, threw dozens of trained divisions against a feeble and weary French force. The end of May seemed to show the tide was turning toward the Germans, and the route to Paris was open to the invaders. Then, at the height of the German offensives, the French high council asked for American intervention. As the Germans moved through Chateau-Thierry toward the Marne, the Allies saw a vast throng of young Americans singing, as a huge convoy spit dust down the long, winding roads. Winston Churchill observed how this first blush of Yankee youth and vigor raised French morale along the line, but the Americans were not immune from the terrible toll that had characterized each major battle. At the battle of Belleau Wood in May–June 1918, a brave Marine Corps of 8,000 was reduced by 5,183 men killed or wounded. Other costly battles at St. Mihiel, Meuse-Argonne, and the taking of Sedall followed, as Americans received a true taste of twentieth-century warfare. Then suddenly, on November 11, 1918, the war came to an abrupt end.[21]

Controlling the War Effort

During this time, Wilson had delegated considerable responsibility to Baker and Daniels and to Chief of Staff March. Because of the distance between the United States and France, the president additionally had granted Pershing great leeway to run the American military abroad as he saw fit. The reconstituted chief of staff system had speeded up the training and supplying of troops, to the astonishment of both the Allies and Germany. In the process, though, the United States had entered a total war, one in which military, economic, social, and propaganda efforts were fused under the national government. Gone forever was the war of part-time soldiers, of summer battles and winter rests, of early armistices and gentlemanly codes of war. War was to be even more a total effort of the nation-state, which led to victory or defeat.

Wilson in the First World War extended the boundaries of presidential power beyond what even Lincoln employed in the Civil War. To the vast powers of commander in chief, Wilson added important controls over the economy. One American commentator of the time, Lindsay Rogers, explained to British readers that the president in 1919 had become king, prime minister, commander in chief, party leader, economic dictator, secretary of state, and general supervisor of the administration.[22]

But as political scientist Clinton Rossiter has noted, Wilson acquired his vast power by statute and not by unilateral executive action. He chose to demand from Congress specific authority to meet the crises before him. Indeed, as Rossiter judged, "The basis of Lincoln's power was the Constitution, and he operated in spite of Congress. The basis of Wilson's power was a group of statutes, and he cooperated with Congress."[23]

Wilson, of course, did use his constitutional authority as commander in chief as well as powers delegated by Congress to further American war interests. He armed American merchant shipmen in 1917 after Congress was deadlocked due to a Senate filibuster; he established the Committee on Public Information to further U.S. propaganda efforts and combat unfavorable stories; and he set up a series of emergency agencies, most important of which was the War Industries Board.

But Congress added whole areas to his authority. The president was empowered to take over and operate the railroads and the water systems, to regulate or commandeer all ship-building facilities in the United States, to regulate and prohibit exports, to raise or conscript an army, to control transportation and the telegraph and telephone systems, to deal with resident enemy aliens, to control the foreign language press, and to redistribute functions among the executive agencies. The Lever Act of August 10, 1917, added even more statutory authority. The president could create agencies to regulate importation, manufacturing, storage, mining, and distribution of necessary goods and commodities; control the distribution of food supplies and fuels; fix wheat, coal, and coke prices; and run factories, mines, packinghouses, pipelines, and major industrial establishments deemed critical to the war effort.

Given his views about presidential leadership of Congress, Wilson was able to head off attempts to curtail his authority, such as the proposal of Senator George E. Chamberlain of Oregon in 1918 to create a war cabinet to include "three distinguished citizens of demonstrated ability" (a reference aimed at including Theodore Roosevelt), which would be set up by the president and the Senate to conduct the war effort.

To exercise his new responsibilities, the president created a series of boards headed usually by conservative businesspeople to oversee critical industries and food production. The most important were the War Industries Board, chaired by Baruch; the Fuel Administration, led by academician Harry A. Garfield; and the Food Administration, run by engineer Herbert Hoover. These boards sought through a web of "volunteer" codes and agreements to regulate industry and commerce, and resorted to price-fixing, license controls, priority regulations, and if necessary, sanctions. Hard-sell appeals to patriotism, threats of higher taxes, and sometimes strong restrictions were generally successful in persuading individuals and companies to meet the government's goals. These boards acted as extensions of the president, exercising the delegated authority given to the executive by Congress. The Overman Act in 1919 granted complete authority to the president over any administrative agency he chose to create for the successful prosecution of the war. Wilson rarely resorted to such broad power, preferring coaxing and softer methods to clear, outright coercion.

Yet the federal government did not prohibit strikes or restrain the right to change jobs. In April 1918, the National War Labor Board was created, and the War Labor Policies Board followed soon after to deal with such difficulties. The president did have the authority to seize companies to get them to cooperate with the government, and he could end draft exemptions for employees who proved to be recalcitrant. Three times during the war, Wilson took control of industries that violated War Labor Board dictates, but strikes were not curtailed, although critical public opinion led to a reduction in work stoppages.

Unlike Lincoln, Wilson refused to suspend the writ of habeas corpus and opposed military trials for sedition and espionage, arguing that they were unconstitutional. Congress, at the president's request, passed a series of laws aimed at curtailing sedition and espionage; these statutes made it a crime to aid the enemy, hinder the United States, spread false reports, and incite to disloyalty by obstructing the recruitment of soldiers. They also prohibited people from speaking, printing, writing, or publishing "any disloyal, profane, scurrilous, or abusive language" about the government, the president, the armed forces, the flag, and the Constitution, and they curtailed any language that would bring the above "into contempt, scorn, contumely, or disrespect."

Wilson delegated the administration of these laws to his zealous Department of Justice, and over two thousand indictments were made throughout the nation; about half of those charged were found guilty. Although Congress refused to approve of prior-restraint censorship, the government did use the Espionage and the Sedition acts to prosecute individuals, curtail cable traffic and foreign-language papers, and close the mails to some printed organs of opinion. In addition, although it was never approved by Congress, the Committee on Public Information, headed by George Creel, worked closely with federal authorities as it directed propaganda efforts and helped suppress critical information on military activities and what it deemed seditious activities.

By the summer of 1920, however, Congress overwhelmingly repealed sixty wartime measures that had delegated vast authority to the president. Wilson unwisely pocket-vetoed the repeal attempt, and the Republicans in the election attacked "the executive dictatorship." The Supreme Court during this period did uphold the vast extension of the war powers of the president; only in 1923, for example, did it end rent controls in Washington, D.C., arguing that the emergency was over.[24]

It is interesting to compare Wilson's activities with those of his two allies: David Lloyd George, the able, charismatic British prime minister, and France's Georges Clemenceau. Lloyd George, who took over the flagging war effort from Prime Minister H. H. Asquith on December 1916, was an artful manipulator, a brilliant orator, and a person given to high purpose and cheap intrigue—a successful combination for most politicians. In comparison to Asquith with his collegial and lackluster style, Lloyd George was a dynamic and hardworking leader. He was, in the words of one observer, the real British war cabinet himself.

As prime minister, Lloyd George used the war cabinet, made up of five people, to coordinate and centralize the whole war effort. He met almost daily with the new cabinet, and that group in turn was informed by a collection of ad hoc and standing committees served by a variety of ministers and specialists. Only the Foreign Office, under Lloyd George's close personal supervision, seemed outside this orbit. The war cabinet reported directly to the prime minister, who set the agenda of cabinet business and was assisted by a cabinet secretariat. He was also aided by a personal circle of associates (which was seen as the equivalent of American presidents' so-called kitchen cabinet) called the "garden suburb," originally housed in huts in the garden of the prime minister's residence at Number 10 Downing Street. In addition, Lloyd George created in March 1917 an imperial war cabinet under his chairmanship, which was used mostly in preparing for the postwar peace conference in autumn 1918.

Lloyd George accumulated vast personal and political power through these interlocking agencies and even sought to impose his control over land and naval war strategy. In 1917, he forced and won a confrontation with the First Sea Lord John Jellicoe to establish convoys to deter U-boats. He was even willing to use the French to conspire against British military leaders on the issue of a unified military command. By early 1918, he challenged his own chief of staff and finally extended his control over military policy as well. Although he lacked a true parliamentary majority in the House of Commons, as Churchill would have during World War II, Lloyd George ruled by the sheer sway of his personality. He was also involved in the details of domestic policy, from the fixing of wheat prices to the duty placed on gloves. His ascendancy continued throughout the war, the peace negotiations, and beyond until October 1922. The *London Times* was to call it "the greatest experiment in political improvisation which Great Britain had ever known."

In France, the seventy-six-year-old Georges Clemenceau, a former radical journalist and longtime parliamentarian, took over in November 1917 amid increasing disillusionment in the Allied ranks over the stalemate. Like Lloyd George, Clemenceau was a master of intrigue and was committed to action and victory over the Central Powers. He recast the cabinet with six departments—navy, foreign affairs, armament, blockade, finance, and war—and he emphasized greater civilian and military cooperation. Clemenceau kept the critical war minister post for himself. Of his predecessors, he said, "Nice fellas. They had only one fault. They were too decent. They weren't meant for war." In addition to his cabinet, he also had a group of more intimate associates, a "cabinet of reference," as it was called. Clemenceau purged the army of old and inept officers, opened up the military promotion lists to new men, and spread his influence over the "departements" and prefects. He skillfully used U.S. aid and intervention at the end of 1917 to revive French morale and pushed for a joint Allied command under the direction of the French general staff. Clemenceau was a strong advocate of a Supreme War Council of the Allied Powers, although deep down he trusted neither his allies nor his own generals. The public at first called him affectionately *Pere-la-victoire*; the infantry, however, respectfully labeled him "The Tiger."

By 1917–1918, as Wilson assumed responsibility for U.S. entrance into the war, the Allies were weary and disillusioned by the carnage and stalemate on the western front. They turned to political radicals and veteran parliamentarians who were pledged to the aggressive pursuit of victory and to new strategies; later, some were to say that European leaders acted like American wartime presidents. But in the United States with its shorter war effort, Wilson approved a network of national planning agencies to wage that war and to redirect domestic life in ways unprecedented in American history.

The same phenomenon was taking place under the German industrialist Walther Rathenau, who created for the Wilhelmine Empire a system for the distribution and manufacturing of war materials. Rathenau was supposed to have said that all he learned about planned economies he learned from his father, who was managing director of the German Electric Company. In April 1914, Rathenau was granted extensive powers, and the War Raw Materials Department was established to deal with conservation, production of substitute materials, and planned distribution. By the end of the year, his control extended over critical materials such as metals, wool, and timber. The war agencies were tightening the ties between the Reich and business, with more emphasis being placed on price controls and manpower distribution. Toward the end of the war, Rathenau exercised vast powers under the military dictatorship that had taken over control of the Reich from the emperor. His position was a forerunner to Albert Speer's similar role in Hitler's regime. Thus, the war had not only changed the nature of the military, but it also deeply affected the home front and taught a new generation of leaders on both sides of the Atlantic how to use the government to control economic and social life.

The Battle for a Peace

Wilson had played a greater role in tipping the scales toward war than any other president in American history. No one at the time realized the consequences of that conflict. At one point, the president had been concerned about the future of "white civilization," as he certainly should have been, for the war ended the naive notions of progress and the inevitable advance of Western civilization. The vast losses from the war created legions of grieving parents, young widows, and prematurely old men. The war and its aftermath upset forever the patterns of deference and class structures that went back even to the Middle Ages in some nations. The war had stripped away the illusions of life, fostered a horrendous mechanization of conflict, and unleashed right-wing and left-wing extremist movements.[25]

It is hard to say that the sacrifices of the war were worth it. The world of 1930 was far worse than that of 1910. The way was paved for weak democracies and the rise of Mussolini, Hitler, Lenin, and later Stalin in the west. Without these severe dislocations, rampant fear, and economic disintegration, the twin evils of fascism and communism would probably be esoteric ideologies confined to beer-hall riffraff and eccentric professors living in shabby flats in Europe. Instead, they became the moving forces that challenged representative governments and gave the world genocidal ventures, gulags, and an even worse Second World War.

But by 1919, the task facing Wilson was a far different one. He was sworn to transform the vague, stirring rhetoric of his speeches into a foreign policy of reconstruction and forgiveness. Like Lincoln, he promised reconciliation; like Lincoln, he favored a reconstruction based on new institutions. But unlike Lincoln, he would live to see his ideas fail, rather than bequeath them to a luckless successor.

Presidents, like the people they lead, are given to emotional judgments and are obsessed about the terrible toll that war takes. Men such as Wilson and Lincoln were not Caesars and Napoleons; they were sharply affected by the carnage around them. Lincoln turned a civil war into a quasi-religious referendum about liberty, and in the process he raised the moral stakes by ending slavery forever. His actions have been seen as a shrewd calculation aimed at appeasing British public opinion and recognizing the growing number of African American troops in the Union army. Perhaps it was a political judgment. Yet in a larger sense he seemed to have consecrated the Union cause, almost as a response to the terrible toll he played a part in exacting.

So Woodrow Wilson, this principled, moralistic son of a minister, reacted similarly after the First World War. Before America's entry into France, Wilson had found the war to be confusing, its causes unclear, and the hope for a stalemate acceptable. But as he experienced the carnage, as he also led the nation into war and its sons to death and dismemberment, Wilson cast the conflict into a far different light. His plea to make the world safe for democracy was not a slogan meant simply for the masses. He surely believed that he was God's instrument to bring about a different world order. He was not alone in that belief; throughout Europe, Wilson was received at first with an awe very different than that reserved for the other victorious Allied leaders. In homes across the ocean, American observers were startled to find over peasant hearths two pictures: Jesus Christ and Woodrow Wilson.[26]

It is too easy to dismiss Wilson as a man who failed; it cannot be denied that he established a hold over large segments of the public imagination. In a mystical way, they seemed to agree with him that young boys should not go to an early death and ancient nations not be ravished of their history and treasure just to reestablish some balance of power among Western imperialistic states. And so, with peace at hand, with famine threatening Europe, Woodrow Wilson sailed from America, not as a triumphant victor, but as a prophet in his own time.

The Versailles Settlement

For several years, Wilson had thought about the type of peace that must be guaranteed—a peace without victory, he called it. To the European leaders who had been involved in the war for thirty-two months longer, the attractiveness of retribution, territory, and even vengeance were much stronger. They could not go back to their nations with what appeared a status quo ante, and they were less willing than Wilson to speak about the legitimate role that Germany could play in Europe. France was deeply troubled as long as it faced a large and powerful Germany, and Britain opposed German hegemony on the Continent and on the seas, since it threatened its own Royal Navy and might compromise the empire. Italy, allied before the war with the Central Powers, had switched sides in May 1915 and was belligerently demanding at the peace conference not only the cities of Trieste and Trentino but also the port of Fiume and other major concessions from Austria-Hungary.

To many people, these European diplomats schooled in the Old World traditions of balance of power and imperial aggrandizement represented the very reasons why the war broke out in the first place. They had sanctioned unsteady and overreaching alliances, played havoc with nationalities, and used patriotism as the cover for national ambition. This age-old game with its cool air of cynicism and hauteur still dominated the European elites. To these diplomats and politicians, Wilson was naive and unrealistic, a moralistic man who did not understand the basis of world politics as it must be played. It has become commonplace in the United States to accept that judgment and to draw from it the bitter lesson that world politics is best devoid of idealism, that it is best rooted in an acceptance of the cynical assumptions of realpolitik. Yet these very practitioners of such a "realistic" worldview and their colleagues led Europe into a series of wars and mis-calculations that culminated in the devastating conflicts of 1914–1919 and the even more horrendous conflagrations of 1939–1945.[27]

Wilson's basic peace proposals were in one sense an accumulation of ideas that had been surfacing in different nations over the years, which reflected the great humanitarian traditions of Western civilization. On both sides of the Atlantic, liberals repudiated the old gospel of the balance of power, of elite secret diplomacy, and of shifting alliances drawn up by bewildered politicians and unsteady monarchies. In their place, they pro-posed an international organization charged with peacekeeping that would make agreements in public. They saw the large military establishments as one of the causes of tension and not just a consequence of that tension, and they supported the creation of a League of Nations to enforce the peace. These proposals were to be included in the early Wilson platform, as he embarked for Europe. The American president came to Versailles not as a victor in search of spoils or as a conqueror ready to inflict retribution but as the most forward-looking liberal on the world stage. He recognized his unique role, and so did the Allied leaders, who were to lock horns with him.

Perhaps for this reason, Wilson had kept from the beginning some distance between himself and the others during their common war. He called the United States an "associate" in the struggle to defeat the Central Powers and not an ally. He knew many but not all of the provisions of the secret agreements that the Allied leaders had consummated and refused to acknowledge them as binding on his nation. Even during the early stages of the war effort, Wilson tried to exert pressure on the Austro-Hungarian nation to withdraw from the war by promising that the Allies would not dismember the empire but would allow it to continue if it were trans-formed into a federation. Remarkably, he tried the same approach with the Germans in December 1917, saying that the United States did not desire to interfere in their internal politics nor to threaten the existence and in-dependence of the German empire. As for the Allies, they were growing increasingly dependent on the United States, and Wilson judged that they would be "financially in our hands."[28]

In September 1917, he had Colonel House call together a group of experts called "The Inquiry" to look at the war aims of the nations and spell out U.S. objectives. As a consequence, Wilson laid out publicly his famous Fourteen Points, which included general principles and particular dispositions on difficult territorial issues. Overall, the speech promised open covenants, freedom of the seas, general disarmament, removal of trade barriers, impartial settlement of colonial claims, and a League of Nations. Wilson also included the independence of Belgium, self-determination for Russia, the evacuation of French territory and the return to it of Alsace-Lorraine, autonomy for the minority nationalities in the Austro-Hungarian empire, a readjustment of Italy's borders, self-determination in the Balkans, autonomy for subjects of the Ottoman Empire, free access through the Dardanelles, and the guarantee of an independent Poland with access to the sea.

To the Germans, Wilson promised a "place of equality among the peoples of the world." But by March 1918, the Germans had taken advantage of the Bolsheviks' weariness and forced upon them a vindictive peace treaty. Wilson realized that moderate civilians were not in charge in Germany and that the war was not going to end as he had hoped. His response was clear: "Force, Force to the utmost, Force without stint or limit, the righteous and triumphant Force which shall make Right the law of the world, and cast every selfish dominion down in the dust."[29]

To Clemenceau, Wilson's intentions for a moderate peace were unrealistic from the start. He sarcastically remarked that God had given mankind ten commandments and they were broken; Wilson had given the world fourteen points—"We shall see." The French leader's intention was to prevent the rise of a strong Germany again. Having seen defeat in the Franco-Prussian war in 1870 and the horrendous losses in the First World War, Clemenceau agreed with Marshal Ferdinand Foch that the west bank of the Rhine had to be stripped from Germany, that in its place there would be one or more Rhenish republics under French control, and that his nation would also permanently govern the Rhineland. Under tremendous pressure from Wilson and objections from British Prime Minister Lloyd George, Clemenceau had to back down and accept instead a fifteen-year occupation of that region and a mutual defense treaty with the United States and Great Britain if Germany attacked France again. These concessions, bitterly negotiated, saved the peace conference from total collapse, but they also forced Wilson to give in on other points about which he felt strongly.

The second major issue was the question of reparations and indemnities. Lloyd George and Clemenceau pushed for Germany to be liable for the total costs of the war. Wilson recognized the enormous weight of British and French public opinion on the issue and had to give some ground. Germany was thus forced to pay the cost of disability pensions to

Allied veterans and their families, to cover Allied war losses incurred by civilians, and also to accept the seizure of $5 billion of German property, French ownership of the coal mines in the Saar Valley, and the occupation of the Saar for twenty years. The French also had the right to occupy the Rhineland beyond the fifteen-year limit if the German government did not pay the reparations on time. The terms seemed harsh even at that time, and Hitler later would use those provisions to inflame German opinion a generation after the treaty was signed. One observer, the British economist John Maynard Keynes, argued that the terms of the treaty were impossible for the Germans to meet. But more recent analysis shows that while the terms were steep, the Germans at the time did have the ability to meet these obligations and that Hitler himself spent many times more money in rearming Germany in the 1930s.

The third issue Wilson had to face was the future of Germany's colonies. His position was clear: they would be supervised by small nations acting under the League of Nations' stewardship. The British and their allies in the empire and Japan insisted on annexation instead. In the end, Wilson won and a mandate system was created—the first major international blow against colonialism, a development that accelerated after World War II. In terms of Japan, Wilson had an even more difficult time, especially concerning the Shantung Province in China, where the Imperial Japanese Army had defeated the Germans in 1915 and taken control. Wilson argued passionately for self-determination, and although he was forced to compromise on the issue, the Japanese ultimately granted China full sovereignty in the province.

One of Wilson's bitterest disputes, though, was closer to home with the desire of Italian Prime Minister Vittorio Orlando to take the port of Fiume as well as Trentino and Trieste. After a long contest of wills, the Italians gave in on their plans to control the Adriatic Sea. As the conference continued, Wilson and Lloyd George insisted on creating an international port at Danzig and allowing the people of Upper Silesia to determine how their land should be partitioned between Poland and Germany. As for the Austro-Hungarian empire, that old regime broke up into several nation-states, ending the alternative of federation proposed by Wilson, among others.

The great difficulty left was Russia, and here too Wilson insisted on self-determination. He opposed the Allies' plans for intervention to topple the Bolsheviks and was willing to send American troops only for very limited purposes, and only for a brief time, to Archangel and Vladivostok. He told Churchill that Allied troops had to leave Russia, and while he

distrusted the Lenin government, Wilson seemed to remember the difficult lessons he had learned in Mexico about the limitations of using armed
forces in civil wars.

Above all, Woodrow Wilson achieved his objective of creating a
League of Nations. The League was composed of an international assembly
in which all member states were represented and an executive council in
which the great powers with some of the other states would sit. There was
also an international court and a secretariat and various commissions. The
critical article in the League charter was the first one, which guaranteed
collective protection against aggression.

Wilson's work was done, and he sailed home to a mounting controversy about the new treaty and the role of the United States in the
world. It has become standard historical judgment to say that Wilson
failed at Versailles, and in the sense that he could not establish a true
peace without making major concessions to the victors, perhaps he did.
The Germans called it a "diktat," a dictated peace. But considering their
demands at Brest-Litovsk after the Russian surrender, it is hard to press
a sympathetic case. In fact, Wilson had protected German interests even
more than they had a right to expect or probably deserved. Historian
Arthur Link concluded that the president fought tenaciously and elo-
quently, was more prepared for the conference than his counterparts, and
was the wisest of the Big Four leaders. He was not outfoxed by the Old
World diplomats or overwhelmed by their skill or insight. In fact, the
president assumed a task that no one, even a leader of his considerable
talents, could totally succeed at. He sought to change the whole character
of the nation-state system, to challenge the alliance and balance of power
mentality, and to insist on a magnanimous settlement to nations that had
exerted themselves for nearly a full three years before America's entrance
into the war.[30]

By the time of Versailles, Wilson lacked much leverage over the Allies,
for the Germans and the Austrian forces were totally routed, and the war
was done. The Allies also knew that Wilson's political base was eroding
at home. Yet the president did bring back a comprehensive treaty that
restored Belgium and Alsace-Lorraine, created an independent Poland,
recognized the demands for self-determination in the Balkan and Central
European corridors, and established an international League as he promised. In 1926, Germany was admitted to the League of Nations, and in
the decade that followed the war, naval disarmament was prominently accepted in the West. Wilson had muted the demands for vengeance more
than the Germans had realized. If one looks at their harsh treaty at Brest-

Litovsk and compares it with Versailles, one can perhaps get an idea of what a difference a Woodrow Wilson can make.

The Battle for the Treaty

Wilson's return home and his abortive fight for the treaty and the League of Nations is frequently portrayed as the final act in a dramatic classical tragedy. The president, who was facing the hostility of narrow-minded partisans in the Senate, took his case to the people, suffered a debilitating stroke from the exertion, refused final compromise, and lived out his remaining years in stoic calm. Historians have looked to his early character and to his battles at Princeton for clues to his final demise. Others have cited his long history of illnesses—illnesses that he overcame—and have postulated that his alleged rigidity in Paris and in the League fight was due to physiological causes.[31]

Yet a closer examination shows that Wilson, while making some serious mistakes, followed a course of behavior that was quite logical. Once again, as in Paris, he took on immense burdens of leadership, burdens that even he could not carry alone. One mistake was the president's appeal on October 25, 1918, for the election of a Democratic Congress—an action perfectly in keeping with his conception of being a sort of prime minister, but one that deprived him of the nonpartisan mantle of chief of state he had assumed so successfully during most of the war. Still, he lost twenty-one House seats and in the 1942 election a noncampaigning FDR lost forty seats; in the Senate, Wilson had six fewer Democrats while FDR had a net loss of nine. And despite his homilies on constitutional collegiality, Wilson's idea of leadership was to lead with the Senate following.

Returning to the capital, the president was ready to do battle and spurned compromise with his Senate opponents. As he phrased it, how could the United States "dare reject it [the League] and break the heart of the world?" He believed that once more he could appeal to the people and sway them as he had done so often, this time on the major controversies that centered on the League of Nations and its guarantees of collective security to repel aggression. Under the American Constitution, the right to declare war belongs to Congress—a statement of sovereignty that is exercised in varying ways by all nation-states. The Republican strategy was to approve the treaty and enter the League but to insist on amendments and reservations that significantly altered the original charter. Most of these changes were minor, but one clarification mandated that the United States could not guarantee the territorial integrity or political independence of any other nation unless Congress approved such a commitment. In addition, three of the four major Allied powers had to accept these reservations for the treaty to go into effect for the United States.

Wilson tried to gain the support of the Republican moderates, and in late July, he held a series of meetings with eleven senators. In August, he met with the Foreign Relations Committee, headed by his archfoe Henry Cabot Lodge, for three hours. Wilson was unsuccessful, and even though he was physically under par, he took his case to the people.

In September, Wilson went into the far-reaching Midwest, the isolationist stronghold, and then down the northwest and Pacific coast toward the southwest. In twenty-two days and over eight thousand miles, he delivered forty addresses, an incredible demonstration of presidential leadership. He explained the provisions of the treaty, especially Article X, which he called "the test of the honor and courage and endurance of the world." Wilson pointed out that the Senate's reservation was unnecessary if it was meant to protect the Constitution. Any decision of the executive council to go to war needed unanimous approval, which included the United States. America could not turn away from its new role "that is the leadership we said we wanted, and now the world offers it to us. It is inconceivable that we should reject it."

Then on September 25, 1919, after his address in Pueblo, Colorado, Wilson began to collapse physically, and on October 2, he suffered a severe stroke, which paralyzed the left side of his face and body. As Wilson struggled to recover, the Senate continued its debate of the treaty. Lodge was successful in stopping the more moderate alternatives and pushed for the Senate to curtail the reaches of Article X. Wilson let it be known that he would not accept the Senate's proposal, and so the Democrats joined with hard-core Republican isolationists to defeat ratification with the Lodge reservations.

For several months, the nation debated the final disposition of the treaty, and pressures mounted for some compromise. Moderate Republicans like former president Taft and Harvard University President A. Lawrence Lowell joined with Democrats like William Jennings Bryan and Colonel House to find common ground for a settlement. As Wilson recovered somewhat in the winter of 1920, he opposed any compromise and began talking of running again for president, promoting his reelection as a solemn referendum on the League. Once again the Senate rejected the treaty with the Lodge reservations.

Wilson's stubborn refusal has been a source of continued controversy, a commentary on his failure to provide that critical element of leadership—

compromise—in his own cause. To Wilson, the issue was whether the United States would be willing to assume the world role that was awaiting it. When it appeared that his nation was not so inclined, Wilson judged it best not to accept a treaty that undercut the very principle of collective security. For only under this rubric, with this type of commitment, could the new world replace the balance-of-power approach that had led to the Great War in the first place. Like an Old Testament prophet, Wilson sat in judgment over the world he had partially formed. Even after his death, his influence on American political figures continued, and his failings and dreams were lessons to Franklin D. Roosevelt, his protégé and assistant secretary of the navy.

Would the League with the United States in it in the 1930s have prevented the rise of Hitler and the development of a conflagration far worse than even the First World War? The shortcomings of the Western democracies were not grounded in the weaknesses of the League but more basically in the failure of nerve and leadership in Britain, France, Italy, Germany—and yes, the United States. And the record of the United Nations has not led to universal acclaim for collective security organized in international organizations. Wilson was correct in his judgments about the failures of the Old World diplomats, but his solution—the solution of liberals of his age—was not and is not now viable in the age of garrison states and ethnic tribalism.

Wilson's problem then was not that he was repudiated at home. Many of the war leaders were repudiated at home: even Orlando and Clemenceau were cast out of power after the war, partly as a consequence of its disruptions. The ancient empires of the Ottomans, the Habsburgs, the Hohenzollerns, and the Romanovs were crushed in this one war. The events unleashed by this conflict led to the paralysis of the Western democracies, the rise of the fascist states, the opportunity for a communist takeover, and the legacy that fed World War II. No leader controlled these events, none foresaw their advance, and no person could approximate their cataclysmic consequences.

Wilson was not totally successful; who could be under those conditions? But he did prevent German hegemony in Europe, he did insist on a more generous peace than his allies, and he did seek to break the cycle of war fed by imperialism and power politics. Yet all of this seems modest within the perspective of what followed Versailles. History has unfairly remembered him for a "lost peace" and for lost opportunities. It has sought to find in his personal character and idiosyncrasies some guides to this unhappy train of events. These examinations have conferred a tragic aura, a sense of failure to Wilson's presidency. In fact, he was one of the most brilliant leaders this nation has produced—a true democratic executive who worked well in his first term with Congress on domestic reform and who inspired his fellow citizens. Then, in war, he sought to avoid American involvement, pressed for a mediated compromise, and even after April 1917, positioned America away from reparations, colonial aggrandizement, and a vindictive peace. Wilson asked much of his nation and too much of himself. Any student of the presidency can be more understanding of the shortcomings of both.

Franklin D. Roosevelt: The Establishment of the Modern Presidency

8

THE AWESOME CHALLENGES OF BOTH the Great Depression and World War II led to the conditions that clearly established Franklin D. Roosevelt as the most important president of the twentieth century and probably the most powerful chief executive in American history. Only Lincoln's term can compare in the magnitude of the domestic crisis facing the presidency at that time, but even so, Roosevelt's impact on international politics was far more significant. In dealing with the Depression and the war, Roosevelt changed the nature of the presidency, the alignment of the political parties, and America's role in the world.

Those three terms, those twelve years, mark a clear watershed, or, more accurately, a cleavage between what occurred before FDR and after him. Even "weak" presidents who followed FDR appear strong in comparison to most of the powerful pre-1933 executives; even later presidents who distrusted FDR have in many ways lived off his legacy. For over two generations, liberals and conservatives, Democrats and Republicans, have operated under the model of the Rooseveltian presidency. And yet, of all our "great" presidents, FDR remains somewhat suspicious, with a reputation for suppleness that is frequently seen as deviousness. If, as biographer James MacGregor Burns says, he was both a lion and a fox, Americans are still wary of the fox. This sentiment is partly due to the ambiguity of the man and partly to our national ambiguity regarding power, the welfare state, and the outcome of the last terrible world war.

The Squire of Hyde Park

Franklin Roosevelt was born into a well-connected and doting family with an estate and deep roots in the Hudson River region of rural Dutchess County, above New York City and its immediate suburbs. There Roosevelt lived the life of a son of a country squire, acquired the security of a warm if not overly protective family, and grew up free from many of the anxieties of the rest of his generation. At an early age, he modeled himself after his colorful older cousin Theodore and consciously imitated his political rise. As part of the Roosevelt clan with loyalties to the Democratic Party, Franklin entered politics, ran for the state senate, fought Tammany Hall, and landed a post as assistant secretary of the navy—the path TR used to reach the White House. When World War I came, Franklin Roosevelt sought to join the combat, hoping to emulate further TR's legendary Spanish-American War record. But Wilson insisted that his ambitious assistant secretary stay home, and the war ended more quickly than Franklin anticipated. In 1920, the Democratic Party looked around for a vice presidential candidate to complement the lackluster James M. Cox on the ticket and chose the thirty-seven-year-old bearer of the famed Roosevelt name. After the landslide Democrat defeat, Franklin finished up his time in Washington and headed for the Canadian coast to vacation with his family. There, suffering from stress due to the controversies resulting from some of his decisions in the navy and exposed earlier to the polio virus, Roosevelt contracted the crippling disease, and its effects were to stay with him for the rest of his life.[1]

For several years, Roosevelt fought to regain some physical mobility while he continued dabbling in national Democratic politics. In 1924, he placed the name of Alfred E. Smith, the governor of New York, in nomination for the presidency in the famous "Happy Warrior" speech, reestablishing himself in the process as a major figure in the party. In 1928, the party leaders in New York, guided by Smith and probably encouraged by Eleanor Roosevelt, insisted that FDR run for governor to bolster Smith's chances of carrying that state in the upcoming presidential election. Preoccupied with his physical therapy in Warm Springs, Georgia, Roosevelt reluctantly accepted. Although Smith lost New York and the nation, Roosevelt squeaked by and became governor of the most important state in the Union. Overnight he was recognized as the leading Democratic politician, and he and his advisers calculated on a 1936 attempt at the presidency, following an expected two terms for Hoover.

But from 1929 to 1932, the economic depression proved to be more acute than anyone had imagined, and Roosevelt decided to run in 1932 instead. After a monumental reelection victory as governor in 1930, FDR was clearly the frontrunner for the nomination. But knowing that any candidate needed two-thirds of the delegates under the party's rules, he realized he would have a difficult time in the convention. Roosevelt's managers made several compromises to assure his nomination. Most critically, FDR repudiated his old Wilsonian faith in the League of Nations, thus encouraging John Nance Garner of Texas and publisher William Randolph Hearst in California; they threw their support to Roosevelt in order to stop Wilson's secretary of war, Newton Baker, from gaining the nomination. Breaking the tradition that candidates waited to be notified by the convention, Roosevelt flew from New York to Chicago and personally accepted the nomination. Thus FDR showed himself as a man not bound by old conventions and physically equipped for the presidency and able to overcome one of the most debilitating diseases.

Roosevelt's name was known across the nation, for he was in some ways a linear descendant of TR: a progressive, a vigorously handsome and captivating figure, and an official in the last Democratic administration. But on a personal level, Franklin Delano Roosevelt, even to those who served him over the years, seemed a bit of a charming enigma, an asset he used well and often. Early in his political career, Roosevelt was seen as ambitious, superficial, and sparklingly buoyant—a man who wore lightly both commitments and intellectual achievements. He was a publicity-seeking state senator and a driving and competent assistant secretary, but he remained a cut below his cousin in political skill and personal curiosity about the world around him.

Then in the 1920s, while he fought the effects of polio and matured emotionally, Roosevelt seemed to change. Earlier, his relationship with his wife Eleanor had become chilly due partly to his marital infidelities, but now she went on to nurse him and also chart out her own life. They became allies in a common political career but were no longer husband and wife in an intimate sense. Both looked for affection elsewhere and devised networks of other supportive relationships. FDR became more guarded and manipulative than in the past. He had been throughout his life a charming fellow, a person so confident and ebullient that it was assumed he was somehow hiding his real frustrations and disappointments behind a mask. In fact, young Roosevelt was simply what he seemed—a pleasant Boy Scout blessed with good looks, important connections, and a bright future. But after his battle with polio, FDR experienced, as he never had before, anger, fear, and deep frustration. Out of that dark night of the soul, his biographers often say, he emerged more sensitive to the problems of the vulnerable.

Actually, Roosevelt's afflictions may have increased his personal complexity. In order to be a strong candidate for public office, he and his associates erected a facade that denied the effects of his disease, and the media helped by never showing him in a wheelchair or as handicapped. His disability led him to be more manipulative and devious, tendencies he exhibited often but usually filtered through layers of calculated charm. The Roosevelt of the 1930s was a public figure with a carefully concealed private world, and this may have contributed to the reputation for shiftiness that has clouded his record and real achievements to this day.[2] That Franklin Roosevelt was a great president there is no doubt, but why he remains less revered than Lincoln or Washington is a mystery. Perhaps the reason is that FDR's personal characteristics seem less noble than those of the other two individuals. There is surely evidence that FDR seemed to enjoy the game a bit too much, that he relished using and confusing people unnecessarily, that his idea of leadership was just too Machiavellian for a people in love with the ethos of common sense and straight shooting.

Roosevelt, then, in the privileged world of his youth and in the life of an invalid, developed personality traits that served him well at times and yet left a legacy of distrust in how he approached the use of power. Years later, some historians and political scientists would look at Roosevelt's chaotic administration of public affairs and canonize it as true genius. Since FDR could not run the huge bureaucracy he was creating, he had fostered jurisdictional disputes, overlapping responsibilities, and organizational competition in order to create a situation where he alone held real power. While there is some truth to that observation, a better explanation was that Roosevelt was simply overwhelmed in his first two terms with the miasma he had created, and confusion was the result. Both as assistant secretary of the navy and as governor, FDR was a rather traditional administrator; during the war, the president delegated many of the day-to-day military responsibilities to General George Catlett Marshall and to aides who accepted the importance of coordination and decision-making. However, in terms of domestic mobilization, confusion and disorganization seemed to be often the order of the day. Overall, Roosevelt was neither a brilliant administrator who saw order in chaos nor an initiator who pioneered a novel way to use presidential power by creating competing advisers. Franklin Roosevelt was a skilled politician who was preoccupied with public opinion, who rarely shared his true emotions with even his closest associates, and who was uncertain about which domestic policies would work and which would not.[3]

Justice Oliver Wendell Holmes Jr. once concluded that Roosevelt had a second-class intellect but a first-class temperament—an observation that FDR's biographers have obediently followed. But in fact, Roosevelt had a quick mind, a retentive memory, and an ability to understand the complexities of popular opinion and public policy. He was not extremely knowledgeable about economics, but the conventional wisdom of that discipline had little to offer politicians at that time. Liberal economists lament the president's ignorance of the theories of John Maynard Keynes, feeling that Keynes's theories of "priming the pump" in the Depression economy by incurring more deficits would have led to the golden road to recovery. Conservative economists equally deplore that Roosevelt went off the sacred gold standard and never appreciated the need to restore business confidence in America, which in that vocabulary meant business dominance. But in the early 1930s, Roosevelt, like mostly everyone else in politics, did not understand what had happened, only that the economic downturn had destroyed the Republicans' lock on the national government and opened up the way for the Democrats once again.[4]

The First New Deal

In his first inaugural, FDR captivated the American people with his admonition that the only thing they had to fear was fear itself. It was a brilliant and reassuring expression of confidence—just what the people needed—but of course, it was quite incorrect. With over one-quarter of the wage-earning population unemployed, with hundreds of banks closed, with mortgages unpaid and foreclosures on farms dramatically up, desperation was quite in order. But Roosevelt perceived that the country needed to first believe again in itself, and to do that, he assumed, it had to believe in him. What has been less commented on was FDR's startling determination that he wanted speedy action from Congress on his recovery recommendations, and that if

> Congress shall fail to take one of these two courses, and in the event that the national emergency is still critical, I shall not evade the clear course of duty that will then confront me. I shall ask the Congress for the one remaining instrument to meet the crisis—broad executive power to wage a war against the emergency, as great as the power that would be given to me if we were in fact invaded by a foreign foe.

Clearly, he was the linear descendant of Theodore Roosevelt. And as the crowds cheered, the New Deal advisers dealt with the most apparent crisis—the collapse of the nation's banking structures. Many states had already closed banks, and Roosevelt's declaration of a "bank holiday" was a defensive move to buy some time. He called a special session of Congress on Thursday, March 9, and asked the legislative branch to confirm his initial proclamation and grant him new powers over banking and commerce. The reaction was spontaneous—without much debate and concern for its usual procedures, Congress approved the bill, and FDR signed it that evening.

Sensing the mood of Congress, the president on the next day requested powers to cut government spending, but strong opposition from veterans organizations led to an open revolt among Democrats in the House of Representatives. With the support of sixty-nine Republicans, the House, however, backed the chief executive. Meanwhile, Roosevelt began his fireside chats, the homey talks that added immensely to his personal popularity and imprinted the office on the needs of his fellow citizens, whom he addressed simply as "my friends." Humorist Will Rogers was to remark that FDR explained the banking crisis so clearly that even the bankers understood it.

Within the next several months, called "The Hundred Days," the president asked Congress for additional powers to deal with the Depression. In the process, FDR put his prestige behind a cornucopia of measures that flooded the legislative branch and revamped forever the role of the federal government. The president urged a new agriculture bill to raise farmers' purchasing power, ease farm mortgage terms, and deal with the problems of farm loans. The Agricultural Adjustment Act passed the Congress in mid-May by a three-to-one majority; several weeks later, Congress approved the Civilian Conservation Corps, which was to employ a quarter of a million young men in reforestation, fighting forest fires, and building dams. The president also pushed for direct federal grants to the states for unemployment relief and for a major overhaul of the securities markets. He followed up with a proposal for the Tennessee Valley Authority, legislation to save home mortgages from foreclosure, reform of the railroads, and a far-reaching cooperative effort for industry. Called the National Industrial Recovery bill, it provided for codes limiting competition and some recognition of the rights of workers to unionize.

"The Hundred Days" became an impressive legislative feat closely identified with FDR's dazzling leadership. Obviously it was, but in another sense, the president acted as a brake on Congress, which was willing to go even further in authorizing public expenditures to fight the Depression. FDR did believe in a balanced budget, and while he recognized the obvious state of the emergency, he periodically went on binges of parsimony and cost cutting. Roosevelt's style, though, was broad and eclectic; he was the honest broker among power blocs, the leader whose greatest gift was an incredible sense of confidence. Confined to a wheelchair, he reminded a paralyzed nation of the curative powers of laughter, optimism, and American common sense. It was a prescription any doctor could profitably prescribe. Even usually critical commentators suspended judgment. Kansas editor William Allen White wondered what had happened to Franklin Roosevelt. Before, he seemed like the typical progressive governor who had fallen under the influence of TR and LaFollette but was not really presidential timber. Now Roosevelt seemed to have "developed magnitude and poise, more than all, power!"[5]

In those early years, FDR insisted on being a nonpartisan leader of the nation, even to the extent of avoiding the Jefferson Day dinners so beloved by the Democratic faithful. He had the support of right-wing agitators and left-wing crackpots, of labor leaders and business people afraid of the very system they had left prostrate. Even Adolf Hitler wrote, "I have sympathy with President Roosevelt because he marches straight to his objective over Congress, over lobbies, over stubborn bureaucracies."

Taking a lesson from his old mentor Woodrow Wilson, the new president delivered his messages in person to Congress. He sent up detailed proposals often drafted jointly by selected congressmen and bureaucrats working together, a practice Lyndon Johnson would revive in the 1960s. He was willing to veto legislation he disagreed with and used the full patronage resources of the office to push his proposals. On one occasion, he approved the appointment to the post of U.S. marshal of a man who was an ally of Senator "Cotton Ed" Smith but also had been found guilty of homicide. In return, Smith concurred in the nomination of leftist academician Rexford Guy Tugwell as undersecretary of agriculture. Roosevelt gleefully confronted Tugwell, saying, "Today I traded you for a couple of murderers!"[6]

Congress continued to be receptive to other presidential initiatives: a reciprocal tariff, a gold reserve act, and the ending of Prohibition. In addition, Roosevelt decided to recognize the Soviet Union and unsuccessfully pushed for a waterway between the United States and Canada. The most controversial act passed during this period created the National Recovery Administration—the government's major attempt to get businesses to draw up codes of fair competition in each area of industry and commerce. Headed by the blustery General Hugh Johnson and symbolized by the Blue Eagle emblem, the National Recovery Administration (NRA) represented the corporate state grafted onto the American voluntary marketplace. It led to some stabilization in the economy, an increase in the power of the organized special interests, and a mass of red tape and endless codes for subcategories and tiny shares of industry. As early as 1934, FDR felt the heat of complaints, and he finally appointed radical lawyer Clarence Darrow to investigate the problems. Darrow's conclusion was that powerful economic interests controlled the code process. FDR cut back on the NRA's powers, fired Johnson, and tried to recoup his losses. Finally, the Supreme Court put the NRA out of business.

The rural counterpart of the NRA, the Agricultural Adjustment Administration, realized a better fate, but not without controversy. The AAA was meant to restore farm prices to parity, which was defined as the relationship they had to nonagricultural prices in the 1909–1914 period. Processing taxes, passed on to the consumers, financed the subsidy, and farmers were urged to curtail production and keep lands out of use. Stories appeared of crops being allowed deliberately to rot in the fields and warehouses, and of baby pigs being slaughtered to stabilize prices—the destruction of surplus crops and animals in a nation facing urban famine and general distress. As with the NRA, organized farm groups and wealthier farmers controlled the AAA, and the new restrictions on the use of their land forced many tenant farmers and sharecroppers out of agriculture altogether.

By the fall of 1933, FDR concluded that enough people were still not employed, and he pushed for a rapid increase in public works spending and an end to the rigid gold standard. Under the aegis of Harry Hopkins, the New Deal's Civil Works Administration spent a billion dollars on quick relief programs, aimed at putting money in the pockets of poor people. Some of those jobs were make-work, leaf raking and lawn cutting, but they provided funds in the worst part of 1933–1934. Hopkins acted quickly to meet the obvious emergency; when told about the virtues of long-run projects, he snapped that people "don't eat in the long run—they eat every day."

As for Roosevelt, he presided over a host of reforms without much of a cohesive philosophy or overall public policy. His view was simply experimental—to try a variety of programs and keep what worked. As expected, he relied on divergent experts, resurrected old collectivist notions of governmental regulations from World War I, experimented with new approaches of cooperation, moderated disputes and personality conflicts, and restrained an inflation-oriented Congress. He avoided partisanship and insisted on staying above the numerous frays that dotted the landscape.[7]

In the 1934 congressional elections, the Democrats won even more seats than they had two years before. The usual pattern then and now is for the majority party to lose some seats, often forty or so. Instead the Democrats picked up nine seats in the House, running up their total to 319, and added nine seats in the Senate, bringing their total there to 69. They gained some additional state governorships as well. It was an incredible vote of support for FDR, even as he donned his nonpartisan mantle. Yet just as this popular vote was being counted, strong right-wing opposition was gathering among the business classes and a group called the American Liberty League. Wealthy industrialists and manufacturers, such as the Duponts, William S. Knudsen, J. Howard Pew, and Sewell L. Avery, joined with conservative Democrats, such as Al Smith, John Davis, and Bainbridge Colby, to oppose Roosevelt and further the league's philosophy of safeguarding the uses of private property and free enterprise as they defined them. More subtly and more pointedly for Roosevelt, the wealthier classes—from which he came and among whom he had spent his life socializing—began to question his personal motives and his commitment to their interests and values. By the end of his first term, FDR was seen by many of the rich and well-born as "a traitor to his class" and was attacked with a ferocity that was stronger than even that directed toward TR during his Bull Moose days.[8]

Roosevelt was first bemused and then baffled by right-wing criticism, seeing himself quite rightfully as a champion of capitalism rather than the enemy. But the heavy weight of opposition on the scales fell out not on the right but on the left. The misery in the land was very real, and in that land new leaders arose promising redistribution of the wealth and greater security for the common people. While FDR talked vaguely of the "forgotten man," these radical leaders promised a better future.

Some important reformers and agitators who had large popular followings were at the height of their appeal in the early 1930s. For FDR, the most accomplished and therefore the most dangerous to him was Senator Huey P. Long of Louisiana. Long was one of the most fascinating political leaders of his generation—a Southerner who generally avoided race baiting, attacked the powerful economic oligarchy in his state, and accomplished genuine populist reforms for the poor. He was also an autocrat, a person who ripped asunder normal political processes, and a true demagogue. Long's career was partially the basis for Robert Penn Warren's novel *All the King's Men* and the popular film by the same name, which chronicled the times of the fictional dictatorial governor Willie Stark. To break Long's hold on Louisiana, FDR actually considered sending federal troops into that state at the time, but he decided against it. By the mid-1930s, Long had won national attention with his "Share the Wealth" program, which promised a $2,000 annual income, free education and homesteads, cheap food, veterans' bonuses, and a limit on private fortunes. He would make "every man a king," and consequently Long was titled "the Kingfish" (after the character in the popular radio show *Amos and Andy*).

Equally prominent was the Roman Catholic priest from Royal Oak, Michigan, Father Charles E. Coughlin, an eloquent orator who had originally supported Roosevelt. But after a personal falling out, Coughlin charged that Roosevelt was in league with "godless capitalists, the Jews, Communists, international bankers, and plutocrats." Added to Long's and Coughlin's following was a movement in California named after Dr. Francis E. Townsend, who devoted his efforts to aiding the old and destitute and advocated guaranteed pensions.

Roosevelt's allies in 1934–1935 were concerned that this attack from the left, especially from Long, might lead to a third major political party and deprive him of enough votes to win reelection. An opinion poll done by Postmaster General James Farley's agents for the National Democratic Committee indicated that Long had remarkable appeal across the United States and not just in the Gulf region, as had been thought. If the Republicans in 1936 nominated a progressive candidate for president and if Long also ran, FDR might be in serious trouble.

Roosevelt, with his superb sense of timing, decided to let the protest leaders play out their hand in 1935, observing that the public's attention "cannot, because of human weakness, be attuned for long periods of time to a constant repetition of the highest note in the scale." He concluded that people grow tired of seeing the same name in front of them, and that he could not keep up the pace of 1933 and 1934 without losing his audience. Yet behind the scenes, he moved to counter the protest leaders' appeals. First, he cut off all patronage to Long and his allies. Then he used the services of Catholic businessman Joseph P. Kennedy to deal gingerly with Coughlin; by 1942 the Vatican silenced the priest after his anti-Semitic rhetoric and pro-fascist leanings became too much of an embarrassment. As for Townsend, FDR suddenly attached himself to the movement for a Social Security Act, which would cut into the physician's major appeal.

Also by 1935, FDR embraced the collective bargaining movement, adding an important component to the Democratic Party, the unions. The president supported in a nonchalant way the incorporation into the NRA of Section 7a, which recognized the right of collective bargaining, but he was not particularly an ally of organized labor, especially in his earlier role as a national broker among groups. Then, in 1935, he enthusiastically embraced the proposal of Senator Robert Wagner of New York, which encouraged employee representation instead of company unions. Originally, FDR opposed the Wagner bill, but after the Supreme Court ruled the NRA unconstitutional and Section 7a was declared void, the president embraced the new bill.[9]

Clearly, by 1935 Roosevelt had decided to abandon his posture as mediator among diverse interests and to throw the full weight of his office into a partisan and aggressive defense of his administration. Some historians have seen his shift as a simple calculation that the population wanted a more radical approach to complex problems, and FDR as usual followed the crowd. In addition, Roosevelt was being severely attacked by conservatives, especially by big business and by the Supreme Court, which was declaring major New Deal initiatives unconstitutional. Unlike Lincoln, FDR was not a person given to absorbing abuse; he struck back and in the process effected a split from the business and financial communities that lasted until the onset of the war.

In the Seventy-Fourth Congress, the legislators limped along, approving several additional New Deal acts, but then in the summer of 1935, that body and the president came forth with a second burst of energy—one so exuberant it was labeled "The Second One Hundred Days."[10] It is this session and not the earlier two years that set in law many of the true historical achievements of the Roosevelt years. However, in the beginning of 1935, FDR was not clearly in charge. The president told Congress that he wanted stronger laws concerning unemployment insurance, old age benefits, work relief, conservation, and other areas. Yet he criticized the federal government's role in providing "relief" jobs and asked for $4.8 billion for related programs, a lower estimate than many proponents in the Senate wanted to aid the poor and unemployed. Thus, for all his conversion to the left, FDR in 1935 still shared Hoover's concerns that federal relief, or welfare, would destroy personal initiative, even in an economy where such enterprise would find no access to employment. However, when the bill ran into opposition in the Senate from conservatives and progressives alike, FDR was out fishing, and it was left to his capable aides and legislators to work out a compromise. In April, he asked the Senate to approve U.S. participation in the World Court and ran into tremendous opposition. In addition, his Social Security bill was stalled in Congress, and an unwanted veterans' bonus bill was making its way though the legislative mill. In May, the Chamber of Commerce attacked FDR publicly, and a group of progressive senators demanded more assertive leadership. On top of those pressures, the Court in the same month declared the NRA invalid.[11]

Now as summer approached, Roosevelt roared back. Applying enormous pressure and the full powers of patronage, he demanded action from a recalcitrant Congress. The Wagner Labor Relations Act was approved, the Social Security Act passed, a stronger TVA bill was accepted, and a holding company bill to curb utility company prices was enacted into law. The president asked Congress for new taxes on gifts, inheritances, and corporations, and preached the beginnings of a "soak the rich" philosophy. Then, like God after six days of creation, the president rested, leaving on a trip across the country in late 1935.

The Mandate of 1936

As Roosevelt pushed for domestic reforms and recalibrated his political stance to the left, the world situation in Europe was rapidly deteriorating. While Americans clamored over the increased role of government in their lives, the Fascist and Nazi regimes came to power and began their descent into the hell of war. The history of that period is the chronicle of the failure of nerve on the part of democratic governments, old settled aristocracies, and flaccid Socialist parties. In the Soviet Union, an even more brutal Joseph Stalin was consolidating his power, putting to an end the myth that communism was democracy by another name.

Roosevelt was genuinely disturbed about the turn of events in Europe, but even though he expressed public concern, his primary focus was on domestic recovery and on his own reelection. FDR did not look any the poorer for his term in office. He still responded to life with a sense of zest and cheerfulness that was contagious to those around him. By his own account, he was an actor, a gifted master of poses, gestures, and expressions. The alphabet agencies of the New Deal went off in all sorts of directions, some of them novel and untried, some cynical, a few naive, many idealistic, and in the process they attracted all sorts of people. In a few instances, even Communists found their way into the New Deal bureaucracy—although far fewer than Republican orators liked to imagine or feared.

Roosevelt was less the chief executive than a sort of sensitive nerve center that judged public opinion, matched strategy to tactics, and left open options while pressing the vague goals of recovery and reform. To many of his subordinates, he was increasingly an enigma, and they grew dismayed by his guile and unreliability under pressure. But in 1936, the popular impression of the man had been set in the first gruesome months of 1933 and then in the achievements of the following legislative session. FDR was the individual who saved the banks and small passbook savings accounts, the leader who stayed mortgage foreclosures, pushed for work relief, cared deeply about conservation and the Dust Bowl, furthered labor's organizing efforts, and created Social Security. The New Deal was seen as a cornucopia of benefits and Roosevelt the funnel of hope. Glumly, Al Smith concluded that FDR would be reelected; nobody shoots Santa Claus, he observed.

Smith was right; the New Deal pumped $5 billion of work projects and relief programs into the limp American economy, over six million new jobs were created, and the unemployment rolls dropped by four million people. Boys left the street corners and went to work reseeding forests and wrote home proudly about it. FDR knew that reelection was in the wind, especially after the assassination of Huey Long in Louisiana. But now the president wanted to make the election "a crusade." The Depression was not over, unemployment was hovering at eight to nine million people, and conditions in 1936 were not back to the inflated times and expectations of pre-1929 levels.

For Roosevelt, there was only one issue: "It's myself, and people must be either for me or against me." At the Democratic National Convention in Philadelphia, FDR accepted renomination, this time having also ended the two-thirds rule once and for all. He attacked "the royalists of the economic order" and "dictatorship by mob rule." Roosevelt went on philosophically, "Governments can err, presidents do make mistakes, but the immortal Dante tells us that divine justice weighs the sins of the cold-blooded and the sins of the warmhearted in different scales. Better the occasional faults of a Government that lives in a spirit of charity than the consistent omissions of a Government frozen in the ice of its own indifference." Then he pronounced that his generation of Americans had a "rendezvous with destiny."

As for the Republicans, they nominated Governor Alf Landon, a moderate from Kansas who turned to the right as he joined the main chorus of opposition to FDR. But the issue clearly was Roosevelt as a leader, as a president, as a friend to those who had known fear and desperation four years before. As the campaign progressed, the president relieved some of his pent-up resentment about the attacks that had been unleashed against him: a traitor to his class, a destroyer of American free enterprise, and even a sick cripple given to bouts of madness. At the end of October, he baited those forces in bitter rhetoric rarely matched by any president before or since: "Never before in all our history have these forces been so united against one candidate as they stand today. They are unanimous in their *hate for me—and I welcome their hatred.* I should like to have it said of my first administration that in it the forces of selfishness and lust for power met their *match.*"

In the raw meat of democratic politics, Roosevelt had few equals, and the populace loved it and loved him. He carried every state but Maine and Vermont, won the electoral vote 523 to 8, and beat Landon 27,752,309 to 16,682,524 in the popular tally. His proportion of the vote, 60.7 percent, was the highest margin in modern American presidential history up to that time. In addition, the Democratic majorities in Congress swelled to an even higher number: 331 seats to 89 in the House and 76 to 16 seats in the Senate. The GOP seemed on its way to becoming an extinct species.[12]

The election sealed the popular impression that Roosevelt was a flawless politician and invincible in national politics. But like a great classical tragedy, pride cometh before the fall. The large increase in the size of the Democratic forces in Congress led to a decline of party cohesiveness and more factionalism. The fruits of overwhelming victory in electoral politics are frequently disappointing, especially in a nation without a strongly disciplined parliamentary party system like Britain's. Roosevelt felt that he had received a personal mandate to continue his programs, a vote of confidence in himself, and that his party must follow.

One of his most astute biographers and a student of leadership in general, James MacGregor Burns, attributed FDR's early success to several factors. First, the president had a fine grasp of public opinion and its moods and was one of the first politicians to use opinion polls systematically. He also had a good sense of timing, of when to move and when to stand still until an issue matured. As FDR himself said, "I am like a cat. I make a quick stroke and then I relax." For example, he would wait until the ferocity of an opposition's attack toned down before he responded. He also paid attention to political detail, to the minutiae that separate good politicians from memorable ones. In the same way, he kept himself abreast of the internal operations of various groups and could split the rank and file from opposition leaders. He picked his fights and carefully staged when they would take place. Above all, Roosevelt was personally charming and adept at reading the minds, intentions, and agendas of the ambitious.

Setbacks for the Chief

The American political system places a premium on controlling power, checking leadership, and curtailing popular passions. The system has prevented classical types of tyranny and modern versions of totalitarian states, inclinations the United States is probably not fertile territory for anyway. In 1937, Franklin Roosevelt took aim at two major checks in that system: the Supreme Court and the loose party allegiances of elected officials. By the end of the year, the president suffered a major defeat in the Court-packing battle, and after the election of 1938, he hit a brick wall in his attempted purge of Democratic conservatives. By that time, the New Deal's legislative agenda ran into increasing difficulties, and by the end of the 1940 campaign, FDR talked foreign policy instead.

Did Roosevelt by these major miscalculations destroy his political base and thus end prematurely the cycle of recovery and reform? And why did an unusually astute judge of the popular mood and legislative folkways stumble so badly after such a monumental victory only months before? The Supreme Court seemed to many observers as the last bastion of conservative political strength, the nemesis of New Deal liberals, and the salvation of the business classes. When on May 6, 1935, the high court in the Schechter poultry case struck down unanimously the NRA, its decision was welcomed in more than conservative quarters. The act, drawn up in the period of the bank crisis in 1933, was poorly drafted and terribly administered by Hugh Johnson and his staff. Roosevelt himself called it "an awful headache." But the Court's rationale was somewhat disturbing—it found that the NRA was an unconstitutional delegation of legislative power and an unwarranted effort to control interstate commerce. Roosevelt's response was to argue, somewhat justifiably, that the nation had been "relegated to the horse and buggy definition of interstate commerce."

In 1935, the Court voided the AAA on the grounds that the processing tax, which financed the subsidies, was an expropriation of money from one group to another. The majority in the six to three decision ruled that agriculture should be a state rather than a federal responsibility. The intent of the decision was clearly to undercut the ability of the national government to use its powers to effect social regulation, since any effective agricultural policy had to transcend state boundaries. The minority on the court, led by Justice Harlan Stone, warned that the courts "are not the only agency of government that must be assumed to have the capacity to govern." The Court then upheld the Tennessee Valley Authority Act (TVA)—to Roosevelt's regret, as he had planned to campaign for a constitutional amendment to change the court after the election in 1936.

In May, the Court also turned around and ruled against an attempt by Congress to regulate the bituminous coal industry, finding that the federal government could not justify its contention of a substantial impact on interstate commerce. Having zealously defended the province of the states in previous cases, the high court struck down New York State's minimum wage law for women, saying that it violated the employer's and employee's right to bargain conditions—a right not particularly strong for women in the middle of massive unemployment. One-third of the states had similar protections, and the Court's philosophy seemed based less on law than on a laissez-faire, uncaring caprice. Even some Republican leaders shuddered at the decisions, and their party platform supported state laws guaranteeing a minimum wage. The Court itself was badly split, five to four, with even Chief Justice Hughes voting at times with the liberal bloc. Critics noted that three members of the conservative wing had been corporate lawyers and the average age of the court was seventy-one, rather advanced for the population at that time.

The Court also voted five to four against the Municipal Bankruptcy Act, saying it infringed on the rights of states to control their own municipalities, a position more rooted in legal imagination than contemporary realities. The opposition to the New Deal seemed more philosophical than strictly legal—it was a matter of power and privilege in the eyes of some liberals and conservative alike. And Roosevelt's response was interesting. Harold Ickes reported, "The president said today and has said on other occasions, that he is not at all adverse to the Supreme Court declaring one New Deal statute after another unconstitutional. I think he believes that the Court will find itself pretty far out on a limb before it is through with it and a real issue will be joined."[13]

Roosevelt, though, did not make the Court an issue in the campaign. Instead, he sought a broad victory—a personal mandate but not a programmatic one. Elections in America, unlike in parliamentary systems, are personal triumphs or retrospective judgments. They are not seen as mandates for more change or as a carte blanche for leaders. Yet after his reelection, the president seemed to judge that the people, and the Congress that was elected with him, would concur in his future moves. And high on his agenda was bringing the judiciary to heel.

After weeks of quiet planning, the president decided to present a plan aimed at changing the composition of the Court. However, rather than confronting the issue directly, once again he relied on a back door approach—seeming sly and wily rather than open. He argued that the issue was judicial efficiency and the congestion of cases in the court system. His reform was to ask for the power to appoint a new justice to the Supreme Court for every justice over seventy who did not retire. Under this scheme, FDR could name six new justices. The number of justices is not set by the Constitution, and in fact it fluctuated in the early and middle years of the republic. Jefferson, Jackson, and even Grant had been critical of the Court, but no president directly confronted it as FDR proposed. With no discussion with his cabinet and little more with his own Democratic leaders in Congress, the president dropped his bombshell. Oddly enough, a similar proposal had been put forth back in 1913 by Wilson's attorney general, James C. McReynolds, who was one of the conservative justices being criticized.

It was a typical Roosevelt ploy: dramatic, secretive, shrewd, and clever. The results, though, were almost uniformly negative. Among the Senate progressives, Burton Wheeler and Hiram Johnson refused support, as did the prestigious George Norris. Conservatives this time lay back and watched the Democratic Party divide and the progressive leaders struggle with Roosevelt's stratagem. FDR clearly misjudged the opposition, writing to a friend, "What a grand fight it is going to be! We need everything we have got to put in it!" And he concluded to visitors, "The people are with me." But Congress found itself inundated by mail, newspapers warned of dictatorship, law associations recalled the sanctity of law and the hallowed place of the Court's history, and New England town meetings passed resolutions criticizing the plan. In addition, in early 1937, industrial labor unions fostered an epidemic of sit-down strikes, events that represented to many a challenge to property rights. Elements of the middle class began to see the Court as a safeguard against the more radical segments of society that the president seemed to dally with in the election. And abroad, the presence of legal safeguards had been starkly wiped away in the Soviet Union, Fascist Italy, and Nazi Germany.

Concerned about the opposition, FDR dropped the efficiency argument and directly attacked the Court's philosophical underpinnings. Once again the party whips were cracked and patronage flowed, but still Congress appeared recalcitrant. Then, in the midst of the battle, Chief Justice Hughes wrote a letter to the Senate explaining that an increase in the size of the court would lower its efficiency, and that the "old men" were actually keeping up with the pace of work. Shrewdly, he took FDR's weakest point and rammed it home tellingly.

In April 1937, the Supreme Court found the Wagner Act constitutional and later upheld the Social Security Act. Pro–New Dealers remarked that a switch in time saved nine. The chief justice, working with his fellow conservative Owen J. Roberts, added two swing votes to the liberal bloc, and consequently FDR lost his main issue. As the Court changed suddenly and the reform bill languished in Congress, FDR claimed a moral victory.

Then on May 18, conservative Justice Willis Van Devanter formally submitted his resignation. Eventually, Roosevelt's measure was mercifully buried.[14]

Liberals have argued that FDR achieved his objectives—to curtail the Court and break the laissez-faire bloc that had so dominated it for generations. To conservatives, the battle was another example of the insatiable desire for power by "that man in the White House." Having mastered Congress and wooed the public, he tried to take on the judiciary. Most historians have seen the battle, though, as a serious miscalculation that proved the president was vulnerable and led to an abrupt end to New Deal reform. The court fight showed all the shortcomings of what FDR had earlier created: he lost in part because he never built a new Democratic Party, one bound by philosophy and not based on his personality. He continued to be evasive, almost for the fun of it, and paid a terrible long-term price—the destruction of the fruits of his election victory only months after his triumph.

Clearly, a great deal of New Deal legislation, drawn up quickly, was poorly drafted and devoid of any constitutional base that would appear familiar in the vocabulary of the 1930s. Not just the Supreme Court but also lower court judges raised valid points of concern. But the record of the Supreme Court up to that period was not the chronicle of independent philosopher-kings devoted to promoting rights and liberties. Historically, the high court has been interested in expanding the authority of the federal government over the states under John Marshall, of protecting slavery and slave interests, and of fostering nearly unbridled power for new industries in corporate America. In the process, the Court took the Fourteenth Amendment, aimed at protecting the rights of freed black slaves, and suddenly covered these new corporate aggregates with what were guarantees of personal rights. The Court did this at the same time it upheld segregation and Jim Crow laws. To see the Supreme Court as a guardian of individual liberties over these years is a misreading of history. As Oliver Wendell Holmes Jr. observed, it is the elected representatives who have been the most responsible branch of government in that regard.

Those opposing Roosevelt in the Senate were motivated by many objectives: some philosophical, some political, some stirrings of conscience. But a crucial element among the Borahs and the Wheelers in the Senate was a desire to beat the president, to restore a sense that the executive is only one baron dealing with others in the disjointed, almost feudal landscape of American politics. When FDR misjudged public opinion, they saw this opportunity and exploited it to the fullest. Despite the view that

American politics is a debate of philosophies and ideologies, it is more often about the balance of power, deference, and egotism. The Supreme Court was indeed attacking the reforms put together and passed by popularly elected congressmen and the president. Many of the same men who so loudly tagged on to FDR during election time were willing to allow that unraveling to continue.[15]

FDR had personalized politics, and to many of his enemies the time had come to cut him back down to size. Those liberal opponents, those Democrats who ran below him on the ticket in 1932 and 1936, became the point men in the court battle and were joined by progressive Borah and even Norris. Wheeler, for example, encouraged both Hughes's letter and its timely release and urged Van Devanter to announce his resignation earlier than expected. To paraphrase David Lloyd George, politics is less the allocation of values than posturing, handbills, and blood on the floor.

From Mastery to Drift

Publicly FDR remained jovial, but in private he erupted against the press and "the fat cats" who had taken him on. In addition to the difficult world situation, Roosevelt now had problems with the pace of recovery at home. By October 1937, the nation began to slip back into a deep depression. His secretary of the treasury, Henry Morgenthau, warned, "We are headed right into another depression. The question is, Mr. President—what are we going to do about it?" As matters worsened, a sense of paralysis set in. The cabinet was deeply divided on whether to expand the New Deal or to quiet things down and court business in order to restore confidence.

Roosevelt seemed genuinely unable to make sense out of what was happening. He reached out for more and more advice and could not get any consensus. In exasperation, he uncharacteristically said of the presidency, "God, what a job!" When Congress convened in November, the president expressed concern about the downturn, but he was unable to get anything of note through that body. The magic had worn off. By the beginning of the year, the president was still bewildered and seeking some solutions. Business leaders blamed the New Deal for failing to restore confidence in the economy, and the president for his attacks on their morality and achievements. Many New Dealers desperately fought to protect and expand their bureaucratic turf. FDR in 1936 and in 1937 swore up and down that fiscal year 1938 would bring a balanced budget. Meanwhile, groups of big spenders were meeting in 1937 and promulgating the economic theories of John Maynard Keynes, who had suggested the seemingly absurd idea that a government in a depression should not cut expenditures but deficit-spend its way to recovery. It was a prescription that made little sense in terms of traditional economic doctrine and conventional American wisdom, but Keynes's ideas were to be used successfully later in the United States and abroad.[16]

As for Roosevelt, the eclectic style that seemed so appropriate in the experimental groupings of this first New Deal now led to disorganization and drift. The president organized meetings with business people, attacked monopolies and profiteering, and gave his approval to a symbolic crusade against trusts. An exasperated ally, Henry Wallace, pleaded with him that he "must furnish that firm and confident leadership which made you such a joy to the nation in March of 1933." Finally, Roosevelt moved—this time to push for more government assistance, and he prepared a $3 billion spending program. Congress passed the bill overwhelmingly; the legislators also knew little about what to do. Then going back to the comfortable certainties of the past, the administration and Congress began a full-scale campaign against the trusts and concentrations of wealth. Somehow, Theodore Roosevelt's earlier tactics seemed more reassuring than Keynes's unproven theories.

In this period, it has generally been assumed that FDR must have lost considerable popularity in order to explain Congress's recalcitrance. Actually, the polls showed very little slippage from his 1936 ratings. Instead, the Democratic Party—with its bloated majorities in the legislative branch—and its cohesive conservative wing became undone as a governing coalition. There seemed to be no viable alternative to Roosevelt. Even in drift, he commanded the heights. But Congress stalemated over his agenda, and FDR's allies asked for an end to controversial legislation. Congress approved a reformulation of the Agricultural Adjustment Act and a modest reorganization of the bureaucracy, but a more extensive proposal for overall reform led to charges of executive dictatorship and the threat of an end to constitutional government.

Disgusted with disloyalty in his own party, including many who used his name and prestige in their campaigns, FDR decided to purge some of his opponents in the 1938 election. It was another major miscalculation, this one firming up the conservative wing of his own party. He argued that as head of the Democratic Party, he had a right to speak about contests where "there may be a clear issue between candidates for a Democratic nomination involving these principles, or involving a clear misuse of my name." Yet once again, he moved circuitously in identifying and attacking those apostates. In the end, except in one instance, FDR's opponents were reelected. The purge failed, and so did this seeming last gasp of Roosevelt's domestic leadership. The Republican ranks in the House increased from 89 seats to 164, and they picked up 7 seats in the Senate. The GOP also carried the governorships of Ohio, Massachusetts, and Minnesota. The new Republican–conservative Democratic coalition would prove congenial to stopping any New Deal initiatives. But by then, Roosevelt's attention was shifting from domestic concerns to the worsening international situation.[17]

The Domestic Record

It is commonplace to state that the New Deal did not end the Great Depression—the war did. In one narrow sense, the conditions of depression persisted, especially in the 1938 downturn, until the expenditures for defense rapidly expanded. Keynes had been correct: government deficits—whether for domestic programs or military preparedness—would liven up a prostrate patient. But the New Deal did provide for both relief for the needy and some substantial reform. What major elements of the welfare state America has—elements the conservative Junker Chancellor Otto Bismarck instituted in Germany in the nineteenth century—came mainly from New Deal initiatives and, to a lesser extent, subsequent Great Society legislation. The Social Security Act, TVA, stock market controls, federal insurance of bank deposits, aid to dependent individuals, farm subsidies, and a host of other reforms stayed with the American people. Work relief, welfare, employment opportunities, handouts—all of them prevented even more misery, and some of the make-work efforts left the nation with forests, dams, post offices, libraries, and public works that built up the country's infrastructure.

The New Deal did not destroy capitalism; it propped it up, smoothed some of its rougher features, and made it more hospitable to the America of the 1930s. Roosevelt was no socialist, nor was he a closet conservative, as the left believed. Roosevelt identified with planned change and progressive reforms. In the convention and election of 1932, FDR was the most liberal candidate who had a chance of winning the presidency. If at times he covered up confusion with a generally buoyant confidence, Roosevelt viewed leadership more as an emotional than an intellectual activity.

However, the New Deal was not a short-run success; it did not end the Great Depression. When Roosevelt took office, he tried a host of experimental programs, many of them ideologically at variance with one another. Liberals have praised this eclectic approach, seeing it as a welcome contrast to Hoover's narrow-gauged responses. But FDR allowed those initiatives to proliferate because he simply did not know what would work, and rather than go down to defeat with one concerted and systematic program, he hoped that a collection and then a succession of activities would allow him to ferret out the worthwhile ones. Yet he remained committed to a balanced budget, disliked federal bureaucracy, and generally disavowed relief and make-work efforts.

In the first New Deal of 1933–1934, this very openness seemed to bring benefits and allowed FDR to be chief broker and friend to all people and all interests. But the criticism of the administration from the very circles that had benefited the most from his dramatic actions, the business interests and upper classes, confused and then angered Roosevelt. To him it was simple avarice, and with a strong challenge from the left both in Congress and in the country, he responded with a "second New Deal," featuring rhetoric and proposals clearly antibusiness and hostile to inherited money.

Thus, by 1937–1938, the New Deal was in a quandary. To bring full recovery, the administration had to restore business confidence, resort to governmental ownership of selected businesses, or engage in massive spending. FDR's personalized campaign of 1936 and the ferocious and often mindless attacks by the rich on him prevented the first course of action; the American people would probably not have approved of government ownership beyond a TVA type of innovation, except perhaps in 1933 for the collapsed banking community; and as far as the third alternative was concerned, the president was unwilling to buy wholeheartedly a Keynesian approach to recovery—a blind spot shared by most educated Americans, including many economists. So the New Deal, which was a product of the "middle way," may have been undone in the end by that very confusion that compromise and moderation bring.

Watching FDR operate in this domestic context has led some observers to see persistent patterns in his leadership: a tactical skill, an unwillingness to commit himself wholeheartedly to anyone or any program, a style of dealing with conflict that depended on personal charm, a superficial attention to detail, a sense of timing that often followed public opinion rather than forming it, and a guarded view about the efficacy of being able to educate the populace and the elites. FDR could stir the masses, charm the malcontents, and cajole and bargain with the professional politicians. But in some ways, he lacked Lincoln's ability to link up tactics and purpose, to take the hurt and pursue some overall sense of direction. To Roosevelt, the issue often was himself—all else seemed secondary.

That style served him well at first. By 1940, FDR had been over-whelmingly elected president twice and could have the nomination again if he so indicated. His domestic record was more impressive than that of any president before him, and his very name remained magic in the air. His enemies were well heeled and well established, but "that man in the White House" retained a hold on the public imagination. And even though he was privately an unhappily married man who craved attention and ap-proval, to the public FDR seemed buoyant and immensely successful.

The greatest failure in public policy, the persistent Depression, re-mained as the bad times of 1939 continued, but that too gave way—not to the charm of FDR or to the concerted efforts of ardent New Deal activities, but to the harsh realities of the war in Europe. Making America an arsenal of democracy, Roosevelt was able to end the Great Depression more quickly and more permanently than anyone could have imagined.

Early International Concerns

By background and experience, Franklin D. Roosevelt was an interna-tionalist. His family had made its fortune in part from the Asian trade, and many of the Hyde Park mementos were partially bought from the profits of its exotic fare. FDR knew world history and geography, spent summers abroad, and watched as cousin Theodore positioned the United States to be a world power. During World War I, FDR absorbed the Wilsonian internationalist doctrine and went down to defeat in 1920 on a ticket com-mitted to the League.

But Roosevelt was not one to wear his ideology heavily; he soon argued that the League of Nations was not Wilson's original dream, and in 1932, he shocked his old Wilsonian friends by caving in to Hearst's demand that he repudiate the international organization. He did so and probably got the nomination in part because of that betrayal. In the early 1930s, FDR learned quickly that anti-international feeling was strong, as the Senate rebelled and refused to approve his modest proposal to join the International Court of Justice in The Hague. During those years, he initially encouraged the London Economic Conference in 1933 and tried to play a leadership role in dealing with the international depression, high tariffs, and the debts owed to the United States by the European democ-racies. But faced with the choice between making real commitments on these issues or adjusting the American dollar to help recovery at home, FDR chose the latter course, dashed the hopes he had raised, and incurred severe criticism abroad.[18]

During the early 1930s, FDR tried to interject himself repeatedly into the affairs of Europe and Asia, but he was unwilling to extend any efforts to garner domestic support for his proposals. These abrupt stops and starts have given the mistaken impression that he was either a true isolationist or a weak-kneed Wilsonian who waited for the war in order to resurrect his predecessor's dream of a true family of nations. FDR was neither; he understood rather well what was happening in Europe, was unwilling at first to expend his political capital generally to explain those events to the American people, waged an undeclared war to aid Britain months before Pearl Harbor, and placed his hopes on a postwar alliance of the great powers rather than on his own United Nations. The last misconception about Roosevelt is that having led the nation brilliantly during the military effort, he then sold out Eastern Europe to the Soviet Union, leaving a legacy that became the Cold War. A more correct appraisal is that FDR did little in the day-to-day operations of the war, delegating those to gifted subordinates, most especially to General Marshall, but that he still probably made a half dozen key strategic decisions that set the framework for the Allies' marches. As for his wartime diplomacy, much of the criticism is misdirected and historically unfounded, even though legions of Americans and Europeans have linked up FDR, Yalta, and appeasement as if they were modern synonyms.[19]

In March 1933, while Roosevelt sought to restore to Americans' faith in themselves, he also encouraged the World Disarmament Conference taking place in Geneva. He pushed for a nonaggression pact, the end of offensive weapons, and a curb on arms and armed forces. But with Hitler's rise to power, Germany withdrew from the conference and from the League of Nations. The newly inaugurated American president was also concerned with both naval disarmament and Japan's demand for parity. Consequently, Roosevelt sought to get the British to stand firm against parity, but the British were more concerned with a newly aggressive Germany than with the Japanese.

Roosevelt's secretary of state, Cordell Hull, at the same time had pushed hard for trade agreements and for an end to interference in the affairs of Latin America. Roosevelt and Hull laid aside the Platt Amendment, which allowed the United States to intervene in Cuba, and FDR also pulled the marines out of Haiti and made friendly overtures to Panama. The administration called its new sensitivity the "Good Neighbor Policy" and presented it as a more fruitful direction than the mixture of marines and economic imperialism that had so marked administrations before Roosevelt.[20]

The Isolationist Fervor

From his first inaugural to Pearl Harbor, FDR had to face the consequences of widespread American disillusionment with World War I.
That sentiment was fed by the hearings of Senator Gerald P. Nye and his
committee, which investigated the munitions industry. Amid charges of
bribery, collusion, gross profiteering, and tax evasion, the committee laid
the groundwork for linking up munitions makers and the advent of the
war. These "merchants of death" had been responsible for encouraging
America's entry into the conflagration, and throughout the country, peace
societies and isolationists pledged to prevent a repetition of those mistakes.

Oddly enough, FDR also denounced the arms trade and granted Nye
access to documents that were to assist his committee with its allegations.
As isolationist feeling grew, Congress was pressed to enact legislation that
would require the president to embargo the export of arms to all belligerents in the case of war abroad. The president pushed for some provision
to discriminate between aggressor and victim, but the tide in Congress
overwhelmed him, and FDR signed a bill that would in the future severely
tie his hands.

As the president approved the Neutrality Act, Benito Mussolini's Italian
forces invaded Ethiopia. A U.S. arms embargo under the law would work
against Italy, which had the ability, more than the Ethiopians, to buy and
ship significant amounts of arms. But neither France nor Britain seemed
willing to stop Mussolini, and the League of Nations proved to be ineffectual after the attack. The president retreated even further behind the
isolationist curtain.[21]

Thus, the early pattern of FDR's behavior seems clear. He was genuinely concerned about the deteriorating state of affairs in the world, and
he tried to use suasion, moral appeals, and goodwill to foster disarmament,
peaceful settlement of conflicts, and economic prosperity. But behind these
mild and well-meaning intentions, there was strong public isolationist
sentiment, which Roosevelt was unwilling to confront. Thus, despite his
personal reservations, FDR approved the initial neutrality law and watched
as Italy invaded Ethiopia, Japan gobbled up China, and Hitler took over
the Sudetenland, Austria, and Czechoslovakia. The foremost study of
Roosevelt's foreign policy, done by Robert Dallek, has shown that the
president was very well informed and quite involved in a detailed way with
the full international picture. Yet again and again, his modest advances
were followed by retreat in the face of congressional opposition or the
suggestions of public disapproval. At times, it appears that FDR bent not

with the wind but with the zephyr—that he did not inspire but responded on a calibrated range so fine that the possibilities of leadership were too easily forfeited. James MacGregor Burns concluded, "As a foreign policy maker, Roosevelt during his first term was more a pussy-footing politician than political leader."[22]

During that term, FDR was obviously more concerned with domestic politics and was unwilling to offend the isolationist bloc—many of whose members were supporters of the New Deal. But it is also probable that he shared many of the assumptions of the isolationists. In his speeches and in his personal correspondence, Roosevelt insisted that the United States should stay out of future conflicts. He counseled the American ambassador to Germany, William Dodd, "I do not know that the United States can save civilization but at least by our example we can make people think and give them the opportunity of saving themselves."[23] In August 1936 in a Chautauqua address, FDR took up the merchants of death theme and warned about the "fool's gold" of trading with belligerents. Then, in one of his most powerful appeals, Roosevelt remarked,

> I have seen war. I have seen war on land and sea. I have seen blood running from the wounded. I have seen men coughing out their gassed lungs. I have seen the dead in the mud. I have seen cities destroyed. I have seen two hundred limping, exhausted men come out of line—the survivors of a regiment of one thousand that went forward forty-eight hours before. I have seen children starving. I have seen the agony of mothers and wives. I hate war.

Perhaps it was just a 1936 campaign speech finely tuned to a pacifist audience. But more likely it was a genuine expression of Roosevelt's horror of war, the consequences of which he had seen only late on his trip to Europe as assistant secretary of the navy. But by 1935, the president clearly comprehended the rising threat of the totalitarian states. He allowed Hull to promote a coordinated and publicly indignant policy, which was aimed at supporting the League of Nations' sanctions against Italy for its invasion of Ethiopia. But when the League failed to act, and the British and the French agreed to the dismemberment of a large portion of Ethiopia, the issue became moot. Whether Roosevelt would have persevered if it mattered is not clear, but he definitely did try to prevent American citizens from profiting from such conflicts.

A similar dilemma faced FDR with regard to Japan's invasion of China in the summer of 1937. An arms embargo in that case would have worked against the Chinese, and the president decided to withhold a neutrality proclamation unless a formal declaration of war came. Despite his sympathies for China and strong U.S. sentiment against the Japanese, Roosevelt feared a conflict on the high seas with the Japanese navy. He ended up announcing new restrictions on American trade with China.[24]

Then on October 5, 1937, FDR decided to make a major address on aggression and "the reign of terror and international lawlessness" that was taking place. With the Japanese attacks on China obviously in mind, he deplored the bombing of civilians, the sinking of ships on the high seas, and the brutality of conquest. Then he warned that the New World would not ultimately be spared the horrors of war. He called war a contagion and argued, "When an epidemic of physical disease starts to spread, the community approves and joins in a quarantine of the patients in order to protect the health of the community against the spread of the disease." He went on to request vaguely that there should be "positive endeavors to preserve peace." The speech seemed a clarion call to action, but what did Roosevelt have in mind? It is difficult to say, for no sooner had FDR staked out a position than he equivocated and backpedaled. Privately, he wrote his old headmaster at Groton, "As you know, I am fighting against a public psychology of long standing—a psychology which comes very close to saying, 'Peace at any price.'"[25]

Indecisiveness characterized Roosevelt's behavior toward Nazi Germany as well. As Hitler rearmed Germany in 1935 and later marched into the Rhineland, the administration said nothing. When Neville Chamberlain reached an agreement with Hitler at Munich, Roosevelt seemed to be of two minds. He was relieved that war was temporarily averted, and yet he was privately skeptical that peace was at hand. War would mean the loss of millions of lives "under circumstances of unspeakable horror," and yet negotiations would postpone "what looks to me like an inevitable conflict within the next five years." The president retained the same standoffish attitude concerning the Spanish Civil War. In 1936, during the presidential campaign, FDR insisted on the United States being neutral and placed an embargo on the export of arms to either side. As time passed, though, the president recognized that noninterference would really end up assisting the pro-fascist regime of General Francisco Franco. At one point in the spring of 1938, he proposed to lift the embargo on arms, but then he decided against a change of policy. The president understood that the munitions would not go across the Spanish frontier anyhow, but his real concern was alienating the Catholic vote. Even Ickes was disgusted that these foreign policy determinations were being dictated, in his opinion, in the United States and Great Britain by Catholic minorities. Thus, by the end of 1938,

FDR had made his own transition as he came to view the world as a more hostile and threatening place than before. But his own leadership remained vague and almost shadowy.[26]

In July 1939, the president warned Congress that "philosophies of force" were threatening the American way of life and that no nation would be safe where aggression went unchecked. He counseled, "There are many methods short of war, but stronger and more effective than mere words, of bringing home to aggressor governments the aggregate sentiments of our own people." The president asked for a revision of the neutrality laws, which "may operate unevenly and unfairly—may actually give aid to an aggressor and deny it to the victim."

After Hitler's conquest of the rest of Czechoslovakia in March 1939, an attempt was made in the Senate to repeal the arms embargo and permit U.S. citizens to trade with nations at war on a cash and carry basis—terms that would favor the British and French. The president, though, remained silent on the debate, and only when it was too late did he strongly push for revision of the arms embargo. Then on September 1, 1939, the Germans invaded Poland, and FDR proclaimed U.S. neutrality and enacted an arms embargo. Again the president pressed for a revision of the Neutrality Act and insisted that his purpose was to keep the United States out of the war, not to help the British or the French. He concluded, "My problem is to get the American people to think of conceivable consequences without scaring the American people into thinking they are going to be dragged into this war."[27]

The Nazi Onslaught

The American people were indeed to do more than ponder the conceivable consequences of war: they were to see the Nazi forces sweep over Norway and Denmark into the Low Countries and France. The "phony" war gave way to the war of lightning movement—the blitzkrieg. As the British scrambled from France and imprinted their retreat on Dunkirk, Americans of many persuasions realized that German advances were certainly a threat to U.S. interests. Roosevelt knew what he could not probably admit: that his nation's security was dependent on the ability of the British and the French to stop the Nazi armies. But he was unwilling to confront directly the isolationist and pacifist elements in America. Indeed, the best summary of American public opinion was that it supported the British and the French against the Germans, but it wished that the United States would stay out of the war.

On June 14, 1940, French Premier Paul Reynaud asked for American troops and supplies to save his nation. Roosevelt's response was to praise French valor and resistance and to increase arms and munitions. But he would make no military commitments because of Congress. Two days later, the French surrendered to the Nazis, leaving the British to fight alone.[28]

By May 1940, the new British prime minister, Winston S. Churchill, pleaded for American destroyers to protect the Atlantic supply lines from German submarines. Roosevelt hesitated, unsure what to do. He insisted that he needed an act of Congress to transfer destroyers to Great Britain. His own cabinet pressured the president to meet Churchill's demands, while Congress insisted that the executive could not transfer any warships until the chief of naval operations certified they were "not essential" to the defense of the United States. Roosevelt's response was again inaction. Churchill pleaded, "Mr. President with great respect I must tell you that in the long history of the world this is a thing to do NOW." But the president seemed undecided as to how to proceed.[29]

By August, several people had proposed a trade—American destroyers for British bases. Roosevelt, though, still believed that the agreement needed congressional approval, and he was concerned the Republicans would use the deal as a campaign issue. Thus, some four months after Churchill's desperate appeal, Roosevelt acted—but only after public support had swung over to strongly favor the British, after Wendell Willkie privately promised not to raise the matter in the campaign, and after FDR's advisers found a way to avoid having to go to Congress over the deal.

Roosevelt was especially sensitive to criticism in 1940. After some real hesitation and deliberate coyness, he had decided to challenge the two-term tradition and run for a third term. To his surprise and that of many political observers, the Republican Party did not turn to established politicians such as Thomas Dewey, Robert Taft, or Arthur Vandenberg. Instead the Grand Old Party nominated Wendell Willkie, an activist, energetic, rumpled utilities executive. Roosevelt had shrewdly reached out to the traditional Republican elites before the election by bringing two well-known Republicans into his cabinet: Henry L. Stimson as secretary of war and Frank Knox as secretary of navy. Knox had been a Rough Rider and Landon's running mate in 1936, and Stimson was a cabinet member under Taft and Hoover.

Willkie ran a strong challenge against the president and openly charged that FDR was preparing to lead the nation into the European war. FDR had already hesitated on the destroyer deal until Republican cabinet members Stimson and Knox pressed him on the bases swap. Then he faced an even touchier subject: compulsory military service. Throughout the summer until August 2, FDR simply avoided providing any leadership on the bill that Secretary Stimson pressed for. He instead visited defense installations, stressed the importance of preparedness, and warned about the gravity of the European situation.

Still, FDR knew that Willkie's charges were making some headway. People had reservations about a third term, strong executive power in a world of totalitarian states, and the abuses of some New Deal programs. But the most explosive issue was the advance of war. Roosevelt faced not only the powerful forces of isolationism and pacifism but also the reservations of Italian American, German American, and Irish American voters. The polls in October showed that Willkie was cutting into FDR's large early lead.

Roosevelt, who had played a waiting game all summer, swung into action and launched a powerful offensive against the Republican Party. He recalled once again the world of the Great Depression, the economy before the New Deal, and its cornucopia of benefits. He attacked the party of "Martin, Barton, and Fish"—three conservative Republican leaders in Congress who went rhythmically together in his ridicule. But most importantly, the president went into Irish-dominated Boston and pledged, "Your boys are not going to be sent into foreign wars." In the past, he usually added "except in case of attack." Now, facing Willkie's sharp criticisms, he deleted the commonsense guarantee and simply told advisers, "If we're attacked, it's no longer a foreign war."

The final results gave FDR a popular vote of 27,243,466–22,304,755 and an electoral vote of 449–82. The president lost only ten states, although Willkie picked up five million more votes than Landon in 1936. The Democrats lost three seats in the Senate and gained seven seats in the House. Roosevelt's victory, then, was a personal vote of confidence and a rare opportunity for him to exercise leadership in the explosive events unfolding.[30]

Hesitations in 1941

With the election behind him, Roosevelt seemed to be somewhat detached from the terrible fate that was about to fall on Britain in late 1940. The president made no shifts in the cabinet, indicated that he would not ask for any changes in the Neutrality Act, and did not respond to Churchill's frantic calls for still more assistance. But then in December,

Roosevelt began to lay out the general outlines of what became known as "Lend Lease." The United States would send the British government munitions without requiring payment, and when the war was over, the British would repay in kind, not in dollars. He presented his plan in a homey analogy—lending your garden hose to your neighbor, whose home was on fire. To the American people, he insisted, "Our national policy is not directed toward war. Its sole purpose is to keep war away from our country and our people." The president summarized the U.S. role in the struggle: "We must be the great arsenal of democracy. For us this is an emergency as serious as war itself."

In the early weeks of 1941, the polls showed that the American people favored Lend Lease by a margin of two to one, with opposition strongest in the isolationist areas of the Midwest and the Great Plains states. That opposition was most pronounced in the Senate, where the opposition was spearheaded by some major leaders, such as Hiram Johnson of California; Burt Wheeler of Montana; the younger Robert LaFollette of Wisconsin; Arthur Vandenberg of Michigan; Bennett Clark of Missouri; Gerald P. Nye of North Dakota; and the newly prominent senator from Ohio, Robert Taft, son of the former president. Against the combined forces of isolationism, the president proceeded cautiously, even avoiding responding to personal attacks on his motives.[31]

In addition, FDR established an advisory commission to the Council of National Defense, a collection of advisers that included William S. Knudsen of General Motors; Edward R. Stettinius, a wealthy financier; labor leader Sidney Hillman; and Leon Henderson, a dedicated New Dealer. Later, Roosevelt set up the Office of Production Management, with Knudsen, Hillman, Stimson, and Knox, to deal with production problems and national mobilization of resources. Bernard Baruch, who had served Woodrow Wilson in a similar capacity in the last war, advocated a centralized agency to oversee allocations, priorities, and price-fixing. Roosevelt opposed any czar, arguing that only the president had such authority, and he opposed delegating it.

It was this decentralized style, the overlapping jurisdiction of many layered agencies, and, above all, Roosevelt's fear of political competition that were to plague the American war effort. The techniques that seemed so creative in the early ferment of the first New Deal had led to immobilization and domestic near deadlock in the late 1930s. Those same techniques applied to preparedness worsened critical production delays and led even Stimson to conclude that Roosevelt was the worst administrator he had ever worked for.[32]

Some of his closest advisers in early 1941 added to the informal criticism of their beloved leader. Felix Frankfurter wondered why the president did not seize the initiative, and Stimson told Roosevelt directly in April that his leadership was clearly lacking. But the president was carefully weighing public opinion before the next guarded and tentative step. Even Frances Perkins and Frank Walker were amazed at the ignorance and public apathy they saw as they crisscrossed the nation over this most basic issue of war and peace.[33]

Halfway around the world, Hitler continued his record of awful successes and pondered his boldest move, an attack in the east on the Soviet Union, a nation that he characterized as "the scum of humanity" led by "common blood-starved criminals." At the end of April, five weeks before his planned attack, Hitler was sure: "We have only to kick in the door and the whole rotten structure will come crashing down."[34]

The British, thrown back on their own reliance and courage, worried about Nazi threats to their traditional ally Greece, endured the rapid successes of General Erwin Rommel's attacks in North Africa, and experienced the loss of Crete. Churchill openly faced his critics in the House of Commons; he was stoically to conclude only that "defeat is bitter." In his darkest hour to date, the prime minister implored Roosevelt for more support. Then, on May 10–11, the Nazis attacked London and damaged much of the Houses of Parliament.

In Asia, the flow of events was equally ominous. Japan seemed committed to an expansion of its "Greater East Asia Co-Prosperity Sphere," but the exact direction of the advance was unclear. The most obvious objective was to take control of the rest of China, a nation further split by the rise of the Communist Chinese rivals to Chiang Kai-shek's regime. Engaged in fighting in other theaters of action, the Soviets and Japanese agreed to a nonaggression pact, one consequence of which was to increase anxiety in China. In mid-April, FDR quietly approved an executive order that allowed U.S. airmen to resign from the military service in order to form volunteer civilian groups to go to China. This move led to the formation of the Flying Tigers under Colonel Claire L. Chennault, which was pledged to assist Chiang's forces.

In the crucial months of late 1940 and early 1941, FDR still refused to commit himself to long-term action. He warned Secretary of Navy Knox to avoid making authorizations that extended beyond July 1, 1941, and he refused to allow his military chiefs to engage in military planning with the British. American military leaders had insisted on the need to coordinate intelligence and planning with the British. After the presidential election, the chief of naval operations, Harold Stark, put forth four basic scenarios for the United States: (1) emphasize hemispheric defense; (2) concentrate on stopping Japan; (3) commit equal forces to the Atlantic and Pacific theaters; or (4) give the Atlantic operations priority over the Pacific war.

The president did not approve any of Stark's options, but he did permit some conversations with the British. By 1941, the army and the navy chiefs had apparently come to favor the last of Stark's options—an "Atlantic First" strategy if war came. As for the president, he seemed at times eclectic if not confused in his approach to the complex crisis; he did recognize the need to choose a strong army chief of staff, and his choice was career officer George Marshall. Marshall provided a sense of cool efficiency, organizational comprehensiveness, and genuine strength of character that later earned him the title "architect of Allied victory." In this period, he too was struggling with Roosevelt's facile charm, disorganized ways, and seemingly short-term commitments to plans and people.[35]

As the American and British military leaders prepared some joint agreements, Roosevelt stayed somewhat away from the plans. Inevitably, the Atlantic First strategy became firmed up, without any serious strategic discussion at the presidential level about the feasibility of other options. The United States was committed to providing Britain with all aid short of going to war itself. But Hitler's forces were brutally impressive, and by April, there was serious doubt that Britain could survive. A worried Roosevelt authorized the repair of British ships in American docks, allowed British pilots to be trained in U.S. airfields, widened the American neutrality patrol zone, transferred ten Coast Guard cutters to the Royal Navy, and put Greenland and the coast of West Africa under navy surveillance. With the Danish government's agreement, FDR first placed Greenland under the aegis of the United States and then started the construction of military bases there.

As the Nazis continued to sink British convoys in the Atlantic, the president faced intense pressure from his own cabinet to provide some protection for shipping. But FDR again hesitated, waiting, it seemed, for some provocation from Hitler. He confided to Morgenthau in May, "I am waiting to be pushed into the situation." Stimson also thought that the president was waiting for some incident to move the nation closer to war, but Ickes wrote FDR that Hitler was not going to allow that to happen.[36]

Roosevelt carefully watched the May Gallup poll, which indicated that about one-quarter of the respondents thought the president had not gone far enough to help Britain, the same number thought he had gone too far, and half pretty much approved of his actions. As Roosevelt struggled with a public statement on the convoy question, the German battleship *Bismarck* swept across the North Sea, threatening Britain. The president wondered if the *Bismarck* would show up in the Caribbean and if U.S. submarines should attempt to sink it. He speculated that he then might be impeached for such an action. Two days later, the British sank the great invader, and the president rested more comfortably, not having to make a decision. The president's speech resulted in a proclamation of unilateral national emergency, but he neither made plans for American convoys nor advocated revising the Neutrality Act. Once again, FDR backtracked, waiting for an event to bring about the opening his leadership skills could not provide. Then, in June 1941, Hitler invaded the Soviet Union.

FDR's attitudes toward the Soviet Union were more guarded than has generally been portrayed. Although he recognized the Soviet Union diplomatically early in his first term, he retained a basic antipathy toward Bolshevism. When the Soviets suddenly became Britain's necessary allies, FDR indicated in general terms that he would be willing to extend aid to the Soviet Union as well. He wrote one editor, Fulton Oursler, that he "would write an editorial condemning the Russian form of dictatorship equally with the German form of dictatorship—but at the same time, I would make it clear that the immediate menace at this time to the security of the United States lies in the threat of Hitler's armies."

His cabinet pushed for an immediate and major commitment to the Soviet Union before Hitler could effectively sweep through the western part of that vast nation. Then the cautious FDR approved navy escorts for American shipping and that of other countries that were joining the U.S. convoys west of Ireland. That decision represented some movement on Roosevelt's part, but he still refused to protect all friendly shipping in the west Atlantic, a step Secretary of the Navy Knox had insisted on. The president desperately sought not to raise the level of opposition in Congress by bolder actions; he waited for an incident in the Atlantic, but Hitler, in turn, had commanded his admirals not to rise to the bait.

In the Pacific, FDR was even more cautious. He argued that since trouble was coming in the Atlantic, it was important to avoid conflict in the Far East. When Ickes told him to cut off oil to Japan, FDR warned, "It is terribly important for the control of the Atlantic for us to help to keep peace in the Pacific. I simply have not got enough Navy to go around—and every little episode in the Pacific means fewer ships in the Atlantic."[37]

In Japan, various factions were vying for control of the government and the emperor's favor, until finally the militarists seized power. As their armies swept through Indochina and ripped deeper into decaying China,

Roosevelt made some modest moves. He froze all Japanese assets in the United States, closed the Panama Canal "for repairs," and placed Lieutenant General Douglas MacArthur in command over the Filipino military.

Faced with British demands for more war supplies and the new list of Soviet needs, Roosevelt had to deal with the consequences of the disorganized production mechanisms he had insisted on. In March 1941, he created the National Defense Mediation Board to deal with the increase in industrial strikes. A month later, the president added the Office of Price Administration and Civilian Supply, and then in May, he had the energetic and flamboyant mayor of New York City, Fiorello LaGuardia, head up the Office of Civilian Defense. The problems he faced were by no means minor ones. In April, John L. Lewis took four hundred thousand coal miners out on strike, and the president had to intervene in getting a settlement in that crucial industry. Then, in the summer, a wildcat strike hit North American Aviation Company, and Roosevelt eventually ordered the secretary of war to take over the plant. Thus, while the Nazis were at Britain's throat and the Soviets were forced into their frozen positions, it was business as usual in the United States, and the president did not seem to be too far in front of popular sentiment.

The British economist John Maynard Keynes warned that the mobilization efforts were deficient and that a stronger conversion program had to be pushed through. In Congress, the Senate Special Committee to Investigate the Defense Program pointed out a host of delays and production problems. One committee member, Tom Connally of Texas, concluded, "We are just advertising to the world . . . that we are in a mess." To increasing charges that he had not exhibited forethought, FDR seemed oblivious. On one hand, the president may have had a better sense of the divisions on Capitol Hill than anyone recognized. In the summer of 1941 the Selective Service Act renewal passed the House by only *one* vote. The supposedly stronger consensus on preparedness was just as Roosevelt had assumed—much more fragile and tentative than other people had asserted. Amid all those pressures, FDR received increasing complaints about racial discrimination in defense industries. African American leaders, led by A. Philip Randolph, insisted on an executive order barring discrimination, but FDR resisted. Randolph threatened a march on Washington to press the case, and the president capitulated with a high-sounding and rather vague document that finally created the Committee on Fair Employment Practices.

In August, FDR agreed to a surprise meeting with Winston S. Churchill off the coast of Newfoundland. While the military staffs on each side presented their differing perspectives on the war, the president and the prime minister agreed to a statement of principles, later called the Atlantic Charter. Roosevelt assiduously avoided making any commitments that could be interpreted at home as "secret agreements." Churchill, not surprisingly, pressed for some evidence of greater support, some hope for a struggling ally.

Back in the United States, Roosevelt was indeed faced with charges of planning a secret invasion of Europe and of leading the nation into another foreign war. Every move the president made resulted in bitter scrutiny and charges from isolationists. Yet his own cabinet, led by Stimson, insisted the nation needed more leadership to meet production schedules and that military strategists needed more of a sense of FDR's views. And despite his assurances to Churchill that he would act more forcefully in his dealings with Tokyo, FDR was still cautious about his moves in the Pacific. The Japanese government responded with vague assurances of goodwill and a pledge to withdraw from Indochina. As the two governments parlayed, the imperial armed forces prepared for war. Initially, the emperor insisted that he would not approve going to war unless all possibilities for peace had ended. Finally, the Japanese empire was geared up to go to war by the end of October 1941 unless its demands were met. Basically, its leaders wanted an end to American and British interference in China, support for the Chungking regime there, and cooperation in Japanese economic development.[38]

As Roosevelt and Hull were pondering the reality of Japan's expressed objectives, an American destroyer, the Greer, began trailing a German U-boat and reported the latter's position to a British plane. The U-boat fired on the Greer, and FDR took this incident as the occasion for a major change of policy. He announced to the American people a policy of "shoot on sight"—in effect, a declaration of naval war against Germany. The U.S. Navy was ordered to protect all shipping of any nation in convoys going to Ireland. It was a clear challenge to Hitler, but the Führer again refused to respond.

The polls showed a two to one approval rating for the shoot-on-sight policy, and FDR moved to modify the Neutrality Act, emphasizing the need to arm American merchant ships. Then on October 16, 1941, a convoy of forty ships escorted by four corvettes was attacked by a group of U-boats; one of the American destroyers rushing to give assistance, the USS Kearney, was hit by a torpedo. As the House of Representatives debated a revision of the Neutrality Act, the report of the attack tipped the scales and the act was changed after a vote of 259–138. The bill moved to the Senate, and FDR helped lay the groundwork there by disclosing he had two important documents in hand. One was a Nazi map of South and Central America that divided those regions into states; the other was a Nazi plan to abolish all religions if Hitler were successful in his conquests. The Senate supported some revision of the Neutrality Act by a vote of 50–37. Several days later the American destroyer *Reuben James* was torpedoed and went down with 115 members of its crew.[39]

Decision in the Pacific

Roosevelt thus was able to get some moderate changes in congressional policy with these inflammatory incidents, but he still lacked any consensus on going to war or facing Hitler directly. By November 1941, the "Old Master" had no more options to play out; he was stalemated in his policies and he refused to be too far in front. His admirer and speechwriter Robert Sherwood concluded, "He had no more tricks left. The bag from which he had pulled so many rabbits was empty." FDR systematically avoided a showdown with Japan, expecting the need to move fast in the Atlantic theater. But there Hitler refused to be Roosevelt's foil and give him the clear attack necessary to mobilize the American people. So in late 1941, the Americans waged an undeclared war in the North Sea and watched uneasily as the Japanese navy seemed to be on the move in the Pacific. The administration had decided in November 1941 to augment the defense of the Philippines and had planned in two or three months to make it viable in case of attack.

The president also waited until Congress passed the Lend Lease bill before he notified the Soviets that they could expect aid totaling $1 billion. To circumvent Catholic opposition to aiding a Communist regime, the president quietly appealed to Pope Pius XII for some understanding. The Vatican was not impressed by his plea but indicated that there was a distinction between aiding the Soviets in war and aiding the Communist regime.

In any case, by November the Japanese government had its own timetable for the completion of talks with the Roosevelt administration. Some bitter Roosevelt haters have charged that FDR knew about Japanese designs on Pearl Harbor before the attack and allowed American forces to be left vulnerable there, realizing that such aggression would end the debate over American foreign policy once and for all. The general weight of the evidence, though, favors the view that FDR did not know about the specific targeting of Pearl Harbor. Still, in early December, the president seemed to sense that war was in the immediate vicinity. On December 1 he told Morgenthau, "It is all in the laps of the gods." And five days later he told another associate, "We might be at war with Japan, although no one knew." However, he expected that the Japanese would move in the Dutch East Indies or Thailand, rather than in the Philippines or Hawaii. He miscalculated that the Japanese would first attack the smaller nations before encircling the larger ones in the region. Then on December 6, the president received reports of a large Japanese convoy and ship movements in the southwest Pacific. He observed, "This means war." But when Hopkins lamented that the Japanese would pick the target and the United States couldn't strike the first blow, FDR replied, "No, we can't do that. We are a democracy and a peaceful people. . . . But we have a good record." A little after 7:30 a.m. on December 7, 1941, the Japanese attacked with a fury at Pearl Harbor.[40]

Roosevelt at first seemed calm, in fact relieved, that the long debate had ended; only later was he sobered by the terrible list of losses, especially to his beloved navy. Stimson pressed for a declaration of war against Germany as well as Japan, but the president again cautiously refused. When he approached Congress on December 8, he called the surprise attack "a date which will live in infamy" and pledged the nation to the inevitable triumph with the help of God. Only one member of Congress, Jeannette Rankin, who had opposed going to war in 1917, voted against the war declaration. Still, it was only half a war until Hitler and Mussolini decided to honor their loose alliance with Japan and declare a formal state of war with the United States as well.

As for Roosevelt, he acknowledged the serious setbacks in the Hawaiian Islands and in the Philippines. He expected heavy casualties and concluded, "It will not only be a long war, but a hard war." Events were to prove him correct. But with the brutal sneak attack on Pearl Harbor, isolationist and peace sentiment ended almost totally. After years of hesitation, false starts, and lethargic leadership at times, Franklin Roosevelt got the dramatic event he needed to unite the nation, an event more final and more traumatic than even the banking crisis that greeted him in 1933. More than Wilson or Lincoln, FDR entered the war with little domestic carping and fifth-column activity. And because of the Nazi attack on the Soviet Union, the organized left, traditionally opposed to the American military and defense preparedness, now welcomed U.S. participation in the war. As the record of atrocities of the Nazis became more visible, this conflict between and among great powers for position, empire, living room, and colonial expansion took on a different tone. The Second World War became a great moral crusade in which the simplicities of good and evil seemed to be a truthful relief on which the ambiguous battles became memorialized. Because Hitler, Mussolini, and the Japanese warlords seemed so truly evil, the Allied leaders stood out in heroic terms. The buoyant FDR, the gallant Churchill, and the prickly Charles DeGaulle became international figures to freedom-loving peoples. Even the tyrannical Stalin became in World War II metamorphosed for a time into a father figure, although a suspicious one. Only later was he more appropriately measured beside Hitler and Mao Tse-tung of China in his deeds of butchery. Together, they became the nightmare of the twentieth century—the demons of the left and the right. But in the depths of the war, Stalin was a critical, if not indispensable, ally. When asked to explain why he was willing to make common cause with the Soviet dictator, Churchill told the House of Commons that he would make an alliance with the devil to defeat the Nazis. He did, and so did FDR.

The year 1942 would prove to be a very bad start for the formal Anglo-American alliance. The Japanese swept across the Pacific basin and beyond, taking the Philippines, Guam, Midway, Singapore, Thailand, Hong Kong, and other strategic points. The Americans had to pay the piper for their slow mobilization, the transfer of Lend Lease to Europe, and the neglect of the armed forces for a generation. The president and his advisers faced not one front but two, and Roosevelt made the first critically important decision of his wartime stewardship: despite the American outrage over Pearl Harbor, the United States would concentrate on an Atlantic First strategy so as to join the British in defeating the Nazis and Fascists before turning full force on the Japanese. "Plan Dog," as it was called, was an important commitment to the British, and Churchill was unashamedly delighted.

At a Christmas-time meeting, the prime minister, and his major associates Lord Beaverbrook and Lord Halifax, were better prepared than the American staff for a discussion of strategy. The British expected the Germans to move down the Iberian Peninsula into North Africa, and they were ready to check the advance by having the Americans invade near Casablanca and drive toward their forces in the east in the direction of Tunisia. Roosevelt at first seemed amenable to the idea, but then he downplayed the initiative.

The Americans and British joined in a spirit of common defense while insisting on important differences in strategy. The American military chiefs, true heirs of the tradition of Grant and Sherman, believed in the need to build up their force strength and then begin a massive thrust toward the heart of Germany. The British, remembering the terrible stalemate of trench warfare in the previous war, insisted on a strategy of moving at soft spots of opportunity and enemy imbalance. The Americans regarded that approach as a wasteful expenditure of resources, a "peripheralism," as it was called, that had led to the type of disaster in the Dardanelles with which Churchill had been associated in the previous war.

Actually, both staffs were correct in some ways. The Allies in 1942 were not ready for the type of concentrated invasion the Americans were contemplating, and yet the war could only be won by a bloodletting across the European continent. Meanwhile in the Pacific, the Japanese advance continued as the Christmas strategy session took place. General Marshall insisted on a unified Pacific command, and the Allies agreed, thus placing the troops of the Americans, British, Dutch, and Australians under the command of British general Archibald Wavell. The Allies accepted a combined British-American chief of staff command, which in the long run would give the United States increasing ascendancy in the direction of the war. Since FDR still had no real "joint chiefs" structure similar to that of the British, he created such a component made up of Marshall, Admiral Ernest J. King, the chief of naval operations, and General Henry Arnold. As a result of their deliberations, the Allies agreed on the North African campaign "Operation Gymnast"—more as a recognition that victory had to be garnered somewhere and that Europe was not the place. It is sometimes forgotten that while the Americans were mobilizing for action and the British held to a defensive strategy by the skin of their teeth, the real battle against the Nazi war machine was being waged in 1942 in the eastern theater. There the Soviet soldiers, fighting for the survival of their nation and not any particular ideology, waged a terrible struggle against the advancing Germans. Stalin's demand to the Allies was brutally simple and easily explainable: a second front, a major assault on the Nazis in the west to divert troops away from his theater. The Anglo-American strategy, its mobilization problems, and its frequent postponements on that front in 1942, 1943, and 1944 led him to suspect that the real strategy was to let the Nazis and the Soviets bleed each other dry.

Wisely, Stalin had decided to avoid declaring war on Japan, and the Japanese likewise wanted to avoid fighting on a second front. The combined Allied command under General Wavell did not stop the Japanese as they moved effectively across the Pacific and threatened even Australia. Roosevelt desperately tried early in the war and insistently throughout it to prop up the Chinese regime headed by Chiang Kai-shek. Churchill, while expressing his respect for the Chinese "as a race," thought the president greatly overestimated their importance in the world. In this disastrous theater of the Pacific, the Untied States was to find a hero: General Douglas MacArthur. MacArthur was vain, difficult, disobedient, and a publicity hound of the first order, but he was also a brilliant and creative American military strategist. In 1942, he insisted on staying in the Philippines as it fell to the Japanese forces. Roosevelt had other plans—he ordered the Filipino President Manuel Quezon and MacArthur out of the country to Corregidor. MacArthur was to prepare for the defense of vital Australia, but not before he dramatically pledged to the Filipino people, "I shall return." Thus, by springtime, the Japanese were approaching the Australian perimeters and moving on India.

To Churchill, India was the very center of his vision of an extended British domain, and its possession still fired up his Victorian imagination. But to Roosevelt, the true future was clear: the war would sound the death knell for British and French imperialist aspirations. When FDR raised the issue right after Pearl Harbor, Churchill was passionately opposed to any independence; when the president suggested various compromises, including an Indian Union modeled on the U.S. Articles of Confederation, he made no real headway.

As his navy regrouped and began its defensive operations in the Pacific, the president offered no advice; he followed the train of events carefully but stayed out of tactical matters. Admiral King in the capital and Admiral Chester W. Nimitz in the Pacific laid out in 1942 the basic strategy for the war in that region. In the equally disheartening Atlantic theater, the president watched as Hitler ordered his troops to wipe out the Soviets. Stalin insisted on more aid and a cross-Channel invasion. The Communist chief would have been surprised to find that the American high command was agreeing with him. Secretary of War Stimson, Marshall, and his aide Lieutenant General Dwight D. Eisenhower were all pushing for an end to the waste of resources and valuable time. German victories in Libya had led to the postponement of the Allied invasion of North Africa, and the American staff was pressing FDR for a major assault in April 1943 across the English Channel. Marshall and Stimson expected from Roosevelt a vague dismissal or a continued capitulation to British thinking, but the president in fact supported their decision and sent Marshall and Hopkins to convince Churchill. The president wrote the prime minister that the people were demanding action, and that "these people are wise enough to see that the Russians are today killing more Germans and destroying more equipment than you and I put together. Even if full success is not attained, the *big* objective will be." As Marshall was to learn later, for democratic politicians in a war, there is nothing worse than the impression of no military engagements being fought. To the surprise of the Americans, the usually skeptical Churchill did not dismiss the plan, probably because he feared that FDR might concentrate then on the Pacific or that Stalin would negotiate a separate treaty with the Nazis.

Stalin agreed to send Vyacheslav Molotov to Washington to confer on the matter, and the president blithely observed that he could handle Stalin better than the British Foreign Office or the State Department since he "thinks he likes me better and I hope he will continue to do so." To a later generation of Americans, such remarks provided convincing proof that FDR was naive in dealing with the Soviet leader, a naïveté that led to a miscalculation of Soviet intentions and trustworthiness. Yet the truth is that Stalin, who was highly suspicious, if not a classic paranoid, probably did prefer FDR to Churchill, although his decisions were not likely to be influenced by the president's considerable charm. Stalin had grown up in a world of brutal party intrigue, lived by peasant cunning, and survived in a world of grim shadows and dark experiences. He did not choose the name Stalin ("Steel") for nothing. Roosevelt, and Harry S Truman for a while after him, tended to deal with Stalin as if they were dealing with a difficult urban party boss or an obnoxious labor leader like John L. Lewis. Stalin, however, was a different type of animal.

Molotov's instructions seemed clear—to get a second front going as soon as possible. The Soviets wanted to have the Allies in the west drain off forty German divisions in 1942; if that occurred the war would be over in the late months of that year or its outcome assured by then. In their planning for such a front, the Americans focused on the problems—the difficult landings and the need to provide adequate air cover. But FDR promised, at least in Molotov's eyes, a cross-Channel landing in August or September. Churchill, when he was informed, was clearly upset—1942 was not reasonable. The prime minister decided to visit Washington to press for more time, and he volunteered to break the news to Stalin, arguing that a North African invasion was the best plan of attack. Stalin was bitterly disappointed and criticized the valor of the Royal Air Force. As his English visitor was counseling delay on starting the second front, the Soviet leader was receiving grim news of Nazi movement toward Stalingrad.

In October 1942, the Soviets were to hold out in that critical battle, and in the Pacific, the Americans stopped the Japanese at a tiny island called Guadalcanal. The president had the Joint Chiefs transfer weapons in short supply elsewhere to turn the tide in what would be the first of a string of costly American victories in that region. And in late 1942, the Allies launched "Operation Torch"—the attack on North Africa. Just before the congressional elections and against the advice of most of his inner military circle, Roosevelt approved the operations. The public demanded action, and this was the theater the commander in chief had chosen. At one point, FDR playfully implored the Almighty in front of others, "Please make it before Election Day." But instead it came five days after the election, and the Americans were successful beyond their hopes.

FDR himself appealed to the French (in their own language) over the BBC, asking them in North Africa to oppose the crushing yoke of Nazism and to end the degradation of France. In North Africa, though, the quicksand of political factionalism in Vichy France with its Nazi agents clouded up the great cause. American military personnel began dealing with pro-Nazi sympathizers, headed by General Jean Francois Darlan, a move that bitterly offended Free French leader General DeGaulle and caused liberal criticism for FDR at home. In later December 1942, Darlan was assassinated, some said by the Free French leadership, and the Allies were relieved of what had become an acute embarrassment.

Thus, by the end of 1942, the wearying string of defeats seemed to have come to a merciful end. The Allies had diverted some Nazi strength away from the eastern front, although surely the laurels for heroism and determination rightfully belonged to the Soviet warriors. The Americans had waged quite successfully their first major engagement by landing and moving into North Africa. And in the Pacific, the Japanese empire was reaching what would be its farthest boundaries; the tenacity of the navy and the leapfrogging strategy of MacArthur's armies and the marines would begin to turn the tide in the Pacific.

In all of this, Roosevelt remained consciously, almost self-consciously, calm and self-assured. He had his press secretary, Stephen Early, stress right after Pearl Harbor that the president had been through this before in World War I, had visited many defense establishments at home and abroad, and had seen more of the previous war in Europe than most other Americans. For Roosevelt, who was always defensive about not having served in that conflict, this was the chance to leave his mark on the great successor conflagration. In 1942, the president had begun to work out the command structure for the war, although in typical Rooseveltian fashion it was overlapping, frustrating to subordinates, and designed to leave ultimate power in his hands alone. But war has an impetus all its own, and as it ground slowly, more of the decisions flowed to the military, especially to General Marshall.[41]

Still, the important objectives set early in the war were clearly the president's, made sometimes in the face of opposition from his own military chieftains. Roosevelt was responsible for sending scarce supplies to the British and later the Soviets before Pearl Harbor; although Americans may have regretted the loss of these supplies, it was surely a correct judgment. It was FDR who, for better or worse, insisted on proclaiming unconditional surrender as Allied policy, FDR who accepted an Atlantic First strategy, and FDR who against his counselors' advice approved the North Africa invasion. And by the end of 1942, Roosevelt was clearly an international figure, eclipsing even Churchill in the role as democracy's premier spokesman. Faced with those accomplishments as a backdrop, the president still suffered from the vices of his virtues. He had an unparalleled grasp of world politics, yet seemed superficial at times in his judgments of events, as if he were a bright boy who skimmed across the surface of life, learning enough for the tests but doing poorly on the final exam. He managed to stay in touch with a variety of administrative military matters, yet he confused his major advisers about his initiatives and how they could help him. Last, he inspired the nation's mobilization efforts, but his management style sometimes helped stymie the very process he so exhorted.

Managing the War at Home

One of America's greatest roles, perhaps its most essential contribution, was being the arsenal of the Allied effort. The British fully admitted, and the Soviets grudgingly so, that the United States provided a veritable seat-rain of supplies, food, and war armaments to buttress the war effort against the Nazi and Fascist forces. Unlike the previous war, the conflict was not for Americans an eighteen-month affair characterized by deadlocks, stalemates, and pauses. The war in 1942 was going poorly for the British and Soviets, and Lend Lease and related programs were the major American contributions through most of that year as they had been before.

Roosevelt recognized that stark fact, and he tried wholeheartedly to gear up the nation quickly for war production and, more extensively, national mobilization. It is quite possible that a free people do not respond well to total war on the home front—even when united by direct attack and motivated by a clear need for survival. On one hand, the American mobilization was often characterized by greed, selfishness, and short-term concern for profit and salary increases in specific areas. On the other hand, however, those American efforts represented a powerful mobilization through influence, pressure, and government coercion to fight a long and costly war.

Like most leaders of his generation, FDR had one major experience in the domestic politics of war mobilization, and that was after the U.S.

entrance into World War I. As assistant secretary of the navy, he had on one occasion at least advocated a unified structure to deal with domestic priorities. It was a commonsense position, one that he rejected again and again in the 1940s conflict in order to keep that power in his own hands. But pressed with military command decisions, diplomatic conferences, and his own failing health, even Franklin Roosevelt could not make sense at times out of the ad hoc structures he had erected. He changed staff, combined agencies, redesignated them, and exhorted their efforts. In one sense, his management style contributed to his difficulties, but in another sense, his wartime predecessors Lincoln and Wilson were no more successful in mobilization in the long run—indeed, considering the magnitude of the task, probably less so.

The major advocate of centralizing the war mobilization effort was Bernard Baruch, the head of Wilson's War Industries Board (WIB) during that earlier war. Not unexpectedly, Baruch pushed FDR publicly and had in mind resurrecting old WIB alumni to run it. Unfortunately for Baruch, his two senior aides—Hugh Johnson and George Peek—had opposed FDR's reelection, a fact the president was not prone to overlook. Baruch's message was remarkably similar over the years; conversion demanded the five M's: mobilization (the draft), minds (propaganda), money (taxation), materials, and manufacturing. Throughout the 1930s, Baruch pushed for more planning and foresight in mobilization and gathered about him many military men as well as politicians who were beneficiaries of his considerable campaign largesse. Roosevelt, who liked to be the only king on the hill, listened to Baruch, courted him, gave him seeming access, and went his own way.[42]

In one sense, FDR had used these emergency agencies during the New Deal, with Johnson and Peck heading up two such establishments, and he was not pleased with their inability to work with the cabinet departments. Then, too, Roosevelt was leery of creating agencies filled with businesspeople, many of them unsympathetic with the domestic goals of reform. During the war, New Dealers remained alert to short-term policies that would lead to eventual rollbacks of domestic legislation. Because of Baruch's power base in Congress, FDR avoided putting him in a position of authority that could challenge his own prerogatives.

When the army came in with a proposal for a Baruch-style "war cabinet," the president's antennae went up. He saw it as an attempt to cut him out of the direct control of industrial mobilization, and he bluntly warned associates, "What do they think they are doing, setting up a second Government?" Aware of Wilson's need to go back to Congress for many administrative changes, FDR insisted on keeping the war management free of legislative interference. He refused to delegate powers to a committee or a czar and insisted that mobilization agencies report to him. On May 25, 1940, the president had quietly signed an executive order creating the Office of Emergency Mobilization; invoking the Defense Act of 1916, he established an advisory commission that reported to him. When one of the members asked Roosevelt, "Who is the boss?" the president characteristically responded, "I am."[43]

In December, the president created the Office of Production Management (OPM) under the joint leadership of William Knudsen of General Motors and Sidney Hillman, a high-ranking labor leader. But soon even Roosevelt's Bureau of the Budget chief was complaining that OPM lacked the ability to pressure business into recognizing the need to meet national rather than market demands or profit expectations. In late August, FDR placed into OPM a Supply Priorities and Allocation Board with OPM's purchasing director, Donald M. Nelson, as its executive director. Yet the mobilization effort lacked what Baruch and others insisted on—one final authority. FDR wanted to make sure he was that authority. Thus, by Pearl Harbor, the United States still lacked a system to coordinate priorities and a price controls policy.

By early 1942, FDR created the War Production Board (WPB) with Donald Nelson as chairman. Nelson, however, left the procurement of supplies to the military, and the armed services found a strong advocate in the Army-Navy Munitions Board headed by an energetic Wall Street lawyer, Ferdinand Eberstadt, who supported their proposals before the WPB. Still, the president's role was critical. When the war brought forth a quick shortage of rubber, FDR was compelled to deal with the issue himself. Congress, concerned about the critical shortages, had passed a bill to create a rubber supply agency to be run by a czar appointed by the president and approved by the Senate. Roosevelt vetoed the bill and appointed a committee headed this time by Baruch. When the report recommended rationing, the president used the findings as an excuse to move ahead.

The war, of course, involved not just problems of supply and priority but also price control. The Office of Price Administration (OPA) created a general maximum price policy that aimed at freezing all retail prices at the highest levels of March 1942. FDR had been warned by his Bureau of the Budget people that in 1915–1916, before the United States entered World War I, the cost of living had shot up 15 percent and that that rate of increase could be repeated in 1942. A concerned president undertook a fireside chat to warn the public, and he pushed for an anti-inflation policy.

Workers feared that price controls were simply wage freezes by another name. Some liberals saw this step as a smoke screen for repealing the New Deal and were urging in its place trust-busting. Then Roosevelt, who had generally avoided becoming associated with rationing and carefully sidestepped talk about taxation, decided to announce publicly that nobody during the war should have an income in excess of $25,000 per year. The remark created an uproar in Congress, and the president was forced to back down.

By the fall of 1942, production had fallen far short of the goals Roosevelt established. As the civilian and military sectors locked in conflict over appropriate spending levels and production for each area of need, the controversy again landed on Roosevelt's desk. Since he had created a system (or nonsystem) that resulted in overlapping levels of jurisdiction and no final authority but "Papa," as he phrased it, it was obvious that the president would have to deal with these problems. But FDR hated conflict, and so he urged both sides to work out the problem amiably.

Concerned again about the lack of coordination in the production crisis, Congress pushed for a single czar, a proposal FDR opposed. As intrigue mounted, Roosevelt created still another agency—the Office of War Mobilization, headed by former Supreme Court Justice James Byrnes. The deficiencies of the mobilization effort were becoming clearer in the areas of manpower. The administration had no real policy, and by 1943, the West Coast aircraft factories were in competition with the armed forces for men. The problem led to a proposal from Baruch that there be local commissions in each community to deal with deferments for men in critical industries. That recommendation in the West Coast controversy became the policy followed across the nation. But throughout late 1943, strikes sprung up and hampered the war effort.

These problems were confounded by plans for peacetime conversion being drawn up already in various parts of the executive bureaucracy. The issue once again turned New Deal liberals and businesspeople into enemies, and in October, FDR authorized Byrnes to deal formally with the prospective issues. Some liberals wanted to return to the familiar public works projects, while businesspeople instead placed their faith in private enterprise. The president, facing a reelection campaign in 1944, was reluctant to begin any reconversion or incur unemployment and warned that the war was still going on. After the German counterattack at the Battle of the Bulge, talk of reconversion quieted down.

Roosevelt then insisted throughout most of the war on avoiding creating a czar, fearing it would undercut his own power, lead to congressional control over mobilization as in World War I, and encourage end runs around the established departments. But at times, even the president grew weary of the system he had partially wrought; on one occasion he complained, "I get so many conflicting recommendations my head is splitting." But the constant reshuffling of agencies, inconclusive directions, and loose priorities did not prove, as has been noted, his style to have been any more or less successful than Lincoln's or Wilson's. Perhaps the difficulties of mobilization are a telling commentary on FDR's loose management, or perhaps a free people just do not lend themselves too well to protracted total war.[44]

The war took a toll on the democratic fabric of America, just as it had under Wilson. Despite his reputation as the archliberal of modern America, FDR in fact incurred serious blemishes on that record, especially in dealing with some ethnic minorities before and during World War II. Although African Americans were an important part of his political coalition, Roosevelt shied away from civil rights. His New Deal, of course, did provide some economic relief to African Americans, especially in the urban areas, although less so in the poorest farm regions. But FDR needed the cooperation of Southern congressmen, and he avoided any overtures on civil rights, anti-lynching legislation, or fair employment practices until black leaders forced action on the last demand. His neglect was partially a political calculation, but FDR knew few African Americans in his personal life and cultivated a public image as an honorary Georgian due to his Warm Springs attachment. Still, African Americans proved to be the most loyal and grateful of the New Deal Democratic constituencies from 1936 down to the present.

Roosevelt's record in dealing with Japanese Americans is less ambiguous and more stark. After Pearl Harbor, waves of hysteria swept across the Pacific coast, and political leaders in California pressed for their removal. Anti-Japanese and anti-Japanese American sentiment had been historically intense in that state, often encouraged by national leaders over the years and pushed by various economic interests.

Ironically, FBI director J. Edgar Hoover, who had interred 942 Japanese aliens right after Pearl Harbor, informed Attorney General Francis Biddle that the push for mass evacuation was based on hysteria and political pressure rather than the facts. The federal authorities met with Governor Culbert L. Olson of California and agreed that all Japanese, including those born in the United States, had to be removed from the state. Even before the president received their report, he had approved of the evacuation, adding only that the government officials should be "as reasonable as you can" in implementing the order.

As a result of the executive order of the president, and against the advice of the Justice Department and the FBI, some 120,000 Japanese on the West Coast were forcibly relocated. In addition, the president pushed for the evacuation of 140,000 Japanese from Oahu, where some espionage had occurred, and wrote that he was not worried about the constitutional questions.[45]

The internment, which was upheld by the Supreme Court in 1944, lasted until the end of that year, although Secretary of War Stimson and others argued for a quicker end. Only in the 1980s did lower federal courts begin to question critically the executive order and did Congress consider giving compensation to the evacuees. In 1988, the surviving Japanese Americans who were removed were granted $20,000 in compensation from the federal government. The historical record shows that there was not one single hostile act by Japanese Americans against the United States during the war period; in retrospect, it appears that J. Edgar Hoover's early judgment in 1942 was correct. The removal of these people, many of them native-born U.S. citizens, is the single gravest example of presidential abuse of civil liberties in American history. The president's decision showed the thinness of traditional liberalism in the United States, especially during crisis, and it also is a sad example of the superficiality, racism, and crude political calculations that sometimes warped FDR's usual decent inclinations.

On a vaster scale, Roosevelt's moral blindness is even more apparent in the genocide of the Jews and other ethnic groups targeted by the Nazis for extermination. There were very few Western leaders who showed much concern about the reports of mass murder taking place in the concentration camps sprawled across central Europe. However, at times, FDR did express some interest in resettling Jews in sparsely settled areas, and he spoke to King Abdul ibn Saud about admitting Jews to Palestine. Yet the president declined to support the modest Wayne-Rogers bill to admit twenty thousand refugee children in 1939–1940 on top of the quota system. At first in September 1942, Roosevelt refused to believe that a "final solution" was occurring. On several occasions, the State Department seemed to stymie various proposals for rescue, including a Treasury Department plan in June 1943 to evacuate seventy thousand Jews from Rumania at a cost of $170,000. Secretary Morgenthau was shocked to find out that the State Department had created a commission to rescue European art and museums but not to save the Jews. By February 1944, the War Refugee Board, created by the administration, began work to help deal with the calamity of obvious genocide.

Roosevelt's inaction is usually attributed to his preoccupation with the war and a reluctance to divert resources away from that vital struggle. But in fact, FDR was rather remarkable in his ability to both direct the war effort and retain a staggering command of detail about the complexities of borders, strategic advances, and internecine political battles across the globe. In fairness, he did try at times to raise the Jewish refugee question, but when he found domestic resistance to quota changes or international resistance to Jewish settlements, he simply refused to overcome the lethargy, if not hostility, of his own State Department and others. The United States and the Allies in general had refused to bomb the death camps and upset their normal extermination processes. Assistant Secretary of War John McCloy called such a step a diversion in the effort to win the war. But in fact, the Allies had in other instances diverted substantial war resources to aid other Hitler victims, especially the heroic Polish resistance in Warsaw in July 1944. In the end, Roosevelt was a bystander, as were so many other Western political and religious leaders, on the question of genocide.[46]

There are other less momentous but somewhat troubling lapses in FDR's liberal record. He received reports from the FBI director on his political opponents and on potential troublemakers. There is also some evidence, although it is not conclusive, that Roosevelt allegedly had men he thought were close to his wife, Eleanor, placed under surveillance during the war period. Taken together, the Roosevelt record then has its troubling episodes, its genuine blind spots, and a certain dark side that only the most partisan observer can ignore. Just as FDR laid the groundwork for the contemporary presidency, he also exhibited in many ways the objectionable abuses of power that mark that great and at times frightening office.[47]

The Strategy of 1943

Franklin Roosevelt saw 1943 as the major year of change in the difficult defensive strategy of the Allies. He was correct: 1943 proved to be the turning point—if one can be so defined—in the war. At the end of the previous year, Nazi Germany suffered reverses in North Africa and at Stalingrad. The Fascist Spanish forces stayed neutral, the Turks began to listen to Churchill's warnings against the Nazis, and the Allies were regaining the offensive in the Atlantic. The crucial question was when there would be an invasion of France.

In November 1942, FDR asked for a conference of the three Allied leaders to deal with future military strategy. Stalin refused to attend, citing pressing military matters. Churchill and Roosevelt did meet at Casablanca in North Africa and laid out the major differences between the two sides. The British insisted on an attack on Italy and a postponement of the cross-Channel invasion until August or September. The Americans pushed for such an invasion as their primary objective and reminded their ally of the Pacific war as well. FDR seemed unclear about the feasibility of a July invasion and thus left for Casablanca not totally committed to the advice of Marshall and other advocates of the invasion.

The president, denied some quick victories for home consumption and facing a division among his own advisers, supported Churchill's plan to move into the Mediterranean. But in typical fashion, he also reasserted his firm support for the invasion of France. At the conference, FDR insisted on bringing DeGaulle and his rival, General Henri Giraud, together for a joint meeting. And the president, surprising Churchill, cited Ulysses S. Grant in pronouncing a policy of "unconditional surrender." Later, critics of the president were to characterize his remarks as ill advised, leading to a declaration that complicated surrender at the end of war. But the Casablanca meeting was a meeting of minds at least on the highest levels. A pleased Churchill concluded, "I love those Americans. They have behaved so generously."[48]

Churchill notified Stalin of the Casablanca decision. The Soviet leader was not happy with a further delay of the much-promised second front. He bitterly wired back that since December the Germans had transferred twenty-seven divisions from the western front to the Soviet battle line. Then, in March 1943, Stalin received notice that shipping losses in the Atlantic had caused his two allies to postpone convoys to Europe. Understandably, Stalin felt betrayed and bitter. Meanwhile, in their chosen battlefield, North Africa, events were not going well. In February, German General Rommel had proved a difficult competitor, and the expected final victory in that theater was slow in coming. In April, American General George Patton's armies pushed eastward, hoping to rout the Nazi forces. Finally, Allied forces won a major victory at Tunisia and took a quarter of a million prisoners. Stalin wired his congratulations.

In March, Churchill sent his foreign secretary, Anthony Eden, to confer with FDR on major territorial issues arising out of the war. Both sides were concerned about Soviet intentions in the Baltic states, East Prussia, and, above all, Poland. FDR was especially sensitive to the effect Soviet domination would have on Americans, especially those with relatives in Poland and the Baltic nations. The president seemed to hope that Stalin would arrange a plebiscite, even a phony one, to offset some of the criticism. W. Averell Harriman, U.S. ambassador to the Soviet Union, recorded that in May 1944 FDR indicated that he did not care if the countries bordering the Soviets became Communist, and the president was supposed to have told Francis Cardinal Spellman of New York that Eastern Europe would simply have to get used to Soviet domination. The Allied leaders explored the idea of dividing Germany up and establishing a worldwide international organization after the war. Roosevelt, however, was not committed to a new Wilsonian League; to him, the Big Four (which included a divided China) would police the world.[49]

When in May Churchill visited FDR, the president insisted on a cross-Channel invasion in spring 1944 and avoided putting troops into Italy after the landing in Sicily. Again, Churchill, representing his own fears and those of the British staff over a war of attrition in France, pushed for knocking Italy out of the conflict and encouraged Turkey into the Allied camp. Marshall, though, insisted on the Channel landing. Finally, the British agreed to an invasion in May 1944 and an increase in bombing missions over Germany, while the Americans supported an attack on Italy with some additional troop commitments going to that front.

For Stalin, it was another postponement, on top of all the others. In addition, FDR expressed his concern once again about the future of Poland. He wanted some sort of rapprochement between the Poles in exile in London and the Soviet-backed partisans. The president clearly let Stalin know that he was concerned about the impact on domestic Polish American public opinion as well. But Stalin distrusted the London Poles, seeing many of them as Nazi sympathizers, and knowing the history of Poland as a corridor to the Soviet Union, he insisted on imposing a friendly regime there. No wartime decisions have been as criticized as FDR's "sell-out" of Poland at this time and later at Yalta. In fact, Roosevelt did try to mediate between Communist and noncommunist forces as best he could. The determining factor in the future of Poland was not to be FDR's naïveté or inattentiveness but the presence of the Red Army in that region. FDR never sold out Poland, because it was never his to give. In 1941, 1942, and 1943, the Soviet armies had carried the brunt of the war against the Nazis, and as they moved west, many chaotic lands and regions freed from the Germans fell under the Soviet sphere of influence.

In July, Patton and General Bernard Montgomery, with a sense of professional rivalry only conquerors know, successfully stormed the island of Sicily; two weeks later, the king of Italy, Victor Emmanuel II, dismissed Mussolini from power. Now Roosevelt had to confront the problem of how to implement his "unconditional surrender" edict. Did it apply to deposing the king of Italy? Did it apply to all of Mussolini's senior aides? The president pleaded for "common sense" and said that he didn't care with whom he dealt, including the king, as long as it wasn't a "definite member of the Fascist government."[50]

The president tried to finesse the question by allowing Churchill to negotiate with the caretaker Pietro Badoglio in Rome, while the British prime minister worried that the end of fascism would lead to a very strong Communist presence that could take over parts of Italy, especially the industrial northern cities. A pragmatic Roosevelt wanted Eisenhower to honor the meaning of unconditional surrender, but he gave clear indications that the Allies would be lenient, especially if Italy gave aid to the cause against the Nazis. Under pressure, mainly from Marshall and Stimson, the president pushed now for a cross-Channel invasion while the British temporized. The British argued for a larger offensive in Italy as a way to prepare for the French cross-Channel invasion. But the Italian campaign was much more difficult than the Allies had imagined, as they moved slowly up the peninsula and finally captured Naples on October 1, 1943.

In November, FDR decided to visit Churchill and then Stalin to discuss strategy and postwar security. At Cairo, he joined the prime minister and Generalissimo Chiang Kai-shek. The president reiterated his pledge of a major role for China in the postwar world, extensive reparations, the return of Taiwan and the Pescadores, and joint occupation of the Ryukyus with the United States. Chiang, though, needed more immediate American support, troops, and supplies—commodities already stretched thin in the twin theaters. When the president and Churchill finally met with Stalin, his immediate salutation was "Let us get down to business." The marshal's demand was a second front moving across the continent toward Germany. In the face of Stalin's logic and Roosevelt's agreement, even Churchill had to approve a 1944 landing. In their conversations, FDR curiously proposed an Allied offensive near the Adriatic to join with the Yugoslavs and push east toward the Soviet armies. Churchill still advocated a Mediterranean operation, Stalin proposed a swift advance into the heart of Germany, and Roosevelt seemed to vacillate, probably trying to mold some consensus.

Stalin later expressed some reservations about FDR's Big Four arrangement, arguing that the smaller nations would oppose their domination and indicating that he was skeptical about the future of China as a major power at the end of the war. He wondered if the U.S. Congress would approve American forces being a part of a European alliance that could insist on U.S. troops. Stalin had already pledged to come to the aid of the Allies in the Pacific against Japan once the Nazis were defeated. Now he agreed to help get the Turks into the war and demanded the division of Germany and reparations from Finland. As expected, Stalin and Roosevelt could not agree on the future of Poland. FDR insisted on the need for some agreement that did not alienate the six to seven million Polish Americans, and he discussed with Stalin the new borders that would expand the Soviet Union in the west at Poland's expense and shift Poland in the west into Germany. Such were the spoils of war. The Allies finally accepted Stalin's borders but did not agree on the government. In terms of the Baltic states, FDR tried again, stressing the sensitivities of American voters of Lithuanian, Latvian, and Estonian descent. But Stalin's argument was that these states had been part of Russia under the last czar and no one had complained.

The Tehran conference held in Iran featured FDR, Churchill, and Stalin. It ended with a commitment to the cross-Channel invasion, with Stalin's pledge to enter eventually the Pacific war against Japan, and with a clear division of opinion on the fate of Poland. Roosevelt had to make a major decision concerning the command of the invasion "Overlord," as it was called. He passed over General Marshall and named Dwight D. Eisenhower to lead it. And in the Pacific, the military chiefs prepared for a massive attack along two lines: the New Guinea–East Indies–Philippines region and a thrust into the Mandated Islands.[51]

The Last Election

In January 1944, the Soviets bested the Nazis and broke the Leningrad blockade; in April they captured Odessa. As the president returned from Tehran, he was experiencing some of the symptoms that could prove to be telltale signs of declining physical health. By early 1944, he seemed to be weary but politically still a colossus. Yet FDR had clearly lost his great ascendancy in the legislative process, even in the firestorm of the war. Inflation was worsening in late 1942, and still Congress was unwilling to enact his policy of taxes and food and price controls. In the area of wage policies, the president seemed reluctant to take the lead, and his War Labor Board reacted on a case-by-case basis. Disgusted with Congress and its delays in passing his tax and farm mobilization policies, the president bluntly warned in words rarely heard in a democratic society: "I ask the Congress to take this action by the first of October. Inaction on your part by that date will leave me with an inescapable responsibility to the people of this country to see to it that the war effort is no longer imperiled by threat of economic chaos. In the event that the Congress should fail to act, and act adequately,

I shall accept the responsibility, and I will act." Clearly, he was expanding the definition of the commander in chief's war powers. Congress obediently passed a modest bill in early October.

FDR visited defense establishments, insisted on nonpartisanship, and became increasingly the voice of the democratic alliance. At home, he avoided Wilson's mistake in 1918 and refused to counsel the public to vote for the Democratic Party's candidates. The 1942 election, however, had led to the Republicans picking up forty-six seats in the House and nine seats in the Senate, or about double Wilson's losses in 1918. The New Deal was surely dead as a domestic reform movement, but its legacy had become institutionalized, and so it seemed had Roosevelt in the American mind.

In early 1943, an embattled president felt compelled to defend the emergency management of the mobilization effort. The major problem, manpower, was still apparent, and yet Roosevelt shied away from the issue. The American economy was plagued by strikes in civilian industries (especially coal mining), absenteeism, and high turnover. The influx of African Americans to industrial jobs and women into the workforce would be expedients that later ended up changing the nature of American society.

Both the legislative and executive branches tried to deal with the difficult problem of labor-management unrest at home. Congress overrode FDR's veto and passed a law restricting the right to strike. Faced with continuing problems in the coal mines, the president had considering seizing the mines and drafting striking miners between the ages of thirty-eight and forty-five. The railroads presented an equally troubling situation. In late 1943, FDR ordered Stimson to seize and operate the railroads; three weeks later, the president himself arbitrated the dispute. When he turned over to Byrnes considerable authority to run the mobilization effort, the press promptly dubbed him "assistant president" and "chief of staff"—concepts inimical to FDR's temperament.

Still, the president had little choice. The public outcry and congressional pressure required more coordination if not centralization of policy than he had implemented. His own head of the Bureau of the Budget had warned him of the breakdown of his earlier approach. In February 1943, the bureau director, Harold Smith, enumerated the duplication, confusion, disorganization, and fragmentation. One of Roosevelt's most astute observers quoted his attitude at the time: "A little rivalry is stimulating. . . . It keeps everybody going to prove he is a better fellow than the next man. It keeps them honest too." On another occasion, FDR demanded teamwork, remarking, "I am the boss. . . . I am the one who gets the rap if we get licked in Congress. . . . I am the boss. I am giving the orders." By the end of the year, though, FDR had moved toward a greater emphasis on a larger White House staff—the beginnings of the contemporary presidency. Earlier in 1937, a presidential commission headed by Louis Brownlow proposed a stronger executive office, arguing that the president needed help in performing his augmented responsibilities, and the war showed the wisdom of those prescriptions for the new American presidency.

FDR's span of attention swung also to military procurement. He created the Office of Scientific Research and Development and also set up an American-British committee on scientific exchanges. Unlike in previous wars, civilian businesspeople and scientists increasingly became a regular part of the military's weapons development programs—not just tanks, rockets, planes, and radar, but also the initiation of the first atomic bomb, originally suggested to FDR in a letter from physicist Albert Einstein.

Amid all of this, Roosevelt had promised that "Dr. New Deal" had given way to "Dr. Win-the-War." But in January 1944, FDR lashed out at self-seeking promoters, profiteers, and those who feathered their nests while the young went to war. He asked for new taxes to control high profits and for more authority over the terms of war contracts and food distribution. In addition, he proposed a national service law to prohibit strikes. The president then asked Congress for a "second Bill of Rights"—an economic charter that would out-deal the old New Deal—and he clearly confronted the Republicans with a demand for easy registration of servicemen, which the GOP took as a ploy by the commander in chief to win reelection with the soldiers' vote.[52]

Thus in early 1944 Roosevelt was ready to wage his last campaign, adopting Lincoln's slogan that one does not change horses in the middle of the stream. But as much as the "Old Master" tried, it was clear to all who wished to observe that FDR looked tired and sick. His doctors had confidentially diagnosed that he was suffering from hypertension and heart disease, and he might have had cancer as well. He seemed more preoccupied, less interested in the job at times, and more annoyed by persistent press criticism. He pressed his attorney general, Francis Biddle, to push for trials for right-wing extremists who had attacked the president and preached anti-Semitism. The trial judge had the indictments dismissed. The most troublesome single opponent for a time proved to be Sewell Avery, the head of Montgomery Ward, who refused to negotiate with the CIO unions. After a strike was called, FDR ordered the Chicago plant seized by the secretary of commerce and tried persuasion to get Avery's cooperation, but to no avail. The secretary of war eventually took over operations.

But the great event of 1944 was not the recalcitrance of corporations like Montgomery Ward or even the presidential campaign—it was the long-awaited invasion across the English Channel. That landing, "Overlord," was to be the greatest amphibious invasion in the long annals of warfare. On D-Day, June 6, 1944, forty-nine hundred warships and over two and a half million Allied troops started the waves of assault that were to destroy the Nazis in the west and alleviate pressure on the Soviet Union. In the evening, the president asked God's good blessings on "our sons, pride of our Nation" and commended faith in God, in the soldiers, in each other, and in the great crusade. Once again, American and British strategy began to divide, as the former wanted to invade southern France and the latter emphasized the importance of moving up the Italian peninsula. Churchill apparently considered promoting again the idea of Western forces in the Balkan region as a counter to the advancing Soviet armies. Roosevelt, with a long Pacific war ahead of him and the need to show Stalin some Allied unity, bluntly refused. The president's decision was clear, and he added to Churchill, "For purely political considerations over here, I should never survive even a slight setback to 'Overlord' if it were known that fairly large forces had been diverted to the Balkans." Years later, Churchill was to judge in retrospect that his counsel would have enabled the Allies to reach Vienna before the Soviets, which would have had important consequences for the postwar world.

But in fact, the American insistence to join the "Overlord" forces and the "Anvil" armies in southern France was a correct one. The problem with Churchill's penchant for attacking the soft underbelly was that the underbelly in World Wars I and II was not soft after all. The diversion of troops from France to Italy and on into the Balkans might have imperiled the major offensive that meant the beginning of the end of Nazi power. There is little evidence that Allied troops moving toward Vienna, if indeed that march could have occurred as easily as Churchill foresaw, would have changed the postwar world appreciably. It might have cut the Soviet postwar empire somewhat, although by 1954 Austria was given its autonomy. Actually, Churchill had already recognized many of Stalin's claims in the Balkans when he made a private deal between the two of them that established British hegemony over Greece and Soviet control over Rumania, with Yugoslavia and Hungary being split fifty-fifty. The Polish issue remained, unless the Allies were willing to move toward a possible confrontation with the Soviets.

In the Pacific, FDR had divided the military command into several sectors, which once again left him with the final say. Now, as the fighting grew more intense, some major strategic decisions had to be made. The navy, under Admiral Nimitz, pushed for bypassing the Philippines, while MacArthur insisted on fulfilling his promise to return. Not coincidentally, FDR chose to go to San Diego to inspect the troops while the Democratic Party renominated him for a fourth term. Then the president left for Honolulu and a meeting with MacArthur and Nimitz. MacArthur insisted on the liberation of the Philippines and warned that the American people would vote against the president if he deserted their old allies and "wards." Consequently, FDR approved MacArthur's plan and returned home in time for his last campaign.

His own nomination was assured, but pressure had built up in the party for a replacement to the mystical progressive, Henry Wallace. FDR, in typical fashion, assured Wallace of his support and also encouraged others—notably James Byrnes, Senator Harry S Truman, and Justice William O. Douglas, among others. As for the president, he insisted before he began that this was his final campaign, stressing also his commander in chief role and his apparent zest and good health to offset rumors to the contrary. With some carefully crafted speeches and after several difficult days of campaign ordeal, FDR refurbished the image that he was still the grand master of American politics. He rebuffed the Republicans by citing their alleged attacks on his dog Fala, and in New York and later in Philadelphia, he endured rain and long hours to show the people that he was indeed fit for the years ahead. Roosevelt carried 432 electoral votes to Dewey's 99; the Democrats gained twenty-four seats in the House of Representatives, but lost two seats in the Senate. His popular vote was 25.6 million to Dewey's 22 million. The fourth inauguration was a simple, almost perfunctory ceremony. A gaunt president took the oath of office, celebrated American courage and fortitude, and then, in the evening of his life, he nostalgically returned to his boyhood—to the wisdom of "my old schoolmaster, Dr. Peabody," that life was not always smooth sailing.[53]

The Ordeals of Alliance

The movements of the Allied armies into France led FDR to deal face to face with General DeGaulle, the inspiring leader of the Free French. Churchill, recognizing DeGaulle's popular appeal and sympathizing with his pride and patriotism, urged Roosevelt to acknowledge the general as the major force in that nation in 1944. But FDR insisted, almost petulantly, that the French should choose their leaders uninfluenced in any way.[54]

Of more critical concern, though, was the continuing problem of Poland, where Stalin refused to give the London-based Poles a role in that government. In conversations with the Soviets, the future of the alliance seemed unclear. The Soviets insisted on Big Four unanimity in any international organization and demanded that all sixteen Soviet republics be seated, with each having a vote. Roosevelt had reservations about the veto power of the Big Four, but the Americans themselves had cited the veto as a guarantee they could present to the Senate when the treaty came up for ratification.[55]

The question of Germany also again presented difficulties. American councils were divided. Stimson wanted to punish Nazi leaders, destroy their army, and partition the nation. But the secretary of treasury, Henry Morgenthau, insisted on reducing Germany to an agricultural society—an approach that Churchill and FDR seemed to agree with at first but later backed away from.

The Roosevelt aspirations for China also began to fall through. Chiang Kai-shek's forces were no match for the Japanese, and a concerned FDR implored Chiang to put American General Joseph Stilwell in charge. The president also sent a personal emissary, Major General Patrick J. Hurley, to mediate between the Communist Chinese and Chiang's Kuomintang. There is some inconclusive evidence that FDR had grown disgusted with Chiang and ordered at the Cairo Conference a contingency plan drawn for his assassination. Overall, the president hoped to use China as a mainstay of the Allies and as a center from which to attack Japan.[56]

Bone-weary and ailing, Roosevelt tried once again personal diplomacy with Stalin on the question of Poland, the proposed United Nations, and the Pacific war. In early February 1945, the three leaders met at Yalta, near the Crimean Sea. Stalin dropped his request for seating sixteen republics in the United Nations and proposed instead the admission of the Ukraine, White Russia, and Lithuania. The British, with their Commonwealth, supported the general approach, and FDR gave in. He later asked for two extra votes for the United States, which was agreed upon but never implemented.

On Poland, though, Stalin stood firm. He regarded the London Poles as pro-Nazi and definitely anti-Soviet. Stalin did agree to some minor concessions—a recognized government with broad representation—but it was clear that the Soviets saw the issue as central to the security of their country. For two generations, FDR would be criticized for appeasing the Soviets and selling out Poland. But then and now, the Soviet army was the telling point. Roosevelt neither sold out Poland nor undermined

American policy through his poor health or diminished capacities. Most importantly for the Americans, Stalin reaffirmed his intention to attack Japan, and he insisted that the Kurile Islands and lower Sakhalin be returned to the Soviet Union. Although there was some disagreement over the fate of Manchuria and other areas, the Soviets did not push aggressively for more concessions to guarantee their entry into what promised to be a very bloody war against determined Japanese forces.

Tensions between the Big Three continued even as the war was coming to a successful conclusion in the west. Soviet promises on Poland were proving to be meaningless, and Stalin feared that the Americans and British were negotiating peace behind his back. Then as he was dealing with the conclusion of the western war, the climax in the Pacific, and the shaky edifice of postwar cooperation, Roosevelt suffered a massive cerebral hemorrhage and died at Warm Springs, Georgia. Stalin was sure he had been poisoned by Churchill and so informed Roosevelt's son. Churchill paid his profoundest regrets but strangely did not choose to attend the president's funeral. The long eventful presidency of Franklin Delano Roosevelt ended far from the capital he so dominated and far from the ancestral estate where he grew up and which he so loved.

The Other Warlords

Another perspective on Roosevelt's war leadership can be obtained by examining the control exercised by the other major leaders of this period. In Japan, the conduct of the war had shifted to the military, of course, but in Europe, the civilian chiefs of state, in various ways, assumed the role of commander in chief. Their styles were very different, the national systems of military command were diverse, and their subtle uses of power are still not fully apparent. Their prosecution of the war and the resulting domestic mobilizations were complex matters, untidy to historians and participants alike. But still, some generalizations can be made. As one moves from Churchill to Stalin to Hitler, the measure of direct control increases as influence changes to unvarnished power. In war, as in science, measures of degree lead to changes in kind.

Of the principal leaders during the Second World War, none had a greater breadth of experience in government than Winston S. Churchill. By the beginning of the war, he had held nearly every major cabinet position in the British government except foreign secretary and had been extensively involved in the conduct of the previous war. One of Churchill's advisers during this period and probably the greatest military strategist of his time, Basil Liddell Hart, has provided a balanced historical assessment of the prime minister's role. Churchill above all exhibited a fighting spirit that inspired the beleaguered democracies during their darkest hour—1940. But in his exuberance, he was involved in some major miscalculations. His public appeals to the Belgians, the Dutch, and the Norwegians probably encouraged the Nazis to move into those areas before they intended in order to forestall the possibility of the British taking over. Churchill clearly overrated the power and fortitude of the French army (as did Stalin), and after its surrender, he insisted on attacking the French fleet to prevent it from falling into German hands. His own admirals had judged the move as unnecessary, countering that the French admirals had promised that they would never surrender their ships or allow them to be seized.

Churchill's best move in 1940 was his decisive step to send reinforcements to Africa, but he continued to divert resources to far too many theaters of action. Once again he tried to open up an avenue of advance by attacking the Balkans, and the British drew the Nazis into Greece—an area they probably would not have gone into so soon. And then, the British had to retreat as at Dunkirk. Many historians have argued that it was Hitler's attack on the Soviet Union that saved Britain and prevented a crushing and final fate. After that invasion and Pearl Harbor, Churchill's preeminence slipped away. The Soviets provided the armies and the United States the matériel in 1942 to begin to turn the tide. Churchill became, in his own words, "President Roosevelt's lieutenant."

And so, Churchill's role as senior partner declined as the war progressed—it was a harbinger of things to come as the world slipped into great power constellations in which Britain was a satellite and not a sun. But what of Churchill in his own land—was he as singularly powerful a military warlord as has been generally assumed? Liddell Hart provided a clear picture when he called Churchill "the great animator of the war," and he marveled at the prime minister's "fertility, versatility, and vitality." Churchill's mind ranged over vast areas of diplomacy and military strategy, and he was constantly pushing and coaxing his ministers, officials, and generals to greater activity and progress in the war effort. Yet this very approach leads one to conclude that his actual influence was not as great as has been previously assumed. He frequently hesitated to insist on his views prevailing, even when they were well founded. Liddell Hart wondered if Churchill's deference to officialdom was due in part to his firing in World War I when he opposed the weight of such opinion.

Churchill himself recorded in his history of the latter war, "The reader must not forget that I never wielded autocratic powers, and always had to move with and focus political and professional opinion." At one point after the Germans took Crete, he concluded, "This is a sad story, and I feel myself greatly to blame for allowing myself to be overborne by the resistances that were offered [to his original plan for more troops there]." On another occasion, he admitted, "I print these details to show how difficult it is to get things done even with much power, realized need and willing helpers."

Liddell Hart also rejected the view, so prominent among critics of FDR, that Churchill in contrast had a grand strategy that superseded the daily necessities of war. He found that for Churchill the goal was "the defeat, ruin and slaughter of Hitler, to the exclusion of all other purposes." Indeed, Churchill tended to concentrate his energies on one objective, often to the neglect of equally important other ones. The contemporary view that he saw more clearly than FDR the likely future is probably not substantiated, and Roosevelt was not as oblivious to the character of Stalin and the historic ambitions of the Soviet Union as has been charged; with regard to the future demise of the colonial empires, the president had far greater foresight than Churchill.

Churchill's overall reluctance in exercising control, then, may be due to many causes: the British coalition government, the cabinet government tradition, and the prime minister's own experiences in World War I. One of his colleagues, Lord Boothby, concluded that Churchill learned two great lessons from Lloyd George's leadership in World War I: first, the loss of political power that arose from the lack of party leadership; and second, the price of continuing and costly clashes between the prime minister and his military advisers. To avoid these problems, Churchill pushed for a close working relationship among his officers, the chiefs of staff, and the departments.

Unlike Lloyd George, who inspired and welcomed men of brilliance and talent, Churchill often seemed to surround himself with lesser men as colleagues and assistants—men less threatening and less likely to break with him over disputes. Toward the end of his life, Churchill despondently observed that the political results that came from victories were less clear-cut than the stirring wartime leadership itself. Judged by that standard, he concluded on one occasion, "I am not sure that I shall be held to have done very well." And later he glumly added, "I have achieved a great deal to achieve nothing in the end." It was a melancholy he shared with his great ancestors, the Marlboroughs, and one that would be alien to a Roosevelt.[57]

Churchill as warlord exercised considerable influence, especially in the 1940–1941 period, but he remembered all too well the lessons of World War I and struggled to avoid the acrimony and personality struggles that characterized the brilliant but divisive term of Lloyd George. As a parliamentary leader, he drew his institutional power from the House of Commons and, unlike FDR, did not have to run for reelection during the war; also in contrast to FDR, he did not have a separate source of legitimate power outside the legislature.

In the Soviet Union, Stalin maintained a fairly tight control over the military, especially in the early years of the war. He had been responsible for the purge of the upper echelons of the military, having had shot over a thousand Soviet generals between 1938 and 1940, and had misjudged Hitler and signed a pact with the Nazi regime. When the Germans turned and attacked the Soviet frontier, it was Molotov and not Stalin who broke the news to the general population. For weeks, from June 22 to July 3, Stalin did not choose to address his people, and even later his first address of the war was poorly given and uninspiring. His initial defensive policy was one of "scorch the earth," destroy everything of value before retreat, just as Russia had done against Napoleon in 1812. Privately, a shaken Stalin even welcomed American troops on any part of the Soviet front under U.S. command—an incredible concession from a Bolshevik who remembered the Allied occupation after World War I.

Stalin's major British biographer, Isaac Deutscher, concluded that he was "his own commander in chief, his own minister of defense, his own quartermaster, his own minister of supply, his own foreign minister, and even his own *chef de protocole*." Stalin insisted on being in constant and direct communication with his field officers, oversaw the evacuation of 1,360 plants and factories in the western Soviet Union and the Ukraine, and was involved in detailed decisions on moving supplies, ammunition, and men.

Stalin initially divided the front into three huge regions and assumed supreme command himself. The State Defense Committee, which included Stalin, Molotov, Kliment Voroshilov, Lavrenti Beria, and Georgi Malenkov, was given the task of running and coordinating the total war effort. As the Nazis advanced toward Moscow, coming within twenty or thirty miles of their target, Stalin rallied the Soviets, this time citing the great heroes of imperial days as well as the more familiar Lenin. Most importantly, while the government planned to leave the capital, Stalin stayed, thus becoming a symbol of perseverance and constancy.

He avoided visiting the front, but he had a superb command of the vast operations in which his army was engaged. Stalin oversaw the logistics of the enormous effort, raising armies, rerouting them, massing them at critical junctions, and ensuring that supplies found the troops. Logistics were even more critical in a nation that was having its western industrial sector devastated. At the end of 1941, the occupied section embraced the regions where 40 percent of the population lived and from which came 65 percent of the coal, 68 percent of the pig iron, 58 percent of all steel, 60 percent of the aluminum, 38 percent of the grain, and 41 percent of the railroad lines. All this boded poorly for the Soviets and Stalin's war leadership; then the harsh winter, and later the mud, came, and the Nazis knew what Napoleon had found out—one does not invade and conquer that vast nation easily.

By the end of 1941, Pearl Harbor had occurred, and Stalin began to pull away from supporting international Communist parties and proletariat revolutions against capitalist states that were fighting his enemy. To stiffen resistance in the all-important Stalingrad defense, the Soviet leaders issued a simple order: "Not a step back." Throughout September, October, and November, the two titanic armies clashed in a series of costly battles that led to an important Nazi defeat. As early as 1941, Hitler was supposed to have seen the Moscow campaign as spelling eventual defeat for him; to other observers, the Stalingrad campaign was the turning point. As for Stalin, he refused all attempts to divert resources from the Moscow front even for this climactic campaign. He instructed his chief of staff, "No matter how they cry and complain, don't promise them any reserves. Don't give them a single battalion from the Moscow front."

In the middle of the Stalingrad campaign, he did away with political commissars who previously oversaw the military. Recalling the reforms of Peter the Great, Stalin also abandoned old Bolshevik egalitarianism and reinstituted guard regiments and divisions, formations, saluting, officer messes and clubs, and even epaulets, and took for himself the title of Marshal. He brought in promising young officers and promoted them rapidly after they succeeded, and in one month alone 360 new generals were named while attempts were made to restore military pride and privileges. To prop up the war effort, he even reached out for support to the Russian Orthodox Church.

Unlike Hitler, Stalin did not usually ride roughshod over his generals, and as he had been in his early years in the Communist Party, he became the arbitrator once again. He collected opinions, weighed them, relayed viewpoints back and forth, and tried to fit the particular judgments into the general state of conditions. And like his colleagues at the top of the other war machines, he spent hours and days trying to relate diplomacy to the confusions of inconclusive campaigns and the battles of awesome destruction.[58]

Of the four major war leaders in the West, Hitler undoubtedly was even more openly involved in the day-to-day military operations. The others may have periodically interfered or intervened, but Hitler regarded himself as the "greatest military strategist of all times," and he acted accordingly. Some of his intuitive military judgments were bold and brilliant in their effectiveness; his mind was quick, retentive, probing, and often daring. But in the final analysis, within the balance of history, it is clear that his military leadership led to disaster, ruin, genocide, and defeat. In the heady atmosphere of idealizing the war, he moved beyond the grandiose rhetoric of sacrifice used by the others. When told that Germany might lose the war, the Führer's summary observation was that if that happened, it proved that the Germans were unworthy of him. That perverse identification shows much about the Nazi world and its immoral architect.

As a corporal in the First World War who became the supreme commander in the Second, he reduced his greatest generals to agents of his will. One of his field marshals, Baron Wolfrom von Richthofen, called the commanders in chief and the commanding generals under Hitler "highly paid noncommissioned officers." One of Hitler's closest associates, the historian Percy Ernst Schramm, has concluded that over the years Hitler consolidated his dictatorship over all elements of society, including the armed forces. In the process, he extended his surveillance over the military, not respecting or trusting most of his senior officers—a suspicion that proved to be well founded in light of the officers' plot to kill Hitler in July 1944.

He encouraged the growth of the Waffen-SS, which in time became independent of the military. And for reasons of his own, he permitted conflicts between the General Staff of the army and the Operations Staff of the OKW (High Command of the Armed Forces), a continuation of the World War I antagonism between the Eastern High Command and the Imperial Supreme Headquarters.

Like Roosevelt, he encouraged a divide-and-conquer approach, but unlike FDR, Hitler directly dictated military movements, often against the advice of the field commanders. Two days before his suicide, an order was issued that major military plans had to be presented to the Führer with thirty-six hours' notice. "Independent decisions are to be justified in detail," the order read. In his hands Hitler held the positions of chancellor, foreign minister, Nazi Führer, supreme commander of the armed forces, and commander in chief of the army. As the war effort began to go against the Nazis after 1942, Hitler accepted even less advice than before. He opposed retreats, checked regroupings or realignments, and even punished a general's daughter for her father's misfortunes on the battlefield. As the war worsened, Hitler's directions were replete with "no retreat," "only with permission," "accepting the risks," and "swift mopping up operation." He became more committed, more obstinate, more fanatical, as he appropriately phrased it. Early in the war, a general could appeal an order that he disagreed with; soon, though, Hitler ended that practice.

Hitler saw the drift of the war, apparently after his failure to conquer Moscow in the winter of 1941. But he insisted that the Allies would be unable to maintain their coalition. Without realizing it, he had helped create the cement that held them as one. Despite the deep differences among the British, American, and Soviet leaders, they together and singularly had come to hate with a personal vengeance the Nazi regime and the man who controlled it.[59]

FDR as Commander in Chief

More than Wilson and even Lincoln, Roosevelt enlarged the commander in chief role of the presidency. Wilson interfered little in the detailed work of his secretary of war, his chief of staff, or the generals in the field. Lincoln, of course, did intervene frequently, but he presided over a nineteenth-century military establishment with a weak general staff and a rather unformed command system. Roosevelt, however, as early as 1939 moved to exert his authority over the uniformed services. In July, he signed an executive order transferring the Joint Army-Navy Board, the Joint Army-Navy Munitions Board, and several other military procurement agencies into an executive office of the president. The assistant secretary of war became the president's chief deputy dealing with mobilization—independent of his superior, the secretary of war. Thus, the military chiefs were placed directly under the president, leading Admiral William Leahy to conclude years later that the war was run without any civilian control except for FDR. In fact, the secretaries were not included in the distribution lists for Joint Chiefs of Staff papers, even though these reports dealt with the basic questions the secretaries were legally responsible for.

Once again, while these boards and chiefs operated in their separate spheres, the president alone was the coordinating link, sharing power with no one and giving him considerable authority over the military chiefs. In the years before Pearl Harbor, the president was willing to override his military advisers; for example, he disregarded their production goals in 1940 and pushed aside their caution in supporting Britain. When the Pacific Fleet commander, Rear Admiral James O. Richardson, appealed to

Washington in autumn 1940 to shift the fleet out of Pearl Harbor to San Diego, he felt the commander in chief's annoyance.

Secretary of War Stimson, observing FDR's lack of coordination, recorded, "He has no system. He is haphazard and scatters responsibility among a lot of uncoordinated men and consequently things are never done." Oddly enough, it was Assistant Secretary of the Navy Franklin D. Roosevelt who had called on Wilson in 1919 to create a joint planning agency to lay out American objectives and capabilities in the previous war.

After Pearl Harbor, though, significant changes began to occur. FDR had to allow the major theater commanders considerable discretion over operational commands. And by early 1942, the Americans had come to establish a military high command, in part, to interface with the British system. On some matters, as in war production, however, FDR was remarkably laissez-faire, allowing each separate service to set its own requirements. In addition, the president did little to influence strategy in the Pacific, except in 1943, when he refused to accept the Joint Chiefs' recommendations for an offensive in Burma and the Bay of Bengal.

At times, especially at the Quebec and Tehran conferences with Churchill, FDR became a mediator between his own military chiefs and the British strategists, including Churchill. As has been noted, the president overruled his divided military leaders and sided with Churchill in the North African campaign. In 1942, an aggressive FDR made it abundantly clear to his advisers that he had accepted the Atlantic First strategy and intended to reach an agreement with the British on the first great Allied offensive. After the debate, FDR underscored his decision in writing, signing the agreement, "Franklin D. Roosevelt, Commander-in-Chief." The point was clearly made. A disappointed General Marshall noted, "In wartime the politicians have to do *something* important every year."

In July 1942, the president appointed Admiral Leahy as his chief of staff, a position that FDR described as "a sort of leg man." After differences of opinion over the North Africa campaign, however, the Joint Chiefs and the president rarely disagreed on major strategy, but that consensus may have been due to their anticipating his reactions rather than his deference to the professionals.

By 1943, though, the president supported his chiefs often against the British, and as has been seen, he finally ended up pushing for "Overlord" and preventing another diversion of forces. By late 1943 and 1944, the conduct of the war moved along accepted lines agreed to by nearly all major figures in the U.S. government. The president and the chiefs recognized the need to defeat Germany decisively and quickly and return the troops home in preparation for the final campaigns in the Pacific. FDR did not envision that American public opinion would support the stationing of U.S. troops in Europe, and he wanted to stay away from the morass of postwar Central and Eastern Europe. In the Pacific, however, he did seem to anticipate a more interventionist role after the war.

There was much of the isolationist in the early years of FDR's presidency. He spoke of avoiding the problems of Europe, of its "ancient hatreds, turbulent frontiers, 'the legacy of old forgotten, far-off things and battles long ago.'" In 1944, he wrote,

> I do not want the United States to have the post-war burden of reconstituting France, Italy and the Balkans. This is not our natural task at a distance of 3500 miles or more. . . . Our principal object is not to take part in the internal problems of Southern Europe, but is rather to take part in eliminating Germany as a possible and even probable cost of a third World War.[60]

Roosevelt in Retrospect

For twelve years, Franklin Delano Roosevelt led the nation through two of its most severe crises. He found a nation with limited federal responsibilities and presided over and fostered actively a patchwork of domestic programs that comprise the welfare state. He inherited a nation committed to isolationism and redirected its massive energies into war and far-flung diplomacy. In the process, he reoriented American partisan allegiances and created the framework that led to the modern executive office of the presidency and the antecedents of the military-industrial complex. No president was so powerful, no president so self-assured in his love of executive authority.

Yet FDR was no revolutionary or radical; he was a conservative patrician who retained a flexible mind—suspicious of ideology and open to ambiguity. His New Deal did not restore the nation to prosperity; mobilization for war and the expansive role of government spending prevented another Great Depression. But his leadership did provide an early sense of inspiration, faith in the future, and confidence in the viability of the American dream. Leadership is more than process, it is inspiration and energy, and FDR epitomized both. Even acknowledging the limitations of the New Deal and its neglect of the unorganized segments of society, many of its basic initiatives remain institutions in American life. In comparison with the welfare states in Europe, even in Bismarck's Germany in the late nineteenth century, it may seem modest, but within American history, it is the culmination of the progressive impulse and its greatest triumph. Roosevelt moved across the political spectrum in that first term from a nearly nonpartisan executive to a fierce reformer, smiting the evils of selfishness, monopoly, and corporate greed. The liberals remembered him for this latter pose—they loved him for the enemies he made. His open and loose administrative manners may have hindered his leadership at times, but the chaos of the 1930s led many citizens to accept experimentation and uneven management. And such a style, for better or worse, was endemic to FDR, as he showed in his confusing domestic mobilization during the war.

Roosevelt was so concerned with keeping power in his own hands that he tolerated, if not promoted, the types of sloppy, uneven, and competitive morass that hurt the mobilization of resources and manpower and taxed an already overburdened and ill president. But the Roosevelt most criticized is the FDR who conducted personal diplomacy with Stalin at Tehran and Yalta. Some seventy years after these conferences, Roosevelt's name is linked in many circles here and abroad with naïveté and appeasement.

Partly, he gave some fuel to those charges by announcing that he knew how to deal with Stalin. Stalin, however, was a brutal, dedicated party functionary who sincerely believed in communism, who ruthlessly crushed the old Bolsheviks who brought it forth, and who seemed to share in many of the historical memories and ambitions of the czars. When FDR met him, the president confided to Frances Perkins that he just did not understand the Soviets. He seemed to believe that by the sheer charm of his personality and humorous jibes at Churchill and Britain's pretensions, he could win "Joe's" favor. That strain of superficiality was a part of Roosevelt's personality. He could ignore what was disturbing, the same way he ignored the plight of African Americans in the United States, the Japanese Americans in U.S. detention camps, and the Jews in Hitler's Europe. Behind the mask was a complex personality and also a certain hollowness of character.

Still, much of the criticism of FDR's diplomacy is misguided. None of the Allied leaders, including Stalin and Churchill, placed diplomatic objectives before the immediate and final defeat of the Nazis. Stalin's great triumph was not any brilliant ploy—he took what the Red Army basically won by its blood and sacrifice. It is possible that the Western Allies might have moved more quickly through Germany, and it is less likely that they might have gone up the Balkans to cut off the Red Army. But in 1942, 1943, and even 1944, the campaigns in Italy and France and the prospects of a long war in the Pacific gave FDR legitimate reasons for pursuing his strategy of trying to keep the Soviets as allies.

Somehow the Second World War is seen as a triumph for Stalin in the eyes of FDR's detractors. But from Stalin's perspective, what had it wrought that so eclipsed FDR's record? After massive sacrifices, the Soviets controlled Eastern Europe and consequently brought forth a united Western alliance with a string of nuclear warheads encircling its bloc until the late 1980s. Stalin created in large part the conditions that led to an American presence that even FDR never contemplated—a long commitment of U.S. combat troops in Europe and an economic plan to rebuild the Atlantic nation-states. Historian A. J. P. Taylor has said that Roosevelt was the really astute leader who emerged from the crucible of war. The United States lost comparatively few soldiers and emerged as the most powerful nation on the earth. In the world of realpolitik, FDR is an outstandingly successful and shrewd national leader, overshadowing the Bismarcks and the Pitts of different eras.[61]

But FDR was not that sort of practitioner of realpolitik, although Taylor is correct about the outcome of his leadership and the modest price the United States paid. Nor was FDR Stalin's foil or Churchill's lesser light. He did not see the United States as a land power in Europe after the war, and he prepared his nation to be one of the policemen of the world in an alliance with Britain, the Soviet Union, and a romanticized version of China. He knew the suspicions of Stalin toward the West and honestly tried to calm them. Today it seems a bit unrealistic, but in the context of waging war in the West and preparing for what was supposed to be a terrible struggle in the Pacific, it was common sense to keep in the war the nation that had tied up 80–90 percent of the Nazi army in 1942—the Soviet Union. As late as 1945, Eisenhower was asking Stalin for help in order to alleviate the pressure on the Allied armies moving into Germany. And Stalin complied.

Roosevelt, in one important sense, did foresee the future course of imperialism and the collapse of colonial empires more clearly than any of the other major statesmen of his time. He not only predicted the end of traditional colonialism but also welcomed it, although he did not shrink from the policy of the big powers as trustees policing the world.[62] Still, there is the question of Poland. FDR tried to convince Stalin of the need for an open government, but at times he seemed more concerned that the Soviet marshal give a public show of good faith just to keep Polish American voters and others pacified. Perhaps he was simply phrasing it so in order to appeal to Stalin's appreciation of self-interest. FDR's weakness, though, was not one of intention or commitment; as has been noted, Poland went to the Red Army and not Stalin's shrewd diplomacy. And as for Stalin, his objectives were clear; they were echoes of the ambitions of the czars: control the flatlands of Poland, the Slavic peoples of the Baltic, and the warm-water ports of access on the borders of the Soviet Union.

Lastly, it must be remembered that Roosevelt's leadership was important in the defeat of fascism, the Nazi war machine, and Japanese militarism in three years' time. That achievement, the negative one of preventing the triumph or at least a deadlock with those forces, was no cheap victory. When FDR demanded unconditional surrender, Churchill and Stalin both had reservations. It would steel the enemies' resolve and determination, they feared, but FDR sensed, perhaps intuitively, that the war demanded a moral crusade that portrayed the enemy as not simply a threatening force but also as a criminal mutation of the human spirit. A simplified credo, a propaganda ploy, perhaps—but one with a powerful ability to inspire captive peoples and sustain the war weary. FDR was a manipulative and, at times, deceitful person, but he sincerely held to a common morality and accepted its pieties. In a world of amoral war barons, genocidal demagogues, and paranoid autocrats, FDR was a pleasant, rather admirable shaft of light. Roosevelt's diplomacy was more circumscribed by real constraints than American conservatives have admitted, and he was more skeptical of Soviet intentions than the radical-left historians like to believe.

The Roosevelt presidency represents the high point of executive leadership in the sheer scope of its sweep and in the lasting consequences of its changes. Admire him or not, Franklin Delano Roosevelt, like Shakespeare's Caesar, was a colossus that bestrode the American political scene and the Second World War, and his personality and achievements profoundly reshaped the office and influenced his successors of both parties for generations to come. The Age of Roosevelt is still with us and has become the centerpiece of the modern presidency.[63]

Harry S Truman: The First Imperial President

9

HE DECADES THAT HAVE FOLLOWED Roosevelt have seen a
much-changed America and a much-changed executive branch
of government. From a provincial, isolationist nation, the United
States emerged as a superpower with an expensive standing army, a nuclear
arsenal of indescribable power, an activist intelligence service with a capacity for far-reaching covert activities, and a strong alliance of privilege and
power encompassing government, business, universities, and the military.
The presidency became the center of this very transformation; it became
an office sitting on top of the bureaucracy perched above the executive
branch of government. While Truman had thirteen assistants, the Obamas
have 480. Offices dealing with economic projections, culture, ethnic affairs, national security, overseas intelligence, and science and technology
were grafted onto the more prosaic traditional presidency.

Yet the post-Rooseveltian presidency revolved around two great issues
that FDR was partially responsible for in his eventful tenure, one emerging out of the New Deal and the other from the uneasy wartime alliance
with the Soviet Union. First, the political parties continued to redefine
themselves from 1945 on partially in terms of the development of and the
opposition to the social welfare state. And second, the foreign policy preoccupation of the postwar presidents through George H. W. Bush was the
power, ambition, and the expansion of the Soviet Union.

On a personal level, most of these presidents were either protégés of
FDR or deeply influenced by his personality and politics. Truman was his
vice president; Eisenhower was plucked from obscurity by FDR and General George C. Marshall to head the Allied forces; John F. Kennedy knew

and admired the president and watched as his father, Joseph P. Kennedy, fell in and out of FDR's favor; Lyndon Johnson was an actual political satellite in the Roosevelt New Deal constellation; Ronald Reagan, while serving to destroy the underpinnings of the welfare state, came from a family that directly benefited from the New Deal administration and was genuinely enamored with the liberal president of his youth; and George H. W. Bush fondly remembered serving as a teenager under FDR, commander in chief.[1] Of course, after the elder Bush, FDR became just a part of the distant past to his successors.

Truman and the Uncertain Legacy

On the eighty-third day of his vice presidency, Harry S Truman received the news of FDR's death. Although Truman was a Roosevelt loyalist, and the president surely had intimations of his own mortality, the usually secretive FDR had not shared any information with Truman about the major decisions made at Yalta and Tehran or the development of the atomic bomb.

In many ways, this unusual team that won the 1944 election seemed to be very different. Truman was the only person to sit in the White House in the twentieth century whose education ended in high school; he later enrolled in a few law courses in night school but never completed the program. He had been a farmer in Missouri, a haberdasher who went bankrupt at age thirty-eight, and a local boy who joined the state National Guard, and he ended up a captain in World War I. He then entered politics, became an honest acolyte in the corrupt Pendergast machine, was elected judge (commissioner), and went on to the U.S. Senate. Over the years, Truman compiled a record for personal honesty, doggedness, and a strong allegiance to the New Deal. In 1944, widespread opposition to the erratic Vice President Henry Wallace led the Democratic Party leaders to look for a replacement. FDR, devious as usual, encouraged Wallace, let it be known he would accept Truman or Supreme Court Justice William O. Douglas as a running mate, and made very favorable comments about James Byrnes of South Carolina.

Truman represented the values that Americans like to believe are characteristic of themselves: he was hardworking, honest, simple, and free of ostentation and pomp. He was the product of machine politics, of men who attended funerals and loved parades, who drank bourbon and protected each other with a fierce communal bonding. Truman never abandoned those values and, for better or worse, continued to exhibit a sense of loyalty that at times impeded his performance as president. He held on to the Democratic Party as surely as he held on to his Baptist religion. One was born and died in those faiths.[2]

Because of his poor eyesight, he wore glasses, avoided sports, fought the sissy label, and read extensively history and biography—making him in some ways the most knowledgeable president since Professor Woodrow Wilson. He was a man given to some profanity, except in the company of women, and he was proud of his rather extraordinary rise in station. Then, at the age of sixty, this interesting American success story was propelled onto the international stage. The Truman presidency was surely one of the most eventful and consequential in U.S. history. It was a presidency of great policies, petty partisanship, and deep public disillusionment. Speaker of the House Sam Rayburn predicted, "Truman will not make a great, flashy president like Roosevelt. But, by God, he'll make a good president, a sound president. He's got the stuff in him."

Truman, though, added to his critics' early underestimations by declaring that at least a million other people were more qualified than he to be president, and he once commented to Senator George Aiken of Vermont, "I'm not big enough. I'm not big enough for this job." In his first term, he had a portrait of Roosevelt hung up in his office, and when faced with a decision he would ask, "Would he think this is the right thing?"

Looking at Truman in his first cabinet meeting, FDR's press secretary, Jonathan Daniels, saw him as "a little man." New Deal partisans could not imagine that this parochial and seemingly unlettered individual could replace the political giant who so dominated American politics. But even Truman, looking at the ashen and worn FDR in 1945, realized that the president's days were clearly numbered. Truman was sworn to uphold his predecessor's legacy—but what was that legacy, what did FDR agree to or believe in about the unformed issues that were being crystallized as the war in Europe was coming to an end?

The central confusion was FDR's policy toward the Soviets. By late March 1945, FDR himself clearly had become fed up with Stalin. At one point he simply concluded, "Averell [Harriman] is right; we can't do business with Stalin. He has broken every one of the promises he made at Yalta." The Soviet Maxim Litvinov placed the blame elsewhere when he said to Edgar Snow in Moscow in 1945, "Why did the Americans wait until now to begin opposing us in the Balkans and Eastern Europe? . . . You should have done this three years ago. Now it's too late and your complaints only arouse suspicion here."

Immediately on taking office, Truman was notified that the war against Germany would last another six months, and the war against Japan another year and a half. Cooperation with the Soviet Union was important in that long struggle, and Truman reaffirmed FDR's controversial objective—unconditional surrender of the Axis Powers. He quickly nominated James Byrnes as secretary of state and set a different tone at press conferences. Where FDR had been jaunty and cagey, Truman answered questions quickly and straightforwardly. His Gallup poll rating climbed to a phenomenal 87 percent—three points higher than FDR ever received at the apex of his popularity. And although he was loyal to the New Deal and its master, Truman disliked professional liberals—"the lunatic fringe," as he called them. The new president concluded, "The American people have been through a lot of experiments and they want a rest from experiments." Yet Truman did associate himself with the New Deal's programs for the future—pushing for more public electric power, full employment, expansion of Social Security, and broad unemployment compensation. Soon he would surprise Southerners and African Americans alike by extending liberalism into the realm of civil rights, a move FDR would never have undertaken.[3]

But Truman soon learned that Congress was not willing to follow a liberal domestic agenda and that the alliance with the Soviet Union was a fragile marriage, coming undone over the contentious issue of Poland. As Truman read the diplomatic messages between the Soviets and the United States, he grew angry over Stalin's insults and accusations concerning American motives. When he first met Soviet Foreign Minister Molotov, Truman bluntly demanded a truly representative government in Poland as provided for in the Yalta accords. To Truman, this was in keeping with FDR's legacy; in reality, it was a hardening of attitudes toward the Soviet Union and Stalin. The new president also adopted the general State Department line in opposing spheres of influence. For Stalin, though, the eastern territories were the bounty of the Red Army's costly victories and, equally important, a series of friendly buffer states that would eventually be linked economically and militarily to the Soviet state.

On May 8, Truman formally announced victory in Europe, "VE Day"; in terms of the Pacific theater, he gave formal assurances that unconditional surrender would not mean "the extermination or enslavement of the Japanese people." Sticking with what he thought were FDR's promises, Truman honored the agreement on occupation zones and refused to accept Churchill's advice that he keep American troops in the Soviet zone. Seeking to overcome postwar difficulties, Truman, Stalin, and Churchill met in Germany at Potsdam from July 17 to August 2, 1945. Churchill expressed approval with his new American partner, concluding to a friend, "He is a man of immense determination. He takes no notice of delicate ground, he just plants his foot down firmly upon it." As for Truman, he also eyed up his colleagues at the conference, comparing the ruthless Stalin to Tom Pendergast and to the New York Tammany Hall boss William Marcy Tweed. He quickly got a taste of the Soviet leader's thinking, however, when he asked what had happened to thousands of Polish army officers massacred in the Katyn Forest. Stalin's response was brutally succinct: "They went away."[4]

Truman had initially refused to support the Morgenthau Plan to agrarianize Germany, and he suggested instead a trade link between the food-producing areas of Hungary, Rumania, and the Ukraine with the coal-producing regions in the West. As after the First World War, the reparations issue also came up at Yalta. The reparations figure debated there was $20 billion, half of which would go to the Soviet Union. But since the Soviets were proving to be so difficult, the administration now saw no compulsion to expedite reparations. Meanwhile, the Soviets turned over to its client government in Poland a major part of Germany within their zone of occupation. In return, the Soviets insisted on taking a portion of what was eastern Poland, consequently pushing both Soviet and Polish borders west at the expense of a defeated Germany—a settlement discussed by the Big Three leaders before.

At Potsdam, Truman's style was rather different from what the Allied leaders had seen with FDR. Charles Bohlen concluded, "Where Roosevelt improvised, Truman stuck closely to positions worked out in advance. Where Roosevelt, in his argumentations, would work in extraneous ideas, Truman was crisp and to the point." But Truman found, as FDR and Churchill had discovered, that Stalin did not intend to allow any reorganization of the Eastern European states then under his control.

Having received confidential notice about the atomic explosion at Alamogordo, New Mexico, Truman's position was strengthened, and he insisted again that the Soviets honor their commitments at Yalta concerning Poland. In their discussions, Stalin decided to link up the future of Italy with that of Eastern Europe, and he concluded that the latter governments were closer to the people than the Italian regime was. Truman was blunt in his response: "I have made it clear—we will not recognize these governments until they are reorganized." The debate on reparations became intertwined with the future of Poland and the fate of other eastern states, as Secretary of State Byrnes pronounced it: an all or nothing deal. Stalin continued to resist. Thus, Four Power administration (France had joined the Big Three) over a divided Germany began, and eventually the reparation agreements broke down altogether.[5]

As suspicions mounted among the Allies, the war in Asia continued. A major and costly offensive against the Japanese was a critical part of the administration's calculations to end the conflict. The development of the bomb and the decision to drop it in two locations over Japan upended all those calculations. The use of the atomic bomb remains one of the most controversial aspects of the American conduct in the war. Truman did not know of the existence of the bomb until after he took office, and despite his own comments later, the new president was less responsible for the decision than is usually assumed. The ultimate decision to drop the first bomb was surely his. But in fact the bureaucratic process to go ahead and develop and use it had moved along like a juggernaut. The only decision Truman could have made was to stop that process, one that had acquired a momentum of its own. The most important figure in the decision was Secretary of War Henry Stimson, and Truman concurred in order to end the war and avert the frightening prediction of enormous American casualties in order to subdue Japan. In addition, the administration came to see the atomic bomb as a bargaining tool with the recalcitrant Soviets and a way of averting their intervention in the Pacific war—an intervention the Americans had vigorously insisted upon previously. And so on August 5, 1945, the first atomic bomb was dropped on Hiroshima.

Stimson was undoubtedly correct when he wrote, "At no time, from 1941 to 1945, did I ever hear it suggested by the president, or by any other responsible member of the government, that atomic energy should not be used in the war." Years later, Truman was to dismiss criticism of the decision with almost facile disdain, but at the time he told an associate, "I'll make the decision, but it is terrifying to think about what I will have to decide." On August 9, he had received a telegram from a religious official asking him not to use the bomb again, and he responded, "Nobody is more disturbed over the use of the atomic bomb than I am but I was greatly disturbed over the unwarranted attack by the Japanese on Pearl Harbor and their murder of our prisoners of war. The only language they seem to understand is the one we have been using to bombard them. When you have to deal with a beast you have to treat him as a beast. It is most regrettable but nevertheless true."

He later concluded, "It occurred to me that a quarter of a million of the flower of our young manhood were worth a couple of Japanese cities, and I still think they were and are." Truman, though, told Stimson at Potsdam he hoped that only one bomb would be dropped, but as biographer Robert Donovan concluded, "this wish was not translated into policy." And so a second and probably unneeded atomic bomb was unleashed on Nagasaki on August 9.[6]

With the quick end of the war in the Pacific after the use of the atomic bomb, Truman refused to share the occupation of Japan with the Soviets. Stalin's response was curt: "I and my colleagues did not expect such an answer from you." The abrupt end of the war also had an impact on the government's reconversion plans, which were geared to an end of the war sometime in 1946. Roosevelt, who had been less than successful in mobilization, had even less control over demobilization planning. Remembering the dislocations after the previous war and the terrible Depression of the 1930s, many feared the worst. And within ten days, 1.8 million people did lose their jobs. It seemed like a repeat of past miseries. On August 18, Truman directed that government agencies move as rapidly as possible to remove wage, price, and production controls. The president and the nation soon faced the prospect of rampant inflation, labor strikes, and enormous pressure to cut back the army and bring the troops back home. In the end, however, the Great Depression did not resume. The balancing effects of the New Deal welfare state, the backlog of consumer demand from the war, remobilization for the Korean conflict, and continued pressures of a Cold War economy all infused the types of stimuli that economist John Maynard Keynes had insisted would bring prosperity.

Lacking a liberal majority in Congress, Truman faced the same intransigence that FDR confronted after 1938. Indeed, a coalition of conservative Democrats and Republicans successfully blocked major legislation from the end of Roosevelt's second term until the 1960s. As for the president, he generally held high the liberal banner, but he rarely pushed for social welfare legislation once he introduced it.

To Err Is Truman

By late 1945 and early 1946, Truman faced a series of problems that seriously undercut his initial public support and left him battered and besieged. Faced with strikes in some essential industries, the president vigorously opposed some stoppages and alienated segments of labor. On top of that problem, postwar shortages of food supplies added to the president's woes, a problem complicated by real fears of famine in Europe.[7] In November 1945, the U.S. ambassador to China, Patrick J. Hurley, abruptly resigned and charged that Chiang Kai-shek did not have the full support of the State

Department because of a "pro-Communist, pro-imperialist" faction there. It was the beginning of a bitter and grossly unfair campaign against the administration, leading to the overall judgment that somehow the United States had "lost China" when Mao Tse-tung took over.

The president's foreign policy got further muddled when his secretary of state, James Byrnes, negotiated in Moscow an agreement with the Soviets on atomic energy, military forces in Iran, and other disputed matters. Byrnes had not kept the president properly informed on the developments, and Truman resented his show of independence. The president concluded that Byrnes "had taken it upon himself to move the foreign policy of the United States in a direction to which I could not, and would not, agree." Increasingly, the president believed that the Soviets understood only military power, and their willingness to negotiate in good faith was being increasingly called into question. The wartime alliance was quickly becoming undone once the common foes were vanquished.[8]

On the Soviet side, Stalin increased pressure on Iran, Greece, and Turkey; on February 9, 1946, he praised the might of the Red Army and pronounced that peace was not possible because of the forces of capitalism and imperialism. Nine days later, evidence of Soviet atomic espionage was made public in Ottawa, Canada. Then, in March, Churchill gave his "Iron Curtain" address, with Truman sitting on the commencement platform at Westminster College. The aging British leader concluded that "from Stettin in the Baltic to Trieste in the Adriatic an Iron Curtain has descended across the Continent." The speech called for a union of "English-speaking peoples"—an old idea of Churchill's, but one that Stalin surely interpreted as an anti-Soviet alliance in the making. At the same time, the State Department sent a forceful protest to the Soviets about their military forces in Iran. By the end of the month, however, the Soviets and Iranians had made major progress in working out an agreement after all.

At home, Truman continued to face an increasing number of strikes and work stoppages from restive labor and toughening corporate management. In 1946, over 4.6 million workers went on strike, with the loss of the equivalent of 116 million days. The president also had to deal with staff turnover in the government, and the burdens of creating a modern executive branch were taking their toll. His budget director, Harold D. Smith, warned that while the president was "an orderly person, there is disorder all around you, and it is becoming worse. . . . For one thing, you need good, continuous staff work, and you are not getting it." Truman complained of an enormous amount of paperwork—some thirty thousand words of memoranda a night. Part of the problem was his inability to put his own brand on the administration he inherited, part of it was a legacy of FDR's freewheeling style, but a good deal of the difficulty came from the transition period Truman was in. He was, in effect, the first "imperial president," the first president as a matter of course and not crisis to sit on top of the expanding bureaucratic executive branch. As the welfare state became institutionalized and as the United States became a global power, the modest federal government grew enormously, and the presidency as the hub also had to change. In his time in office, Truman would expand the executive office of the White House, bringing in specialists in economics, resource management, labor, atomic energy, and other areas. He would push for some centralization of the armed forces, a large standing army, an intelligence agency, and a strong military and foreign policy establishment. In many ways, it is Truman more than even FDR who created the modern presidency as we and his heirs have come to know it.[9]

In steering his own course through all of this, Truman was more often a man of tenacity than of subtlety. He quickly welcomed the departure of Harold Ickes in Interior and fired Henry Wallace in Agriculture. Ickes, the crusty New Dealer par excellence, blasted "government by crony" and then left the cabinet. Wallace, farmer, mystic, and makeshift expert in foreign policy, had decided to depart from the administration on the question of how to deal with Stalin. He would later coalesce his group of fervent New Dealers, Communists, and some fellow travelers into a presidential bid in 1948. Parts of the New Deal coalition were spinning off as the president faced the difficulties of 1946. As for labor, Truman refused to allow strikes in critical industries to go unchecked. He threatened to take control of the railroads when a settlement seemed beyond reach, and in one year he seized the coal mines (twice), 134 meatpacking plants, 91 tugboats, and the facilities of 26 oil producing and refining companies, as well as the Great Lakes Towing Company. Fed up with railroad strikes, on May 8, 1946, the president decided to draft the strikers and then order them back to work on the railroads. Truman dramatically appeared before Congress with a tough message, and as he reached his conclusion, he was handed a note indicating an agreement had been reached. Triumphantly, he announced, "Word has been received that the railroad strike has been settled, on terms proposed by the president!" It was a major victory for Truman, one that he needed desperately to reassert his leadership.[10]

Then the president took on John L. Lewis of the United Mine Workers, a tough negotiator who had challenged Roosevelt's authority even during the war. On November 20, 1946, the mine workers went on strike even after extensive efforts by the administration to work out a fair settlement. The Truman administration's tactics were to take Lewis to court, and the labor leader was fined $10,000 personally and the union $3.5 million. The showdown worked and Lewis called off the strike, citing the Supreme Court's review of the injunction. The high court finally upheld the convictions for contempt of court but reduced the fine.

By the end of 1946, Truman seemed to go from one crisis to another, some of his own making, but most due to the difficult postwar problems of reconversion and social dislocation. In terms of foreign policy, the president was moving away from what he initially perceived as FDR's legacy of cooperation with the Soviets to a hardheaded and often belligerent confrontation with Stalin and his imperialist ambitions. To replace Byrnes at State, Truman named retired General Marshall—a person the president was to call the greatest living American of his time. But even Marshall, the organizer of victory in World War II, could not succeed in ending the civil war in China. American foreign policy was contradictory: the administration claimed to be an honest broker between Chiang and Mao, but it opposed the Communists in their bid for power. With a declining military establishment, serious problems in Europe, and a crumbling Chinese Nationalist regime, the Americans could not dictate a settlement in China, try as they might.[11]

Republican critics of Truman's foreign policy were correct on one count: The administration was primarily concerned in 1947 with the fate of Europe, which tottered on the brink of catastrophe, social chaos, and, in some cases, Communist takeovers. First food and later fuel shortages became critical, and only the United States could respond with much-needed supplies. Through 1947, faced with British withdrawal in Greece, Turkey, and the Middle East, the administration moved with unaccustomed brilliance into the gap. First, the president proposed granting aid to Greece and Turkey as a way of curtailing Soviet influence. Republican Senator Arthur Vandenberg, the symbol and carrier of bipartisan foreign policy, was clearly stunned and implored the president to tell the Congress and the country about the crisis in the most threatening terms. Thus the Truman Doctrine, as it was called, was born. To get congressional support, the president heeded Vandenberg and accentuated his anticommunist rhetoric. The Cold War heated up.

The administration followed up its requests with a major rehabilitation program for Europe, named after General Marshall. The Marshall Plan included large-scale U.S. assistance for the recovery of Europe and did not initially exclude Eastern Europe. Luckily for the administration, the usually suspicious Soviets saw it as an attempt to isolate the Soviet Union, and so the plan also became a tool in the arsenal of Western democracies. Thus, within a relatively short period of time—about eighteen months— the Truman administration, in a flurry of activity and with some broad conceptualization, changed the very basis of American foreign policy. It put in place the Truman Doctrine, the Marshall Plan, Point Four (expert economic assistance), and later the Western military alliance called the North Atlantic Treaty Organization (NATO).

The policy behind these initiatives became known as "containment," the encircling of the Soviet Union with military bases and the establishment of a tougher line drawn in the sand. Considering the isolationist history of the United States and its genuine war weariness, the Truman foreign policy was an incredible political achievement. Its successes were due to the president's persistence, his advisers' care, Republican cooperation, and, above all, Stalin. In the last years of his brutal regime the Soviet dictator had reached too far and too fast after the war to both recoup Soviet losses due to the Nazi onslaughts and also to extend Soviet control over the eastern sectors of Europe and beyond. Soviet apologists would later say that Stalin was simply pursuing the age-old policies of the czars; in large part, though, his reactions were excessive, those befitting a man of incredible brutality and true paranoia. Truman's responses were clear and blunt—no more Hitlers, no more Munichs, no more appeasement.[12]

To win congressional approval, he was not above overdramatizing the Soviet threat and using the anticommunist rhetoric so popular in Republican and conservative circles. Partly, but not totally, as a result, Truman later found the Communist issue turned on him and the Democratic Party. Unable to gather public attention with their laissez-faire social philosophy, the Republican leaders used the Red Scare issue to garner support. Truman tried to stop the rush by announcing his own internal security program, which aimed at dismissing government employees who were found to be disloyal. Investigators had access to FBI files, military and naval intelligence, the information of the House Un-American Activities Committee, and records of local law enforcement agencies. Loyalty boards were set up, and employees were not guaranteed the right to confront their accusers. Without realizing it, Truman helped lay the groundwork for the assaults of Senator Joseph McCarthy and a whole generation of attacks on due process and basic American civil liberties. In politics, halfway steps are often more dangerous than wrong policies, for the latter are easier to see and to challenge. But in any case, by April 1947, Truman's approval rating bounced up to 60 percent—nearly double his low point of a year before.[13]

Truman's standing fluctuated wildly in his first term, his popularity being linked up with the difficult concrete problems he faced and how he dealt with them. He lacked the great resources of public affection that FDR and later Ronald Reagan would have. Like Lincoln, he was never a beloved figure while in the White House, and the controversies in which he was embroiled took a toll. At times, Truman seemed, like all of us, to be his own worst enemy. He was tolerant of diverse opinions, then resentful when those advocates went public with their differences. He seemed at first to be deferential to Roosevelt's memory, wondering what the great man would have done on this matter or that. Then Truman, especially in his second term, seemed too self-assured, if not cocky. Still, in the period of 1947–1948, Truman became president in his own right, and in the crucible of events, he laid the groundwork for the strange election before him.

Fortunately for Truman, the Republicans decided to go beyond the president's tough stand against strikers and take on the whole organized labor movement. In April 1947, the GOP-controlled House of Representatives passed the Hartley bill to limit the power of organized labor. The Senate passed a milder bill, and a conference committee compromise was sent to Truman in June. Union halls and closed shops (which required union membership to hold a job) were forbidden; states could pass "right to work" laws, which outlawed union-shop agreements; and various unfair labor practices were prohibited. Injunctions were permitted, and the president could ask for an eighty-day cooling-off period to delay a shutdown. Although the bill does not seem, after nearly seventy years of implementation, to have been so devastating to organized labor, in 1947 the unions regarded it as a clear attack by their traditional enemies, which it certainly was. The president vetoed the Taft-Hartley bill, sending back a stinging message. Congress quickly overrode his veto, but for Truman, the controversy added to his shaky coalition the powerful labor constituency. Thus, the Republicans would help reelect Truman in 1948 without realizing it. In addition, the American Federation of Labor (AFL) and the Congress of Industrial Organizations (CIO) became more partisan and politically active than ever before, making organized labor one of the most important sources of strength for the Democratic Party nationally and often locally, well into the present.[14]

In the fall of 1947, Truman was facing another explosive situation that in the end would add to his political problems and then political clout—Palestine. Truman's position on a homeland for displaced Jews was a moderate one: in mid-1946, he encouraged the immigration of one hundred thousand European Jews to the region but reserved judgment on the future of Palestine. While the president seemed sympathetic to the plight of the survivors of the Holocaust, he deeply resented pressure from American Zionist leaders. The British had proposed a Palestine federation with four areas: Arab and Jewish provinces, a district of Jerusalem, and a district of the Negev. Truman seemed to support the idea at first, but the reaction at home was so critical that he backed off. Senator Robert Taft attacked the plan, Jewish groups demanded that it be repudiated, and influential Americans spoke out against the compromise. An angry Truman focused only on Jewish criticism and harshly concluded to an associate, "Jesus Christ couldn't please them when he was here on earth, so how could anyone expect that I would have any luck?" But after all was said and done, Truman saw the political realities and abandoned U.S. support for the compromise.[15]

Yet the president did retain a genuine sympathy for Jewish refugees and began to push, often against State Department advice, for support for a Jewish homeland. When the issue went to the United Nations, administration representatives heavily pressured smaller nations to support such a homeland, although Truman may not have been aware of the threats or heavy-handed methods used by his own delegation. After the General Assembly voted, fighting broke out in the region, and the president grew concerned about having to send U.S. troops there. While Jewish demands in the election campaign mounted, the State Department feared that a separate homeland would alienate the Arabs. Dissension in the administration led to differing views being made public, and the president's own position seemed to be unclear or undercut by his own subordinates. Clark Clifford and others warned Truman of the political ramifications of not recognizing a separate Jewish state, while Secretary of State Marshall insisted that he himself would vote against Truman if he succumbed to the pressure. While the American representatives at the UN were discussing the issue, the president decided to recognize the State of Israel. On May 15, 1948, Arab armies invaded Israel and war began. As for Truman, it is easy to cite political considerations in his defense, but probably he was also just weary of the controversy and the alleged confusion on America's position. He correctly judged U.S. sentiment and surely considered the long campaign ahead of him.

Just as FDR had been able to finesse the Jewish homeland–Arab issue, he had also been able to sidestep civil rights. Truman, however, did not have that luxury, and he had to deal with the latter controversy as well. At first it seemed to bring him toward political disaster, but once again, controversy rebounded to his credit and to his advantage. Ironically, this small-town Missouri politician who was not averse to racial epithets became the most pro-black president since Lincoln. Truman at first simply misjudged the intensity of Southern opposition to his civil rights program. He pushed for support of a special government commission's recommendations: a permanent commission on civil rights, a civil rights section in the Justice Department, an anti-lynching law, and a statute to curb police brutality. The commission also advocated an end to the poll tax, protection of qualified voters, an amendment to give residents of the District of Columbia the right to vote in presidential elections, and home rule for the predominantly black District. The commission attacked segregation in a variety of ways, insisting, for example, on a pledge of nondiscrimination from recipients of any federal program and an end to racially restrictive covenants that were especially prominent in housing deeds at that time.[16]

The president supported the thrust of the report and ran into a buzz saw of Southern political opposition. One minister wrote Truman from Florida, "If that report is carried out you won't be elected dogcatcher in 1948. The South today is the South of 1861 regarding things your committee had under consideration." The president at first remarked that he hadn't really read the report, but in December he instructed his staff to present a civil rights program to go to Congress early in 1948.

Thus, as he faced the nominating convention, Truman had compiled an impressive record and an impressive list of foes. On the left, Henry Wallace had begun his own quixotic campaign, attacking Truman's "global Monroe Doctrine" and his supposed abandonment of FDR's policy of cooperation with the Soviets. He even criticized the Marshall Plan, saying it was a tool of U.S. domination. To much annoyance, Truman watched as some of the hard-core New Dealers, mainly in the liberal Americans for Democratic Action, wooed General Dwight Eisenhower as a Democratic candidate for president. FDR's sons backed the nonpolitical military man, as did Hubert Humphrey, Arthur Goldberg of the CIO, Walter Reuther of the United Auto Workers (UAW), Harold Ickes, and other liberals. Eleanor Roosevelt was also supposedly "discussing" whether to grant her support.

But as that intrigue continued, Truman was adding Democratic delegates and state caucuses to his cause and relying on the Democratic National Convention's leaders and old congressional friends to put his candidacy over. Then Eisenhower announced that he was not interested, and the opposition to Truman had no viable alternative at that late date. The hard-core liberals had not only misjudged Truman and the American electorate but, almost humorously, they had also misjudged Eisenhower, as his time in office would bear out.

   The Democratic Convention supported a strong civil rights plank, much to Truman's dismay, and Southern delegates left the floor; later, some established a states' rights presidential ticket of Strom Thurmond of South Carolina for president and Fielding Lewis Wright of Mississippi for vice president. Truman thus began the so-called Impossible Campaign of 1948—an ordeal for a modest man facing monumental domestic and international problems, lacking a Southern base so essential to any Democrat, and hurt by attacks on the left. Truman insisted, though, that he would win, and throughout the long summer, he whistle-stopped throughout the great heartland of America, into its unsettling cities, and through the mixed landscapes of the South. The underdog suddenly emerged as the prosecutor. He threw away his set speeches, which he fumbled through, and talked as an old stump speaker to his fellow citizens. To cries of "Give 'em hell, Harry," he did. He called the Republican Congress back into session on "Turnip Day" and gloated as they defeated liberal legislation. He branded them the "Do-Nothing Eightieth Congress," and the title stuck. The Republicans called him the worst president in history; the *Chicago Tribune* insisted he was a "nincompoop." Among newspaper editorials, 65 percent favored Dewey, and only 15 percent supported the president.

   The Republican candidate, Thomas E. Dewey, had been criticized in 1944 for attacking FDR too harshly, so in 1948 he acted boringly "presidential" until it was too late. The public overall seemed genuinely disgusted with Wallace's attacks on his own country's foreign policy, and Stalin's behavior lent more credibility to Truman's view of the world than that of the progressives and their fellow travelers. Surprisingly, the states' rights ticket did not prove as powerful a draw in the South as some had expected. The issue was still the New Deal, and Truman wrapped the cloak of FDR around himself. Added to that, a misbegotten farm policy hurt the Republican Congress and Republican candidates in the Midwest. When election day came, Dewey was considering cabinet appointments, and Truman sat counting the remaining pieces of the old Roosevelt coalition. Remarkably, it held—Truman garnered 303 electoral votes and carried twenty-eight states, including Arkansas, Florida, Georgia, Kentucky, North Carolina, Tennessee (eleven of twelve electoral votes), and Texas in the traditional solid South; he also carried, in the Midwest, Iowa, Illinois, Minnesota, and Wisconsin. In addition, the Democrats regained control of both houses of Congress. Enough of the New Deal political alliance stayed together in the end.[17]

The Cold War and Limited War

But the pleasure of public vindication gave way to a heightened sense of personal responsibility. Even during the hijinks of the campaign, Truman had to stop and consider the problem of Soviet threats over the future of Berlin, which was also divided into zones. When the Allies moved toward a single German government in their joint sectors, the Soviet Union responded with an attempt to curtail movement into West Berlin, which lay within the Soviet sector. Truman supported a massive airlift of supplies to the city and ignored American General Lucius Clay's proposal to give the Soviets an ultimatum by announcing that a land convoy would come through their sector to the beleaguered city.

Faced with a distraught secretary of defense, James Forrestal, who could not pull together the new unified services command and was always suspicious of the military mind, the president himself exercised considerable civilian control over the armed forces and specifically kept custody of the atomic bomb in his hands alone. Then, in July, he issued a dramatic executive order to end racial discrimination in the military and to ensure equal opportunity in the civil service as well.

At the beginning of his second term, Truman proposed a tax increase, a modest military budget, and new programs in low-cost housing, higher Social Security benefits, and federal aid to education. In his 1949 State of the Union address, he observed, "I expect to try to give every segment of our population a fair deal." But in Congress, the conservative alliance of Southern Democrats and Republicans lined up even more, and the GOP, stunned by unexpected defeat, turned ardently to the right.

The new generation of Republican congressional figures concentrated a drumbeat of attack on what was previously a bipartisan foreign policy. The focal point became China, and the charge was that the Democratic administration and the State Department were allowing, if not encouraging, a triumph by Mao and his Communist armies. To add to Truman's woes, in December 1948, Alger Hiss, a high-ranking State Department figure and friend of Secretary of State Dean Acheson, was accused of perjury in denying that he passed on government documents to a Communist agent. To many, it seemed that the reckless charges of people like Senators Joe McCarthy and William Jenner were not without some foundation. The president unwisely agreed in an answer to a reporter's leading question that the Republican subversive hunting campaign was nothing more than "a red herring to divert public attention from inflation." The red herring remark was to haunt him later. Hiss was eventually found guilty of perjury

and one of his main accusers, Congressman Richard M. Nixon of California, was to become a household name.[18]

Meanwhile, Truman's and Acheson's battle against the forces of communism abroad accelerated. The blockade of Berlin by the Soviets pushed
the Allies closer together on the need for a strong Atlantic alliance and
encouraged the creation of a West German government. On April 4, 1949,
twelve nations signed the North Atlantic Treaty and laid the groundwork
for the military and political alliance that became NATO. For Americans
it was an extraordinary break with tradition; Truman concluded that if the
treaty had existed in 1914 and in 1939, it would have prevented two terrible wars. Stalin seemed almost on cue to buttress the arguments for the
alliance as Czechoslovakia went Communist, Finland was pressured by the
Soviets, and Norway also expressed public concerns about its Communist
neighbor's intentions.

The keystone of that Atlantic alliance would be the military strength
of the United States, but at that time, the nation was struggling to cut the
armed forces, hold down the budget, and reorganize the military services.
The United States had slashed its military force strength from nearly 12
million at the end of the war to 1.5 million in the summer of 1947. The
budget cap caused a major row within the armed forces hierarchy, especially in the navy, where the public was treated to a steady stream of pan-
icky complaints from what became known as the "revolt of the admirals."
In addition, Congress proved again unwilling to enact universal military
training, a favorite notion of Truman. Although the president retained
what was by American postwar standards a large standing army, the new
role he was leading the nation into required even more conventional military might. The administration seemed to both count on the atomic bomb
in its defense calculus and shy away from the use of that terrible instrument
ever again. The revolt of the admirals was only the first problem that Truman would face with a strong, assertive military establishment. He would
end up firing one of the most accomplished and insubordinate generals in
U.S. history at the height of the Korean War that was to come.[19]

In addition, two major events rocked American self-confidence: first,
the fall of China; and second, the Soviets' detonation of their own atomic
bomb. The president had at first followed FDR's quixotic support of
Chiang Kai-shek's government and also attempted to moderate Mao's war
aims. With the Soviets in Manchuria, the Communist Chinese received
additional support and encouragement from their allies. Truman tried in
vain to strengthen the Chiang regime and curtail Soviet influence in the
region. As noted, he finally sent George Marshall to mediate the differences

between the two Chinese regimes while at the same time insisting on preserving Chiang's government as the legitimate one. The result was a predictable failure; in addition, Marshall, distressed by what he saw, insisted that the United States should avoid military intervention even as a last resort to rescue the Nationalists. Preoccupied with European problems, troubles at home, and his own reelection, the president spent little time informing the people or Congress about the steady deterioration of Chiang's regime. Mao was clear in his objective in 1948; it was "to drive out aggressive forces of American imperialism . . . and establish a unified democratic people's republic." Soon after Truman's inauguration, all of China north of the Yangtze River had fallen under Mao's control. Republicans howled at the contrast between broad support for Europe and the alleged meagerness of aid to China. Secretary of State Acheson declared that American policy in China was waiting until "the dust settles." Critics concluded that the State Department regarded the Communists as simple "agrarian reformers" and charged that the trail of appeasement starting at Yalta was continuing. By October 1, 1949, the People's Republic of China was established, and Chiang fled to Formosa (Taiwan), converting it into the last bastion of his Nationalist government. With a Communist China and a divided Korea, the administration began to support a stronger Japan and reassessed the importance of Formosa in that region.[20]

Then in late August 1949, the Soviets detonated an atomic device—the American monopoly on nuclear weapons ended much earlier than the administration and the public expected. Vandenberg wrote, "This is now a different world." Thus, the keystone of the Truman military strategy, the awesome bomb and the U.S. monopoly of it, lost much of its potency. In a bipolar world, or at least within a bipolar military strategy, the existence of Soviet nuclear capability made that alien nation even more feared and more mysterious. Some Americans insisted that the breakthrough was possible only because of Soviet espionage; a backward country could not by itself compete with U.S. science and technology. But the results were clearly the same. Soon the administration would be debating the creation of a more devastating weapon: the "superbomb," or hydrogen bomb, a development Truman approved only because he feared the Soviets would move ahead on their own. They did, and so did the United States—in the first round of nuclear escalation and supposed deterrents. As Truman was making that decision, reports came in of another high-level espionage case: Dr. Klaus Fuchs in the British atomic energy research establishment was charged with passing on secrets to the Soviet Union.

Faced with an increasingly hostile world, the administration drew up in spring 1950 a major policy statement on national security—NSC 68—that advocated a massive upgrading of the nation's military might. Acheson candidly observed later, "The purpose of NSC 68 was to bludgeon the mass mind of 'top government' that not only could the president make a decision but that the decision could be carried out." The administration was contemplating an increase in the defense budget from $13 billion up to $40 billion and a vast upgrading of U.S. and Allied military strength.[21]

At home, the steady assaults on Truman continued. The opposition and the press found additional evidence of Democrats who had used their influence to win government contracts or garner special treatment for clients. One particularly vulnerable target was Truman's friend and military aide, General Harry Vaughan. The president, loyal to old acquaintances, refused to discharge him, and so the controversy continued. In Congress, the majority refused to support the president's major recommendations on social legislation. Federal aid to education got caught up in the church-state issue, as Francis Cardinal Spellman of New York and Eleanor Roosevelt became involved in a nasty spat on the issue. The administration's farm program, pressed by Agriculture Secretary Charles F. Brannan, went down to defeat with its attempt to support farm income rather than stabilize or inflate farm prices. Oddly enough, President Richard Nixon in 1973 would approve that same approach in trying to deal with similar problems. And Truman's attempt to promote national health insurance fell victim to a well-organized campaign by the medical profession; a partial initiative for the elderly was finally enacted by Congress and approved by President Lyndon B. Johnson in 1965, and a comprehensive plan was passed by President Barack Obama in 2010.[22]

Then in late June 1950, as Truman took stock back home in Missouri of the postwar world he faced, he received shocking news: North Korea had invaded South Korea—a new war had begun. The president's initial response was to downplay the crisis, hoping that U.S. support and supplies would turn the tide. But it quickly became apparent that the South Koreans were on the way to being routed. To the president and his senior advisers, it was a choice of following the course that had led to appeasement and World War II or of standing firm. Truman saw it as a test of collective security, the first real trial of the United Nations. Would that body go the way of the League of Nations? Also, the Americans viewed the North Korean invasion as a cat's-paw of Stalin's ambitions. They assumed, probably incorrectly, that the Soviets had provoked the invasion rather than having simply accepted their allies' plans.

The administration sought UN support for South Korea and, since the Soviet delegate was fortuitously absent, they received it. The Seventh Fleet was interposed between Formosa and mainland China to protect Chiang; MacArthur, in Japan, was ordered to send supplies and a survey group to Korea, and the air force was to draw up plans (but not to take action) to destroy Soviet air bases in the Far East. Previously, both Secretary of State Acheson and General MacArthur had excluded South Korea from their calculations of the American sphere of defense interests. But now, the attack on the lower peninsula was seen as a direct challenge to U.S. power and influence. Politically, an administration charged with the loss of China would not stand by and see the loss of Korea, regardless of its real significance to American interests. Support for Truman's actions was nearly unanimous. Even Henry Wallace expressed approval.

The military situation rapidly deteriorated, and the president soon faced fateful decisions to commit first naval and air support and then American ground troops. The president viewed Korea as the Greece of the Far East, concluding, "If we are tough enough now, if we stand up to them like we did in Greece three years ago, they won't take any next steps. But if we stand by, they'll move into Iran and they'll take over the whole Middle East." Faced with these problems, the president reversed his direction and committed himself to the military defense of Formosa. Aid was also sent to French Indochina—a decision of monumental importance later. Congress cheered Truman's commitment of naval and air forces in the Korean conflict, as Republicans and Democrats temporarily closed ranks. It would be a brief marriage of true minds.[23]

Truman's initial concern and his continuing preoccupation was that the United States avoid any war with the Soviets. "We must be damned careful. We must not say that we are anticipating a war with the Soviet Union. We want to take any steps we have to push the North Koreans behind the line, but I don't want to get us overcommitted to a whole lot of other things that could mean war." His goal was to drive the North Koreans back to the thirty-eighth parallel dividing line, and he asked the Soviets to use their influence to get the victorious North Koreans to withdraw. They refused.[24]

Faced with continuing bad news of South Korean defeats and General MacArthur's urgent appeals, Truman on June 30 crossed the political Rubicon and authorized a regimental combat team. American ground troops entered the war in earnest. In response to MacArthur's appeal to accept Chiang Kai-shek's offer of Chinese Nationalist troops, Truman at first agreed. But Acheson insisted that it would bring the Communist

Chinese into the war, and the Joint Chiefs of Staff cited logistics and supply problems if such a step took place. Truman backed down and laid the groundwork for one of the major criticisms that MacArthur would later level at the administration's handling of the war.

The administration, though, should have noticed the early storm warnings in Congress over the president's unilateral commitment of troops in Korea. Early in the Senate deliberations, right after the commitment of naval and land forces, the question was raised as to whether the executive could respond without Congress's approval. The Democratic leader, Scott Lucas, noted, "More than a hundred occasions in the life of this republic the president as commander in chief has ordered the fleet or the troops to do certain things which involved the risk of war." Later, Republican Senator Taft charged that "a complete usurpation by the president of authority to use the armed forces of the country" was taking place. He then made political hay out of Acheson's speech on January 12, which did not include South Korea and Formosa in the U.S. defense perimeter. Yet Taft made it clear that he would support the president's policy if it came to a vote. When Secretary of the Army Frank Pace wondered why the president did not push for a resolution of support, Truman responded, "They are all with me." He insisted that the United States was not at war with North Korea but was a member of the United Nations going to the relief of the Korean Republic to "suppress a bandit raid." Later he was to agree to characterize the war as "a police action"—a term that would come to haunt him as American sacrifices increased dramatically in the war.[25]

Truman had considered a message to Congress, but fearing a wave of panic over economic controls and hoarding, he delayed and then finally abandoned the move. To buttress the administration's position, Acheson had the State Department draw up a position paper listing historical and legal precedents for the commander in chief's use of military forces. Eighty-five instances, many of them rather limited, were cited as providing a basis for Truman's decision not to go to Congress.

The onslaught of the war had laid the basis for the rapid increase in military expenditures projected originally in NSC 68 and led to an institutionalization of the National Security Council. Once again a president asked for authority to allocate resources, control credit, and undergird the war effort at home. Money flowed into upgrading the armed forces and creating tactical nuclear weapons. By 1951, the budget for defense and related matters jumped from $17.7 billion to $53.4 billion.

As American commitments increased, the North Korean armies continued their assault across the peninsula, driving the Republic of Korea and the UN forces farther south. The Republicans supported the war but attacked the administration for its lack of military preparedness. To some extent, they were correct. General Omar Bradley was to admit, "It is a bruising and shocking fact that when we Americans were committed in Korea we were left without an adequate margin of military strength with which to face an enemy at any other specific point. Certainly we were left without the strength to meet a general attack . . . except for the atomic bomb." Recent liberal critics have argued that Truman carefully supported the confrontations of the Cold War in order to assert U.S. strength or imperialist intent, yet his policies of frugality and civilian control over the military seem at variance with such a view.[26]

No Substitute for Victory

By the fall of 1950, MacArthur had eight U.S. divisions, some regimental combat teams, a modest collection of UN forces, and a beleaguered South Korean army at his disposal. MacArthur obviously felt the frustrations of such limited support. To him it surely was another example of shortsightedness, similar to the lack of commitment in Washington that he had seen in the last war in the Pacific. As for Truman, he had already formed a negative opinion of MacArthur even though he had never met him. He referred to him as "Mr. Prima Donna, Brass Hat," a "bunco man." Concerned about MacArthur's independence, Truman sent Averell Harriman to assure the general of his personal support and to warn that Chiang must not become the cause of a war with the Communist Chinese. MacArthur promised to abide by his commander in chief's directives. But by late August, the general issued a statement declaring his views on the strategic importance of Formosa—a challenge that the administration chose not to unfurl at Mao's regime. Truman forced a retraction, but Republicans made political capital charging that the general had been unfairly censured and chastised.

Truman then had to face the question of whether to fight up to the thirty-eighth parallel and let the North Koreans retreat to the spot of their initial advance or to push them back toward the Yalu River and the Chinese border. The risks were obvious: such a step would pressure the Communist Chinese to enter the war and, worse still, the Soviets to add their support. On the other hand, should the North Koreans be allowed to stay above the line, able at a later date to resume their drive south? Should they not suffer because of their initial aggression? Now the State Department and the American advisers chose to raise the ante by agreeing that "it is

U.S. policy to help bring about the complete independence and unity of Korea." The CIA had warned of "grave risks" in crossing the thirty-eighth parallel, but, as Averell Harriman reflected later, "it would have taken a superhuman effort to say no. Psychologically, it was almost impossible not to go ahead and complete the job."

Then, on September 15, MacArthur conducted one of the most brilliant strategic maneuvers in military history. Against incredible odds, he implemented an amphibious assault two hundred miles behind enemy lines at Inchon. Suddenly, the tide of war and, even more importantly, the scales of morale tipped heavily in favor of the United States and the forces of the Republic of Korea. An emboldened Joint Chiefs of Staff sent MacArthur the fateful directive: "Your military objective is the destruction of the North Korean Forces." Marshall on September 30 informed MacArthur, "We want you to feel unhampered tactically and strategically to proceed north of the 38th parallel." The general's response was clearly in line: "Unless and until the enemy capitulates, I regard all of Korea open for our military operations." The Joint Chiefs' order, though, had contained one important caveat: MacArthur was not to move forces above the thirty-eighth parallel if there were a threat from Chinese or Soviet forces.

By fall 1950, the president's advisers were counseling a meeting with the victorious MacArthur, a meeting less to clear up ambiguities than to help Truman and the Democrats politically in the upcoming elections in 1950. The president at first refused, but later he agreed to go to Wake Island to see MacArthur personally. Although there has been a variety of accounts about personal bitterness and protocol disputes during the visit, it appears that the two got along fairly well. MacArthur was supposed to have apologized for the controversy surrounding his statement to the Veterans of Foreign Wars on Formosa and assured Truman that the Chinese Communists would not enter the war. The general hoped to withdraw the Eighth Army by Christmas. The president was clearly relieved by the prediction, and overall they avoided discussing basic U.S. and UN objectives in Korea and what practical limitations were imposed on the field commander. Truman bestowed an additional citation on the general, ironically praising "his vision, his judgment, his indomitable will and unshakable faith." Later, Truman called MacArthur an intellectually honest man and a loyal member of the government. It was a short and eventful honeymoon.[27]

Back home, the elections of 1950 were not affected by the staged Wake Island meeting or by the changes in the fates of the war. Senator Joseph McCarthy continued his assaults on the administration, and in several key races, his influence seemed to turn the tide in favor of the Republicans. The reckless senator from Wisconsin became a feared commodity on Capitol Hill, a bully doing what bullies do best, intimidating the timid. In California, Richard Nixon skillfully used the Communist issue to defeat Helen Gahagan Douglas for the Senate; in Illinois the Democratic Senate leader, Scott Lucas, was defeated by Everett McKinley Dirksen; in Maryland, a McCarthy foe, Millard Tydings, went down to defeat; in Utah, liberal Democratic Senator Elbert Thomas lost as well. In Massachusetts, former ambassador Joseph P. Kennedy and his son John quietly contributed to Nixon's election, and their family members defended McCarthy publicly. McCarthyism seemed to be sweeping across the land. The Democrats lost twenty-eight seats in the House and five in the Senate, not an unusually high number for the majority party in an off-year election, but it left little support for the Fair Deal's domestic reforms. A depressed president surveyed the results grimly.

Truman's real problems, though, were ahead of him—another and more dismal turn of events in Korea was in the works. MacArthur, high in the saddle, had interpreted his mandate to unite the peninsula and to destroy the North Korean army as broadly as he could. Without consulting the Joint Chiefs, he ordered a major bombing attack on all enemy facilities in North Korea and the blowing up of the bridges over the Yalu River. Truman asked for a review of the general's intentions, fearing that they would lead to a Chinese attack. The Joint Chiefs, in part in deference to MacArthur's immense military prestige and unwilling to second-guess the field commander, wavered. MacArthur appealed to the president and warned of a "calamity of major proportion" unless he were allowed to continue. The president approved the bombings but had the Joint Chiefs warn MacArthur about possible Soviet involvement.

By early November, MacArthur asked for the right to pursue North Korean aircraft as they returned to Manchuria, and the administration approved "hot pursuit" engagements—an unclear line at best. Under heavy pressure from the Allies, however, that approval was withdrawn. The president sought to assure the Communist Chinese that he did not desire to widen the war and threaten their borders, but they refused to accept such assurances; on November 29, their armies launched a major assault across the Chinese borders and flooded into North Korea. MacArthur's response was brief and frightening: "We face an entirely new War."

The general's Christmas pledge came back to haunt him, as Marshall advocated finding a way out without a loss of honor, and Acheson pushed for an exit as well. Truman added to the panic by indicating that he might give MacArthur authority to use the atomic bomb at his discretion. Immediately, British Prime Minister Clement Attlee flew to Washington to insist on prior consultation before any such serious actions were undertaken.[28]

MacArthur continued to emphasize his own line of attack. He told the editors of *U.S. News and World Report* on December 1 that the inability to pursue enemy pilots into Manchuria was an "enormous handicap, without precedent in military history." Faced with this new war, the president declared a national emergency and applied selective controls on the economy. Some Republican leaders pushed for unleashing Chiang to conduct a second front on the mainland Chinese, and a series of resolutions were introduced in Congress that opposed sending U.S. troops without legislative approval. The once much-cheered bipartisan police action had become "Truman's war."

The Joint Chiefs told MacArthur to fight on as long as possible, inflicting maximum losses but being ready to retreat to Japan if necessary to protect his armies in Korea. Then, in mid-January, the Joint Chiefs presented MacArthur with a draft document that would have approved a blockade of China, unleashed Chiang, and allowed naval and air attacks on China if the Communists there attacked U.S. forces outside of Korea. Thus, it appears that there is some justification to MacArthur's charge later that the Joint Chiefs had been close to approving an enlarged war. At the same time, Truman wrote MacArthur that if the UN forces were expelled from Korea, "We shall not accept the result politically or militarily until the aggression has been rectified."[29]

Washington's siege resolve may have been lessened by the fortuitous appointment of General Matthew Ridgway, who quickly reorganized and upgraded the Eighth Army and the Tenth Corps in Korea. As those forces improved, the extreme choice MacArthur sought to force on the administration was reexamined. Then, while the administration was pressing for a cease-fire, MacArthur issued his own declaration on March 24, offering to meet with the enemy commander in chief and outlining what could be topics of negotiation. The objectives were clearly to upstage the president, issue an ultimatum to the Red Chinese, and lay out again the general's political objectives. In addition, the general had written to Republican Congressman Joseph Martin that the war had to be won for the good of Asia and Europe: "We must win. There is no substitute for victory."

Truman had had enough; he began discussions that would lead to the firing of MacArthur. At first, Marshall and General Omar Bradley favored a reprimand, but in the end, the Joint Chiefs and the major civilian advisers were unanimous in approving MacArthur's removal. After reflecting on

Lincoln's agony over McClellan, Truman moved decisively and brought on himself a firestorm greater than any other that had confronted the president.

Cries of impeachment rang through the halls of Congress, as the general returned home to an admiring and somewhat alien land for him. His speech to Congress—one of the genuine pieces of high drama and great oratory—gave way to an old soldier's good-bye. But public sentiment ran its course, and Truman watched as the fervor and intensity died down. With some sympathetic Senate supporters, a congressional investigation revealed that the Joint Chiefs of Staff unanimously disapproved of MacArthur's course of action. The most telling conclusion was General Bradley's observation: "This strategy would have involved us in the wrong war, at the wrong place, at the wrong time, and with the wrong enemy [China]." The firing stuck, Truman was battered but prevailed, and the war became enmeshed in a deadlock hovering around the thirty-eighth parallel again.[30]

There is little debate today that MacArthur was clearly insubordinate and merited firing and that Truman had both sound reasons and constitutional justification for his actions. But one can also appreciate MacArthur's position a bit more in historical hindsight. The orders of the Joint Chiefs did lend encouragement and support to his strategy and his boldness. The Chiefs individually and collectively were less than a towering source of strength and were unclear and often deferential to the prestigious field commander nominally under their supervision.

At Wake Island, and on numerous other occasions, the president had the opportunity to rein in the general, and he too passed up the opportunities. They all expected MacArthur to win a war they chose to fight and then dangerously enlarged, and when he pushed on, they demanded some assurance that the Communist Chinese would not enter it. And when the Chinese did, the administration seemed to blame MacArthur as if he betrayed them or deliberately misled them.

MacArthur, looking for that last great victory, unnecessarily raised the ante in 1951; the response of the Joint Chiefs and the president seemed clear: no escalation, but they too considered the very steps that they later chastised him for considering when they finally testified before Congress. If, as General Bradley said, it was the wrong war, at the wrong time, with the wrong enemy, it was the president and the Joint Chiefs who injected U.S. troops into that regional theater in the first place and allowed them to go north of the thirty-eighth parallel. While MacArthur was excessively pessimistic about the Eighth Army and the UN-ROK (Republic of Korea) effort in 1951, the administration also probably seriously misjudged Stalin's willingness to go to war over Korea. His preoccupation was the Soviet empire, and while he would acknowledge North Korea's intentions and support his Asian allies, he was not going to follow up the destruction of the Soviet Union in the west in World War II with a war with the United States in Asia, especially using nuclear arms.

The Truman administration pleaded the wisdom of a "limited war"— one that ended where it began. MacArthur was pictured as reckless and uncompromising, a figure from the distant past. In part, he was a true soldier who loved the cadence, the loyalty, the grandeur of war as a profession, as he had been taught at his father's knee and at his beloved West Point. He warned that there is no substitute for victory—but what is victory in a world of nuclear weapons, biological warfare, and doomsday devices? And how can one ask a generation of young men to give up their lives for a limited war, a war without a cause, a war of political objectives where the battlefields deny one a sense of progress or liberation? Paid mercenaries in the past had fought such wars, but not democratic armies mobilized since the time of the French Revolution to fight for great causes and hopeful ideals. The Truman administration sought to fight the first, but not the last, limited war—and it ended without triumph, without parades, with only a terrible sense of public frustration and private loss.

As that war continued through 1951, the nation also heard of other espionage cases, most tellingly the alleged spying of Julius and Ethel Rosenberg. Pressure built up on Truman to deal with subversion, and on April 28, 1951, he issued an executive order that allowed government employees to be dismissed if "there is reasonable doubt as to the loyalty of the person involved." Ironically, as the president moved farther away from protecting constitutional liberties and due process, he expressed concern to his associates over the looseness of the very loyalty boards he created.[31]

The Conclusion of the New Deal Reign

By the end of the year, the president had little political capital left to draw on. Congress refused to enact tough price, credit, and rent controls; a rash of scandals broke out in the Bureau of Internal Revenue; and Truman moved to dismiss his attorney general, James McGrath, for firing Newbold Morris, whom the president had appointed to investigate government corruption. Then, to add to his problems, the president precipitated a major constitutional crisis—and lost. In April 1952, Truman seized the steel industry to avert a strike, which he argued would damage the war effort. Privately encouraged by his friend Chief Justice Fred Vinson, the president refused to use the Taft-Hartley Act and instead relied on his powers as commander in chief to stop the threat. He could have invoked the law and asked for a cooling-off period, or seized the steel industry under the Selective Service Act if defense materials were not delivered as contracted for, or he could have simply gone to an unsympathetic Congress for new legislation.

The district court judge, however, refused to uphold the president's action, calling it "illegal and without authority of law." Truman's response was that if he were wrong, so were Jefferson, Lincoln, Wilson, and FDR in their exercise of prerogatives, and he insisted they were not. The Supreme Court heard the appeal, and by a vote of six to three, the Court also found Truman's action unconstitutional. The decision is normally seen as a rebuff to the notion of executive powers. But the opinions of the majority are in fact confusing, and one can read some of those opinions and those of the minority of the Court as giving a president the authority Truman wanted if emergency conditions were graver than existed in 1952. What seems like a clear precedent on the limitations of executive power is, on reflection, more ambiguous than meets the eye. In any case, Truman obeyed the court, ended the steel seizure, and asked Congress for new legislation—which it in turn refused to pass, citing the Taft-Hartley remedy. The strike ended in late July with basically the wage and price terms that were presented four months earlier.[32]

The year 1952 was a time of presidential election politics, and although Truman toyed a bit with another term, he was genuinely tired of the demands of the office. The Republicans, looking for a winner, finally swayed Dwight Eisenhower—who, much to Truman's dismay, criticized elements of the very foreign policy he himself had helped the Democratic presidents put into place. To add to Truman's annoyance, even his own party's candidate, Governor Adlai E. Stevenson of Illinois, promised "to clean up the mess in Washington."[33]

After twenty years of rule, the Democratic Party had left a rich legacy of social legislation and had forged a Western alliance that destroyed the Nazis and the Japanese empire and held in check somewhat Stalin's ambitions. But the public grew weary of sacrifice, of scandals, of war, and of the strange sense that American achievements were traded away by spies, fellow travelers, and naive State Department dupes. Nixon, running with Eisenhower, called the Democrats the party of communism, corruption, and Korea—and as unfair as it was, the seeds of discontent sprouted in many American minds.

Truman remained one of the most vilified and unpopular presidents of his time, but a president whose reputation soared after his retirement. He became the common man made good—the honest, dedicated servant in the cause of democracy around the world. His record is a mixed one to assess. Speaker of the House Sam Rayburn once observed that Truman was wrong on the small things but right on the big decisions that often recast America's international responsibilities. Revisionist and left-wing historians have seen him as the cause of the Cold War, as if Stalin were a sensitive soul seeking only secure boundaries for his troubled state.

There is no question that Truman hired many mediocre people, fired too many individuals, and, like Lincoln, was plagued by his poor choices. Perhaps the United States was not ready for the burdens of postwar global leadership any more than it was ready for the protracted Civil War. Yet, as noted, in a mere eighteen months, the administration recast American foreign policy in the most creative and lasting period in its history. Like the assumptions or not, Truman and his small band of brothers were effective in mobilizing public support, compromising with Congress, supporting allies in Europe, and laying the groundwork for a rebirth of the Atlantic community, the economy, and military might. He had, of course, considerable assistance from Stalin in selling that harsh view of reality.

On the home front, amid all the controversies, half turns, and twists, the United States did a fairly good job at reconversion, and some of that credit goes to Truman. Surely, the United States handled its recovery better than after the Civil War, World War I, or Vietnam. Most of his domestic proposals did not see the light of day, and some liberal critics argued then and later that the president proposed but did not press. That is somewhat true, but after 1938, even the skillful FDR had been blocked. The New Deal was over, and recasting it as the Fair Deal fooled or pacified no one. Only in 1964–1967 did Lyndon Johnson, an uncommonly skilled practitioner of congressional politics and a president with a solid liberal majority in those two houses, enact the Fair Deal agenda in housing, education, medical care, civil rights, and other areas.

Truman as president went from being excessively modest in 1945 to cantankerous and often cocky by the end of his second term. He was blunt, too opinionated, often loyal to the wrong people, and continually contentious, almost like a bantam rooster out to show the political barnyard his stuff. But he was also an ardent patriot and an honest commoner sworn to the public interest. It was noted that he put his own two-cent stamps on his personal letters, never profited from public office in any way even after he retired, and was deeply committed to the dignity of the position he inherited.[34] Truman also put in place the institutions of the new executive office—the National Security Council, the Council of Economic Advisers, the Joint Chiefs of Staff, the CIA, and other bodies that surround the contemporary office. It may be said that FDR was the first modern president in what he did and the office he created. But it was Harry S Truman who institutionalized the modern or so-called "imperial" presidency, transforming it by crisis and practice into the nerve center of the national government and of the Western alliance. He was later asked what was the first thing he did after giving up the immense burdens and powers of the office and arriving home. Characteristically, he responded that he carried the "grips [suitcases] up to the attic."[35]

Ronald Reagan: Unleashing Right-Wing America   **10**

P OLITICS IS OFTEN A DERIVATIVE profession, drawing men and
women who have been molded and succeeded or failed in other
walks of life. They bring with them the habits of a lifetime to
politics and to the leadership of an often fickle people. Washington and
Eisenhower remained military men in many ways long after their service
was done; Wilson lectured Congress and the nation as a good Calvinist
schoolmaster; Hoover and Carter analyzed public policy through the rigid
and exacting eyes of engineers. Ronald Reagan was, in one sense, in a
perfect profession for the late twentieth-century presidency—he was an
actor, a master of space and place and impressions.

Ronald Reagan led the charmed life of a handsome, personable, small-
town boy who progressed from being a sports announcer to a movie star,
to the leader of a visible Hollywood labor union, and finally to a citizen
politician in the most populous state in the Union. He was the son of a
strong-willed mother and an alcoholic father who was intensely committed
to and benefited from the Democratic Party. For most of his early years,
Ronald Reagan was an admirer of the liberal New Deal and the towering presence of Franklin D. Roosevelt. In fact, he insisted on linking his
conservative administration and his own attitudes to the life and times of
FDR. Characteristically, his use of television and radio was patterned on
Roosevelt's own immensely successful radio addresses to the people.[1]

It has been fashionable to belittle Reagan's abilities as an actor, but
he was one of the most popular movie figures of that period. With some
pride, he called himself the "Errol Flynn of the B-movies." After World
War II, however, his career began to flounder, and he headed up the

Screen Actors Guild and defended performers before Senator Joseph Mc-
Carthy's committee, publicly upholding their civil liberties while secretly
serving as an occasional informant for the FBI called T-10. He developed
a deep fear of Communists, whom he claimed had targeted him for elimi-
nation during this period because of his opposition to their feeble attempts
to infiltrate the movie industry. Ironically, he had unknowingly flirted
with Communist fellow traveler organizations and was seen by some as a
rather extreme New Deal liberal. From his union presidency, he went on
to host a television series and became a spokesman for General Electric.
Reagan started giving uplifting quasi-political speeches for that company
and gravitated toward the conservative orbit of his second wife and his
new father-in-law. He also came to the attention of a small group of very
wealthy Californians who supported him financially and calculated that
he could become governor of their state and the president of the United
States. They were correct, as Reagan in 1980 rode to a landslide victory,
becoming the fortieth president.[2]

Unlike some other conservative politicians, Reagan was able to fuse
traditional small-town Republicans on Main Street with Wall Street
operatives and religious fundamentalists—many of the last group once
Democrats like himself. By 1980, large segments of the population felt
threatened by the social movements of the 1960s and 1970s. The changing
role of women, the new legal rights of racial minorities, the open advocacy
in some quarters of easy sex and drugs, and the breakdown of middle-class
family morality upset a good number of moderate voters. The backlash
against the civil rights bills ended once and for all the Democratic hegemony over white voters in the South, as Lyndon Johnson predicted when
he signed the Civil Rights Act in 1964. And as civil rights moved from the
heady days of the 1960s toward affirmative action, protected categories of
people, and goals for preferential hiring, white resistance began coalescing.[3]
In addition, some of the large generational cohort born in the late 1940s
challenged the mores of their parents and of postwar American society.
That twenty-year span starting in the 1960s led to greater self-expression,
creativity, and social reform, and it also led to hedonism, self-righteousness,
and crude individualism.

It is ironic that the first television president and the first divorced president, whose own family life with his children was strained, should have
become the bearer of the flag of the old values. It is odd that the strongest
advocate of a war-centered patriotism should be a man whose military
career involved only making training films in California while other men
fought and died at Anzio, Omaha Beach, and Guadalcanal. But what was

even more remarkable was that Ronald Reagan was never troubled by the gap between his life and his rhetorical descriptions of it. He could urge that the federal government stamp out social welfare programs and let private philanthropy take its place, while he himself was at best a modest giver to charities. He could describe in vivid detail the sacrifices of World War II veterans at Normandy as if he were there himself, explaining once that he frequently visualized as real what were fictional occurrences. But those blurrings between reality and make-believe did not matter, for the American people had become a television generation, and many of them lived for images and judged their political leaders accordingly.

It was the show that mattered, and few could rival Reagan as the master showman. His friends and his critics alike called him "the Great Communicator," but nearly every one of his associates who has shared his or her views of him publicly has reported that Reagan was remarkably aloof and distinct from the very world about which he was communicating. His foremost biographer, Lou Cannon, attributes that attitude to the fact that he was the child of an alcoholic, and that it is not uncommon for such offspring to be loners who withdraw into their own world. The difference with Reagan was that his world was one of optimism and light, one in which an aged man could still dream captivating dreams of youth. And in the end, it was Reagan who gave the best definition of his time in office when he said that politics was like acting—you start quickly, coast along, and end up with a fast finish.

The Tax Cuts

Reagan is a difficult act for historians to judge. He was able brilliantly to mobilize people and to convey and motivate confidence in the presidency and in the special mission of America.[4] Although liberals hate to admit it, his sterling repetitions of the moral superiority of democracy and freedom helped inspire beleaguered dissident elements, especially in Communist Europe. One may scoff at those flights of rhetorical fancies at home, but in the grim rooms of the Soviet Union and the sullen parlors of Warsaw and Budapest, Reagan's expressions were part of the explosives that by 1989 destroyed communism as a philosophy and as a world order.

But the darker side of Reagan's terms became starker as the nation paid the bills for an eight-year period of social neglect and political paralysis. In 1981, his administration began with a major tax cut that was meant to give people back more of their own money and to slice the federal government down to size. But the president was committed to a massive military build-up (actually begun under President Jimmy Carter), which ended up costing nearly $1 trillion and which was characterized by incredible waste, misallocation of resources, and a total lack of strategic priorities. He ended up raising taxes seven times in eight years, and he tripled the federal budget deficit.

It is clear that the president had no real idea what his own economic policy was, and his budget director, former congressman David Stockman, bluntly confessed that there were no philosophical underpinnings, except self-interest and greed.[5] Reagan believed, according to his son Ron, that the poor were poor because it was their fault. He obviously had forgotten about his family and the assistance of the New Deal in the 1930s. The administration claimed that it was committed to supply-side economics that stressed tax cuts, limited government, and unbridled consumption. Some Reaganites argued that supply-side economics was not a new idea with this president, but that in fact it had been discussed in congressional committees as a way to encourage savings and higher productivity.[6] But the critics of such a cut saw the Reagan rescissions as another version of the 1920s trickle-down theory: lower the taxes of the rich, and benefits will eventually drip down to the masses. What the Reagan tax cut of 1981 did was to slash the rates (especially for the wealthy), reduce the domestic welfare state, and use the savings to upgrade the military. The results were not just a shrinkage in the scope of the federal government's concerns but also a major shift of money from domestic to military spending. The tax cuts helped lead to massive deficits in that period; the national debt jumped from $908 billion in 1980 to $2.68 trillion in 1989. Under Reagan, the debt accumulated was greater than the total from the administration of George Washington to that of Jimmy Carter.

The tax cut bill ran into initial rough sledding in Congress, especially in the Democratic-controlled House of Representatives. The Republicans had captured the Senate as a result of the 1980 election (53–46), while the House remained Democratic (242–189). Then, on March 30, 1981, the president was seriously wounded in an assassination attempt outside the Washington Hilton hotel where he had made a speech. Reagan, in the first harrowing hours of his ordeal, was so heroic and good-natured that his courage and poise impressed the nation, and his popular stock rose markedly and probably aided his domestic proposals. The tax reduction package had several important effects besides cutting revenues and increasing the national debt. The cuts did help stimulate the economy and played a role in what became a decade of good economic times, especially for the rich, and eliminated the financial base for new liberal spending programs from the Democrats.

The Pyramid of Wealth

The 1980s became a time of great accumulation of wealth for the upper classes, as the average income of the top 1 percent of the nation doubled.[7] By 1990, even some conservative writers, such as Kevin Phillips, were aghast at the massive shift of wealth to the very rich, their often tasteless ostentations, mindless mergers of corporations and financial institutions, and unregulated foreign investment.[8] By the late twentieth century, the United States led all other major industrial nations in the gap dividing the upper fifth of its population from the lower fifth. The number of millionaires increased from 574,000 in 1980 to 1.3 million by 1988, and America's top 420,000 households accounted for 26.9 percent of the nation's wealth. While the salaries and benefits of corporate CEOs and presidents increased astronomically, the number of middle-management jobs during the 1980s declined by as many as 1.5 million positions. Worse off were female-headed households, especially those with children, where poverty levels, especially among minority women, reached frightening levels. The percentage of children living in poverty was double in 1986 what it was in 1967. For the first time in memory, commentators were talking about the next generation having a permanently lower standard of living than its parents.

The number of those under twenty-five years old who owned their own homes dropped from 21.3 percent in 1980 to 16.1 percent in 1987. And the same downward trend occurred among those in the various age brackets from twenty-five through thirty. As for Ronald Reagan's reactions, he simply offered the view that a rising tide lifts all boats—that is, better breaks for the wealthy would benefit everyone, sooner or later. His personal philosophy was best spelled out in his declaration, "What I want to see above all is that this remains a country where someone can always get rich." But it would be a mistake to say that Reagan's appeal was simply to the top 10 percent of Americans. His constituency was not just the rich but also those who have an ambition to be rich; for them, the American dream is predominantly circumscribed by wealth, the accumulation of goods, and the visceral pleasure of deal making. And in the first years of Reagan's initial term, the Democrats in Congress seemed disjointed, defensive, and distracted in their opposition to this new, and very old, public philosophy.

One unexpected occurrence was that as the federal government cut taxes, the states and localities had to assume more obligations, so that the total tax receipts as a percentage of gross national product by 1984 returned to where it was before Reagan took office. Still, about 27 percent of the gross national product, a relatively low level compared to other advanced industrial nations in the world, went to pay the total federal, state, and local tax bill. The 1980s witnessed a decline in the size and standard of living of the middle class—the traditional bastion of democracy. The adjusted wages of average workers by 1991 were below 1979 levels. Family incomes were maintained by wives going to work, with some social critics citing deleterious consequences for the upbringing of the nation's young. In 1960, 30 percent of wives with children under eighteen worked; by 1987, it was 65 percent. Some went to work because of their desire to continue or to begin a career in the workplace, but many went to work to help make ends meet.

However, the administration delivered on its agenda to cut taxes for the wealthy and to free business from many public restraints and government regulations. The tax bill slashed the top personal tax bracket from 70 percent to 28 percent (to be phased in over seven years), and by 1983, the percentage of federal tax receipts paid through corporate income taxes dropped to a mere 6.2 percent. The administration followed up those cuts with an almost total deregulation of American businesses in some sectors. Much of that deregulation policy was in place before Reagan took office, but his administration allowed massive mergers, corporate raidings, and redeployment of corporate assets, as twenty-five thousand deals worth over $2 billion took place. Most ominously, the administration and several key members of Congress allowed the savings and loan banks to expand their traditionally narrow range of operations and, at the same time, had the government guarantee personal accounts in those lending institutions up to $100,000. In the 1990s, when many of the savings and loan associations ended up in trouble because of bad lending practices, the American taxpayers were left with an enormous and almost incalculable liability to fund irresponsible speculations, incompetent management, and rampantly deficient business practices in what was once one of the most conservative and responsible fields of American corporate life.

Equally ominous was the great transfer of economic power away from the United States to Western Europe and Japan. Obviously, the near monopoly of America in setting the world's economic directions had to end after the headiness of post–World War II experiences. But because of its loose business practices, its speculative economy in the 1980s, and its rampant consumerism, the United States became the prime target for foreign investors and exporters. When Ronald Reagan became president, the United States was the largest creditor nation in the world, but by the time he left office it had become the largest debtor nation. Supporters of the Reagan administration have argued that the United States was simply a good investment, with its stable government and its encouraging business climate, and they noted with approval how unemployment had fallen in the late 1980s and how in that period the United States had created more than 90 percent of the total new jobs recorded in the ten leading industrial democracies. Whereas inflation in the last year of Carter was 12.5 percent, the prime interest 15.26 percent, and civilian unemployment 7.1 percent, Reagan's figures eventually were 4.4 percent, 9.32 percent, and 5.5 percent, respectively.

And in American society, the expressions of its way of life on television and in print revolved around the romances of the so-called rich and the famous. The president and his first lady, in the early years of the administration, played to that mythic dream, mining the parts for all they were indeed worth, emulating that upper sliver of the population. Ronald Reagan, the son of a politically liberal shoe salesman, had come half circle to a world he and so many of those who will never know riches loved— the mores and habits of the idle rich. The Reagan administration brought with it a legion of ideological conservatives, not of the Eisenhower or even of the Nixon variety, but men and women whose main themes were a distrust of government and a genuine disdain of liberal programs as the safety net of the losers in society. They began, under the president's benign gaze, a major attack on the liberal legacy, commencing with a challenge to the most popular liberal benefits program, Social Security, and suffered a major setback.

By midterm, the economy had still not turned around sufficiently, and the Reagan revolution was in trouble. By 1982, however, Congress and the president teamed up to pass a "tax enhancement" bill—the largest single increase in U.S. history on top of a major increase in Social Security taxes, which was meant to guarantee the solvency of what was deemed an actuarially unsound program. In the long run, Reagan's tax cuts proved to be actually too large, as David Stockman reported decades later. The result of this latter increase was a major shift or redistribution through a regressive levy of the total tax burden to lower- and middle-income households.[9]

Reagan's budget director, David Stockman, was later to criticize the president for failing to push his "revolution" to its (or Stockman's) logical consequences, and he portrayed Reagan as merely "a consensus politician," a figurehead unwilling to do battle to the death against the liberal welfare state. Reagan was indeed a consensus politician in some ways, but he was also unwilling to antagonize an American public that hates taxes but wants more governmental entitlements. The entitlements that go to the middle class—Social Security, veterans programs, aid to homeowners, Medicare— are firmly entrenched, but programs aimed at the poor lack a strong political base and thus are vulnerable, even though they are no less meritorious than the former category.

Reagan also was worried in his first term that after his first year in office the American economy was still not stimulated enough by the tax cuts or by the president's own bold enthusiasms. The economic decline was one of the worst that the country had experienced since the Great Depression, as more than 11.5 million people were out of work and another 2–3 million still seeking employment but not counted in the figures. Business shutdowns and farm foreclosures rose to startling levels, and advocates of the homeless created tent cities called "Reagan ranches"—a dark memory of the "Hoovervilles" of the 1930s. As Democrats attacked him for his intentions to destroy the very programs they had worked a lifetime to create, the president criticized the basic tenets of the liberal welfare state and insisted that his administration "stay the course." Reagan did not know at that time that his own budget director did not believe in the economic figures he was promulgating, and that the president and his people had been deceived in accepting Stockman's calculations of revenues. That deception was revealed in an article in the *Atlantic* magazine in November 1981 in which William Greider related that Stockman regarded the "supply side economics" of the Reagan administration as simply another form of the trickle-down theory so popularized in the 1920s.[10]

The chief reason for the end of inflation and the increase in unemployment in the first term, however, was the decision of the Federal Reserve Board, headed by Jimmy Carter appointee Paul Volcker, to have that body so tighten the money supply that the inflation rate had to tumble down. But the consequences for job creation and employment were dire, and the housing industry, automotive sales, farmers, and small business felt the effects of such an abrupt contraction. Reagan supported the stiff medicine, as inflation dropped to 5 percent by the end of his first year in office.[11] In the congressional elections in 1982, the GOP gained a seat in the Senate and lost only twenty-seven seats in the House; there seemed to be popular support for harsh measures after all. As the economy began to pick up later and as inflation was no longer a problem, other industrial societies began to look seriously at Reagan's tax cut strategy, and his personal discipline in staying the course became for some a model of tough leadership, so differ-ent from Carter's ways. In 1986, the president changed gears and accepted the proposals from some in Congress to overhaul the tax code, which eliminated many special tax privileges and loopholes—an objective Demo-crats had talked about but could not deliver, even in progressive periods. The old president was proving to be a lithe moving target for liberals, and at times an unpredictable commodity for conservatives. To the chagrin of some of the GOP's right wing, this optimistic man could incorporate in his psychological makeup contradictions about his policy statements and simply reformulate them to prove that he was right all along.[12]

"MAD"

Even more mystifying at times to some of the faithful and some of his most dedicated foes was Reagan's foreign policy. In the beginning of his first term in office, the parody of Ronald Reagan was clear—he was a shoot-from-the-hip conservative cowboy who understood little of the complex world and rode only the traditional hobbyhorse of the GOP, anticommunism. He was especially attacked for his speech on January 29, 1981, when he asserted offhandedly that the Communists, or "one-world Socialists," believed in a morality that allowed them to commit any crime in order to prevail over the Western democracies. Two years later, before a group of evangelical ministers in Florida, Reagan struck a similar theme by denouncing the Soviet Union as an aggressive "evil empire." Later, in 1989–1991, when the Eastern European countries threw off Soviet control of their domestic affairs and the Soviet Union itself came undone, Rea-gan's descriptions did not seem so far-fetched after all.[13]

Early in his first term, then, Reagan easily filled the role of a staunch anticommunist who showed little interest in arms control and was a foe of the policies of détente of former president Gerald Ford and his secre-tary of state, Henry Kissinger. The Soviet leaders responded as might be expected—they were suspicious of Reagan and wary of his assertive ani-mosities toward their way of life. Being traditional ideologues themselves, they understood the dangers of Reagan the ideologue. Added to the Reagan calculation was his religious acceptance of the biblical notion of Armageddon, the fundamentalist view of the imminent end of the world. But Reagan, beyond those mixed considerations, had a strange dream—he hated the then-current American nuclear strategic doctrine of "mutual as-sured destruction," appropriately termed MAD, and sought to terminate it.

That doctrine was based on the notion that the United States must pile up enough nuclear weapons so as never to be challenged in the first place at the brink. Many knew it was a dangerous doctrine, perhaps even an absurd and irresponsible doctrine, but it was the government orthodoxy in the United States, for NATO, and for the Soviet world in its planning as well. The justifications—moral and political—were based on the assumption that arming to the nuclear teeth created a balance of terror that protected the peace. Reagan had the simple-minded credulity to point to the terrible consequences of that view and challenge it with an absurd counterproposal—SDI, the Strategic Defensive Initiative. The president advocated building the ultimate defense—a sort of protective bubble over the entire United States, a view he may have gotten from old science fiction films and/or from casual conversations with some scientists. The proposal was idiotic, but Reagan had undone the old balance of terror viewpoint by simply pointing to its inherent evil, a view shared by many thoughtful people over the years.

Initially, though, Reagan had denounced the SALT (Strategic Arms Limitation Talks) treaties, with their intricate schemes for weighing nuclear advantages, throw weights, and verification. Friends and foes remarked on how little the president knew about the basics of nuclear strategy, the difference between U.S. and Soviet strategic assets, and what was happening at the negotiating tables engaged in disarmament's arcane language. The president started out with a belief that the United States could so outspend the Soviets that they would be forced to seek negotiations to reduce nuclear arms levels. Early in the administration, Reagan startled the Soviets by advocating the "zero-option" proposal, which would remove all Soviet SS-20s in Europe and Asia in return for the United States canceling deployment of cruise missiles and Pershing IIs. Thus the president was building up the military, proposing massive cuts in nuclear weapons, attacking communism at its ideological source, and promoting a new world—all at once! His advisers divided among themselves, moving in and out of ascendancy, and the Soviets, faced with a series of changes in their own leadership, could not figure out how to respond to Reagan.[14]

In reviewing the fate of Eastern Europe, the president predicted that Poland would be the linchpin of opposition to communism and that there would be "repeated explosions against repressions." In the end, Reagan insisted, Marxism-Leninism would join other tyrannies on the "ash-heap of history."[15] He was correct. Soviet leaders obviously did not concur in that pessimism, and they came to regard the SDI not as a bold romantic innovation but as a dangerous beginning of a new antimissile system that would disturb the balance of power between the two superpowers. By Reagan's second term, Soviet leadership had passed to Mikhail Gorbachev, whose time in office would have profound effects on the total geopolitical world. The U.S. president had not had a personal conference with any previous Soviet leader, explaining whimsically, "The only reason I'd never met with General Secretary Gorbachev's predecessors was because they kept dying on me." Indeed, from 1980 to 1985, the Kremlin's leadership went from the slow-moving neo-Stalinist Leonid Brezhnev to KGB leader Yuri Andropov to party operative Konstantin Chernenko to Gorbachev in 1985.[16]

Gorbachev was to begin a process of normalization, which led to the end of communism in most of Eastern Europe and eventually the toppling of that form of government in the Soviet Union and that state's disintegration. Without the Red Army garrisoned in its satellites, the Soviet Union could not keep its influence intact even after forty years of Communist alliance politics. And in that nation, the old security apparatus of party bureaucrats, secret police, and army leaders began to crumble, as strange expressions of democracy and traditional expressions of nationalism, Orthodox Christianity, and Islam played havoc on the old empire.

As Gorbachev confronted Reagan in a series of summit conferences in the late 1980s, his strategy was to press for more extensive nuclear arms reductions similar to what had characterized U.S.-Soviet relations for the last five American administrations. At their various meetings, Reagan and Gorbachev worked on disarmament proposals and debated vigorously the president's dream of SDI, the technology of which Reagan rather remarkably offered to share with the evil empire's leaders! But by the beginnings of the first Bush administration, the scenario was to change, as Gorbachev and later his successors in the Soviet Union and other former Communist states were seriously talking about eliminating whole classes of nuclear weapons, an approach Reagan and Gorbachev started at the end of the president's last term. Reagan was to move far beyond the traditional arms control consensus in his own country, and he startled his conservative supporters as he simply waved aside their fears of the Soviet Union by remarking blithely that he knew what was going on more than they did on the arms control issue. Going to Moscow in May 1988, Reagan pushed for democratic changes and quoted the great Russian poet Aleksander Pushkin: "It's time, my friend, it's time."[17]

Iran–Contra Affair

Reagan's excursions into Latin America and the Middle East were to prove to be less successful, and his serious policy choices had terrible costs at times. In Nicaragua, the president inherited Carter's hostility toward the new Marxist regime of the ruling Sandinistas. He praised the opposition armed forces in that nation, called the "Contras," identifying them with the American Founding Fathers and the leaders of the French Resistance in World War II. But Reagan was careful to avoid listening to the more hawkish conservative advisers, including his first secretary of state, Alexander Haig, who wanted to rid the hemisphere of Castro and the Nicaraguan Sandinistas in one fell swoop. The president went on to approve CIA covert activities and military aid to topple the Sandinistas, but he avoided any talk of using American troops. Referring to the demands of some American conservatives for more support, the president observed, "Those sons of bitches won't be happy until we have 25,000 troops in Managua, and I'm not going to do it." Although Reagan had often praised the American war effort in Vietnam, he did not wish to replicate that experience in his time in office.[18]

The president's main foreign policy advisers were also deeply divided about how to deal with the Nicaraguan situation and later El Salvador. Reagan, a poor manager and an inadequate policymaker, seemed to stay above the Nicaraguan fray, although he offered support to neighboring El Salvador and its president, Napoleon Duarte, to allow it to resist its own leftist guerrillas. Reagan began to accept a strategy of asking foreign governments to sponsor the Nicaraguan Contras in order to get around the increasingly tight restrictions being imposed by the Congress on American government support. He personally solicited the Saudi Arabian government and other nations to fund such arrangements. The director of the CIA, William Casey, and the National Security Council advisers in this period, Robert McFarlane and later Admiral John Poindexter, became advocates of covert activities to help the Contras. Secretary of State George Shultz and Secretary of Defense Caspar Weinberger both distanced themselves from the Contra support activities, fearing congressional and public criticism if those transactions became public, which eventually happened. Like Eisenhower, Reagan turned to the CIA to do what the U.S. armed forces could not do—to wage war through surrogates, without public notice. Thus Reagan, the Great Communicator, gave up communicating with the people over the heads of the liberals in Congress. And in the process, he was able to avoid having to confront the divisions in his own house on the issue.[19]

Under increasing criticism, the president appointed a blue-ribbon committee to look at U.S. policy toward Central America. Headed by former secretary of state Henry Kissinger, it proposed foreign aid to the region, economic development assistance, scholarships for Latin American students, and a literacy corps. But the administration's tone was being set by the more assertive CIA and two successive NSC directors, who pushed for aid to the Contras and direct action against the Sandinistas. The final chapter was a bizarre scheme that came to be labeled the "Iran-Contra Affair," which destroyed the president's ability to govern in his second term. Briefly, American agents led by CIA Director Casey and National Security Director John Poindexter permitted a marine colonel, Oliver North, to organize the sale of American arms to the Iranian government as a way to free U.S. hostages held in Lebanon. The holding of these hostages was deeply troubling to Reagan, and he was genuinely affected by the hostage families pleading with him to do something to bring their relatives home. Reagan was a man of sentiment, and their cause became his. He was not the disengaged executive when he persistently demanded action, and his aides responded accordingly.

The president and some of his advisers believed that they could buy the goodwill of the radical Iranian fundamentalists, who had just waged a costly war against the Iraqis. The United States quietly supplied advanced technical weapons, probably through the Israeli government, to the Iranians and received a very good price for those items. The profits could be used, it was explained to Colonel North by one of the Iranian middlemen, to assist American friends in Central America. North, who was deeply sympathetic to the anticommunist cause, records that he received approval from National Security Council Director Poindexter to proceed along those very lines. Thus, the Iran-Contra connection was established.

At first, the public only learned of the arms-for-hostages deal with the Iranians, which was never completed; that exchange raised serious questions about dealing with terrorists, which the Reagan administration had promised not to do. The president denied that he ever approved any such swap, but his position was untenable as the logic of such a swap was apparent to nearly everyone else. The administration, seeking to avoid another Watergate-type public outcry, asked the attorney general and long-time Reagan loyalist, Ed Meese, to conduct a full investigation. During that review, he found a document in North's files that laid out the second and more damaging link, the diversion of arms profits from Iran to the Contras. The issue now became a constitutional crisis—a direct attempt to circumvent Congress and assert covertly the executive's prescriptions to direct and fund foreign policy as he saw fit. Reagan swore he was unaware of the transfer of funds. The blame shifted from North to Poindexter to Casey to the president and his vice president and a former director of the CIA, George H. W. Bush. Congressional investigations, a special prosecutor, and several jury trials endeavored to find out who knew what when. At first, Poindexter took full responsibility, saying he made the decision to transfer funds from arms sales profits to assist the Contras and that he did not talk to the president about the diversion; the chief executive must have the opportunity for deniability. North, in his memoirs, however, insists that the president was aware of the full transactions but that he may not have remembered or paid attention at the time![20]

A presidential-appointed committee, headed by former Senator John Tower of Texas, found no evidence that Reagan was aware of the transactions, but in a less than ringing endorsement, the panel concluded that his management style was woefully deficient. The president responded that he found good subordinates, appointed them to office, and let them run their agencies and departments uninhibited by him. Even friendly associates have concluded that Reagan had little curiosity about government and its workings, asked few questions even at cabinet meetings, was inattentive and often ill prepared, and was more given to anecdotes than analysis. His was a committed administration with a disinterested executive nominally leading it. Ironically, it was this disinterestedness that made it difficult to link him to the Iran-Contra affair conclusively, thus probably saving his presidency. Actually, though, the president was forceful in insisting on moving on Iran and the hostages, bypassing his own secretary of state and secretary of defense in the process. He was committed enough to personally solicit money for the Contras from outside the country, and he knew full well that if the public found out, the administration would be in serious trouble. When the matter was exposed, he praised Colonel North as a national hero and said his story would make a great movie someday—the finest kudos Ronald Reagan could lay on a mere mortal.

Reagan was also willing to show his commitment to the freedom fighters when he supported the Afghan mujahideen who were opposing the Soviet invasion of their homeland. Eventually, Gorbachev came to see Afghanistan as his Vietnam, and he pulled the Red Army out of that land— although a pro-Soviet regime proved to be viable until 1992, longer than the administration predicted. Also Reagan, under pressure from Congress and some of his own conservative supporters, eventually used his office to ease out the corrupt Ferdinand Marcos regime in the Philippines.[21]

Foreign Ventures

In the Middle East, the president's ambivalent management style and his pronounced inability to resolve intergovernmental disputes led not just to institutional confrontations, as in the Iran-Contra affair, but also to the terrible tragedy of losing 241 marines in a terrorist attack on their temporary barracks in Lebanon. A nation once civil and prosperous, Lebanon by 1982 was a garrison state split by religious and ethnic factions and engaged in a bitter civil war in which nearly one hundred thousand people had died since 1975. The administration itself was deeply divided initially about the importance of Lebanon, although the president pronounced it a vital part of U.S. interests.

On July 17, 1981, Israel bombed the Palestine Liberation Organization (PLO) headquarters in Beirut, and the United States pushed for a cease-fire in that nation between the warring factions, a settlement that lasted for nearly a year. Then, on June 6, 1982, the Israelis launched a major invasion, aimed at crippling the strength of PLO's ally Syria by destroying Syrian surface-to-air missiles in the Bekaa Valley, shooting down more than twenty Syrian planes, and encircling the PLO inside Beirut. Once again the administration pushed for a cease-fire, but the Israelis bombed West Beirut again, intending to end once and for all the presence of their enemies so close to their border. The president's special envoy, Philip Habib, tried to get an American commitment to be a part of a proposed peacekeeping force that would guarantee the removal of the PLO from Lebanon to safe quarters elsewhere. The president unfortunately agreed to put U.S. troops into that morass without thinking about the consequences, American security objectives, and the true mission of U.S. forces there. Throughout his administration, Secretary of State George Shultz and Secretary of Defense Caspar Weinberger had disagreed on the basic tenets of U.S. foreign policy, and once again this lack of consensus led the president to drift into a compromise.

At first, the Reagan policy in the Middle East seemed to work well, and on September 10, U.S. marines were evacuated from Lebanon and went back to their ships. Then, on September 15, the cease-fire ended after the president-elect of Lebanon, Bashier Gemayel, was murdered when a bomb exploded at his party's office. The Israelis entered West Beirut once again to protect their interests. Reagan, ignoring the advice of his Defense Department chiefs, reintroduced the marines into Lebanon to stabilize the situation. Instead, as time progressed, the American presence entered into a more activist posture, one that seemed hostile to the Syrians and supportive of the Christian faction. Then on October 23, 1983, the marine headquarters was bombed by Moslem extremists and 241 servicemen were killed, as the structure they were in totally collapsed. It was the worst disaster of the Reagan administration, and it brought forth a wave of public outcry and deep sorrow. A board of inquiry appointed by Reagan focused on the command problems in the operations and the unclear mission, but the clear culprit for putting the troops in harm's way was the lack of some sense of purpose from the commander in chief. One U.S. senator, Ernest Hollings of South Carolina, bluntly concluded, "They do not have a mission. If they were put there to fight, there are too few. If they were put there to die, there are too many."[22]

As the nation and the president mourned the deaths, the Reagan administration planned its own invasion of the Caribbean island of Grenada, where the Marxist prime minister, Maurice Bishop, who had been under house arrest, was murdered on October 19 by members of his own party. Fearful of anarchy in another part of the world and concerned about the fate of one thousand Americans there, many of them students at the St. George's School of Medicine, the president ordered American troops onto the island. His advisers were especially fearful of another hostage situation similar to what Carter had gone through for 444 days with Iran. The invasion force of five thousand men simply overwhelmed the island's opposition, despite terrible American intelligence and major logistical problems. It was a fine, short war, and the American people responded positively to Reagan's display of leadership. Thirty hours after the invasion, U.S. medical students landed in Charleston, South Carolina, and some kissed American soil. A fine media event was had by all.

In 1984, Reagan ran for reelection and won a huge electoral landslide victory, carrying forty-nine states against Democrat Walter F. Mondale, who barely won his own home state of Minnesota and prevailed in the District of Columbia. The Roosevelt coalition was finally cracked, its great voting blocs split up, as another president caught the American fancy. Reagan appeared as the confident, strong-willed leader with a deep sense of optimism and a real commitment to patriotism and national pride. Privately he was pleasant and disengaged, ill informed, and often passive. But some Americans lived on images, not reality, and Reagan's handlers knew the new political realities.[23]

The president had agreed to a major shake-up of his staff, most importantly the swap of jobs involving Chief of Staff James Baker, a Texas moderate and Bush associate, and Secretary of Treasury Donald Regan. The result was to be unsettling for the president and the administration. There had been some conversations about allowing Baker to go to the National Security Council, but conservatives intervened and Reagan, fearful of controversy as usual, demurred. Later, even the president was astute enough after the Iran-Contra affair to conclude, "My decision not to appoint Jim Baker as national security adviser, I suppose, was a turning point for my administration."[24] But in the glow of victory all seemed well. Reagan and his people cited his restoration of the nation's spirit; their slogan for reelection was "It's morning again in America."

A major anchor of reality for Reagan was his hard-headed wife, Nancy, who was subject to considerable criticism during his time in office but at critical junctures provided some real practicality to his dreamy moods. She was pilloried for her pretentiousness, reliance on astrology, coldness, ruthless style, and conspicuous love of wealth and fashion, but the First Lady occasionally intervened with Reagan and his staff to force him to make necessary and difficult decisions. Her advice did not always prevail, and at times it was petty instead of informed, but overall her views on the inadequacy of his staff, his ill-advised trip to a cemetery in West Germany whose graves included those of Nazis, and her plea for a more accommodationist foreign policy made more sense than his policies or inclinations at the time. In her memoirs, even she drops the adoring tone once in a while to comment that Ronnie was often just too kind.[25]

He was kind and rather uninterested, which made staff changes so very important. Unlike Eisenhower, Reagan had little high-level administrative experience to fall back on when staff members went awry. James Baker, his first chief of staff, was a man given to slow, methodical steps, the type of process that would have probably prevented Iran-Contra adventures. Secretary of Treasury Donald Regan, a brusque Wall Street executive, disliked compromise and political jockeying—the very stuff of White House life. He had worked hard on the Tax Reform Act of 1986, the most comprehensive reform and loophole-closing package in American history. The president praised the bill, but once again he was not involved in its passage except for signing the final proposal.[26] By the end of Reagan's first term, Baker and Regan had the president's approval to change jobs—with consequences no one could foretell. The inadequacy of Donald Regan's White House staff was obvious early in his handling of a request for the president to visit a German military cemetery to symbolize the "end" of World War II animosities. It was a magnanimous act on the president's part, one aimed at placating German Chancellor Helmut Kohl's desire to show that the legacy of the war was indeed forgotten. But unfortunately, the cemetery, located in Bitburg, was also the resting place of some of the hated Waffen-SS troops. The world Jewish community and numerous veterans groups, as well as others, expressed outrage; Reagan, a man of his word, stubbornly insisted on honoring his commitment to Kohl. One survivor of the Holocaust, Jewish writer Elie Wiesel, pleaded with the president, "That place, Mr. President, is not your place. Your place is with the victims of the SS."[27] It was a mistake compounded by insensitivity, one that showed early on the cracks in the edifice of the White House staff. The incident was to be a preface to the Iran-Contra affair in which the NSC and the CIA upstaged the major cabinet secretaries and set for the nation a clandestine policy of hostage-arms trading and a diversion of funds to the Contras. As has been noted, it threatened the integrity of the president and undercut his final years as chief executive.

The full measure of Ronald Reagan's presidency began to move from the passive buoyant optimism of the actor's repertoire to the harshness of controversy and personal vilification. Baker and his associates had kept the wolf away from Ronald Reagan's door. They directed and protected the aged president, often from himself, and filled America with images of easy hope and the vibrancy of its special destiny. After Reagan's first term, the stage directors changed, and the star stood at times naked and vulnerable in a hostile world.

Angry cries of impeachment once again filled the air—this time not over Watergate but over the Iran-Contra affair. And then the president moved onto the world stage dealing directly with the Soviet leader Gorbachev. Their meetings progressed from confrontation and ideological debates to a final positive accommodation that led to arms agreements that were startling in their size and scope. The Cold War was ending, and incredibly it was Reagan who had both helped encourage resistance to Soviet occupation and led the way to a reconciliation with their leaders while that very empire was collapsing. With self-confidence once again, Ronald Reagan concluded his time in office, saying, "We meant to change a nation, and instead we changed a world."[28]

The Reagan years provided an important reaffirmation of American self-confidence at home. But it was also a time of immeasurable greed, corporate irresponsibility, and an unparalleled number of federal government officials accused of malfeasance and influence pedaling. To Reaganites, the American dream was simply individual economic success; there was no real concern about the family, the community, or the social fabric of the nation except as campaign slogans. There also was no recognition of the wisdom of the great British conservative Edmund Burke, who concluded that a nation is more than a holding company—it is a union of the past, the future, and the present generations.

Abroad, the Reagan administration did change the world—often not for the better. Its interventions in Nicaragua, Honduras, and El Salvador extracted heavier costs in terms of human life than were warranted. However, in the first instance, the Sandinistas were indeed a curse on their land and were voted out in an election that the United States—that is, the Reagan administration—was instrumental in holding. Overall, Reagan and his followers would credit the president with inspiring the forces of democracy all over the world, especially in the Soviet Union and its client states. America's old enemy and its empire ended up in disarray and crumbled by 1990–1991; Reagan surely deserves some credit for that collapse, along with the powerful tides of nationalism and ethnicity that swept over Eastern Europe. Love him or hate him, Ronald Reagan did restore the notion of an activist presidency, despite his own passive temperament; he insisted that the presidency was capable of working changes in the nation. In the process, he vanquished the sense that the post-Roosevelt presidency was filled with tragedy, political humiliation, and popular despair.

He helped fracture the durable FDR coalition, and he put together a new conservative coalition for fiscal conservatives, social conservatives, and Christian fundamentalists, all joined to fight the advancing liberal and more tolerant welfare state. By the centennial anniversary of his birth in 2010, he was an American icon of the right, most of whom did not know his complex record as governor and as president.

Reagan thus was a substantial president, but there was still a void, an insensitivity to the plight of the most vulnerable in society that will be linked with the Reagan years and the president himself. For what differentiates a Reagan from a Roosevelt—Franklin or Theodore—is that sense of fellow feeling or sympathy with the suffering in society. It is the margin of hope that separates politics as mere intrigue from politics as moral leadership. Yet, as far as Reagan was concerned, he was pleased as always with himself, recalling once again that, in his vocabulary, politics is like acting: you start quickly, coast a bit, and end with a fast finish.[29]

Conclusion

O N ONE LEVEL, THIS BOOK may give the reader a false impression, for it is an account only of our greatest presidents. As such, it does not cover those men who have been weak, timid, disorganized, and even venial. Instead, I have focused on men of vision, of political acumen, and of deep, lasting impact.

It may be that in the twenty-first century, it is nearly impossible to be a great president as one faces the fierce world of a 24/7 news cycle, mindless partisanship, the growth of ideological commentators and bloggers, the presence of a Congress almost totally preoccupied by local interests, and the need to raise campaign funds for constant and expensive races. The modern presidency may not have the assets to centralize the public debate and guide lasting, loyal coalitions.

Even if one looks carefully at these great presidents, many of them had legislative branches that often provided them with little support. Almost all of the war presidents conducted their military campaigns without much useful congressional help. In terms of diplomacy, the presidents have resorted often to secrecy—not to deny information to foreign powers, but to curtail interventions from Congress and the courts. The Founding Fathers gave us a separation of powers that is often an invitation to conflict.

This is not to say that presidents are always right in their conduct of war and diplomacy, but, for better or worse, they have set the parameters of our foreign policies. Presidential leadership is most apparent in those areas. In terms of domestic policy, it is very difficult to ignore or override the other branches of government or even the division of authority between the federal government and the states. Proponents of the states' domain like to see them as "laboratories of democracy," where solutions can be tried and tested before policies become national. That may have been true in the Progressive era, but today most states do not have the expertise or the vision to deal with great domestic issues. The influence of money, the enticement of patronage, and the siren calls of ideological politics are even stronger in the state capitals than in Washington, D.C.

Even great presidents, though, have a limited window of time for innovation and reform. As a general rule, one can see that in the first year in office, neophyte presidents need time to put together a team, vet their choices, and lay out legislative agendas in concrete terms. It is notably in the second and third years that they take hold and achieve their most likely successes. In year four they are on the road raising money, tuning up the organization, and bouncing from pillar to post running for reelection. In a successful second term, they begin to try to capture some momentum in the first two years, but then they have little left in the last two. There is not much time to govern in an eight-year span. Studies show that very few presidents, even great ones, have very successful second terms. Perhaps it is the turnover of first-rate people, the weakness of being a lame-duck president, the fickle public mood that controls the second term—especially in a republic of limited powers with (now) a two-term limit. Even Franklin D. Roosevelt's second term was a series of many futilities. It was in his third term that his wartime global leadership cast him on a new plane of leadership. Thus, considering all those limitations, some of the presidents have truly performed remarkable and important tasks in the time given them.

It may be that this eighteenth-century office—even with its extensive modifications and augmentations—is just too constricted to be effective in the twenty-first century. Even earlier, in the nineteenth century, Lord Bryce in Britain wondered why great men were not chosen president. The alternative frequently posed to our system is that of a prime ministership, the parliamentary model that just about every Western democracy has. But many of those modern prime ministers have been successful only when they adopted "presidential" practices grafted on parliamentary traditions. Executive accountability is really a very difficult exercise under any system.

When the nation faces a grave national emergency or a terrible catastrophe, the American people turn not to Congress, the Supreme Court, or the state legislatures. They turn to the president, for he is the commander in chief and, at times of grief, our consoler in chief. At their very best, the president explains to the nation the context in which incoherent but important happenings make sense. And it for this reason that we should remember John Adams's words inscribed on a mantelpiece in the White House: "May none but honest and wise men ever rule under this roof."

Notes

Preface

1. Alexander Hamilton in *Federalist Paper*, Number 70, cites energy, dispatch, decision, activity, and secrecy as the major assets of the presidency.

2. "Historical Rankings of Presidents of the United States," http://er.wikipedia .org; Marc Landy and Sidney M. Milkis, *Presidential Greatness* (Lawrence: University Press of Kansas, 2001).

3. Landy and Milkis, *Presidential Greatness*, passim.

4. Ibid.

5. Karl Rove, "What Makes a Great President," June 30, 2003, http://hnn .us/articles/1529.html.

Chapter 1: George Washington: Creating a Nation in War and Then in Peace

1. Background material on George Washington has grown since the bicentennial celebration. Of special importance are the older works. Douglas Southall Freeman, *George Washington*, 7 vols. (New York: Scribner, 1948–1957); James Thomas Flexner, *George Washington*, 4 vols. (Boston: Little, Brown, 1965–1972); Noemie Emery, *Washington* (New York: Putnam, 1976); Catherine L. Albanese, *Sons of the Fathers: The Civil Religions of the American Revolution* (Philadelphia: Temple University Press, 1976); Garry Wills, *Cincinnatus* (Garden City, NY: Doubleday, 1984); Barry Schwartz, *George Washington: The Making of an American Symbol* (New York: Free Press, 1987); Thomas A. Lewis, *For King and Country* (New York: HarperCollins, 1993); Ron Chernow, *Washington: A Life* (New York: Penguin Press, 2010); Richard Brookhiser, *Founding Father: Rediscovering George Washington* (New York: Free Press, 1996); Joseph Ellis, *His Excellency: George Washington* (New York: Knopf, 2004); and Richard Norton Smith, *Patriarch: George Washington and the New American Nation* (Boston: Houghton Mifflin, 1993).

2. Martha J. Lamb, *The Washington Inauguration* (New York and London: White and Allen, 1889); *Wall & Nassau: An Account of the Inauguration of George Washington* (New York: Bankers Trust Co., 1939); Frank Monaghan, *Notes on the Inaugural Journey of George Washington* (New York: n.p., 1939); Rufus Wilmot Griswold, *The Republican Court* (New York: Appleton, 1854); and Frank Fletcher Stephens, *The Transition Period 1788–1789 in the Government of the United States* (Columbia, MO: E. W. Stephens, 1909).

3. Edward S. Corwin, "The President's Removal Power under the Constitution," in *Selected Essays on Constitutional Law*, vol. 4, *Administrative Law*, ed. Douglas B. Maggs (Chicago: Foundation Press, 1938), 1467–1518. See also the debate in *The Debates and Proceedings of the Congress of the United States*, comp. Joseph Gales (Washington, DC: Gales and Seaton, 1834).

4. James Hart, *The American Presidency in Action, 1789* (New York: Macmillan, 1948); Leonard White, *The Federalists* (New York: Macmillan, 1956); Charles C. Thach Jr., *The Creation of the Presidency, 1775–1789* (Baltimore: Johns Hopkins University Press, 1923); and Carl E. Prince, *The Federalists and the Origins of the U.S. Civil Service* (New York: New York University Press, 1977).

5. Essential to a discussion of the debt situation and the banks is Forrest McDonald, *The Presidency of George Washington* (New York: Norton, 1975), 50–59. Also of use are *Papers of Alexander Hamilton*, vol. 6, ed. Harold C. Syrett and Jacob E. Cooke (New York: Columbia University Press, 1961); Robert Hendrickson, *Hamilton II* (New York: Mason-Charter, 1976); Ron Chernow, *Hamilton* (New York: Penguin, 2004); and John Miller, *The Federalist Era* (New York: Harper & Row, 1960), chaps. 3 and 4.

6. Richard Kohn, *The Eagle and the Sword* (New York: Free Press, 1975); Michael P. Riccards, *A Republic, If You Can Keep It: The Foundation of the American Presidency, 1700–1800* (Westport, CT: Greenwood Press, 1987), chap. 18; George D. Hanson, *Sixty Years of Indian Affairs* (Chapel Hill: University of North Carolina Press, 1941); Jennings Wise, *The Red Man in the New World Drama* (New York: Macmillan, 1971); Reginald Horsman, *The Frontier in the Formative Years, 1783–1815* (New York: Holt, Rinehart, and Winston, 1970) and *Expansion and the American Indian Policy, 1783–1812* (East Lansing: Michigan State University Press, 1967); Katherine C. Turner, *Red Man Calling on the Great White Father* (Norman: University of Oklahoma Press, 1951); John W. Caughey, *McGillivray of the Creeks* (Norman: University of Oklahoma Press, 1938); and Randolph C. Downs, *Council Fires on the Upper Ohio* (Pittsburgh, PA: University of Pittsburgh Press, 1940). Also of interest is Anthony Wayne, *A Name in Arms: The Wayne-Knox-Pickering-McHenry Correspondence*, ed. Richard Knopf (Pittsburgh, PA: University of Pittsburgh Press, 1960).

7. Joseph Charles, *The Origins of the American Party System* (Williamsburg, VA: Institute of Early American History and Culture, 1956); William N. Chambers, *Political Parties in a New Nation* (New York: Oxford University Press, 1963); Jackson Turner Main, *Political Parties before the Constitution* (New York: Norton, 1973);

H. James Henderson, *Party Politics in the Continental Congress* (New York: McGraw-Hill, 1974); Bernard Fay, "Early Party Machinery in the United States," *Pennsylvania Magazine of History and Biography* 60 (October 1936): 375–90; George D. Leutscher, *Early Political Machinery in the United States* (Philadelphia: n.p., 1903); Richard P. McCormick, *The Second Party System* (New York: Norton, 1966); and Rudolph Bell, *Party and Faction in American Politics* (Westport, CT: Greenwood Press, 1973).

8. Noble Cunningham, *Jeffersonian Republicans* (Chapel Hill: University of North Carolina Press, 1957); Dumas Malone, *Jefferson and the Rights of Man* (Boston: Little, Brown, 1951); Samuel Flagg Bemis, *A Diplomatic History of the United States* (New York: Holt, Rinehart, and Winston, 1965), chaps. 5 and 6; Frederick Jackson Turner, "The Origins of Genet's Projected Attack on Louisiana and the Floridas," in *Significance of Sections in American History* (New York: Peter Smith, 1950), 52–85; Charles Marion Thomas, *American Neutrality in 1793* (New York: Columbia University Press, 1931); John J. Reardon, *Edmund Randolph* (New York: Macmillan, 1974); and Harry Ammon, "The Genet Mission and the Development of American Political Parties," *Journal of American History* 52 (March 1966): 725–41.

9. Leland Baldwin, *Whiskey Rebels* (Pittsburgh, PA: University of Pittsburgh Press, 1939); Jacob E. Cooke, "The Whiskey Insurrection: A Reevaluation," *Pennsylvania History* 30 (July 1963): 316–46; David O. Whitlea, "The Economic Inquiry into the Whiskey Rebellion of 1794," *Agricultural History* 49 (July 1975): 491–504; William Miller, "The Democratic Societies and the Whiskey Insurrection," *Pennsylvania Magazine of History and Biography* 62 (July 1938): 324–59; and William D. Barber, "'Among the Most Techy Articles of Civil Police': Federal Taxation and the Adoption of the Whiskey Excise," *William and Mary Quarterly* 25, 3rd series (January 1968): 58–84.

10. Bemis, *A Diplomatic History*, chaps. 6 and 7; Alexander De Conde, *Entangling Alliances* (Durham, NC: Duke University Press, 1958); Bradford Perkins, *The First Rapprochement* (Berkeley and Los Angeles: University of California Press, 1955); A. L. Burt, *The United States, Great Britain, and British North America* (New York: Russell & Russell, 1961), chap. 8; Jerald A. Combs, *The Jay Treaty* (Berkeley and Los Angeles: University of California Press, 1970); Gerard H. Clarfield, *Timothy Pickering and American Diplomacy* (Columbia: University of Missouri Press, 1969); and Eugene Perry Link, *Democratic-Republican Societies* (New York: Columbia University Press, 1942).

Chapter 2: Thomas Jefferson: Establishing Popular Rule

1. Marshall Smelser, *The Democratic Republic, 1801–1815* (New York: Harper & Row, 1968); Forrest McDonald, *The Presidency of Thomas Jefferson* (Lawrence: University Press of Kansas, 1976), chap. 1; Rebecca Lloyd Shippen, "Inauguration of President Thomas Jefferson 1801," *Pennsylvania Magazine of History and*

Biography 25 (1901): 71–76; Margaret Bayard Smith, *The First Forty Years of Washington Society* (New York: Scribner, 1906); Herbert Agar, "John Adams and Jefferson," in *The People's Choice* (Boston: Houghton Mifflin, 1933), 32–71; David Brion Davis, *Was Thomas Jefferson an Authentic Enemy of Slavery?* (Oxford, UK: Clarendon Press, 1970); John Dos Passos, *The Head and Heart of Thomas Jefferson* (Garden City, NY: Doubleday, 1954); Henry Steele Commager, *Jefferson, Nationalism, and Enlightenment* (New York: G. Braziller, 1975); David Brion Davis, *The Problem of Slavery in the Age of Revolution* (Ithaca, NY: Cornell University Press, 1975), 169–84; Edward Channing, *The Jeffersonian System* (New York: Harper, 1906); J. M. Merriam, "Jefferson's Use of Executive Patronage," *American Historical Association Papers* 2 (1887): 47; Leonard W. Levy, *Jefferson and Civil Liberties: The Darker Side* (Cambridge, MA: Harvard University Press, 1963); Francis Luther Mott, *Jefferson and the Press* (Baton Rouge: Louisiana State University Press, 1943); and Adrienne Koch, *The Philosophy of Thomas Jefferson* (New York: Columbia University Press, 1943).

2. There is a far-reaching literature on Jefferson and his thought. I have benefited especially from Dumas Malone's magisterial *Jefferson and His Time*, 6 vols. (Boston: Little, Brown, 1948–1981); Merrill D. Peterson, *Thomas Jefferson and the New Nation* (New York: Oxford University Press, 1970); Robert M. Johnston Jr., *Jefferson and the Presidency* (Ithaca, NY: Cornell University Press, 1978); Claude G. Bowers, *The Young Jefferson* (Boston: Houghton Mifflin, 1943), and *Jefferson in Power* (Boston: Houghton Mifflin, 1936); Richard F. Matthews, *The Radical Politics of Thomas Jefferson* (Lawrence: University Press of Kansas, 1984); Daniel Boorstin, *The Lost World of Thomas Jefferson* (Boston: Beacon, 1974); Fawn M. Brodie, *Thomas Jefferson* (New York: Bantam, 1974); Merrill Peterson, *The Jeffersonian Image in the American Mind* (New York: Oxford University Press, 1960); Harold L. Hillenbrand, *The Unfinished Revolution: Education and Community in the Thought of Thomas Jefferson*, 2 vols. (Stanford, CA: Stanford University Press, 1980); Gary Wills, *Inventing America* (New York: Vintage, 1978); George Tucker, *The Life of Thomas Jefferson*, 2 vols. (Philadelphia: Carey, Lea, and Blanchard, 1837); Henry Adams, *History of the United States during the First Administrations of Thomas Jefferson and James Madison*, 2 vols. (New York: Library of America, 1986); Yehoshua Arieli, *Individualism and Nationalism in American Ideology* (Cambridge, MA: Harvard University Press, 1964), 123–80; Marie Kimball, *Jefferson*, 3 vols. (New York: Coward-McCann, 1943–1950); Leonard White, *The Jeffersonians* (New York: Macmillan, 1951); and Peter S. Onuf, ed., *Jeffersonian Legacies* (Charlottesville: University Press of Virginia, 1993).

3. Richard E. Ellis, *The Jeffersonian Crisis* (New York: Norton, 1971); Jerry W. Knudson, "The Jeffersonian Assault on the Federalist Judiciary," *American Journal of Legal History* 14 (1970): 55–70; C. S. Thomas, "Jefferson and the Judiciary," *Constitutional Review* 10 (April 1926): 67–76; Charles Grove Haines, *The American Doctrine of Judicial Supremacy* (Berkeley and Los Angeles: University of California Press, 1932), 241–53; and Julian P. Boyd, "The Chasm That Separated Thomas

Jefferson and John Marshall," in *Essays on the American Constitution*, ed. G. Dietz (Englewood Cliffs, NJ: Prentice Hall, 1964), 3–20.

4. Johnston, *Jefferson and the Presidency*, passim; Everett Lee Long, "Jefferson and Congress" (PhD diss., University of Missouri, 1966); and Noble E. Cunningham Jr., *The Process of Government under Jefferson* (Princeton, NJ: Princeton University Press, 1978) and *The Jeffersonian Republicans in Power* (Chapel Hill: University of North Carolina Press, 1963). Also of special interest is Jefferson to Barnabas, Library of Congress, No. 27995-6, series 1; May 13, 1806–November 1806, Reel 36.

5. Dumas Malone, *Jefferson the President, 1801–1805* (Boston: Little, Brown, 1970), 73, 81, 88; quote to de Nemours on page 91. Norman K. Risjord, *The Old Republicans* (New York: Columbia University Press, 1965); Lance Banning, *The Jeffersonian Persuasion* (Ithaca, NY: Cornell University Press, 1970); Dumas Malone, "Presidential Leadership and National Unity: The Jefferson Example," *Journal of Southern History* 25 (February 1969): 3–17; Carl Russell Fish, "Jefferson's Policy as to Public Office, 1801–1809," in *The Civil Service and the Patronage* (New York: Longmans, Green, 1905), 29–51; Alexander B. Lacy Jr., "Jefferson and Congress: Congressional Method and Politics, 1801–1809" (PhD diss., University of Virginia, 1964); Dumas Malone, *Thomas Jefferson as a Political Leader* (Berkeley and Los Angeles: University of California Press, 1963); Carl E. Prince, "The Passing of the Aristocrats: Jefferson's Removal of the Federalists," *Journal of American History* 57 (December 1970): 563–75; Gaillard Hunt, "Office Seeking during Jefferson's Administration," *American Historical Review* 3 (January 1898): 270–91; and James Sterling Young, *The Washington Community* (New York: Columbia University Press, 1967). Also of interest are David K. McCarrell, *The Formation of the Jeffersonian Party in Virginia* (Durham, NC: Duke University Press, 1937); Harry Ammon, "The Jeffersonian Republicans in Virginia," *Virginia Magazine of History and Biography* 71 (April 1963): 153–67; William Nisbet Chambers, *Political Parties in a New Nation* (New York: Oxford University Press, 1963), 170–90; Alfred Young, "The Mechanics and the Jeffersonians: New York 1789–1801," *Labor History* 5 (Fall 1965): 247–76; William A. Robinson, *Jeffersonian Democracy in New England* (New Haven, CT: Yale University Press, 1916); Alfred Young, *The Jeffersonian Republicans of New York* (Chapel Hill: University of North Carolina Press, 1968); Staughton Lynd, "Beyond Beard," in *Towards a New Past*, ed. Barton J. Berstein (New York: Pantheon, 1968); Charles Beard, *Economic Origins of Jeffersonian Democracy* (New York: Macmillan, 1915); Carl F. Prince, *New Jersey's Jeffersonian Republicans* (Chapel Hill: University of North Carolina Press, 1967); Paul Goodman, *The Democratic Republicans of Massachusetts* (Cambridge, MA: Harvard University Press, 1964); James H. Broussard, *The Southern Federalists* (Baton Rouge: Louisiana University Press, 1928); Richard Buel, *Securing the Revolution* (Ithaca, NY: Cornell University Press, 1972); and David Hackett Fischer, *The Revolution of American Conservatism* (New York: Harper & Row, 1967).

6. Malone, *Jefferson the President, 1801–1805*, 987; Paul E. Norton, "Jefferson's Plan for Mothballing the Frigates," *US Naval Institute Proceedings* 82 (July 1956):

737–41; Donald Jackson, "Jefferson, Meriwether Lewis, and the Reduction of the United States," *Proceedings of the American Philosophical Society* 124 (April 29, 1980): 91–96; Joseph G. Henrich, "The Triumph of Ideology: The Jeffersonians and the Navy, 1779–1807" (PhD diss., Duke University, 1971); Julia H. Macleod, "Jefferson and the Navy: A Defense," *Huntington Library Quarterly* 8 (1945): 153–84; Mary P. Adams, "Jefferson's Military Policy with Special References to the Frontier, 1805–1809" (PhD diss., University of Virginia, 1958); and Theodore J. Crackel, *Mr. Jefferson's Army* (New York: New York University Press, 1987).

7. Malone, *Jefferson the President, 1801–1805*, 105; Raymond Walter, *Albert Gallatin* (New York: Macmillan, 1957); Alexander Balinsky, *Albert Gallatin* (New Brunswick, NJ: Rutgers University Press, 1958); and Joseph Doffman, "The Economic Philosophy of Thomas Jefferson," *Political Science Quarterly* 55 (1940): 98–121.

8. Malone, *Jefferson the President, 1801–1805*, 112.

9. Ibid., 131.

10. Ibid., 176.

11. Ibid., 225.

12. Ibid., 235.

13. Arthur P. Whitaker, *The Mississippi Question, 1795–1803* (Gloucester, MA: Peter Smith, 1962), 25; Stuart Seely Sprague, "Jefferson, Kentucky, and the Closing of the Port of New Orleans, 1802–1803," *Register of the Kentucky Historical Society* 70 (October 1972): 312–17; William Appleman Williams, *The Contours of American History* (Cleveland, OH: World Publishing Company, 1961), 188–92; and Mary P. Adams, "Jefferson's Reaction to the Treaty of San Ildefonso," *Journal of Southern History* 21 (May 1955): 173–88.

14. Whitaker, *Mississippi Question, 1795–1803*, 180.

15. Ibid., 123–38.

16. C. Peter Magrath, *Yazoo: Law and Politics in the New Republic* (Providence, RI: Brown University Press, 1966).

17. Malone, *Jefferson the President, 1801–1805*, 270–79; Napoleon's quote is on page 294.

18. Ibid., 320.

19. George Drago, *Jefferson's Louisiana* (Cambridge, MA: Harvard University Press, 1975); James K. Hosman, *The History of the Louisiana Purchase* (New York: Appleton, 1902); Alexander De Conde, *This Affair of Louisiana* (New York: Scribner, 1976); Lawrence S. Kaplan, *Jefferson and France* (New Haven, CT: Yale University Press, 1967); Arthur Burr Darling, *Our Rising Empire* (New Haven, CT: Yale University Press, 1940); Clifford L. Egan, "United States, France, and West Florida, 1803–1807," *Florida Historical Quarterly* 47 (1969): 227–52; J. W. Bradley, "W. C. Clairborne and Spain: Foreign Affairs under Jefferson and Madison," *Louisiana History* 12 (1971): 297–314, and 13 (1972): 5–26; and R. A. McLenore, "Jeffersonian Diplomacy in the Purchase of Louisiana 1803," *Louisiana Historical Quarterly* 18 (1935): 246–53.

20. Malone, *Jefferson the President, 1801–1805*, 350.

21. Ibid., 436.

22. Ibid., 452; Henry Adams, *John Randolph* (New York: Chelsea House, 1983), chap. 6.

23. Robert Dawidoff, *The Education of John Randolph* (New York: Norton, 1979); and Dumas Malone, *Jefferson the President: Second Term, 1805–1809* (Boston: Little, Brown, 1974), 23.

24. Malone, *Jefferson the President: Second Term, 1805–1809*, 56.

25. Malone, *Jefferson the President: Second Term, 1805–1809*, 60–63; and Bradford Perkins, *Prologue to War: England and the United States, 1805–1812* (Berkeley and Los Angeles: University of California Press, 1961), 3, 5, 23, 50, 92, 112.

26. Malone, *Jefferson the President: Second Term, 1805–1809*, 93.

27. Ibid., 110.

28. Ibid., 193, 208.

29. Ibid., 218; Milton Lomask, *Aaron Burr: The Conspiracy and Years of Exile, 1805–1836* (New York: Farrar, Straus & Giroux, 1982); Dumas Malone and Gary Wills, "Executive Privilege," *New York Review of Books* 21 (July 18, 1974): 36–40; Gary Wills, "The Strange Case of Mr. Jefferson's Subpoena," *New York Review of Books* 21 (May 21, 1974): 15–19, and "An UnAmerican Politician," *New York Review of Books* 21 (May 16, 1974): 9–12; Thomas Perkins Aberbethy, *The Burr Conspiracy* (New York: Oxford University Press, 1954); Nathan Schachner, *Aaron Burr* (New York: Frederick A. Stokes, 1936); and Jonathan Daniels, *Ordeal of Ambition* (Garden City, NY: Doubleday, 1970) and *Reports of the Trials of Colonel Aaron Burr*, 2 vols. (New York: Da Capo, 1969).

30. Edward Corwin, *John Marshall and the Constitution* (New Haven, CT: Yale University Press, 1919), 95; and Malone, *Jefferson the President: Second Term, 1805–1809*, 314–20.

31. Corwin, *John Marshall*, 98.

32. Malone, *Jefferson the President: Second Term, 1805–1809*, 383–85; and Herbert Heater, "Non-Importation 1806–1812," *Journal of Economic History* 1 (1941): 150–78.

33. Malone, *Jefferson the President: Second Term, 1805–1809*, 436, 452, 473; Burton Spivak, *Jefferson's English Crisis* (Charlottesville: University Press of Virginia, 1979); Herbert Briggs, *The Doctrine of Continuous Voyage*, vol. 44 in Studies in History and Political Science (Baltimore: Johns Hopkins University Press, 1926); Douglas W. Tanner, "Jefferson, Impressment, and the Rejection of the Monroe-Pinkney Treaty," *Essays in History* 13 (1968): 7–26; Anthony Steel, "Impressment in the Monroe-Pinkney Treaty," *American Historical Review* 57 (1952): 352–69; James F. Zimmerman, *Impressment of American Seamen* (New York: Columbia University Press, 1925); and Bradford Perkins, *Prologue to War: The First Rapprochement: England and the United States* (Berkeley and Los Angeles: University of California Press, 1955).

34. Reginald C. Stuart, *The Half-Way Pacifist* (Toronto: University of Toronto Press, 1978); Louis Sears, *Jefferson and the Embargo* (Durham, NC: Duke

University Press, 1927); Schuyler D. Hoslett, "Jefferson and England: The Embargo as a Measure of Coercion," *Americana* 34 (1940): 39–54; Richard Mannix, "Gallatin, Jefferson, and the Embargo of 1808," *Diplomatic History* 3 (1979): 151–72; Nelson S. Dearmont, "Federalist Attitudes toward Government Secrecy in the Age of Jefferson," *Historian* 37 (February 1975): 227–40; Merrill D. Peterson, "Thomas Jefferson and Commercial Policy, 1783–1793," *William and Mary Quarterly* 22, 3rd series (October 1965): 584–610; Milton B. Rich, *The Presidents and Civil Disorder* (Washington, DC: Brookings Institution Press, 1941), 31–37; and David Lindsay, "George Canning and Jefferson's Embargo, 1807–1809," *Tyler's Quarterly* 1 (1952): 43–47.

35. Walter Wilson Jennings, *The American Embargo, 1807–1809*, vol. 8, University of Iowa Studies in the Social Sciences (Iowa City: University of Iowa, 1921).

36. Malone, *Jefferson the President: Second Term, 1805–1809*, chap. 31, quotation on page 668.

Chapter 3: Andrew Jackson:
The President as a Tribune of the People

1. Albert Somit, "The Political and Administrative Ideas of Andrew Jackson," (PhD diss., University of Chicago, 1947), 45.

2. Ibid., 19.

3. Ibid., 13. The major biography of Jackson is Robert V. Remini, *Andrew Jackson*, 3 vols. (New York: Harper & Row, 1977–1984). Also of use are his *The Election of Andrew Jackson* (Philadelphia: Lippincott, 1963); *The Revolutionary Age of Andrew Jackson* (New York: Avon, 1976); and *Martin Van Buren and the Making of the Democratic Party* (New York: Columbia University Press, 1962). Of interest are Jon Meacham, *American Lion: Andrew Jackson in the White House* (New York: Random House, 2008); and Ronald P. Formisano, "Towards a Reorientation of Jacksonian Politics," *Journal of American History* 63 (June 1976): 42–65. Other biographies include Harold C. Syrett, *Andrew Jackson* (Indianapolis, IN: Bobbs-Merrill, 1953); J. W. Ward, *Andrew Jackson* (New York: Oxford University Press, 1955); William G. Summer, *Andrew Jackson as a Public Man* (Boston: Houghton Mifflin, 1882); James Parton, *Life of Andrew Jackson*, 3 vols. (Boston: Houghton Mifflin, 1859) and *Presidency of Andrew Jackson* (New York: Harper, 1867); Marquis James, *Andrew Jackson*, 2 vols. (Indianapolis, IN: Bobbs-Merrill, 1933, 1937); and John Spencer Bassett, *Life of Andrew Jackson* (New York: Scribner, 1916).

4. Somit, "Political and Administrative Ideas of Andrew Jackson," 22; and Edwin A. Miles, "The Jacksonian Era," in *Writing Southern History*, ed. Arthur S. Link and Rembert W. Patrick (Baton Rouge: Louisiana State University Press, 1966), 125–46.

5. Robert Remini, *Andrew Jackson and the Course of American Freedom* (vol. 2 of his biography), 16–17.

6. Ibid., 173.

7. Ibid., 179; see also Remini, *Election of Andrew Jackson*, passim.

8. Remini, *Andrew Jackson and the Course of American Freedom*, 189.

9. Ibid., 199.

10. Ibid., 218; Arthur M. Schlesinger, *Age of Jackson* (Boston: Little, Brown, 1945), chaps. 21 and 32, and a useful later review in the *New York Review of Books*, December 7, 1989, 48–52.

11. Remini, *Andrew Jackson and the Course of American Freedom*, 233–35.

12. Claude Bowers, *The Party Battles of the Jackson Period* (Boston: Houghton Mifflin, 1922); Richard B. Latner, *The Presidency of Andrew Jackson* (Athens: University of Georgia Press, 1979); and Sean Wilentz, *The Rise of American Democracy* (New York: Norton, 2005).

13. Remini, *Andrew Jackson and the Course of American Freedom*, 241–47, and "Martin Van Buren and the Tariff of Abominations," *American Historical Review* 63 (July 1958): 903–17.

14. Arthur H. De Rosier Jr., *The Removal of the Choctaw Indians* (Knoxville: University of Tennessee Press, 1970); Michael P. Rogin, *Fathers and Children: Jackson and the Subjugation of the American Indian* (New York: Knopf, 1975); F. P. Prucha, "Andrew Jackson's Indian Policy," *Journal of American History* 56 (December 1969): 527–39; Robert Remini, *The Legacy of Andrew Jackson* (Baton Rouge: Louisiana State University Press, 1988); Ronald N. Satz, *American Indian Policy in the Jacksonian Era* (Lincoln: University of Nebraska Press, 1975); Herman J. Violan, *Thomas L. McKenney: Architect of America's Early Indian Policy* (Chicago: Swallow Press, 1974); and Joseph C. Burke, "The Cherokee Cases," *Stanford Law Review* 21 (February 1969): 500–31.

15. Remini, *Andrew Jackson and the Course of American Freedom*, 293–304.

16. Ibid., 368; Schlesinger, *Age of Jackson*, chaps. 7–10; Leonard D. White, *The Jacksonians* (New York: Macmillan, 1954), chap. 24; and John M. McFaul, *The Politics of Jacksonian Finance* (Ithaca, NY: Cornell University Press, 1972).

17. Remini, *Andrew Jackson and the Course of American Freedom*, 370–72.

18. Ibid., 390–92.

19. Robert Remini, *Andrew Jackson and the Course of American Democracy* (vol. 3 of his biography), passim; Chauncey S. Boucher, *Nullification Controversy in South Carolina* (New York: Russell & Russell, 1968); William W. Freehling, *Prelude to Civil War: Nullification Controversy in South Carolina, 1816–1832* (New York: Harper & Row, 1965); Frederic Bancroft, *Calhoun and the South Carolina Nullification Movement* (Baltimore: Johns Hopkins University Press, 1928); and Paul Bergeron, "The Nullification Controversy Revisited," *Tennessee Historical Quarterly* 35 (1976): 263–75.

20. Merrill Petersen, *Olive Branch and Sword* (Baton Rouge: Louisiana State University Press, 1982).

21. Remini, *Andrew Jackson and the Course of American Democracy*, 70–75.

22. Ibid., 83.

23. Ibid., 106–11.

24. Ibid., 128.

25. Ibid., 143; Schlesinger, *Age of Jackson*, chaps. 18 and 19.

26. Rogin, *Fathers and Children*, passim; Richard Drinnon, *Facing West* (New York: New American Library, 1980); Remini, *Andrew Jackson and the Course of American Democracy*, 300–12; and citations in note 14.

27. John M. Belohlavek, *"Let the Eagle Soar": The Foreign Policy of Andrew Jackson* (Lincoln: University of Nebraska Press, 1985), 2.

28. Ibid., 28.

29. Ibid., 113.

30. Ibid., 119; Carl Schurz, *Life of Henry Clay* (Boston: Houghton Mifflin, 1887), chap. 16; K. Jack Bauer, "The United States Navy and Texas Independence," *Military Affairs* (April 1970): 44–48; E. C. Barker, *President Jackson and the Texas Revolution* (n.p., 1907), 789–809; Joseph C. McElhannon, "Relations between Imperial Mexico and the United States," in *Essays in Mexican History*, ed. Thomas E. Cotnet and Carlos E. Castaneda (Austin: University of Texas Press, 1958), 127–41; Richard R. Stenberg, "The Texas Schemes of Jackson and Houston, 1829–1836," *Southwestern Social Science Quarterly* 15 (1934): 229–50; and Donald Day and Harry Herbert Ullom, eds., *The Autobiography of Sam Houston* (Norman: University of Oklahoma Press, 1954).

31. Remini, *Andrew Jackson and the Course of American Democracy*, chaps. 19 and 23.

32. Ibid., 315–27.

Chapter 4: James K. Polk:
The Arts of Waging Conflict

1. Martha McBride Morrel, *Young Hickory* (New York: Dutton, 1949); Charles Sellers, *James K. Polk: Jacksonian, 1795–1845* (Princeton, NJ: Princeton University Press, 1957), and his companion volume *James K. Polk: Continentalist, 1843–1846* (Princeton, NJ: Princeton University Press, 1966); Eugene I. McCormac, *James K. Polk* (Berkeley and Los Angeles: University of California Press, 1922); and Robert W. Merry, *A Country of Vast Designs: James K. Polk, the Mexican War, and the Conquest of the American Continent* (New York: Simon & Schuster, 2009).

2. Charles A. McCoy, *Polk and the Presidency* (Austin: University of Texas Press, 1960), 53, 70, 74; Albert K. Weinberg, *Manifest Destiny* (Baltimore: Johns Hopkins University Press, 1935); Frederick Merk, *Manifest Destiny and Mission in American History* (New York: Knopf, 1963) and *The Monroe Doctrine and American Expansion* (New York: Knopf, 1966); Thomas Hietala, *Manifest Destiny* (Ithaca, NY: Cornell University Press, 1985); Kinley J. Brauer, *Cotton versus Conscience* (Lexington: University of Kentucky Press, 1967); Richard R. Stenberg, "Polk and Fremont 1845–1846," *Pacific Historical Review* 7 (September 1938): 211–27, and "Failure of Polk's Mexican War Intrigue of 1845," *Pacific Historical Review* 4 (1935): 39–68; William C. Binkley, *The Expansionist Movement in Texas, 1836–1850* (New York: Da Capo, 1970); Fred Somkin, *Unquiet Eagle* (Ithaca, NY: Cornell University

Press, 1967); George L. Rives, "Mexican Diplomacy on the Eve of War with the United States," *American Historical Review* 18 (January 1913): 275–94; Eugene C. Barker, "The Influence of Slavery in the Colonization of Texas," *Mississippi Valley Historical Review* 9 (June 1924): 3–36; John C. McElhannon, "Relations between Imperial Mexico and the United States, 1821–1823," in *Essays in Mexican History*, ed. Thomas Cotner and Carlos E. Castaneda (Austin: University of Texas, Institute of Latin American Studies, 1958), 127–43; and Donald Day and Harry Herbert Ullom, eds., *The Autobiography of Sam Houston* (Norman: University of Oklahoma Press, 1954), chap. 16.

3. McCoy, *Polk and the Presidency*, 82.

4. Frederick Merk, *The Oregon Question* (Cambridge, MA: Harvard University Press, 1967); Norman A. Graebner, *Empire on the Pacific* (New York: Ronald Press, 1955); and Thomas P. Martin, "Free Trade and the Oregon Question, 1842–1846," in *Facts and Factors in Economic History*, ed. Edwin Francis Gay (Cambridge, MA: Harvard University Press, 1932).

5. McCoy, *Polk and the Presidency*, 92.

6. Ibid., 96.

7. Paul H. Bergeron, *The Presidency of James K. Polk* (Lawrence: University Press of Kansas, 1987), chap. 4; John Seigentheler, *James K. Polk* (New York: Henry Holt, 2003); Robert W. Johannsen, *To the Halls of the Montezumas* (New York: Oxford University Press, 1985); Glenn W. Price, *Origins of the War with Mexico* (Austin: University of Texas Press, 1967); David M. Pletchan, *The Diplomacy of Annexation* (Columbia: University of Missouri Press, 1973); John H. Schroeder, *Mr. Polk's War* (Madison: University of Wisconsin Press, 1973); and John Eisenhower, *So Far from God* (New York: Random House, 1989).

8. McCoy, *Polk and the Presidency*, 123, 131.

9. Bergeron, *Presidency of James K. Polk*, chap. 7.

10. McCoy, *Polk and the Presidency*, 155.

11. Ibid., 164.

12. Ibid., 196; Eric Foner, "The Wilmot Proviso," *Journal of American History* 56 (April 1969): 262–79; and Chauncey S. Boucher, "That Aggressive Slavocracy," *Mississippi Valley Historical Review* 8 (June 1921): 113–79.

13. McCoy, *Polk and the Presidency*, 178.

Chapter 5: Abraham Lincoln:
The Commander in Chief Goes to War

1. The historical literature on Lincoln is immense, and I have included only the sources from which I have drawn specific judgments and information. For a good bibliographical essay on the period, see James M. McPherson, *Battle Cry of Freedom* (New York: Oxford University Press, 1988). A useful modern biography is Stephen B. Oates, *With Malice toward None* (New York: Harper & Row, 1977). My favorites, though, are the two volumes by William Lee Miller: *Lincoln's Virtue*

(New York: Vintage, 2003) and *President Lincoln* (New York: Knopf, 2008). The single most important source for this narrative is James G. Randall, *Lincoln the President*, 4 vols. (New York: Scribner, 1945–1955), although I do not accept the basic premise that Lincoln was simply a conservative. Also of use are Norman A. Graebner, *The Enduring Lincoln* (Urbana: University of Illinois Press, 1959); Joel H. Sibley, "Always a Whig in Politics," paper presented at the Annual Symposium of the Abraham Lincoln Association, February 12, 1986; and M. E. Bradford, "Lincoln and the Language of Hate and Fear: A View from the South," *Continuity* 9 (1985): 87–108.

2. This discovery of the nonliberal side of Lincoln is expressed in Richard Hofstadter, *The American Political Tradition* (New York: Knopf, 1948), chap. 5.

3. Randall, *Lincoln*, 1:123. For very different understandings of Lincoln and his formative years, see Dwight G. Anderson, *Abraham Lincoln: The Quest for Immortality* (New York: Knopf, 1982); George B. Forgie, *Patricide in the House Divided* (New York: Norton, 1979); Charles B. Stozier, *Lincoln's Quest for Union* (New York: Basic Books, 1982); Stephen B. Oates, *Abraham Lincoln: The Man behind the Myths* (New York: Signet, 1984); Donald Riddle, *Congressman A. Lincoln* (Urbana: University of Illinois Press, 1957); Gabor Boritt, ed., *The Historian's Lincoln* (Urbana: University of Illinois Press, 1988); David Donald, *Lincoln Reconsidered* (New York: Vintage, 1961), chaps. 4, 7, and 10; Carl Sandburg, *Abraham Lincoln: The Prairie Years* (New York: Harcourt Brace, 1929); Don E. Fehrenbacher, *Prelude to Greatness* (Stanford, CA: Stanford University Press, 1962); and David M. Potter, *The Impending Crisis* (New York: Harper & Row, 1971).

4. Randall, *Lincoln*, 1:206; Reinhard H. Luthin, *First Lincoln Campaign* (Cambridge, MA: Harvard University Press, 1944); and Frederick C. Luebke, ed., *Ethnic Voters in the Election of Lincoln* (Lincoln: University of Nebraska Press, 1971).

5. Randall, *Lincoln*, 1:207; David M. Potter, *Lincoln and His Party in the Secession Crisis* (New Haven, CT: Yale University Press, 1942); Harold M. Hyman, "The Narrow Escape from a 'Compromise of 1860': Secession and the Constitution," in *Freedom and Reform*, ed. Harold M. Hyman and Leonard Levy (New York: Harper & Row, 1967), 149–66; Eric Foner, *Free Soil, Free Labor, Free Men* (New York: Oxford University Press, 1970); and David Donald, *Charles Sumner and the Coming of the Civil War* (New York: Knopf, 1960).

6. Randall, *Lincoln*, 1:215.

7. Ibid., 225.

8. Ibid., 235.

9. The standard study of the Fort Sumter crisis is Richard N. Current, *Lincoln and the First Shot* (Philadelphia: Lippincott, 1963). Also useful is Potter, *Lincoln and His Party*, 337–66; Potter, *Impending Crisis*, 570–83; and Kenneth Stampp, *And the War Came* (Chicago: University of Chicago Press, 1964).

10. Randall, *Lincoln*, 1:344.

11. Ibid., 350.

12. Michael P. Riccards, "The Presidency in Sickness and in Health," *Presidential Studies Quarterly* 7 (Summer 1977): 215–30.

13. David Donald, *Lincoln Reconsidered*, 187–208.

14. Clinton Rossiter, *Constitutional Dictatorship* (Princeton, NJ: Princeton University Press, 1948); and Edward S. Corwin, *The President: Office and Powers, 1787–1984*, 5th ed. (New York: New York University Press, 1984), 167, 264–67, 495–97; see also Charles M. Hubbard, ed., *Lincoln Reshapes the Presidency* (Macon, GA: Mercer University Press, 2003); and Geoffrey Perret, *Lincoln's War* (New York: Random House, 2004).

15. Randall, *Lincoln*, 1:228–30.

16. The best study of these legal problems and difficulties remains James G. Randall, *Constitutional Problems under Lincoln* (Urbana: University of Illinois Press, 1951), which is supplemented in an informed way by Harold M. Hyman, *A More Perfect Union* (Boston: Houghton Mifflin, 1975); and Mark Neely Jr., *The Fate of Liberty* (New York: Oxford University Press, 1991).

17. Randall, *Lincoln*, 2:7.

18. Ibid., 28.

19. Oates, *With Malice toward None*, 224, 225, 241–43.

20. Foreign policy is considered in Norman A. Graebner, "Northern Diplomacy and European Neutrality," in *Why the North Won the War*, ed. David Donald (New York: Macmillan, 1962), 55–78; and Jay Monaghan, *Diplomat in Carpet Slippers* (Indianapolis, IN: Bobbs-Merrill, 1945).

21. For a balanced judgment, see Stephen W. Sears, *George B. McClellan* (New York: Ticknor and Fields, 1988).

22. Randall, *Lincoln*, 2:69.

23. Burke Davis, *They Called Him Stonewall* (New York: Fairfax Press, 1988).

24. Randall, *Lincoln*, 2:92.

25. T. Harry Williams, *Lincoln and the Radicals* (Madison: University of Wisconsin Press, 1960).

26. On confiscation, see J. G. Randall and David Donald, *The Civil War and Reconstruction* (Boston: Heath, 1961), 372–73; Hans L. Trefoussse, *The Radical Republicans* (New York: Knopf, 1969); James A. Rawley, ed., *Lincoln and Civil War Politics* (New York: Holt, Rinehart, and Winston, 1969); Edward Boykin, *Congress and the Civil War* (New York: McBride, 1955); Robert S. Harper, *Lincoln and the Press* (New York: McGraw-Hill, 1951); J. F. C. Fuller, *Grant and Lee* (London: Eyre and Spottiswoode, 1932); and Nancy S. Anderson and Dwight Anderson, *The Generals* (New York: Knopf, 1988). The president's ambivalences are discussed in Kenneth Stampp, *The Era of Reconstruction, 1865–1877* (New York: Knopf, 1965), 44–45.

27. The emancipation question is also presented in James M. McPherson, *The Struggle for Equality* (Princeton, NJ: Princeton University Press, 1964); LaWanda Cox, *Lincoln and Black Freedom* (Urbana: University of Illinois Press, 1985); and

James M. McPherson, *The Negro Civil War* (New York: Pantheon, 1965). The crucial issue of African Americans in the Union army is presented in Joseph T. Glatthaar, *Forged in Battle* (New York: Free Press, 1990). About 180,000 African Americans served in the Union army, and more than 36,000 died in the war. On Greeley, see Randall, *Lincoln*, 2:158.

28. Christopher Dell, *Lincoln and the War Democrats* (Madison, NJ: Fairleigh Dickinson University Press, 1975); Joel Silbey, *A Respectable Minority* (New York: Norton, 1977); and Frank L. Klement, *Copperheads in the Middle West* (Chicago: University of Chicago Press, 1960).

29. William F. Zornow, *Lincoln and the Party Divided* (Westport, CT: Greenwood Press, 1972); William B. Hesseltine, *Lincoln and the War Governors* (New York: Knopf, 1948); Carl R. Fish, "Lincoln and the Patronage," *American Historical Review* 8 (1924): 53–69; Harry J. Carman and Reinhart H. Luthin, *Lincoln and the Patronage* (Gloucester, UK: Peter Smith, 1964); and Allan G. Bogue, *The Congressman's Civil War* (New York: Cambridge University Press, 1989).

30. Oates, *With Malice toward None*, 327–30.

31. Randall, *Lincoln*, 2:241.

32. Ibid., 255.

33. Ibid., 288.

34. Richard E. Beringer et al., *Why the South Lost the Civil War* (Athens: University of Georgia Press, 1986); and David M. Potter, "Jefferson Davis and the Political Factors in Confederate Defeat," in *Why the North Won the Civil War*, ed. David Donald (New York: Macmillan, 1962), 91–112.

35. Clement Eaton, *Jefferson Davis* (New York: Free Press, 1977), 127; Reinbert W. Patrick, *Jefferson Davis and His Cabinet* (Baton Rouge: Louisiana State University Press, 1944); D. S. Freeman, *The South to Posterity* (New York: Scribner, 1939); Paul D. Escort, *After Secession: Jefferson Davis and the Failure of Confederate Nationalism* (Baton Rouge: Louisiana State University Press, 1978); and William C. Davis, *Jefferson Davis* (New York: HarperCollins, 1991).

36. Eaton, *Jefferson Davis*, 139.

37. Ibid., 144.

38. Eli N. Evans, *Judah P. Benjamin: The Jewish Confederate* (New York: Free Press, 1988).

39. Emory M. Thomas, *The Confederate Nation, 1861–1865* (New York: Harper & Row, 1979).

40. Eaton, *Jefferson Davis*, chap. 22.

41. Wilfred Buck Years, *The Confederate Congress* (Athens: University of Georgia Press, 1960).

42. Hofstadter, *American Political Tradition*, chap. 5.

43. Randall, *Lincoln*, 3:135–36.

44. Corwin, *The President*, 166–68; Richard P. Longaker, *Presidency and Civil Liberties* (Ithaca, NY: Cornell University Press, 1961); and Herman Belz, "Lincoln and the Constitution," *Congress and the Presidency* 15 (Autumn 1988): 147–64.

45. Corwin, *The President*, 165–66, 266, 288, 356, 501–2.

46. Randall, *Lincoln*, 3:218.

47. Oates, *Abraham Lincoln*, 120–21, 18–20.

48. Randall, *Lincoln*, 3:208.

49. Dell, *Lincoln and the War Democrats*, chap. 12; quote on Vallandingham in Randall, *Lincoln*, 3:227.

50. Randall, *Lincoln*, 3:130.

51. Oates, *With Malice toward None*, chap. 10.

52. Randall, *Lincoln*, 4:248.

53. Ibid., chaps. 7 and 11; and Harold M. Hyman, "Election of 1864," in *History of American Presidential Elections, 1789–1968*, vol. 2, ed. Arthur M. Schlesinger Jr. and Fred Israel (New York: Chelsea Publishing Company, 1985).

54. William S. McFeeley, *Grant* (New York: Norton, 1981), chaps. 12 and 13; and Randall, *Lincoln*, 4:150. Also of interest are the works of Bruce Catton, some of which are contained in *Bruce Catton's Civil War* (New York: Fairfax Press, 1984); Selby Foote, *Civil War*, 3 vols. (New York: Vintage, 1968); and also Trevor H. Dupuy, *Military Life of A. Lincoln: Commander in Chief* (New York: Franklin Watts, 1969); T. Harry Williams, *Lincoln and His Generals* (New York: Knopf, 1952); Kenneth P. Williams, *Lincoln Finds a General* (New York: Macmillan, 1950); John Shepley Tilley, *Lincoln Takes Command* (Chapel Hill: University of North Carolina Press, 1941); and Gabor S. Boritt, ed., *Lincoln, the War President* (New York: Oxford University Press, 1992).

55. Cox, *Lincoln and Black Freedom*, passim; Eric Foner, *Reconstruction* (New York: Harper, 1988), chaps. 1 and 2; William Hesseltine, *Lincoln's Plan for Reconstruction* (New York: Quadrangle, 1960); William Harris, *Presidential Reconstruction in Mississippi* (Baton Rouge: Louisiana State University Press, 1967); and a more sympathetic Hans J. Trefousse, *Radical Republicans* (New York: Knopf, 1969).

56. Williams, *Lincoln and the Radicals*, chaps. 11, 13, and 14.

57. Randall, *Lincoln*, 4:193.

58. Hyman, *A More Perfect Union*, 267–70.

59. Randall, *Lincoln*, 4:310; Oates, *With Malice toward None*, 404–5.

Chapter 6: Theodore Roosevelt: The Dynamics of Domestic Reform

1. Edmund Morris, *The Rise of Theodore Roosevelt* (New York: Coward, McCann & Geoghegan, 1979), *Theodore Rex* (New York: Random House, 2011), and *Colonel Roosevelt* (New York: Random House, 2010); William Gatewood, *Theodore Roosevelt and the Art of Controversy* (Baton Rouge: Louisiana State University Press, 1970); William H. Harbaugh, *Power and Responsibility* (New York: Farrar, Straus & Giroux, 1961); Carleton Putnam, *Theodore Roosevelt*, vol. 1 (New York: Scribner, 1958); Elting E. Morison and John Blum, eds., *Letters of Theodore Roosevelt*, 8 vols. (Cambridge, MA: Harvard University Press, 1951–1954);

G. Wallace Chessman, *Governor Theodore Roosevelt* (Cambridge, MA: Harvard University Press, 1965); George E. Mowry, *The Era of Theodore Roosevelt* (New York: Harper, 1958), 109; and Thomas Dyer, *Theodore Roosevelt and the Idea of Race* (Baton Rouge: Louisiana State University Press, 1980). On the environment, see Douglas Brinkley, *The Wilderness Warrior* (New York: HarperCollins, 2009).

2. Mowry, *Era of Theodore Roosevelt*, 100.

3. Richard Hofstadter, *The American Political Tradition* (New York: Knopf, 1948), chap. 9. A more critical view is Jim Powell, *Bully Boy: The Truth about Theodore Roosevelt's Legacy* (New York: Crown Forum, 2006).

4. Harbaugh, *Power and Responsibility*, chap. 9.

5. Mowry, *Era of Theodore Roosevelt*, 129.

6. Balthasar Meyer, *A History of the Northern Securities Case* (Madison: University of Wisconsin Press, 1906); Frederick L. Allen, *The Great Pierpont Morgan* (New York: Harper, 1949); and Ron Chernow, *The House of Morgan* (New York: Atlantic Monthly Press, 1990).

7. Henry F. Pringle, *Theodore Roosevelt* (New York: Harcourt Brace, 1931), 253–54.

8. Mowry, *Era of Theodore Roosevelt*, 135.

9. Pringle, *Theodore Roosevelt*, 271.

10. Hofstadter, *American Political Tradition*, chap. 9; and Dyer, *Theodore Roosevelt and the Idea of Race*, passim.

11. Pringle, *Theodore Roosevelt*, 279–300. Other studies of his Latin American diplomacy are Howard Beale, *Theodore Roosevelt and the Rise of America to World Power* (Baltimore: Johns Hopkins University Press, 1956); William E. Leuchtenburg, "Progressivism and Imperialism: The Progressive Movement and American Foreign Policy, 1898–1916," *Mississippi Valley Historical Review* 39 (December 1952): 483–504; Dexter Perkins, *The United States and the Caribbean* (Cambridge, MA: Harvard University Press, 1947), and *The Monroe Doctrine, 1867–1907* (Baltimore: Johns Hopkins University Press, 1937); H. C. Hill, *Roosevelt and the Caribbean* (Chicago: University of Chicago Press, 1927); and S. W. Livermore, "Theodore Roosevelt, the American Navy, and the Venezuelan Crisis," *American Historical Review* 51 (April 1946): 452–71.

12. Pringle, *Theodore Roosevelt*, 298.

13. Ibid., 301–38; Harbaugh, *Power and Responsibility*, 194–204; D. C. Miner, *The Fight for the Panama Route* (New York: Columbia University Press, 1940); and M. P. Duval, *And the Mountains Will Move* (Stanford, CA: Stanford University Press, 1947).

14. Pringle, *Theodore Roosevelt*, 339–58.

15. Beale, *Theodore Roosevelt and the Rise of America to World Power*, passim; Alfred W. Griswold, *The Far Eastern Policy of the United States* (New York: Harcourt Brace, 1938); Tyler Dennett, *Roosevelt and the Russo-Japanese War* (Gloucester, UK: Peter Smith, 1959); Thomas A. Bailey, "The World Crisis of the American Battleship Fleet, 1907–1909," *Pacific Historical Review* 1 (December 1932): 389–

423; Bailey, "The Root-Takahira Agreement of 1908," *Pacific Historical Review* 9 (March 1940): 19–40; Delbar McKee, *Chinese Exclusion versus the Open Door* (Detroit, MI: Wayne State University Press, 1977); and Eugene Trani, *The Treaty of Portsmouth* (Lexington: University of Kentucky Press, 1969).

16. Eugene N. Anderson, *The First Moroccan Crisis, 1904–1906* (Chicago: University of Chicago Press, 1930).

17. Thomas A. Bailey, *Theodore Roosevelt and the Japanese American Crisis* (Palo Alto, CA: Stanford University Press, 1934); and Pringle, *Theodore Roosevelt*, 410.

18. Harbaugh, *Power and Responsibility*, part 4; and Pringle, *Theodore Roosevelt*, 414.

19. Pringle, *Theodore Roosevelt*, 428.

20. Ibid., 442 and passim, which includes Pringle's discussions of the deals.

21. Harbaugh, *Power and Responsibility*, 290–93.

22. David H. Burton, *The Learned Presidency* (Rutherford, NJ: Fairleigh Dickinson University Press, 1988).

23. John Morton Blum, *The Republican Roosevelt* (Cambridge, MA: Harvard University Press, 1954), 2.

24. Ibid., 12.

25. Ibid., chap. 1; and Lewis L. Gould, *The William Howard Taft Presidency* (Lawrence: University Press of Kansas, 2009).

Chapter 7: Woodrow Wilson: The Progressive Agenda at Home and Across the World

1. Any treatment of Woodrow Wilson is heavily indebted to the fine scholarship of Arthur S. Link, the editor of *The Papers of Woodrow Wilson* (Princeton, NJ: Princeton University Press, 1966–1993) and the author of a stream of biographies and monographs on this period, some cited below. Also of interest are John Milton Cooper Jr., *Woodrow Wilson* (New York: Knopf, 2009); Ray S. Baker, *Woodrow Wilson: Life and Letters*, 8 vols. (Garden City, NY: Doubleday; Page; and Doubleday, Doran, 1927–1939); Henry W. Bragdon, *Woodrow Wilson: The Academic Years* (Cambridge, MA: Harvard University Press, 1967); John M. Cooper, *The Warrior and the Priest* (Cambridge, MA: Harvard University Press, 1983); Sigmund Freud and William C. Bullitt, *Thomas Woodrow Wilson* (London: Weidenfeld & Nicolson, 1966); John M. Mulder, *Woodrow Wilson: The Years of Preparation* (Princeton, NJ: Princeton University Press, 1978); George C. Osborn, *Woodrow Wilson: The Early Years* (Baton Rouge: Louisiana State University Press, 1968); James Axtell, *The Making of Princeton University* (Princeton, NJ: Princeton University Press, 2004); W. Barksdale Maynard, *Woodrow Wilson: Princeton to the Presidency* (New Haven, CT: Yale University Press, 2008); Edwin A. Weinstein, *Woodrow Wilson* (Princeton, NJ: Princeton University Press, 1981); Neils Aage Thorsen, *The Political Thought of Woodrow Wilson, 1875–1910* (Princeton, NJ: Princeton University Press, 1988); and Arthur Walworth, *Woodrow Wilson*, 2nd ed., 2 vols. in one (Baltimore: Penguin, 1969).

2. Arthur S. Link, *Wilson: The Road to the White House* (Princeton, NJ: Princeton University Press, 1947).

3. Arthur S. Link, *Woodrow Wilson and the Progressive Era* (New York: Harper, 1954), 40–43.

4. Ibid., 47.

5. Ibid., 80.

6. Selig Adler, "Bryan and Wilsonian Caribbean Penetration," *Hispanic American Historical Review* 20 (May 1940): 198–226.

7. Link, *Woodrow Wilson and the Progressive Era*, 84–85.

8. Issac J. Cox, *Nicaragua and the United States, 1909–1927* (Boston: World Peace Foundation, 1927).

9. Link, *Woodrow Wilson and the Progressive Era*, 103–5, and *Wilson the Diplomatist* (Chicago: Quadrangle Books, 1957), chap. 1.

10. Link, *Wilson the Diplomatist*, 17–24; Howard F. Cline, *The United States and Mexico* (Cambridge, MA: Harvard University Press, 1953); Stuart A. MacCorkle, *American Policy of Recognition towards Mexico* (Baltimore: Johns Hopkins University Press, 1933); and Link, *Woodrow Wilson and the Progressive Era*, chap. 5.

11. Walworth, *Woodrow Wilson*, book 2, 1–12; and Arthur S. Link, *The Struggle for Neutrality, 1914–1915* (Princeton, NJ: Princeton University Press, 1960).

12. Link, *Woodrow Wilson and the Progressive Era*, 221–22.

13. Arthur S. Link, *Wilson: Confusions and Crises, 1915–1916* (Princeton, NJ: Princeton University Press, 1964); and Ernest May, *The World War and American Isolation, 1914–1917* (Cambridge, MA: Harvard University Press, 1959).

14. See Link, *Woodrow Wilson and the Progressive Era*, 253–55; and A. J. P. Taylor, *Illustrated History of the First World War* (New York: Putnam, 1964), for a quick summary aimed at the nonscholarly audience.

15. Link, *Woodrow Wilson and the Progressive Era*, chap. 10; and Richard Piper, *The Russian Revolution* (New York: Knopf, 1990).

16. Taylor, *Illustrated History of the First World War*, chaps. 1–4; Keith Robbins, *The First World War* (New York: Oxford University Press, 1985); Winston S. Churchill, *The Unknown War: The Eastern Front* (New York: Scribner, 1931); George F. Kennan, *The Fateful Alliance* (New York: Pantheon, 1984); Norman Stone, *The Eastern Front, 1914–1917* (New York: Scribner, 1978); D. F. Fleming, *The Origins and Legacies of World War I* (New York: Doubleday, 1968); Fritz Fischer, *Germany's Aims in the First World War* (New York: Norton, 1967); Graydon A. Tunstall Jr., *Planning for War against Russia and Serbia* (New York: Columbia University Press, 1994); John M. Blum, *Woodrow Wilson and the Politics of Morality* (Boston: Little, Brown, 1956); Sidney B. Fay, *The Origins of the World War* (New York: Macmillan, 1949); and Patrick Devlin, *Too Proud to Fight* (New York: Oxford University Press, 1975).

17. F. Lee Burns, *Europe since 1914* (New York: Appleton-Century-Crofts, 1949), chap. 1; and Correlli Barnett, *The Great War* (New York: Putnam, 1979).

18. Robert H. Ferrell, *Woodrow Wilson and World War I* (New York: Harper & Row, 1985), chaps. 1–3.

19. Ferrell, *Woodrow Wilson and World War I*, 36–63; and F. W. O'Brien, ed., *Hoover-Wilson Wartime Correspondence* (Ames: Iowa State University Press, 1974).

20. Josephus Daniels, *The Wilson Era* (Chapel Hill: University of North Carolina Press, 1946), 160–71; Daniel R. Beaver, *Newton D. Baker and the American War Effort, 1917–1919* (Lincoln: University of Nebraska Press, 1966); Edward M. Coffman, *The Hilt of the Sword* (Madison: University of Wisconsin Press, 1966); Peyton C. Marsh, *The Nation at War* (Garden City, NY: Doubleday, Doran, 1932); and Christopher Ray, "Woodrow Wilson as Commander-in-Chief," *History* 43 (April 1993): 24–30.

21. Ferrell, *Woodrow Wilson and World War I*, chap. 5; Kenneth O. Morgan, "Lloyd George's Premiership," *Historical Journal* 13 (1970): 130–57; David R. Woodward, *Lloyd George and the Generals* (Newark: University of Delaware Press, 1983); David R. Woodward, "Britain in a Continental War," *Albion* 12 (Spring 1980): 37–65; John Turner, *Lloyd George's Secretariat* (New York: Cambridge University Press, 1980); Peter E. Wright, *At the Supreme War Council* (New York: Putnam, 1921); Tim Travese, *The Killing Ground* (London: Allen & Unwin, 1987); David R. Watson, *Georges Clemenceau* (New York: David McKay, 1976); Geoffrey Bruun, *Clemenceau* (Hamden, CT: Archon, 1968); Gregor Dallas, *At the Heart of a Tiger* (New York: Carroll & Gray, 1993); Volker R. Berghahn and Martin Kitchen, eds., *Germany in the Age of Total War* (Totowa, NJ: Barnes and Noble, 1981), especially chap. 3 on Rathenau; James Joll, *Intellectuals in Politics* (London: Weidenfeld & Nicolson, 1960), part 2; David Felix, "Walter Rathenau," *European Studies Review* 5 (1975): 69–79; and D. J. Goodspeed, *Ludendorff* (Boston: Houghton Mifflin, 1966), passim.

22. Clinton Rossiter, *Constitutional Democracy* (Princeton, NJ: Princeton University Press, 1948), 242.

23. Ibid., 242.

24. Ibid., 250–53; and Harry N. Scheiber, *The Wilson Administration and Civil Liberties* (Ithaca, NY: Cornell University Press, 1981).

25. Paul Fussell, *The Great War and Modern Memory* (New York: Oxford University Press, 1975); and Arno J. Mayer, *The Persistence of the Old Regime* (New York: Pantheon, 1981).

26. Arthur Walworth, *Wilson and His Peacemakers* (New York: Norton, 1986).

27. Ibid., part 1.

28. Link, *Wilson the Diplomatist*, 100; Watson, *Georges Clemenceau*, passim; and Bruun, *Clemenceau*, passim.

29. Link, *Wilson the Diplomatist*, 105.

30. Ibid., chap. 4; Walworth, *Wilson and His Peacemakers*, parts 3 and 4; David Lloyd George, *The Truth about the Peace Treaties*, 2 vols. (London: V. Gollancz, 1938); Thomas A. Bailey, *Wilson and the Peacemakers* (New York: Macmillan,

1947); Margaret MacMillian, *Paris 1919* (New York: Random House, 2003); Roy W. Curry, *Woodrow Wilson and Far Eastern Policy* (New York: Bookman, 1957); Lloyd C. Gardner, *Wilson and Revolutions* (Philadelphia: Lippincott, 1976); and Arthur S. Link, ed., *Woodrow Wilson and a Revolutionary World* (Chapel Hill: University of North Carolina Press, 1982). The German treaty with the Russians mandated that Russia would lose 32 percent of its cultivable land, 27 percent of its railroads, 54 percent of its industry, and 89 percent of its coal mines. See Alan Bullock, *Hitler and Stalin* (New York: Knopf, 1992), 62.

31. Ferrell, *Woodrow Wilson and World War I*, chap. 10; Lloyd E. Ambrosius, "Wilson, the Republicans, and French Security after World War I," *Journal of American History* 59 (September 1972): 341–52; Daniels, *The Wilson Era*, part 11; and Jeffrey K. Tulis, *The Rhetorical Presidency* (Princeton, NJ: Princeton University Press, 1987), 147–61.

Chapter 8: Franklin D. Roosevelt: The Establishment of the Modern Presidency

1. The secondary literature on Franklin D. Roosevelt's life and administration is extensive, and I have cited only those sources that I have specifically used in this narrative. A useful bibliographical tool is Otis L. Graham and Meghan R. Wander, eds., *Franklin D. Roosevelt: His Life and Times; An Encyclopedic View* (New York: G. K. Hall, 1985). The major studies are Arthur M. Schlesinger Jr., *The Age of Roosevelt*, 3 vols. (Boston: Houghton Mifflin, 1957–1960); Kenneth S. Davis, *FDR*, 5 vols. (New York: Putnam, 1971; Random House, 1985–2007); Frank Freidel, *Roosevelt*, 4 vols. (Boston: Little, Brown, 1952–1973); and Geoffrey C. Ward, *Before the Trumpet* (New York: Harper & Row, 1985) and *First Class Temperament* (New York: Harper, 1989). Also see Jean Edward Smith, *FDR* (New York: Random House, 2007); Bernard Asbell, *The FDR Memoirs* (Garden City, NY: Doubleday, 1973); Raymond Moley, *After Seven Years* (New York: Harper, 1939); Rexford G. Tugwell, *The Democratic Roosevelt* (Garden City, NY: Doubleday, 1957); Frances Perkins, *The Roosevelt I Knew* (New York: Viking, 1946); James MacGregor Burns, *Roosevelt: The Lion and the Fox* (New York: Harcourt Brace and World, 1966); George McJimsey, *The Presidency of Franklin Delano Roosevelt* (Lawrence: University Press of Kansas, 2000); Samuel Rosenman, *Working with Roosevelt* (New York: Harper, 1952); Robert Sherwood, *Roosevelt and Hopkins* (New York: Harper, 1948); Rexford G. Tugwell, *Roosevelt's Revolution* (New York: Macmillan, 1977); and H. W. Brands, *Traitor to His Class* (New York: Doubleday, 2008).

2. Hugh Gregory Gallagher, *FDR's Splendid Deception* (New York: Dodd, Mead, 1985). On FDR and possible brain cancer, see Steven Lomazow and Eric Fetterman, *FDR's Deadly Secret* (New York: Public Affairs, 2009).

3. For the view that administrative chaos was a sign of FDR's brilliance, see Richard Neustadt, *Presidential Power and the Modern Presidency* (New York: Wiley, 1990).

4. Richard Hofstadter, *The American Political Tradition* (New York: Knopf, 1948), chap. 12.

5. Arthur M. Schlesinger Jr., *The Age of Roosevelt*, vol. 2, *The Coming of the New Deal* (Boston: Houghton Mifflin, 1959); Burns, *Roosevelt: The Lion and the Fox*, passim; Elliot A. Rosen, *Hoover, Roosevelt, and the Brains Trust* (New York: Columbia University Press, 1977); Frank Freidel, *Roosevelt: Launching the New Deal* (Boston: Little, Brown, 1973); James E. Sargent, *Roosevelt and the Hundred Days* (New York: Garland, 1981); Ernest K. Lindley, *Roosevelt Revolution* (New York: Viking Press, 1933); Graham J. White, *FDR and the Press* (Chicago: University of Chicago Press, 1979); and Richard W. Steele, *Propaganda in an Open Society* (Westport, CT: Greenwood Press, 1985).

6. Burns, *Roosevelt: The Lion and the Fox*, 188.

7. Paul K. Conkin, *The New Deal* (New York: Thomas Y. Crowell, 1967); and David M. Kennedy, *Freedom from Fear* (New York: Oxford University Press, 1999).

8. Schlesinger, *The Age of Roosevelt*, vol. 2, chaps. 26–31.

9. William Leuchtenburg, *Franklin D. Roosevelt and the New Deal* (New York: Harper & Row, 1963); Irving Bernstein, *The New Deal Collective Bargaining Policy* (Berkeley and Los Angeles: University of California Press, 1950); and Andrew J. Badger, *The New Deal: The Depression, 1937–40* (New York: Noonday, 1989). See also William Ivy Hair, *The Kingfish and His Realm* (Baton Rouge: Louisiana State University Press, 1991), 307.

10. Basil Rauch's *The History of the New Deal* (New York: Creative Age, 1944) is one of the earliest discussions of the distinctions between the first and the second New Deal.

11. Frank Freidel, *Franklin D. Roosevelt: A Rendezvous with Destiny* (Boston: Little, Brown, 1990), chap. 15.

12. Ibid., chap. 16; Burns, *Roosevelt: The Lion and the Fox*, chap. 14, 221, especially as FDR sees himself on the issue as noted below. The "cat" analogy is on page 285.

13. Burns, *Roosevelt: The Lion and the Fox*, 230–34.

14. Ted Morgan, *FDR: A Biography* (New York: Simon & Schuster, 1985); Jeff Shesol, *Supreme Power* (New York: Norton, 2010); Joseph Alsop and Turner Catledge, *The 168 Days* (Garden City, NY: Doubleday and Doran, 1938); William E. Leuchtenburg, "Franklin D. Roosevelt's Supreme Court 'Packing' Plan," in *Essays on the New Deal*, ed. Harold Hollingsworth and William Holmes (Arlington: University of Texas Press, 1969); Paul L. Murphy, *The Constitution in Crisis Times* (New York: Harper & Row, 1972); Robert H. Jackson, *The Struggle for Judicial Supremacy* (New York: Vintage, 1949); and Gregory A. Caldeira, "Public Opinion and the U.S. Supreme Court: FDR's Court Packing Plan," *American Political Science Review* 81 (December 1987): 1139–53. Arthur M. Schlesinger Jr. is quoted (and has reaffirmed to me) as saying that FDR was reportedly willing to defy the Supreme Court to protect economic and political stability in the winter

of 1935, when the Court was expected to overrule the government on gold redemption. FDR was prepared to issue a "dissent" of his own in the form of a set of proclamations and orders nullifying the expected decision. The Court upheld the government, however, by a vote of five to four. See Douglas Muzzlo, *Watergate Games* (New York: New York University Press, 1982), and Noah Feldman, *Scorpions* (New York: Hachette Books, 2010).

15. Burns, *Roosevelt: The Lion and the Fox*, chap. 15.

16. Ibid., chap. 16.

17. Freidel, *Franklin D. Roosevelt: A Rendezvous with Destiny*, chap. 21. FDR feared a rollback of some of the New Deal. He insisted on personal Social Security "accounts" in order to stop Congress from repealing the system later. See Richard Neustadt and Ernest May, *Thinking of Time* (New York: Free Press, 1986). Very harsh conservative criticisms are in Amity Shales, *The Forgotten Man* (New York: HarperCollins, 2007); Burton Folsom Jr., *New Deal or Raw Deal?* (New York: Threshold, 2008); and Eliot Rosen, *Roosevelt, the Great Depression, and the Economics of Recovery* (Charlottesville: University Press of Virginia, 2005).

18. Robert Dallek, *Franklin D. Roosevelt and American Foreign Policy, 1932–1945* (New York: Oxford University Press, 1979), prologue; and Donald C. Watt, *How War Came* (New York: Pantheon, 1989).

19. A strong case that FDR was in the 1930s an appeaser of Hitler is made by Frederick W. Marks II, *Wind over Sand* (Athens: University of Georgia Press, 1988). The opposite view is expressed in Robert Edwin Herzstein, *Roosevelt and Hitler* (New York: Paragon House, 1989), which sees FDR as waging a calculated propaganda war against the Nazis before the attack on Pearl Harbor. See also Arnold Offnet, *American Appeasement* (Cambridge, MA: Harvard University Press, 1969) and *Origins of the Second World War* (New York: Praeger, 1975); Charles A. Beard, *American Foreign Policy in the Making, 1932–40* (New Haven, CT: Yale University Press, 1946); Robert A. Divine, *Roosevelt and World War II* (Baltimore: Johns Hopkins University Press, 1969); and William Langer and S. Everett Gleason, *The Challenge to Isolation, 1937–1940* (New York: Harper, 1952).

20. Marks, *Wind over Sand*, chaps. 1 and 6; and David G. Haglund, *Latin America and the Transformation of U.S. Strategic Thought, 1936–1940* (New York: Harper, 1952).

21. Dallek, *Franklin D. Roosevelt and American Foreign Policy*, chaps. 1–4.

22. Burns, *Roosevelt: The Lion and the Fox*, 262.

23. Divine, *Roosevelt and World War II*, 8. On FDR seeing the horrors of war, see Burns, *Roosevelt: The Lion and the Fox*, 277.

24. Marks, *Wind over Sand*, chap. 2; Henry L. Stimson and McGeorge Bundy, *On Active Service in Peace and War* (New York: Harper, 1947); Frederick C. Adams, "The Road to Pearl Harbor: A Reexamination of American Far Eastern Policy, July 1937–December 1938," *Journal of American History* 58 (June 1971): 73–92; and Dorothy Borg, *The United States and the Far Eastern Crisis of 1933–1938* (Cambridge, MA: Harvard University Press, 1964).

25. Divine, *Roosevelt and World War II*, 18–21; John McVickar Haight, "France, the United States, and the Munich Crisis," *Journal of Modern History* 32 (December 1960): 340–58; and Langer and Gleason, *The Challenge to Isolation*, passim.

26. Divine, *Roosevelt and World War II*, 21; and Burns, *Roosevelt: The Lion and the Fox*, 384–90.

27. Burns, *Roosevelt: The Lion and the Fox*, 390–97.

28. Ibid., 420–21.

29. Divine, *Roosevelt and World War II*, 34; and Wayne S. Cole, *Roosevelt and the Isolationists, 1932–1945* (Lincoln: University of Nebraska Press, 1983).

30. Herbert S. Parmet and Marie B. Hecht, *Never Again* (New York: Macmillan, 1968); Burns, *Roosevelt: The Lion and the Fox*, chap. 21; Joseph Barnes, *Willkie* (New York: Simon & Schuster, 1952); Rosenman, *Working with Roosevelt*, passim; James A. Farley, *Jim Farley's Story* (New York: Whittlesey House, 1948); and Edward J. Flynn, *You're the Boss* (New York: Viking, 1947).

31. Burns, *Roosevelt: The Lion and the Fox*, 457–59; Walter Johnson, *The Battle against Isolation* (Chicago: University of Chicago Press, 1940); Herbert Feis, *The Road to Pearl Harbor* (Princeton, NJ: Princeton University Press, 1950); and William Langer and S. Everett Gleason, *The Undeclared War* (New York: Harper, 1953).

32. Divine, *Roosevelt and World War II*, chap. 2; and James MacGregor Burns, *Roosevelt: The Soldier of Freedom* (New York: Harcourt Brace Jovanovich, 1970), 51–52.

33. Burns, *Roosevelt: The Soldier of Freedom*, chap. 2.

34. Ibid., 72.

35. Ibid., 84–85; Waldo Heinrichs, *Threshold of War: Franklin D. Roosevelt and American Entry into World War II* (New York: Oxford University Press, 1988).

36. Morgan, *FDR*, 589.

37. Burns, *Roosevelt: The Soldier of Freedom*, 109.

38. Ibid., 119–20.

39. Heinrichs, *Threshold of War*, 166–79.

40. Dallek, *American Foreign Policy*, chap. 11; Heinrichs, *Threshold of War*, epilogue; Burns, *Roosevelt: The Soldier of Freedom*, 149–61; Sherwood, *Roosevelt and Hopkins*, 431; and Joseph P. Lash, *Roosevelt and Churchill, 1939–41* (New York: Norton, 1976).

41. This narrative follows along with Burns, *Roosevelt: The Soldier of Freedom*, part 1. See also John Colville, *The Fringes of Power* (New York: Norton, 1985); John Keegan, *The Second World War* (New York: Viking, 1989); and Forrest C. Pogue, *George C. Marshall: Ordeal and Hope, 1939–1942* (volume 2 in series) (New York: Viking, 1966).

42. Gordon A. Schwartz, *The Speculator: Bernard M. Baruch in Washington, 1917–1965* (Chapel Hill: University of North Carolina Press, 1981), chap. 7.

43. Ibid., 366.

44. Ibid., chap. 7; and John Blum, *V Was for Victory* (New York: Harcourt Brace Jovanovich, 1976); Scott Hart, *Washington at War* (Englewood Cliffs, NJ:

Prentice Hall, 1970); David Brinkley, *Washington Goes to War* (New York: Ballantine Books, 1988); and Thomas Fleming, *The New Dealers' War* (New York: Basic Books, 2001).

45. Morgan, *FDR*, chaps. 22 and 23.

46. Burns, *Roosevelt: The Soldier of Freedom*, chap. 19; Arthur D. Morse, *While Six Million Died* (New York: Random House, 1968); Martin S. Gilbert, *The Holocaust* (New York: Holt, 1986); Arno J. Mayer, *Why Did the Heavens Not Darken* (New York: Pantheon, 1988); Sol Stern, "Roosevelt and the Jews: Bystander to Genocide," *New York Village Voice*, September 18, 1984, 29–36; Henry R. Feingold, *The Politics of Rescue* (New Brunswick, NJ: Rutgers University Press, 1970); Patrick S. Washburn, *A Question of Sedition* (New York: Oxford University Press, 1986); Richard Drinnon, *Keeper of Concentration Camps* (Berkeley and Los Angeles: University of California Press, 1986); Jacobus ten Broek, "Wartime Power of the Military over Citizen Civilians within the Country," *California Law Review* 41 (Summer 1953): 67–208; and Arthur M. Schlesinger Jr., "Did FDR Betray the Jews?" *Newsweek*, April 18, 1994, 14. A more sympathetic view is Robert N. Rosen, *Saving the Jews: Franklin D. Roosevelt and the Holocaust* (New York: Thunder's Mouth Press, 2006).

47. Victor Lasky, *It Didn't Start with Watergate* (New York: Dell, 1977), 158–68.

48. Pogue, *George C. Marshall: Organizer of Victory, 1943–1945* (volume 3 in series) (New York: Viking, 1973), chap. 2; and Burns, *Roosevelt: The Soldier of Freedom*, chap. 10.

49. Burns, *Roosevelt: The Soldier of Freedom*, chaps. 10 and 12; and William Larsh, "W. Averell Harriman and the Polish Question, December 1943–August 1944," *Eastern European Politics and Societies* 7 (Fall 1993): 513–54.

50. Burns, *Roosevelt: The Soldier of Freedom*, 384, 390–91.

51. Marks, *Wind over Sand*, chap. 5; Dallek, *Franklin D. Roosevelt and American Foreign Policy*, chap. 14; and Keith Eubank, *Summit at Teheran* (New York: William Morrow, 1985).

52. The election is chronicled in Burns, *Roosevelt: The Soldier of Freedom*, chap. 17, with chaps. 11 and 12 on domestic affairs.

53. Freidel, *Franklin D. Roosevelt: A Rendezvous with Destiny*, chaps. 37–38. In addition, see Bruce Catton, *The War Lords* (New York: Harcourt Brace, 1948); Nathan D. Grudstein, *Presidential Delegation of Authority in Wartime* (Pittsburgh, PA: University of Pittsburgh Press, 1961); Luther Gulick, "War Organizing of the Federal Government," *American Political Science Review* 38 (December 1944): 1166–79; and Jean Edward Smith, *Lucius D. Clay* (New York: Henry Holt, 1990), chaps. 8–10.

54. Milton Viorst, *Hostile Allies: FDR and Charles DeGaulle* (New York: Macmillan, 1965); Jean Lacouture, *DeGaulle: The Rebel, 1890–1944* (New York: Norton, 1990); and Andrew Roberts, *Masters and Commanders* (New York: HarperCollins, 2009).

55. John P. Vloyantaes, "The Significance of Pre-Yalta Politics Regarding Liberated Countries in Europe," *Western Political Science Quarterly* 11 (June 1958): 209–28; Marks, *Wind over Sand*, chap. 5; and Stanislaw Mikolojczyk, *The Rape of Poland* (New York: Whittlesey House, 1948).

56. Ronald H. Spector, *Eagle against the Sun* (New York: Free Press, 1985). On alleged assassination plans, see Marks, *Wind over Sand*, 182.

57. Churchill has become a cottage industry for historians. See A. J. P. Taylor et al., *Churchill Revised* (New York: Dial Press, 1969); Hart's article is on pages 173–228. The early years of Churchill are examined in William Manchester, *The Last Lion*, 2 vols. (Boston: Little, Brown, 1983, 1988). His own history of the period is Churchill's *The Second World War*, 6 vols. (Boston: Houghton Mifflin, 1948–1953). Also of use are Maxwell P. Schoenfeld, *The War Ministry of Winston Churchill* (Ames: Iowa State University Press, 1972), chaps. 3 and 4; Carlo D'Este, *Warlord: A Life of Winston S. Churchill* (New York: HarperCollins, 2008); *Churchill and Roosevelt: The Complete Correspondence*, 3 vols., ed. Warren F. Kimball (Princeton, NJ: Princeton University Press, 1984); Colville, *The Fringes of Power*, passim; A. J. P. Taylor, *The War Lords* (New York: Penguin Books, 1978); William B. Breuner, *Feuding Allies: The Private Wars of High Command* (New York: Wiley, 1995); Martin Gilbert, *Winston S. Churchill*, vol. 6, *1939–1941*, *Finest Hour* (Boston: Houghton Mifflin, 1983), and vol. 7, *1941–1945*, *Road to Victory* (Boston: Houghton Mifflin, 1986); David Irving, *Churchill's War* (New York: Avon, 1990); Alistair Horne, *Harold Macmillan* (New York: Viking, 1989); and R. W. Thompson, *Generalissimo Churchill* (New York: Scribner, 1973). Also see Max Hastings, *Winston's War: Churchill, 1940–1945* (New York: Knopf, 2010); Jon Meachan, *Franklin and Winston* (New York: Random House, 2001); Andrew Roberts, *Hitler and Churchill* (London: Weidenfeld & Nicolson, 2003); John Strawson, *Churchill and Hitler* (New York: Fromm International, 1997); Richard Holmes, *In the Footsteps of Churchill* (New York: Basic Books, 2005); and Richard Toye, *Churchill's Europe* (New York: Holt, 2010).

58. The best treatment of Stalin's wartime leadership is Geoffrey Roberts, *Stalin's Wars* (New Haven, CT: Yale University Press, 2006); also see Isaac Deutscher, *Stalin* (New York: Viking, 1960); Adam Ulam, *Stalin* (New York: Viking, 1960); John Erickson, *The Road to Stalingrad* (Boulder, CO: Westview Press, 1975) and *The Road to Berlin* (London: Weidenfeld & Nicolson, 1983); and Albert Seaton, *Stalin as Military Commander* (New York: Praeger, 1976). The estimate of Stalin's attack on the generals comes from historian W. Bruce Lincoln.

59. Percy Ernst Schramm, *Hitler: The Man and the Military Leader* (Chicago: Quadrangle, 1971); Sebastian Heffner, *The Meaning of Hitler* (New York: Macmillan, 1979); William Carr, *Hitler: A Study in Personality and Politics* (Baltimore: Edward Arnold, 1978); and Richard Overy, *The Dictators* (New York: Norton, 2004). In 1937, Churchill called Hitler one of the "great figures whose lives have enriched the story of mankind" and an "indomitable champion," quoted in Robert R. James, *Anthony Eden* (London: Weindenfeld & Nicolson, 1986), 136.

60. William Emerson, "Franklin Roosevelt as Commander in Chief in World War II," *Military Affairs* 22 (Winter 1958–1959): 181–207; Eric Larrabee, *Commander in Chief* (New York: Harper & Row, 1987); Thomas Parrish, *Roosevelt and Marshall* (New York: Morrow, 1989); Pogue, *George C. Marshall*, volumes 2 and 3; Ed Cray, *General of the Army* (New York: Norton, 1990); and Richard W. Steele, *The First Offensive 1942: Roosevelt, Marshall, and the Making of American Strategy* (Bloomington: Indiana University Press, 1973).

61. Theodore Draper, "Neoconservative History," *New York Review of Books* (January 16, 1986): 5–15, with rejoinder and reply in August 14, 1986.

62. John J. Sbrega, "The Anti-Colonial Policies of FDR," *Political Science Quarterly* 101 (January 1986): 65–84.

63. Later assessments are in Wilbur J. Cohen, ed., *The Roosevelt New Deal* (Austin: University of Texas Press, 1981) and *The New Deal: Fifty Years Later* (Austin: University of Texas Press, 1984); William Leuchtenburg, *In the Shadow of FDR* (Ithaca, NY: Cornell University Press, 1985); and a more critical Steve Fraser and Gary Gerstle, eds., *The Rise and Fall of the New Deal Order* (Princeton, NJ: Princeton University Press, 1989).

Chapter 9: Harry S Truman: The First Imperial President

1. William E. Leuchtenburg, *In the Shadow of FDR* (Ithaca, NY: Cornell University Press, 1985), passim, and *The White House Looks South* (Baton Rouge: Louisiana State University Press, 2005).

2. David McCullough, *Truman* (New York: Simon & Schuster, 1992); Richard Lawrence Miller, *Truman: The Rise to Power* (New York: McGraw-Hill, 1986); and Roy Jenkins, *Truman* (New York: Harper & Row, 1986).

3. The superb Donovan volumes are the best source for any study of the Truman years: Robert J. Donovan, *Conflict and Crisis* (New York: Norton, 1977) and *Tumultuous Years* (New York: Norton, 1980). The Rayburn quote is from *Conflict and Crisis*, 13. Used here is *Conflict and Crisis*, 11, 13, 24, 27; Donald R. McCoy, *The Presidency of Harry S Truman* (Lawrence: University Press of Kansas, 1984), 27; Francis H. Heller, ed., *Economics and the Truman Administration* (Lawrence: Regents Press of Kansas, 1981); Alonzo L. Hamby, *Beyond the New Deal* (New York: Columbia University Press, 1973); and Cabel Phillips, *The Truman Presidency* (New York: Macmillan, 1966).

4. Donovan, *Conflict and Crisis*, 76.

5. Ibid., 81–86.

6. Henry L. Stimson and McGeorge Bundy, *On Active Duty in Peace and War* (New York: Harper & Row, 1948); Martin J. Sherwin, *A World Destroyed: The Atomic Bomb and the Grand Alliance* (New York: Knopf, 1975); Donovan, *Conflict and Crisis*, 49, 96–98; Gar Alperovitz, *Cold War Essays* (New York: Anchor, 1970), chap. 4, and "Did We Have to Drop the Bomb?" *New York Times*, August

3, 1989, 23; and Thomas G. Paterson, "Potsdam, the Atomic Bomb, and the Cold War," *Pacific Historical Review* 41 (May 1972): 225–38.

7. Robert A. Garson, *The Democratic Party and the Politics of Sectionalism, 1941–1948* (Baton Rouge: Louisiana State University Press, 1974).

8. Harry S Truman, *Years of Decision*, vol. 1 of his *Memoirs* (New York: Doubleday, 1955), chap. 36.

9. Donovan, *Conflict and Crisis*, 163–71; and Arthur M. Schlesinger Jr., *The Imperial Presidency* (Boston: Houghton Mifflin, 1973), 127–50.

10. Donovan, *Conflict and Crisis*, 215.

11. Forrest C. Pogue, *George C. Marshall: Statesman, 1945–1959* (New York: Viking, 1987).

12. John Gimbel, *The Origins of the Marshall Plan* (Palo Alto, CA: Stanford University Press, 1976); McCoy, *Presidency of Harry S Truman*, 125–29; Jean Edward Smith, *Lucius D. Clay*, vol. 3 (New York: Holt, 1990); and John Lewis Gaddis, *The Cold War: A New History* (New York: Penguin, 2005).

13. Richard M. Freeland, *The Truman Doctrine and the Origins of McCarthyism* (New York: Knopf, 1972).

14. Harry S Truman, *Years of Trial and Hope, 1946–1952*, vol. 2 of his *Memoirs* (New York: Doubleday, 1956); and Bert Cochran, *Harry Truman and the Crisis Presidency* (New York: Funk & Wagnalls, 1973), chaps. 11 and 12.

15. John Sketsinger, *The Jewish Vote and the Creation of Israel* (Palo Alto, CA: Hoover Institution Press, 1974); and Zvi Ganin, *Truman, American Jewry, and Israel* (New York: Holmes & Meier, 1979). The quote on Jesus and the Jews is from Donovan, *Conflict and Crisis*, 319.

16. Barton J. Berstein, "The Ambiguous Legacy: The Truman Administration and Civil Rights," in *Politics and Policies of the Truman Administration* (Chicago: Quadrangle Books, 1972), 269–314; Donald R. McCoy and Richard T. Ruetten, *Quest and Response* (Lawrence: University Press of Kansas, 1973); and William C. Berman, *The Politics of Civil Rights in the Truman Administration* (Columbus: Ohio State University Press, 1970).

17. Donovan, *Conflict and Crisis*, chaps. 40–43; Cochran, *Harry Truman and the Crisis Presidency*, chap. 26; Irwin Ross, *The Loneliest Campaign* (New York: New American Library, 1968); Allen Yarnell, *Democrats and Progressives* (Berkeley and Los Angeles: University of California Press, 1974); and Richard Norton Smith, *Thomas E. Dewey and His Times* (New York: Simon & Schuster, 1982).

18. Thomas C. Reeves, *The Life and Times of Joe McCarthy* (New York: Stein & Day, 1982); David M. Oshinsky, *Conspiracy So Immense* (New York: Free Press, 1983); and Donovan, *Tumultuous Years*, 32.

19. Richard F. Haynes, *The Awesome Power: Harry S Truman as Commander in Chief* (Baton Rouge: Louisiana State University Press, 1973), 126–27; and Arnold A. Offner, *Another Such Victory: President Truman and the Cold War, 1945–1953* (Palo Alto, CA: Stanford University Press, 2002).

20. Herbert Feis, *The China Triangle* (Princeton, NJ: Princeton University Press, 1953); Robert M. Blum, *Drawing the Line* (New York: Norton, 1982); and June M. Grasso, *Truman's Two China Policy* (Armonk, NY: Sharpe, 1987).

21. Donovan, *Tumultuous Years*, 160.

22. McCoy, *Presidency of Harry S Truman*, chap. 8.

23. Donovan, *Tumultuous Years*, 199–205.

24. Ibid., 212.

25. Robert J. Donovan, *Nemesis: Truman and Johnson in the Coils of War in Asia* (New York: St. Martin's Press, 1984); Donovan, *Tumultuous Years*, 220–22; and Michael P. Riccards, *The Presidency and the Middle Kingdom: China, the United States, and Executive Leadership* (Lanham, MD: Lexington Books, 2000).

26. Lloyd C. Gardner, *Architects of Illusion* (Chicago: Quadrangle Books, 1970); Thomas G. Paterson, ed., *Cold War Critics* (Chicago: Quadrangle Books, 1971); Robert W. Tucker, *The Radical Left and American Foreign Policy* (Baltimore: Johns Hopkins University Press, 1971); and Donovan, *Tumultuous Years*, 255.

27. These expressions of support that gave MacArthur a sense of security are at variance with Truman's later actions and are cited in Donovan, *Tumultuous Years*, 271–90. Also of importance are Haynes, *Awesome Power*, chaps. 11 and 12; Dean Acheson, *Present at Creation* (New York: Norton, 1969), 452–511; and William Manchester, *American Caesar* (Boston: Little, Brown, 1978), chap. 9.

28. Donald R. McCoy, *The Presidency of Harry S Truman* (Lawrence: University Press of Kansas, 1984); and D. Clayton James, *The Years of MacArthur*, vol. 3 (Boston: Houghton Mifflin, 1985), chaps. 17 and 18.

29. Donovan, *Tumultuous Years*, 348.

30. Ibid., 369.

31. McCoy, *Presidency of Harry S Truman*, 274–77.

32. Andrew J. Dunar, *The Truman Scandals and the Politics of Morality* (Columbia: University of Missouri Press, 1984).

33. Maeva Marcus, *Truman and the Steel Seizure Case* (New York: Columbia University Press, 1977).

34. A popular volume that helped set that positive view was Merle Miller, *Plain Speaking: An Oral Biography* (New York: Berkeley Books, 1973).

35. Francis H. Heller, *The Truman White House* (Lawrence: University Press of Kansas, 1980); and Alfred D. Sander, "Truman and the National Security Council 1945–1947," *Journal of American History* 59 (September 1972): 369–88.

Chapter 10: Ronald Reagan: Unleashing Right-Wing America

1. Lou Cannon, *Reagan* (New York: Putnam, 1982); Anne Edwards, *Early Reagan* (New York: William Morrow, 1987); Gary Wills, *Reagan's America* (Garden City, NY: Doubleday, 1985); Ronald Reagan and Richard C. Hubler, *Where's the Rest of Me?* (New York: Dell, 1965); Lawrence I. Barrett, *Gambling with History*

(Garden City, NY: Doubleday, 1983); Ronnie Dugger, *On Reagan* (New York: McGraw-Hill, 1983); and Michael P. Riccards, "Rendezvous with Destiny: The Influence of Franklin Delano Roosevelt on the Life and Presidency of Ronald Reagan," delivered at the Hofstra University Conference on the Reagan Presidency, April 23, 1993.

2. Edwards, *Early Reagan*, passim; and Michael Rogin, *Ronald Reagan, the Movie, and Other Episodes in Political Demonology* (Berkeley and Los Angeles: University of California Press, 1987).

3. Thomas Byrne Edsall with Mary D. Edsall, *Chain Reaction* (New York: Norton, 1991).

4. Charles O. Jones, ed., *The Reagan Legacy* (Chatham, NJ: Chatham House, 1988); especially chapter 1 by Bert A. Rockman; B. B. Kymlicka and Jean V. Matthews, eds., *The Reagan Revolution* (Chicago: Dorsey, 1988); and W. Eliot Brownless and Hugh Davis Graham, eds., *The Reagan Presidency* (Lawrence: University Press of Kansas, 2008).

5. David A. Stockman, *The Triumph of Politics: How the Reagan Revolution Failed* (New York: Harper & Row, 1986); Robert Lekachman, *Greed Is Not Enough* (New York: Pantheon, 1982); and Fred Block et al., *The Mean Season* (New York: Pantheon, 1987). See also Bob Herbert, "Reagan and Reality," *New York Times*, February 15, 2010, which quotes his son, Ron.

6. William Niskanen, *Reaganomics* (New York: Oxford University Press, 1988); Martin Anderson, *Revolution* (New York: Harcourt Brace Jovanovich, 1988); and William G. Hyland, ed., *The Reagan Foreign Policy* (New York: New American Library, 1987). For a more critical view, see Paul Kennedy, *The Rise and Fall of the Great Powers* (New York: Random House, 1987); Robert Kuttman, *The End of Laissez Faire* (New York: Knopf, 1991); Walter Russell Mead, *Mortal Splendor* (Boston: Houghton Mifflin, 1987); and Benjamin Friedman, *Day of Reckoning* (New York: Random House, 1988).

7. Robert Pear, "On Reaganomics' 10th Birthday Not All Celebrate," *New York Times*, August 11, 1991; George F. Will, "Who's Better Off These Days," *Washington Post*, October 31, 1991; and Peter Passell, "Forces in Society and Reaganism Helped Dig Deeper Hole for Poor," *New York Times*, July 16, 1989.

8. The following pages on the economic effects of the Reagan years follow closely Kevin Phillips, *The Politics of Rich and Poor* (New York: Random House, 1990); especially cited are 11, 20, 21, 52, 78, 80, 122, 127, 205.

9. Quote is from Lou Cannon, *President Reagan: The Role of a Lifetime* (New York: Simon & Schuster, 1991), 109. This book is still the major study on Reagan's terms in office and is the background for much of this narrative.

10. Cannon, *President Reagan*, 233, 240, 253; and William Greider, *The Education of David Stockman and Other Americans* (New York: Signet, 1986).

11. William Greider, *Secrets of the Temple: How the Federal Reserve Runs the Country* (New York: Touchstone, 1987).

12. Cannon, *President Reagan*, 271; and Jeffrey H. Birnbaum and Alan S. Murray, *Showdown at Gucci Gulch* (New York: Random House, 1987).

13. Ronald Reagan, *An American Life* (New York: Simon & Schuster, 1990), 569–70; Ron Reagan, *My Father at 100* (New York: Viking, 2010).

14. Cannon, *President Reagan*, 297–303.

15. Ibid., 315.

16. Ibid., 740.

17. Dusko Duder and Louise Branson, *Gorbachev: Heretic in the Kremlin* (New York: Viking, 1990); Cannon, *President Reagan*, 782–86; and Strobe Talbot, *The Master of the Game* (New York: Knopf, 1988).

18. Cannon, *President Reagan*, 337; Roy Guttman, *Banana Diplomacy* (New York: Simon & Schuster, 1988); Alexander M. Haig Jr., *Caveat: Realism, Reagan, and Foreign Policy* (New York: Macmillan, 1984); Mark Hertsgaard, *On Bended Knee* (New York: Schocken Books, 1988); and Stephen Kinzer, *Blood of Brothers: Life and War in Nicaragua* (New York: Putnam, 1991).

19. Bob Woodward, *Veil: The Secret Wars of the CIA, 1981–87* (New York: Simon & Schuster, 1987).

20. Theodore Draper, *A Very Thin Line* (New York: Hill & Wang, 1991); Oliver North, *Under Fire* (New York: HarperCollins, 1991); *Iran-Contra Affair: Report of Congressional Committees*, H. Rep. #100–433 (Washington, DC: Government Printing Office, November 1987); and Constantine Menges, *Inside the National Security Council* (New York: Simon & Schuster, 1988).

21. *The Tower Commission Report* (New York: New York Times Book, 1987); Cannon, *President Reagan*, 704, on his remark; Michael Ledeen, *Perilous Statecraft* (New York: Scribner, 1988); Jane Mayer and Doyle McManus, *Landslide* (Boston: Houghton Mifflin, 1988); and Stanley Karnow, *In Our Image: America's Empire in the Philippines* (New York: Random House, 1989).

22. Cannon, *President Reagan*, chap. 15.

23. Peter Goldman and Tony Fuller, *The Quest for the Presidency 1984* (New York: Bantam, 1985).

24. Reagan, *An American Life*, 448.

25. Nancy Reagan, *My Turn* (New York: Random House, 1989); Kitty Kelly, *Nancy Reagan* (New York: Simon & Schuster, 1991); Don T. Regan, *For the Record* (New York: Harcourt Brace Jovanovich, 1988); and Michael K. Deaver, *Behind the Scenes* (New York: William Morrow, 1987).

26. Birnbaum and Murray, *Showdown*, 286–87.

27. Cannon, *President Reagan*, 580.

28. Ibid., 792.

29. Some of the most critical views of Reagan's presidency and his disengagement come from his own inner circle: Stockman, *The Triumph of Politics*; Regan, *For the Record*; Deaver, *Behind the Scenes*; Haig, *Caveat*; Terrell Bell, *The Thirteenth Man* (New York: Free Press, 1988); Peggy Noonan, *What I Saw at the Revolution* (New York: Random House, 1990); Larry Speakes, *Speaking Out* (New York: Scribner, 1988); and Caspar Weinberger, *Fighting for Peace* (New York: Warner, 1990).

Index

About the Author

Michael P. Riccards is executive director of the Hall Institute of Public Policy in New Jersey and has been the public policy scholar at the College Board in Washington, D.C. He has also been president of Fitchburg State College in Massachusetts; Shepherd College in Shepherdstown, West Virginia; and St. John's College in Santa Fe, New Mexico. He has served as provost of Hunter College in New York City; dean of arts and sciences at the University of Massachusetts, Boston; a faculty member at SUNY College at Buffalo; and special assistant to the chancellor of higher education in New Jersey. In addition, he has been a Fulbright Fellow to Japan, a National Endowment for the Humanities Fellow at Princeton University, a Henry Huntington Library Fellow, and a member of the National Advisory Committee of the Center for the Study of the Presidency in New York City. Dr. Riccards has also been the chair of the New Mexico Endowment for the Humanities, a member of the West Virginia Council for the Humanities, and the chair of the New Jersey Abraham Lincoln Bicentennial Commission. He is the author of numerous books and articles, and fourteen verse plays. He is married and has three children and three grandchildren.